EXECUTIVE EQ

EXECUTIVE EQ

Emotional Intelligence in Business

Robert K Cooper & Ayman Sawaf

ORION BUSINESS
BOOKS

First published in Great Britain in 1997 by Orion Business
An imprint of The Orion Publishing Group Ltd
Orion House, 5 Upper St Martin's Lane, London WC2H 9EA

A CIP catalogue record for this book is available from the British Library

Filmset by Selwood Systems, Midsomer Norton
Printed in Great Britain by Butler & Tanner Ltd
Frome and London

Dedicated to advancing the inner side of leadership
and successful enterprise in which
how we do business together is as important as what we produce,
and how we serve others is as vital as how much we profit.

CONTENTS

THE FIRST CORNERSTONE: EMOTIONAL LITERACY
Being real and *true to yourself:* Builds *personal power* – including awareness, inner guidance, respect, responsibility and connection

THE SECOND CORNERSTONE: EMOTIONAL FITNESS
Being clear and *getting along:* Builds *inspiration* – of self and others – including authenticity, resilience, and trusting relationships

THE THIRD CORNERSTONE: EMOTIONAL DEPTH

Reaching down and *stepping up:* Builds *core character* and calls forth your potential, integrity and purpose

THE FOURTH CORNERSTONE: EMOTIONAL ALCHEMY

Sensing opportunities and *creating the future:* Builds *confluence –* including intuitive innovation, integration, situational transformation, and fluid intelligence

NOTE TO THE READER

Executive EQ is a unique collaboration. In 1989, Ayman Sawaf, an international executive and entrepreneur, began to research emotional literacy. He founded a professional newsletter in the field and became Chairman of the Foundation for Education in Emotional Literacy, a non-profit organization. Robert K. Cooper, PhD, was engaged to conduct a global research survey on emotional intelligence in business and related fields.

Out of this multi-year initiative grew a new company: Advanced Intelligence Technologies. Cooper and Sawaf engaged Esther M. Orioli, CEO of Essi Systems, Inc., a leading corporate data and measurement firm, and her research team, headed by Karen Trocki, PhD, to develop with them the first norm-tested, statistically reliable *EQ Map* and *Organizational EQ Profiles*. At the back of this book you will find a copy of the introductory self-scoring version of the *EQ Map*. As of the date of this publication, it has been tested on thousands of executives, managers, and professionals in more than a hundred organizations in service, technology, and industry.

It was Sawaf who initially suggested the Four Cornerstone Model for *Executive EQ*, and he and Cooper developed an early outline of this book. When the comprehensive research and writing processes began in earnest, the two of them decided that Robert Cooper would research and write *Executive EQ* and convey it in his voice.

THE VALUE AND PROFITABILITY OF EMOTIONAL INTELLIGENCE IN BUSINESS

We are in the beginning stages of what many authorities believe will be the next revolution in business. By design, no blood will be shed in this sweeping transformation from old to new, just a host of preconceived notions.

It all began with a series of studies indicating that people who are intellectually the brightest are often not the most successful, either in business or their personal lives.[1] Which suggests that a technically proficient executive or professional with a high EQ is someone who picks up – more readily, more deftly, and more quickly than others – the budding conflicts that need resolution, the team and company vulnerabilities that need addressing, the gaps to be leaped or filled, the hidden connections that spell opportunity, and the murky, mysterious interactions that seem most likely to prove golden – and profitable.

As you will discover in the pages of this book, there is growing evidence from the latest scientific studies and reports from management confirming the link between emotional intelligence and success. Yet for many years leadership and management has held to the premise that statistics analysis, intellectual digging, disembodied relationships, and conceptual brilliance are what drive an organization to pinnacles of profitablity. All that pure intellect may have been necessary to make America's corporations more competitive, and it certainly has had some payoffs; but not without dramatic costs that most people in organizations feel every day, including crumbling trust, jarring uncertainty, greater distance between managers and those they manage, stifled creativity, festering cynicism, increasingly volatile anger, and vanishing loyalty and commitment.

Something we were withholding made us weak ...

We have paid a drastic price – not only in our organizations, but in our own lives – for trying to disconnect emotions from intellect. It can't be done. Not only do we know intuitively that it can't be done, modern science is proving every day that it is emotional intelligence, not IQ or raw brainpower alone, that underpins many of the best decisions, the most dynamic organizations, and the most satisfying and successful lives. Brain scientists are providing physiological explanations for this connection, and more than a dozen studies cited throughout this book already link the various competencies of emotional intelligence to increased profitability in business.

Robert Frost wrote, 'Something we were withholding made us weak, until we found out that it was ourselves.' Every day an untold number of bright and efficient managers and professionals check the best of themselves at the door before coming in to work – and this takes a direct or indirect human and financial toll on all of us. What gets left behind includes that 'something' Frost was describing: *heart.* Perhaps less poetically, Yale psychologist Robert Sternberg, an expert on successful intelligence, asserts, 'If IQ rules, it is only because we let it. And when we let it rule, we choose a bad master.'

Emotional intelligence emerges not from the musings of rarefied intellect but from the workings of the human heart. EQ isn't about sales tricks or how to work a room. And it's not about putting a good face on things or the psychology of control, exploitation, or manipulation. The word *emotion* may be simply defined as applying 'movement,' either metaphorically or literally, to core feelings. And it is emotional intelligence, rather than intellect, that motivates us to pursue our unique potential and purpose, and activates our innermost values and aspirations, transforming them from things *we think about* to what we *live.* Emotions have long been considered to be of such depth and power that in Latin, for example, they were described as *motus anima*, meaning literally 'the spirit that moves us'.

Contrary to most conventional thinking, emotions are inherently neither positive nor negative; rather, they serve as the single most powerful source of human energy, authenticity, and drive, and can offer us a wellspring of intuitive creative wisdom. In fact, each feeling provides us with vital and potentially profitable information every minute of the day. This feedback – from the heart, not the head – is what ignites creative genius, keeps you honest with yourself, shapes trusting relationships, provides an inner compass for your life and career, guides you to unexpected possibilities, and may even save you or your organization from disaster. It is not enough, of course, just to *have* feelings, or we'd all be geniuses. Emotional intelligence requires that we learn to *acknowledge* and *understand* feelings – in ourselves and others – and that we appropriately *respond* to them, effectively *applying* the information and energy of emotions in our daily life and work. A more complete definition is as follows:

> Emotional intelligence is the ability to sense, understand, and effectively apply the power and acumen of *emotions* as a source of human energy, information, connection, and influence.

It's Time to Roll Up Our Sleeves and Begin Exploring EQ and Its Link to Success and Profitability

Regardless of our current job position or title, each of us is ultimately responsible for being the chief executive officer of our own life and work. A growing number of us are being asked to serve as leaders in one form or another in the workplace and to meet expectations that are getting higher all the time. It's not just that we expect executives and managers to assume responsibility for the enduring success of our group or organization and to share rewards and profits fairly with all involved. We also insist that they demonstrate extensive knowledge and analytical expertise in a vast range of areas, such as finance, statistics, resource allocation, technology, information systems, product development, manufacturing, service delivery, and marketing. That's just for starters.

We also demand competence in writing, speaking, listening, negotiating, strategizing, and influencing. Beyond this, we expect executives and managers to demonstrate virtually every known or suspected attribute of leadership character, including honesty, energy, trust, integrity, intuition, imagination, resilience, purpose, commitment, influence, motivation, sensitivity, empathy, humour, courage, conscience, and humility. On top of this, we want leaders at all levels of an organization to be our mentors, coaches, counselors, allies, guardians, and friends, ever alert to the organization's needs and our personal best interests. Unfortunately, we're still largely in the dark when it comes to learning how to do this – how to become not only exceptional managers and leaders but notable men and women, too. And one of the central missing pieces of the puzzle is emotional intelligence.

The purpose of writing this book is to raise and explore some potentially useful questions about the characteristics and values of developing and applying emotional intelligence in work and life. What you will find in the pages ahead is a comprehensive, integrated working model that offers a starting point based on the insights of leaders and researchers in many organizations around the world.

Contrary to conventional thinking, emotions are rarely intrusions into our lives, but are intelligent, sensitive, beneficial, and even wise.[2] With few exceptions, emotions are not at odds with good judgment and reasoning; rather, they *inspire* and *enliven* good judgment and reasoning and are linked to success and profitability. And, as you will see, everything important that happens to us arouses emotion.

Everything.

The *EQ Map*

For a number of years, I and a group of colleagues have shared the belief that many qualities of emotional intelligence could be identified and measured in a highly personalized way which was markedly different from IQ-type tests. To check our hypothesis, we invited one of America's leading corporate measurement and research firms, Essi Systems, Inc., of San Francisco, to work with us to develop the first *EQ Map*. Using state-of-the-art mapping technologies, a research team headed by CEO Esther M. Orioli and Karen Trocki, PhD, director of research, launched this scientific initiative, drawing on a corporate client base totaling more than 2,000 organizations. From this early collaboration, Q-Metrics was born, with a corporate mission to explore ways to measure and map the dimensions of human intelligence that contribute to personal and interpersonal achievement, the success of organizations, and the benefit of humanity.

As a result of this combined effort, you will find – at the back of this book – your copy of the introductory version of the *EQ Map*, the first extensively researched, nationally norm-tested, statistically reliable measurement method that enables you to begin charting your relative strengths and vulnerabilities across a wide range of characteristics related to emotional intelligence. As of the date of this publication, the *EQ Map* has been pilot-tested on thousands of executives, managers, and professionals in more than a hundred organizations in service, technology, and manufacturing industries in the US and Canada. Modified versions of the *EQ Map* are being developed for the United Kingdom, Europe, Japan, and other nations and regions of the world. We believe the results hold great promise. Already we are learning ways to begin measuring the relationship between emotional intelligence and health, teamwork, innovation, productivity, and profit.

You may be surprised at what the *EQ Map* tells you. Or it may confirm things you have long sensed about yourself. It may also remind you of talents and inherent capabilities you've forgotten and that call for renewed attention. While it may be valuable to concentrate on one or two of the areas, or scales, of the *EQ Map* where your scales indicates a possible vulnerability, it can prove just as important to continue deepening and developing your areas of strength across the full range of emotional intelligence attributes, and counting on them as assets in your life and work. For a computer-scored interpretation to your *EQ Map* and a confidential report based on the latest data and discoveries, see the contact page at the back of the book.

PROLOGUE

We all know the feeling. Usually we are standing spellbound at the edge of a shoreline at sunset or overlooking our favourite wooded park at dawn or as the stars come out, and we sense a powerful presence. I was standing on a mountain in Tibet. Sunlight climbed the distant slopes above blue lakes ringed by converging gorges. Below, the steepling meadows were lined with crystalline rocks, rushing streams and the drift of wild flowers.

The view and atmosphere elicited in me a profound sense of wonder, a heightened curiosity about the meanings of our existence – the mysteries of who we are, of what we live for, and what we may yet achieve. I gazed at the worlds beyond, across the horizons of my imagination, looking out as if, for that string of moments on the rooftop of the world, nothing was hidden from me.

What I could not have known then, on that day years ago, was that I was about to experience something that would change forever the way I felt about courage and compassion, leadership and learning, intuition and trust. Just before reaching the summit, my Tibetan guide had asked, 'Are you ready?' Ready for what? I wondered as I nodded breathlessly. For the rarefield view? For a deep feeling of accomplishment in the climb? Yes, I would be ready.

But I was not ready. Not for what came.

Along with my Tibetan guide, an elder was journeying with us that day. He looked very old when I first saw him; I found out later he was fifty-nine. His skin was creased and wrinkled, a weathered brown. His shining eyes were a sharp blue-black, the whites criss-crossed with blood vessels, giving him a weary, or perhaps strained, look. But this was not borne out in the way he walked and climbed – with a quiet confidence and considerable stamina, despite a slight limp on his left side. He wore old mountain boots and a dark blue heavy canvas coat over grey work trousers and a red sweater that was frayed at the collar. The knucles on his hands were variously enlarged – some looked to have been broken, others gnarled with age or arthritis – and he carried a long ironwood walking staff that the guide told me he had years ago dethorned, smoothed, and oiled by hand, until it gleamed.

I was in Tibet, on the first of several trips there, completing a research project on the inner side of leadership. Prior to this, I had spent a number of years consulting with corporate executives and management teams, and exploring scientific findings on exceptional human performance under pressure. Over a period of two decades, I had also studied the lives of various leaders – some well known and others little known – throughout world history. Since 1973, I'd found myself most intrigued by one man in particular, a leader virtually unheard of in the West, who had lived in Tibet in the seventh century. He faced a daunting series of hardships and rose to prominence through a rare leadership style that combined mind *and* heart, strength *and* compassion – and he built an empire where none had been before, an empire arguably grander in size, scope and influence than those of Caesar, Attila or Alexander. By any standards, his accomplishments, beyond his military victories, were remarkable: a representative government; expansive worldwide trade; advocacy of a moral code and human rights; creation of a written language and plan for national literacy; a medical care system based on the finest traditions from Greece, Persia, India, and China; and promotion of an egalitarian culture, unifying the wild tribes of Central Asia. I had come to Tibet to walk in the footsteps of this leader who lived more than 1300 years ago.

Once we reached the summit, the guide stood with me beside the elder. Together we looked out across the ancient hidden valleys below. It was a wondrous, breathtaking sight. The sun was warm on our faces. Despite the clear blue sky, soft snowflakes were beginning to fall. I turned into the breeze and noticed the source of the snow: a cluster of white clouds, backdropped against the sky, drifting towards us from the east.

'There.' The elder was pointing.

'What is it?' I asked, curious, stepping nearer to the outer edge of the crest.

'There. The mound of rocks.'

At the foot of this face of the mountain, several thousand feet below, caught in the shadowed glow of the afternoon sun, I could see what appeared to be a circular pile of large rocks, as if some wide hole in the ground had been filled in. The elder stared at it and I saw his arms begin to shake. I looked at him, confused now, noticing that tears had started to run down his cheeks. I glanced over at my Tibetan guide. He, too, was red-eyed, visibly moved by something I could not yet comprehend.

'All of my family,' the elder said so softly I almost could not hear him, 'was buried there ... before they took the bodies away.'*

'What do you mean?' I thought there might have been a climbing

*To honour a promise I made to people in Tibet and in an effort to help protect the surviving Tibetans from further persecution at the hands of the occupying Chinese Army, I have altered dates, numbers, times, human and geographical features, and other elements in this composite story.

accident of some kind, recalling our ascent and my apprehension that a gust of wind or misstep could send us plummeting down the mountain face.

'Do you know what this gesture means?' the elder asked me, bringing his hands together, palm to palm, fingers pointing skyward, in front of his chest.

Yes, I nodded. Throughout Tibet and the Himalayas, it was a sign of respect, of greeting, and of prayer.

He peered into my eyes before going on. 'In 1959, the Chinese Army banned us from prayer of any kind. Before the Chinese invasion, I had been chosen by the elders as one of the future leaders of the villages'. He motioned towards the neck of the valley and beyond. That was before I went to the university, and before the Red Army came and destroyed our homes and businesses, our libraries and temples, and raped our wives and children, and forbade us from prayer. For more than a thousand years, for the most part we have been a peaceful people; we had a small defensive force but they were no match for the Red Guard. No other countries came to our aid. It was a dark time for Tibet, and still is for those who survived. . . .' He wiped the tears from his eyes and continued.

'There was a day, years ago, when I was walking along that road' – he pointed to a narrow route which appeared as a slender silver thread across the valley floor. 'I came upon an old friend and, on instinct, out of respect' – he touched his weathered palms together in front of his chest – 'I greeted him in the traditional way and said, "Tashi deley", which means "I honour the greatness in you" and we stopped to talk for a while'.

He went on: 'A Chinese Army officer saw me do this, and he said, "Arrest this man. He is praying and spreading religion. He has defied the law. We will make an example out of him." For years I had spoken out against the way our people were being treated; but I had not attacked anyone or taken up arms. However, there was much unrest in the valley and I believe the Chinese soldiers were watching me, afraid of a rebellion. By the next day the Army had gathered together my surviving relatives – my wife, my brother and sister, father, mother, grandmother, uncle and aunts, and the family's children and grandchildren. At gunpoint, they ordered some of the villagers to watch, they made us dig a hole' – he motioned to the rock-covered mound below. The officers yelled that rules must be obeyed, no matter what. No one must think or feel anything the Chinese group leaders do not tell them to think or feel. Then they told of my crime: I had defied the ban on prayer and religion and was an enemy of the people and government, and announced my punishment while four soldiers held my arms.'

For a few moments he was unable to speak. The wind shifted. My guide was visibly moved, his features charged with emotion. It seemed a long time before the elder went on: 'They ignored my protests. Maybe they had planned this for a long time. To this day, I do not know. I told them again that my prayer was given on instinct, given out of respect for my friend, and I was not promoting religion to him. It was not an act of defiance or rebellion against the government rulers. I pleaded with them to punish *me*, to make me alone suffer, and no one else. They said, "Don't worry, you will suffer plenty." They they ignored me, forcing me to watch.'

He drew a long breath and exhaled very slowly, as if gathering himself. I found myself in the grip of such intense feelings that it seemed I was actually standing there, years before, beside him as he faced a terrible, pivotal moment in his life. What happened next, I wondered, and how did he respond? What would *I* have done?

He began speaking again, his arms still trembling. 'The officers were laughing as a company of soldiers soaked strips of cotton in gasoline and stuffed these down the throats of my wife and relatives and set the cotton on fire and threw them into the hole. The soldiers buried them alive, burning. And the children, the little ones, their cries, their eyes . . .'

He stopped, standing rigid, his hands shaking uncontrollably.

I felt the blood pounding in my chest and searing my throat. I imagined if this had happened to my family. I imagined my wife, son and two young daughters dying that way. The snow was easing up and I watched the blue wind cross the beams of mounting light, in the quiet sigh of a man's life, a man I now knew was the sole survivor of his family, a leader singled out in an atmosphere of fear and repression. This was a man whose crime had been to bring his hands together in prayer to honour the greatness in another human being.

The image burned into my senses.

How many times throughout history have there been such horrors? And where, today, I wondered, are they happening still?

Slowly, the elder turned to me and dried the wetness from his cheeks. His hands were bare and I watched snow fall on them. It didn't melt right away but seemed to rest there, clinging to the old knuckles. The light illuminated his features, worn by weather and life and sun, but his eyes glowed with clarity. He looked into my face; no, he looked through my eyes, as if into my soul. I know no words to describe it, the look he gave.

'Tell me,' his voice grew stronger, 'about your life – and about America.'

I was incredulous. 'My life? America?' I felt a surge of dismay, then anger. 'How can you do that?'

'Do what?'

'Tell someone about a loss so devastating and then, just like that, let it go?'

He tilted his head and stared at me with a curious look on his face. 'Let it go? I can never let it go. They took away from me everything. Except two things, two things no one can take away: first, what I value and believe – what I *feel*, beneath everything else, is true in my heart, even when my mind can't prove or explain it. And second, short of killing me, they could not take away how I express *who I am* on the path of my destiny. These are the things that make me real and give me hope.'

'But how –' I began.

'Robert,' he interrupted me, 'it was the most terrible thing. The hardest thing in my life. I wanted you to know about it. You can learn something from it. Besides, without knowing this, you do not know me. The deep me, the real me. I could never be a leader of you. And you could not wholeheartedly work beside me or follow me. Think of this: could you trust me, or share a purpose or vision with me, simply because someone, like the Chinese officer, commanded you to? No. But now, if you choose to, you can begin to know me, and work with me, and trust me. Now I am real, I am not just a name. I have a heart and a voice and a life story. I am not just some stranger who climbed a mountain with you.'

Now I am real. I am not just a name. I have a heart and a voice and a life story.

'As for your other question,' he added, 'the one about how could I tell you of such a horrifying experience and then turn my attention away from it? It's because of you, you are alive. You are here, now. My family is dead. All things die. Sooner or later. Learning to face that is a hard thing. But I am living. Each day, I tell myself that. And you are here. I can learn things from you. I have work left to do.'

I can learn things from you.

The elder saw my confusion.

'You must understand, Robert, that this is not something only' – he slowly circled his open hand in the air – 'of the mind's making. It is from the heart.' He touched his palm to his chest. 'In Tibet, we call it *authentic presence*. It means, literally, "field of power". When we live from here, from the inside, we can talk openly and honestly with each other, and say the things we deeply feel, even when it's hard to say them. We hold ourselves, and each other, accountable to our best effort in all things. We search for our calling, for the path we are born to take. Every person has this, and can face hardships and problems but not live inside them. This is a very difficult thing to do, but we can do it, we can set them aside.

They do not go away, but we must not miss the chance to keep learning from whatever is here *now*.'

As he said this, I found myself thinking of the business executives, government leaders, and management teams I had worked with over the years. 'But can the rest of us learn that?' I asked. 'What about the times when we're trying to cope with setbacks or difficulties and find ourselves facing another problem, and another? If we turn our attention to these too,' I tried to rationalize, 'won't we get overwhelmed by them? Isn't it better to try *not* to face or feel them until later?'

'No,' he said after a moment's reflection. *No*.

'The bridge,' said my guide.

'Yes,' agreed the elder, remembering. 'The same day I lost my family, the Chinese Army blew up one of the bridges over the river. To punish us more. To force the people, everyone, to suffer. To have to travel far around to cross the river. The officers said, "Build it back if you can. We will not help you."'

The elder explained that he was forced away from the massacre and led, with the others, to the edge of the water near the destroyed bridge. The villagers were crying, overwhelmed. He realized he had to make a choice. To give up his life, then and there, or to lead in some other way. Through the numbness and pain, and the crush of his circumstances, he stared at the smouldering ruins of the bridge. He let his intuition guide him.

He picked up a large rock and, with anguish throttling his chest and tears pouring down his face, he set his jaw and walked, while the battalions of armed soldiers taunted him, into the icy river toward a submerged support pillar of the old bridge, just visible above the water, and set the stone there. The enemy officers had learned that the Tibetan people were, by long tradition, afraid of deep water, and assumed they would not – could not – rebuild the bridge. But they underestimated the depth of one man's emotional courage and character, a man who before 1959 had been chosen to lead his people. The invasion had kept him from that destiny, until a day of terror and explosions. A day that would challenge any leader, any human being, to the core. What would *I* do? I was asking myself. And I ask you, my reader, what would *you* have done?

'I will carry a hundred stones and timbers for each of my lost relatives,' said the elder to the villagers with his eyes on fire. 'How many will you carry?'

At first, no one answered, no one moved. They were watching him, feeling his presence as he responded to fate and the call of leadership. He knew then that he could not give up, couldn't *not* go into the deep water, or they would all die; the hundreds of villagers would give up, not just him. Before long, others were hoisting heavy stones and wading into the river. Eighteen rocks he carried that day when at last the villagers wrapped bankets around him, trembling from head to .toe from the shock of his loss and the cold. In the months that followed, they rebuilt the bridge by hand, with a high arch in the ancient Tibetan design. It stands today, as a symbol, more beautiful and useful than before. I've stood on that bridge. It's a living monument to the memory of one man's heart, and the heart of his community.

For the rest of that long afternoon, the elder, the guide, and I talked about our lives and what it meant to have a purpose and a destiny. I told them what, to me, America stands for; how it was a nation born out of a fierce struggle to uphold human freedom, rights and dignity. Yet I clearly realized the Tibetan elder was demonstrating – and I was trying to learn or re-learn – a long sought-after ability *to be a deeply feeling, authentic human being, no matter what life brings, no matter what challenges and opportunities we face.* And it was then that I began to believe that such an ability requires not just intellect but emotional intelligence' including an *activating energy* that enlivens what we feel and value. We express this in many ways, such as being open, honest, of integrity, courageous, and creative, committing ourselves to transforming even the most daunting circumstances into something meaningful, and valuable, as we shape a new future.

These are some of the qualities of emotional intelligence. When you *think* about them, such attributes are little more than an ideology or principles or good ideas; it's only when you deeply *feel* them that they become active and real, and you are compelled to *act* upon them, to live them. Every business leader wants, or needs, to have qualities such as these. Every employee calls for them in a boss, and every family member hopes for them in a parent, partner or sibling. You know what IQ is; EQ (Emotional Quotient) is the emotional intelligence counterpart to IQ.

The leader in Tibet was forced, through catastrophic change, to start over with little help and few resources, to reach deeply inside himself and find a way to prevail against daunting odds*; similarly, business managers

---

*I have no way of knowing whather the officer in charge of this reported tragedy was a Red Guard rogue or acted with backing from the occupying Chinese Communist government in Tibet, or if he and his soldiers were ever disciplined for their actions. By recounting elements of this tragedy as described to me, as well as writing about some of my experiences with the Tibetan people, I am not intending, in any way, to condemn the Chinese people; they had no say in their government's illegal invasion of the sovereign nation of Tibet or the attempted genocide there and the terror-based repression that is still going. I also want to make it clear that none of the business leaders or organizations I work with were in any way connected with my travels in Tibet, which took place years ago and were purely personal journeys. As Nobel laureate Elie Wiesel has said, 'What is happening in Tibet is a crime against all of humanity.' To learn more, contact the International

are forced to start over many times in their careers, to find ways to prevail in facing layoffs, cutbacks, regulatory changes, market downturns, dwindling resources, limited funding, and cut-throat global competition.

By and large, what we are searching for in business and in life isn't *out there*, in the latest trends or technology; it's *in here*, inside ourselves. It has been there all along, but many of us have not valued it, or respected it, or used it as brilliantly as we are capable. At its essence, a meaningful and successful life requires being attuned to what is on the *inside*, beneath the mental analyses, the appearances and control, beneath the rhetoric and skin.

In the human heart.

No, the heart isn't just a pump, as cardiologists describe it. It is more. Scientists can measure its energy from five feet away.[3] It radiates. It activates our deepest values, transforming them from something we *think about* ro what we *live*. It knows things our mind does not, cannot. The heart is the place of courage and spirit, integrity and commitment. It is a source of energy and deep feelings that call us to create, learn, cooperate, lead and serve.

The leader in Tibet was clearly intelligent. But not only in mind; he had high emotional intelligence. I witnessed numerous small acts of creative, practical leadership during the time I spent with him. I observed him at work in his community, interacting with others, trusting them, holding them accountable to their best efforts, and generating creative ideas and work alliances despite a dearth of resources and absence of funds. Time and again, he demonstrated what can be seen as a hallmark of EQ: *He learned – and taught – through feelings instead of abstract ideas and analysis, relationship instead of rote, authenticity instead of role, deep discernment instead of habit, and through essence instead of surface.*

He was, in sum, the deepest, most authentic leader I have ever met. Who is yours? Take a few moments to remember, to feel what it was like to be with this person. Over the years I have known a number of exceptional men and women who lead and innovate, who have defied the odds and, more often than not, prevailed. You'll meet many of them in the pages of this book. I vowed to find a way to learn what this man had learned, and to measure it if that proved possible, and this eventually led to assembling the team that created the EQ Map™. The poet William Stafford once said that the writer's job is to dig so deep into his own story that he reaches everyone's story. That's what I have tried to do in these

Campaign for Tibet (1825 K St., N.W., Suite 520, Washington, DC 20006; 202-785-1515. Web site on the Internet: http: //www.peacenet.orglict).

pages. That's a leader's job, too. At least one of the reasons you're reading this book is because you're a feeling human being, not a nameless face or a number-cruncher with a job title. In light of this, now is a good time to ask, What are your life stories? What is your sense of personal calling, your deepest feelings about the reason you are alive? What makes you real and worth knowing?

A Starting Point for Exploration

This book is based on a combination of scientific research and personal experience, and on specific insights and practical examples from leaders, managers, and professionals around the world. The essence is this: there's more in human life – and work – than our rigid, time-worn theories allow. There is more depth and wisdom in what we feel, in how the heart holds an image of our unique potential, or destiny, and calls us to it.

This book is about that call.

One of the immediate payoffs is an opportunity to disengage yourself from the constant, numbing struggle to work harder, faster, and longer, and, instead, to begin championing and changing the core of your inner life, your interpersonal life, and your work life. James MacGregor Burns said that 'executives must operate by feel and by feedback'.[4] He was right. An enterprise is what we make it. If we treat it like an altar of facts and logic, like a calculator, machine, or military regiment, that's what it will be. But what if, instead, we treat it as something precious and *alive*, an organization of creative ideas and trusting relationships to be grown and nurtured, valued and celebrated, like a family, a community, or a temple?

I think about many of my corporate colleagues, most of whom, during business school, crunched at least a million numbers and analyzed a thousand balance sheets. But not one of them had thirty seconds' worth of counsel about the ABCs of building deep, trusting relationships, or about respecting and expressing the truth of deeply felt human values and creative intuition – the combined intelligence of the heart *and* head – or holding to credibility and integrity while flowing *with* problems instead of getting overwhelmed or derailed by them.

In the past hundred years, we've capped the rise of academic intelligence and technical rationality. Modern education and training have been built on a much heralded mindset of logic and analysis. A curriculum built on grammar, arithmetic, reductionistic reasoning, formula-driven analysis, and rote memorization of the latest crop of facts. We've tried to use this inert intelligence to fashion ourselves into perfect students and by-the-books professionals. Not practical, adaptive, or creative. Not *real* people but perfect-*appearing* people, with high IQ and achievements, academically speaking. We've excelled at this model. We've taken it to the top.

And what we've discovered is, by itself, it's not the most vital thing and it's not enough.

Not nearly enough.

All of us know people who succeed in school but fail in life, and vice versa. We all know people rich with common sense or creativity who did poorly in academic tests. They are a constant reminder that there is more to success than school smarts. And yet we seem largely oblivious to the findings that IQ may be related to as little as *4 per cent* of real-world success.[5] In other words, 90 per cent may be related to *other forms of intelligence*.

Think about it: all around us, despite the information revolution and a populace with intellectual prowess unequalled throughout history, relationships are crumbling, trust is vanishing, lawyers are thriving, cynicism is rising, hatred is spreading, and the politics of democracy have been relegated to little more than a staged media concoction . At the same time, many of us feel overworked and undervalued. In lots of cases, we've lost our sense of direction. Or our creative spirit is waning. Or we can no longer find any real meaning in much of what we do.

Voltaire pointed out that for the ancient Romans, *sensus communis* meant not only common sense but also humanity and sensibility, including the full use of the senses, the heart and intuition. Yes, business runs on brain power. But to think well and for lasting success, we must learn to compete with every aspect of our intelligence, not just from the neck up. Besides, the latest neurological evidence indicates that *emotion* is the indispensable 'fuel' for the brain's higher reasoning powers.[6] More on that in a moment. When I went through my undergraduate sciences education, I was taught that, on average, an adult used only about 10 per cent of his or her intelligence in the course of a lifetime. Years later, I learned there had been a revised estimate from brain scientists: on average, an adult may actually use only about *one ten-thousandth* of his or her potential intelligence over a lifetime.[7] In short, we have vastly more untapped capacities than we generally give ourselves credit for. Successful individuals and organizations around the world have realized there are many dimensions of practical and creative intelligence beyond IQ.[8] And, as Yale psychologist Robert Sternberg asserts, 'People still count IQ, but IQ doesn't count ...

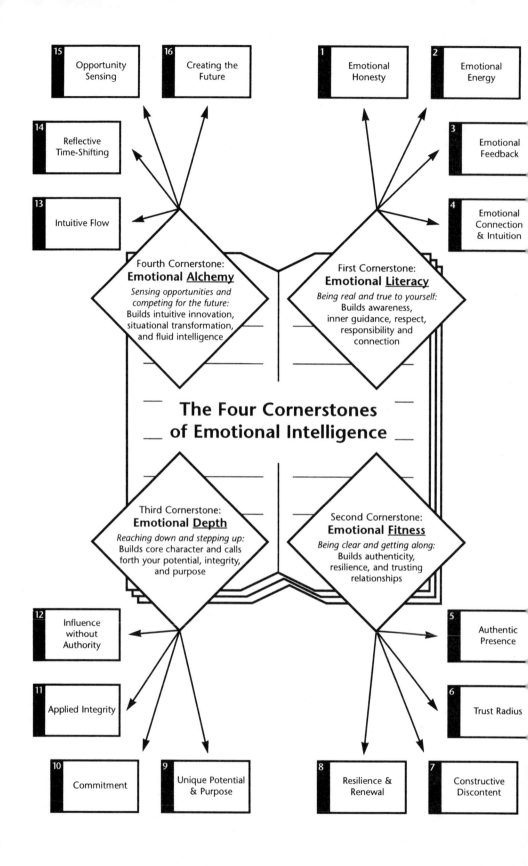

15 Opportunity Sensing

16 Creating the Future

1 Emotional Honesty

2 Emotional Energy

14 Reflective Time-Shifting

3 Emotional Feedback

13 Intuitive Flow

4 Emotional Connection & Intuition

Fourth Cornerstone:
Emotional Alchemy
Sensing opportunities and competing for the future:
Builds intuitive innovation, situational transformation, and fluid intelligence

First Cornerstone:
Emotional Literacy
Being real and true to yourself:
Builds awareness, inner guidance, respect, responsibility and connection

The Four Cornerstones of Emotional Intelligence

Third Cornerstone:
Emotional Depth
Reaching down and stepping up:
Builds core character and calls forth your potential, integrity, and purpose

Second Cornerstone:
Emotional Fitness
Being clear and getting along:
Builds authenticity, resilience, and trusting relationships

12 Influence without Authority

5 Authentic Presence

11 Applied Integrity

6 Trust Radius

10 Commitment

9 Unique Potential & Purpose

8 Resilience & Renewal

7 Constructive Discontent

We must never lose sight of the fact that what really matters most in the world is not inert intelligence.'9

So where do we turn? One place is to emotional intelligence. This book advances an initial working plan to begin discussing and developing EQ in your business and life. What we offer you is a starting point: a Four Cornerstone Model (see facing page) which *moves emotional intelligence out of the realm of psychological analysis and philosophical theories, and into the realm of direct knowing, exploration and application.* Executive EQ begins with the cornerstone of *emotional literacy*, which builds a locus of self-confidence through emotional honesty, energy, emotional feedback, intuition, responsibility, and connection.

The second cornerstone, *emotional fitness*, strengthens your authenticity, believability, and resilience, expanding your circle of trust and your capacity for listening, managing conflict, and making the most of constructive discontent. In *emotional depth*, the third cornerstone, you explore ways to align your life and work with your unique potential and purpose, and to back this with integrity, commitment, and accountability, which, in turn, increase your influence without authority. From here you advance to the fourth cornerstone, *emotional alchemy*, through which you extend your creative instincts and capacity to flow with problems and pressures and to compete for the future by building your capacity to sense more readily – and access – the widest range of hidden solutions and untapped opportunities.

EQ is Essential to Success in the Twenty-first Century

If the driving force of intelligence in twentieth-century business has been IQ, then – in accordance to growing evidence – in the dawning twenty-first century it will be EQ, and related forms of practical and creative intelligence. This book will explore many of the reasons why. Of course, there are still those in management who would dismiss emotions entirely, or see them as a minefield to be avoided at all costs. Yet in many cases these are the very managers who, for all their emphasis on cold, hard numbers and the bottom line, are most out of touch with the heart-level engine that drives human capital and produces the exceptional, creative work required for any company to lead the field amidst the turbulence and confusion of global market changes.

In work today, the stakes are tremendously high. You can be fired tomorrow. Going through the motions just won't cut it. Your company can go under. What this book attempts to demonstrate is that emotional intelligence is one of the most indispensable elements, not only in creating a profitable business but in leading a successful life. It is a primary source of motivation, information (feedback), personal power, innovation, and influence.

As we look out over the growing chasm between executives and managers striving to make the 'right' decisions and the individuals whose lives are stretched to the breaking point by those very decisions, we are often asked to put our faith in the healing power of that rare and ill-defined virtue called 'leadership'. We have been told that if only there were enough leaders at all levels of an organization they could serve as our mentors, coaches, counselors, allies, guardians, and friends. That they could remain ever alert to the organization's needs while at the same time furthering our personal best interests.

But if there was enough tradition-based leadership to solve this problem, we would have found it or created it or bought it by now with the hundreds of millions of dollars spent on leadership development and executive education. The truth is, today there are too many wounds, and the wounds are deep, for the standard leadership healers to mend them by themselves. There are times, of course, when conventional business leadership can be a good and necessary thing, but, as with rationality, its powers stretch only so far.

I believe there is a better way.

According to systems thinking, the deeper structures, or habits, of which we are unaware, hold us hostage. Review the pattern of your life and work: as pressures, uncertainties and change come at you from all sides, are you calling more than ever on your emotional intelligence, or is the altar of intellect – of memorized facts, technical analysis, and reductionistic reasoning – holding you hostage?

Ask yourself: which of these paths am I climbing today, counting on in my career, investing myself in? It is far from an idle question. There is a great chance that your answer will, according to new research, determine your future.

INTRODUCTION

The Call for Leaders and Organizations with High EQ

For decades now, the typical concentration in business has rested squarely on analysis, external power and technical rationality – a shift which can be seen as starting with Voltaire and other thinkers in the eighteenth century. This has served largely to overshadow other human characteristics, such as emotion, intuition, spirit, and experience.

Our emotions, as much or more than our bodies and minds, contain our histories, every line and verse of every experience, deep understanding, and relationship in our lives. They comprise the feeling of who we are, and enter our systems as energy. Energy, as we have been taught, is neither created nor destroyed. It flows.

This energy is a primary source of influence and power. Not all forms are physical. A thought is a form of energy, but what is it formed out of?[11] Light? Electricity? Emotion, too, is comprised of energy that continually pours through you, setting in motion a confluence of deep processes that affect every aspect of your life. When you increase your emotional intelligence, you shift the form of this energy, and it changes your experience of work, life, and relationship.

The passing era of business intelligence has been dominated primarily by IQ and physics, and has centred on a mathematical model that treated nearly everything as if it were inanimate and analyzable, or sequential and reductionist. There are many reasons to believe that the emerging model of business intelligence will be based far more on the principles of EQ and biological systems[12], and that it will treat people, markets, ideas, and organizations as unique and alive, generative and interactive, and inherently capable of change, learning, growth, inspiration, creativity, synergy, and transformation.

In many workplaces, talented, productive people are being thwarted or sabotaged by gaps in emotional intelligence – in themselves, their bosses, and the others around them. In many companies, we're caught up in an atmosphere of autocratic and sometimes abusive management, mountains of rules and red tape, traumatic downsizings, and a fear-laced climate of uncertainty, perceived inequities, resentment, and anger that, at times, can border on hostility and rage. We show up and keep our hearts closed and our heads down, just hoping to get by and collect our pay cheques. The truth is, however, that many people in business have very little energy left; certainly not enough to lead their career, company or industry into a successful future.

If we lack emotional intelligence, whenever stress rises the human brain switches to autopilot and has an inherent tendency to do more of the same, only harder. Which, more often than not, is precisely the wrong approach in today's work world. I remember giving a guest lecture at one of America's best-known business schools. Just prior to my presentation, in an amphitheatre filled with MBA students, an entrepreneur's proposal for starting a new company was being reviewed. The assertive students were calling out points of rejection to the business plan. 'That won't work.' 'A dead end!' 'You'll never have enough quality control!' 'The overheads will kill you.' 'Who would buy this product, anyway?' 'You'll be bankrupt in a year!' 'You're going against every rule of economics!' Point by point, they shot him down.

The entrepreneur stood in silence, eyeing the faces in the audience.

'Yes,' he said at last, 'you are very efficient. You know your business principles and case studies. The investment bankers shot this idea down, too.' He paused. Murmurs of confidence swept the room. Gloating faces. Score another kill for the MBAs. 'However, there's one more thing . . .' said the entrepreneur. 'My partners and I identified the points you raised. We realized each of the objections and reasons why our ideas couldn't possibly work. And then, one by one, we followed our intuition and found a way around them. We believed the "impossible" was possible, and we frankly didn't care if others couldn't see this yet.

'We formed a small company, financed it ourselves on a shoestring, and went into business. This month begins our third year. We're still in business.' A snicker came from the upper left corner of the lecture hall. The entrepreneur looked directly towards the source of that sound of derision as he said, 'We had revenues of $26 million, and profits of nearly $5 million.' A stunned look passed across the faces of these gathered future leaders of enterprise. They were momentarily in shock. One of my good friends, a business school professor for more than a quarter of a century, stood silently at the back of the room, smiling. He knew. Another lesson was being learned about the inherent weaknesses of technical analysis without the sounding board of emotional intelligence – in particular, intuitive creative wisdom.

Think about it. For the most part, *reasoning* has its power and value only in the context of emotion. No matter what the product, idea, service, or cause, we *buy* – or *buy in* – based on feelings; and then, if possible, we rationalize or justify our choices with numbers and facts. No one talks about the *rationale* of a passionate relationship or hobby, or brags about a *reasonable* marriage or *logical* vacation, or requires a *statistical analysis* of deeply felt human longings and dreams. By and large, the *passions* – the word the ancient Greeks used for emotions – are more honest than thought or reason.

In many cases, when I ask professionals to tell me their story, they tell me about their academic achievements, their curriculum vitae or what they have acquired. Yet academic intelligence is an inert and analytical intelligence; it rarely ever sparks creative initiative or leads to purpose-directed accomplishments.[13] The truth is, those of us who can memorize and recall facts well, and may from time to time reason with those facts, don't necessarily rely on them to make a real difference in life or work, either to ourselves or anyone else. When I ask business people to tell me something of their story, I'm asking to know who they are, not what they've done. IQ doesn't measure this at all. What I'm most curious about is what they believe is their unique potential and how they discovered it, what they've struggled with and had to face to achieve what they have achieved, what they have risked, learned, dreamed and drawn upon to do it, what they have felt, feared, learned, imagined, and discovered throughout their life. This is the real story of our work and lives, and it is, above all, a story of emotional intelligence.

> *Business is now so complex and difficult, the survival of firms so hazardous in an environment increasingly unpredictable, competitive and fraught with danger, that their continued existence depends on the day-to-day mobilization of every ounce of intelligence.*
>
> Konosuke Matsushita, Founder, Matsushita Electric, Ltd

Think about yourself and the people you work with. What have you each been through in your life? What got you here? What makes you worth knowing – and trusting? What fires your creativity? What makes you real – and valuable? If I can't know what you feel, what matters to you, then, as the elder in Tibet told me, we are little more than a face and a name to each other; you are not deep or alive to me, nor I to you. This is one reason why an estimated 93 per cent of our believability and credibility are based on EQ – and related practical and creative intelligence – not IQ.[14]

Think about how much time and energy you have wasted protecting yourself from people you do not trust, avoiding problems you cannot talk about, faking acceptance of decisions with which you do not agree, remaining silent despite the intuitive sense that you're missing opportunities, putting up with jobs that aren't right for you, or holding back your insights on current problems and emerging challenges.

Some men and women are blessed with a high level of both IQ and EQ. Some have a paucity of one or other or both. These and other forms of intelligence enhance and complement each other: emotions spark creativity, collaboration, initiative, and transformation; logical reasoning reins in errant impulses and aligns purpose with process, technology with touch. There's another driving force here, too: evidence indicates that a person's fundamental values and character in life stem, above all, not from IQ but from underlying *emotional* capacities.

Emotional Intelligence is a Primary Source of Human Energy, Information and Influence

The shift in leadership capacity and scope that I've been describing is, I believe, neither discretionary nor a fad. It is the result of specific and growing changes in business life, in general, and the realities of dealing with increasingly brief, fast-paced – and necessarily trusting, collaborative, and innovative – human interactions at work. While excessive emotion can temporarily disrupt reasoning or analysis, new research suggests that, in most cases, too little emotion can be even more devastating to a career or company.[15] Many of the insights and points of discussion in this book are referenced to the observations of business leaders and to the findings of a wide range of scientists and specialists, and are also related to our emerging research in developing the *EQ Map* and *Organisational EQ Profiles* with the help of executives, managers, and professionals from more than a hundred organizations. According to Josh Hammond, President of the American Quality Foundation, emotions have a high-performance definition which is present at the heart of nearly every leading enterprise but is little recognized or valued in most of today's other organizations:[16]

EMOTIONS

Conventional vs. High-Performance Meaning

Conventional	High Performance
sign of weakness	sign of strength
no place in business	essential in business
avoid emotions	emotions trigger learning
confuse	explicate (clarify)
table them	integrate them
avoid emotional people	seek out emotional people
pay attention only to thoughts of	listen for the emotion in
use of nonemotional words	use of emotional words

Based on the latest research, I would add the following:

Conventional	High Performance
interfere with good judgment	essential to good judgment
distract us	motivate us
sign of vulnerability	make us real and alive
obstruct, or slow-down, reasoning	enhance, or speed-up, reasoning
form a barrier to control	build trust and connection
weaken fixed attitudes	activate ethical values
inhibit the flow of objective data	provide vital information and feedback
complicate management planning	spark creativity and innovation
undermine authority	generate influence without authority

Studies[17] also reveal that emotions are an essential 'activating energy' for *ethical values* such as trust, integrity, empathy, resilience, and credibility, and for *social capital*, which represents your ability to build and sustain trusting, profitable business relationships.[18] At the centre of these traits is something every great leader must have: the capacity to create excitement. This is similar to what is generally called the ability to motivate self and others, but that's too watered down an expression

> *Without the guidance of emotions, reasoning has neither principles nor power*
>
> Robert C. Solomon, Professor of Philosophy, University of Texas

to signify the inner fire required to build great companies and compete for the future. Even the emotion of anger is imbued with an intelligence that, in the right hands and in the rights ways, can be transformed into creative collaboration and breakthrough innovations.

Much of what you learn in this book may be common sense, but it's not common practice. Fortunately, scientists now consider EQ a *learnable* intelligence, one which can be developed and improved at any time and any age.[19]

Emotional Intelligence is Vital to Reasoning and IQ

Emotions are powerful organizers of thought and action, and are, paradoxically, indispensable for reasoning and rationality. EQ also comes to the aid of IQ when you need to solve important problems or make a key decision, and enables you to accomplish this in a superior fashion and a fraction of the time – a few minutes, or even moments, for example, instead of the entire day or more of the exhausting nonstop linear, sequential thinking that might be required to reach the same decision without the aid of EQ. Moreover, emotions awaken intuition and curiosity, which assist in anticipating an uncertain future and planning our actions accordingly.

'There has never been any doubt that, under certain circumstances, emotion can disrupt reasoning,' explains Antonio R. Damasio, head of neurology at the University of Iowa College of Medicine.

> Yet research indicates that *reduction in emotion may constitute an equally important source of irrational behaviour.* ... In truth, reasoning/decision-making and emotion/feeling 'intersect' in the brain.... There is a collection of systems in the brain dedicated to the goal-oriented thinking process we call *reasoning,* and to the response selection we call *decision making. This same collection of brain systems is also involved in emotion and feeling.* Feelings and emotion are a powerful influence on reason. *I see feelings as having a truly privileged status.* They retain a primacy that pervades our mental life. Feelings have a say on how the rest of the brain and cognition go about their business. Their influence is immense.

For many years, the traditional view from within management was solidly tied to administration and strategy. Executives came to believe that almost everything important to a company's profit could be categorized, analyzed, and predicted. You could always come up with the right strategy to guide your company to enduring triumph in any circumstance if only you *thought* about it hard enough.

Or perhaps not. It turns out that emotional intelligence is, in effect, an indispensable activator and enhancer of intellectual prowess, or IQ. To use a description from physics, if we consider the overall intelligence capacity of a human being as a force field, then IQ and EQ interrelate with each other as constituents of this field, and this creates a dynamic tension, from one to the other, stabilizing their respective energies. And if IQ and EQ are relatively equal, their interaction creates an upward motion – a lift in intelligent energy – which is the key principle, for example, that distinguished Bell helicopter from earlier attempts at flight design.

The fact is, for people with identical IQs, some will outperform others. Something beyond IQ is at work. That something – or a large part of it – is EQ. When emotions are acknowledged and guided constructively, they enhance intellectual performance. Dr Robert Rosenthal, a Harvard psychologist and expert on empathy, has shown that when people administering IQ tests treat their subjects warmly, the test scores are higher.[20]

In meetings and other group settings where people come together to collaborate, there is a strong sense of group IQ, the sum total of intellectual knowledge and skills in the room. However, the single most important element in group intelligence is not the average, or highest, IQ, but emotional intelligence. A single participant who is low in EQ can lower the collective IQ of the entire group. Chris Argyris, from Harvard, asks, 'How can a group where everyone has an individual IQ of 130 get together and collectively end up with an IQ of 65?[21] Yale's Robert Sternberg and Wendy Williams, who studied why some groups are more creative and effective than others, call this 'group IQ', and it reflects how effectively the players collaborate.[22] Though the group may be able to work smarter than its members' collective intelligences would suggest, it can rapidly work dumber by not allowing people to share talents, and by allowing destructive discontent, domineering, or in-fighting to degrade performance and stymie progress.

Today's fast-changing, more open and fluid style of work puts a premium on the combination of intellect and EQ, especially when it comes to trusting and teaming with others to solve problems and seize opportunities. A study[23] of star performers at Bell Labs, the scientific think-tank near Princeton University, reviewed engineers and scientists who are all ranked near the top of academic IQ tests. What makes the difference between the stars in this group and the also-rans was not IQ but other aspects of intelligence, including EQ. They were better able to motivate themselves and take the initiative – willing to take on responsibilities above and beyond their stated job – especially during times of crisis and change. They build rapport and high-trust relationships across the entire organization, and are better able to take full and immediate advantage of informal, highly adaptive *ad hoc* networks and teams to create breakthroughs.

In order to effectively explore and apply the discoveries and principles in this book, my partners and I have developed a variety of tools[24], including the *EQ Map*[25] at the end of the book and a sampling of *EQ-in-Action* application exercises in each chapter.

What you will find in the pages ahead is a comprehensive, integrated working model of emotional intelligence in leadership and organizations. It is my sincere hope that it will serve as a starting point for dialogue in executive and management circles and will encourage some meaningful reflection, exploration, and new learning for us all.

Emotional Literacy

Being real and *true to yourself:*
Builds *personal power* – including self-awareness, inner
guidance, respect, responsibility and connection

We begin our journey through the four cornerstones of emotional intelligence with *emotional literacy*. By way of context: in *academic* literacy, to read is to think about meaning, to write is to make thinking visible as language, to speak is to voice your views to others. In *computer* literacy, to function at a keyboard is to use the language of the screen as interaction of thinking with the software or network. *Emotional* literacy emerges not from the musings of rarified intellect but from the workings of the human heart, from which comes the energy that makes us real and that motivates us to identify and pursue our unique potential and purpose. Emotional literacy centres on learning the alphabet, grammar and vocabulary of EQ and recognizing, respecting, and valuing the inherent wisdom of feelings.

One of the most harmful attitudes our modern work culture has perpetuated is that we cannot, under any circumstances, trust our inner voice or perceptions. We are raised to doubt ourselves, to discount intuition, and to seek outside validation for virtually everything we do. We are conditioned to assume that people other than ourselves know best and can tell us the honest truth more clearly than we could ever tell ourselves. Yet, as we will see, surveys of thousands of successful executives, managers, and entrepreneurs indicate that the majority of them have, for years, counted on gut hunches – as well as many other forms of emotional intelligence – in nearly all important decisions and interactions.

CHAPTER 1

Emotional Honesty

harlie Chaplin, the British-born film actor, once entered a Charlie Chaplin look-alike contest. He came in third. This raises an important issue: how well do you actually know yourself, and let others know you? And how openly and honestly do you listen to and respect what you intuitively sense and feel?

When pure sincerity forms within, it is outwardly realized in other people's hearts.

Lao Tzu, Understanding the Mysteries, Sixth Century BC

Stop for a minute and jot down an answer, rating yourself from one (not very honest) to ten (utmost honesty). Ironically, any attempt to fake such honesty – to profess being truthful yet feel no sense of care or kindness, to go through the motions, as many professionals do each day – blocks us from living it. Contrary to popular opinion, 'being honest' isn't a mind game of putting the 'right' face or spin on things, or being politically correct. It's about paying attention to what your heart says is true.

Cash-register Honesty or *Emotional* Honesty?

Think about it. There's cash-register honesty. That's the looks-good truth that most of us are wont to ensure. You keep your hand out of the till. You make certain to appear at all times to be following the rules. If you find a mathematical error, you fix it. Make a mistake? You admit it. Unless, of course, it affects your status or career, in which case you may choose achievement over honesty, or loyalty or harmony over truth and blame problems on others or on circumstances. If a colleague or employee is going through the motions and reports, 'I'm doing my best,' you nod with understanding. As long as this person shows up for work and acts busy, many of us tend to accept it at face value. 'That's fine,' we say. 'You're giving the organization all you can. That's all I expect. Good job.'

But inside you don't believe it. He could be doing much better serving customers, you feel. She's not fully committed to this creative project, your gut tells you. But with cash-register honesty, you say nothing. No rules are being broken, right? Yet if you value emotional honesty, you will pay attention to what you feel – beneath the motions and words – and you will speak up. You don't get stuck in your head; you connect, too, with your heart. You care. You're committing part of your life to this job, this company. You sense untapped potential, in yourself and others. You have the guts to say so, to put yourself on the line. You listen to your intuition. You ask questions. You learn all you can about others and their unique potential,[1] who they are, deep down. You offer support. You hold yourself accountable for your own best effort, at all times. And you hold others accountable to theirs.

Being *emotionally* honest requires listening to the strong feelings of 'inner truth' – which arises, at least in major part, from your core emotional intelligence as it links to your intuition and conscience – and reflecting on it and acting accordingly and appropriately. This is very different from a traditional analytical style of working, in which control is justified solely by academic credentials, rank, or expertise. In this latter approach, to admit not knowing something or making a mistake is to admit loss of control. Not so with emotional honesty, in which we rebel against repressing honest feelings just to 'put the right face on things' that really aren't right, or to 'go through the motions' to 'look good' and act as if we care. Such actions may be politically correct. They are not emotionally correct. And what you and others *feel* communicates the emotional truth all by itself, in your eyes and body language, in the tone of your voice, beneath the words. Feelings make us real and, despite all attempts to stifle them, they will not sit idly by when potentials are ignored, possibilities get overlooked, or values are being trampled upon.

To prove this to yourself, conduct an EQ self-audit in the days ahead. Monitor your thoughts and feelings. Are you honest with yourself? How deep is this honesty? Is it primarily cash-register honesty, of the head? Or emotional honesty, of the heart? How carefully do you pay attention to your gut feelings, or, by habit, do you often fail to notice them?

It takes courage to acknowledge what you feel, especially when it's at odds with whatever your thoughts may be trying to rationalize. But this is the juncture where emotional literacy is born: in learning to remain aware of your thoughts while acknowledging the inner voice of your feelings. M. Scott Fitzgerald wrote, 'The test of a first-rate intelligence is the ability to hold two opposing ideas in mind at the same time and still retain the ability to function.' Actually, it may be easier than that. A first-rate intelligence combines EQ with IQ and not only retains the ability to function, but *excels* at functioning.

This is the call of emotional honesty: to remain honest with yourself and to respect the wisdom of both the heart and head, which brings us to a related question we'll be discussing in Chapters 5 and 9 but which I believe warrants some initial reflection now: how often do you choose harmony over truth? How often in your life have you been able to express a deeply felt sense of truth or concern at the expense of group harmony? When, specifically, have you stepped forward to voice such feelings, especially when doing so has been contrary, unpopular, or may even put your position or future at risk? Ask yourself, do I have the habit of glossing over my feelings, repressing them for the 'sake of the group', even when my intuition prompts me not to?

Many of us today feel that jobs are so scarce that we're lucky to have one at all. Complaining about perceived injustices and frustrations makes us sound like we're whining, which leaves us feeling guilty and more worried than ever about being laid off. So when problems loom up, we've grown conditioned to assuming that we must solve them silently on our own, if at all, and then simply put on a 'good face' and keep working longer and harder. However, as we will see, this climate of emotional suppression and fear kills all of the ideas that lead to innovation. And when that happens, the company is likely doomed anyway, which is one of the key reasons why we need more emotional intelligence at work – so we can step up and speak out with the greatest chance of helping our career and company, and the least likelihood of losing our job or hurting our chances for another.

Feelings are Indispensable for Insight and Good Judgment

We will argue throughout this book that much of your intuitive creative wisdom exists at the core of emotional intelligence. It is yours to call upon, to draw forth. This kind of practical intuition is a felt sense – an intelligent feeling – of inner knowing. And there is strong evidence that what you *feel* is not at odds with insight and good judgment; it is indispensable for insight and good judgment.[2] Emotions complement reason but do not require its rationalization. Emotions offer us an intuitive, prereflective logic, and one that can be brought into the open upon reflection and made explicit.[3] They are the driving force of a life well lived.

Emotions bestow meaning on the circumstances of our lives. Rather than being disturbances or intrusions, they serve as the heart of our existence, infusing it with richness and providing the system of meanings and values within which our lives and work either grow and thrive or stagnate and die. Emotion, not reason, is also what moves us to face the deep and central questions of our existence.

As for the emotional honesty and its link to intuition, let's consider a revolutionary thinker, Pitirim A. Sorokin. Imprisoned by Lenin and condemned to death, he was banished to exile in the United States, where he flourished in academia to become one of this century's greatest sociologist-philosophers. He dedicated his life to a comprehensive analysis of a human society in which he proposed that the crises we face today require a different approach from accessing knowledge – beyond reason and the five traditional senses. For Sorokin, there are three forms of truth: sensory, rational, and intuitive. The most fundamental and essential, and the deepest, is intuitive.[4] Many business leaders call this 'gut instinct' or 'judgment.'

Intuition, says Sorokin, is the ultimate foundation for our understanding of ethics, of the good and worthy in life. It is well understood in psychology and philosophy that aesthetic and moral judgments are based on deep subjective feelings, not vague musings of intellect. When intuition is actively developed, it expands and heightens your emotional intelligence and is, as Sorokin found, a key source of personal knowledge. This, it should be noted, is in contrast to the way the word intuition is used by rationalists, who write it off as merely some lucky guess or vague intimation of chance collisions of thoughts or ideas already buried somewhere in the brain. As we will see, this is not the case. Intuition is closely tied to emotional intelligence and can be of immense value to professional and personal success.[5] It was Carl Jung who reminded us that the term intuition 'does not denote something contrary to reason, but something outside the province of reason'.

The shortest and surest way to live with honour in the world is to be in reality what we would appear to be.

Socrates

Sorokin, who used the resources of Harvard University to study exhaustively human culture throughout history, found broad agreement about intuition. Among those supporting his view that intuition is the basis of truth are Plato, Aristotle, Plotinus, St Augustine, Thomas Hobbes, Henri Bergson, Baruch Spinoza, Carl Jung, and Alfred North Whitehead.

Even the stalwart proponent of rationality John Stuart Mill stated that, 'The truths known by intuition are the original premises from which all others are inferred.'

Intuition builds on this foundation of emotional honesty. It requires telling yourself the truth about what you are feeling. Only when you can stay in touch with this inner voice can you develop a source of knowing beyond your thoughts. At work, you might begin contrasting your intuitive sense to your rational appraisal. In this way, you can put your ideas and instincts more directly to the test. Observe the results. You'll discover what holds up and what doesn't; who is trustworthy and who isn't; what pays off and what doesn't; what means the most to you, and what doesn't. Along the way, you'll begin developing and accessing intuitive knowledge in ways that are unique to you. One discussion at a time.

Most of us already know that people at every corporate level are clamouring for direct, emotionally straightforward talk. They want us to have the guts to tell the truth, even when it hurts us to tell it, or reveals our humanity and vulnerability. 'Treat us like adults,' they say. 'Be real. Treat us like we can handle the truth about what's ahead. Don't skirt the tough issues and act like nothing's going on.' As Rushmore Kidder, founder of the Institute for Global Ethics, reminds us, the history of those who put loyalty or harmony over truth (loyalty to Hitler, Mao, Stalin, Saddam Hussein, and even Richard Nixon) are capable of doing terrible damage. It's hard to envision that kind of harm arising when we respect, openly express, and are open to discussing what our heart tells us is true.

Emotional Honesty makes You Real and True to Yourself

To the extent that we can be emotionally honest – getting out of our head and into the heart, using well-chosen words to say what we truly feel and believe – we find our voice, we become real. From there, we learn to readily face, and learn from, not only the bright, vigorous, and expansive side of human feelings, but also from the more constricting shadow side of the heart, from which arise our self-doubt, anger, and soul-searching. Without experiencing potent feelings, which can be powerful catalysts for change, we'd never be forced to take a good, clear look at who we are, what we're capable of becoming, and where we're going right now in our life and work.

This brings me to the example of a major service company, whose executives received an unsolicited offer to buy part of its business. The investor who made the bid demanded an answer within twenty-four hours, with 'no excuses or exceptions', which was his well-known policy. Unfortunately, the vice-president in charge of the area of the division targeted for sale happened to be away, as luck would have it, on the final two weeks of a sabbatical in a remote part of the world where he could not be reached. The president and CEO both realized this was an exceptionally generous offer, and they sensed it would prove very smart for the company to accept it.

'But he'll never wait an extra minute, let alone two weeks!' exclaimed the president.

The CEO nodded. The rest of the board members, called to this special meeting, were silent. An executive vice-president stood up at the back of the room and said, 'I believe we should ask the investor straight out to wait. Why not tell him we will not entertain any other offers in the next two weeks? It's what we need to give him a clear answer.'

Reluctantly, the CEO agreed. She was dreading making the call, and felt a gnawing sense of doubt as to the outcome. Meanwhile, the board members tried to come up with some plausible excuse that might convince the investor to delay his decision. They drew a blank. This man was smart and aggressive. He would not be fooled.

The next morning, the CEO called the investor. Without delay, she kindly asked him point blank for a two-week grace period on the decision.

He thought about it for only a second. 'Fine,' he said. 'I'll keep the offer open until then.'

That's what emotional honesty can do.

Ultimately, it's up to each of us to create work environments where cash-register honesty is demanded as the point of entry, but where emotional honesty is of paramount importance. Consider Jan Timmer, CEO of the electronics giant Philips, in the Netherlands, who initiated a deeper level of openness and honesty by printing a newspaper datelined in the future announcing that the company had gone bankrupt.

Or Derek Wanless, head of NatWest Group, one of the United Kingdom's 'Big Four' banks with total assets of $250 billion. He makes it a point to get closer to the emotionally honest voices of his employees by devoting an estimated 30 per cent of his time to meeting them face to face, at sites through his firm.[6] 'It is only by getting out and around that you can see and feel what is *really* happening. I have always done a bit of that, but the percentage of my time spent that way is up very sharply, and it might increase more.'

This is something that a growing number of executives are paying attention to. For example, Colin Marshall, CEO of British Airways, one of the largest single-centre businesses in the world, with $9 billion in sales, believes that openness and emotional honesty are among the vital elements in bringing out the best performance of his organization.[7]

'We don't believe that where we are today is where we should be or where we would expect to be tomorrow,' he says. Over the past five years, British Airways has held 110 seminars, each with twenty-five managers, and at each one, Marshall says, 'I spent two to three hours just sitting there talking openly and honestly with them about various aspects of the business.' Marshall says that, after years of strict control, managers were at first reluctant to speak out, but now they know 'they aren't going to get slayed if they come up with a criticism'. To prove his point, Marshall has fired managers who haven't listened openly to criticism or ideas, and has promoted those with emotional honesty who have challenged the system.

Marshall has found that acknowledging and expressing our honest feelings, and tapping into the intuitive business-improvement wisdom they can hold, takes courage. He's right. Here's a related example from one of the companies I've worked with:

Jackson, a senior partner and operating manager at a large firm, has just announced to a junior partner, Allan, that he is recommending that the board promote Kurt, an outsider from a much larger company, to director of the firm's professional development, a position just vacated by the retirement of its long-time director named Joe. But this announcement obviously doesn't sit well with Allan. Jackson notices the discomfort, but wonders, why can't you just drop it, Allan? This isn't your concern. Let the boss promote whomever he wants. Let's get on with things.

But Allan turns to Jackson and the sparks begin to fly. Allan thinks that Julia, who for seven years has been staff management in professional development, is the best one for the job. Besides, for the past month she's been acting director. Incensed, Jackson snaps that Julia's not had enough experience for the job. Allan disagrees: 'I understand that you may doubt her ability, Jackson, but I feel that's because she was lost in Joe's shadow. I truly feel she's the right one for the job.'

'Don't you think I considered her already?' replies Jackson defensively. 'Why would I spend money on an executive search firm if I thought Julia was right for the spot?'

But Allan stands his ground. 'Jackson, I simply need to let you know how strongly I feel about this: Julia is the one who gets things done in that department. I've worked with her over the years. She's bright.

She's gutsy and resourceful. She's the one with ideas. And she has a good sense of humour, which is something we need more of around here. The people in that department like her. They respect her. Come on, Jackson. She deserves the job!'

Jackson soon realizes, or senses, the depth and intensity of Allan's words, and he draws in a breath while studying Allan's face. At last, Jackson gives a long sigh, and says, 'OK. Let me think about it.'

Within the week, Julia is named director of professional development at the firm.

For me, one of the key points from this story is that whenever you have a 'gut feeling' that an associate or boss may be barking up the wrong tree, don't deny it. Acknowledge it to yourself. Consider saying it out loud. You may be right or wrong; that's not the main point. It's fine to give someone the benefit of the doubt in certain situations, but not if your gut feeling is strongly telling you otherwise. In that case, it can pay to raise the question instead of sweeping your intuition under the company rug. How many times in the past have you kicked yourself for remaining silent when you had thoughts or feelings you could have shared with someone, and hindsight tells you they would have been useful, or could have made a major difference? What kept you from speaking up or forging ahead? By doing so, wouldn't you have earned more self-respect and respect from the associate or boss?

A Grand Simplifier

There is no doubt that complete and unconditional openness and truth-telling can cross the line into absurdity, especially if you were to tell everyone everything you feel. The crux of the issue is *relevance* – appropriately expressing those feelings which are relevant to your purpose and consistent with your ethical values. In the long run – and often in the short term, too – emotional honesty can serve as a significant simplifier in your life and work, energizing and clarifying your path and relationships.

We lie loudest when we lie to ourselves.

Eric Hoffer, American Sociologist

To be emotionally honest is to be more real and authentic, to care about and respect yourself, which is prerequisite of – or at least foundational to – caring about and respecting others. This has little to do with raising your voice or pointing your finger; in fact, emotional honesty is often best served with a simple quiet word or firm glance.

I'm reminded by several of my colleagues that, when many deaf people speak, the stronger their feelings, the smaller and slower their signs become – subtle motions of the hand and simple, intense turns of the wrist, for example. This is worth recalling for all of us who've been conditioned to fear that strong emotions send us into fits of ranting and raving. It is far more likely that, through skills in emotional literacy, the more angered or passionate we may feel about something, the more the intensity of this feeling is conveyed, perhaps without a single word to others, through our strongly felt *presence* and *intently focused actions*. On the other hand, shouting demands or shaking your finger or fist in another person's face may actually undermine your intentions, making others tense, closed, and defensive or adversarial. It's worth thinking about.

The Most Exceptional People You've Ever Known

Consider this simple exercise I use with leadership teams to deepen the context of emotional honesty. Take out a piece of paper and write across the top: The Most Exceptional People I've Ever Known. Now take a few minutes to jot down the names of several of the men or women who have made the greatest difference in your life or work. Reflect on what, exactly, it was about these men and women that made them exceptional and memorable. Was it their intellect or academic record? Chances are, it wasn't.

What I've found over the years is that, by and large, the exceptional people we remember tend to be those with the most heart. Those with intuitive creative genius, perhaps. Or compassion and courage. These are the people who were emotionally honest and refused to live a lie or simply go through the motions for efficiency or a pay cheque. They had the heart to break new ground, question elitist rules, and extend a caring hand or a kind word. They held to personally shaped standards of integrity and kept searching for the deeper meanings of life.

As I write this, I find myself remembering a friend who served in the US Marine Corps with me during Vietnam, a sergeant in Force Reconnaissance who, trapped behind enemy lines, refused to leave a wounded soldier behind, and carried him on his back to safety, evading hostile fire, for nearly fifty kilometres. I also recall a woman friend who, from an automobile accident, was instantly paralyzed from the waist down and began a fight for her life, within a larger struggle to keep her self-pride and hope from becoming paralyzed, too. She called upon her heart and put her life back together, going on to win five gold medals at the International Handicapped Olympic Games and an award from the President of the United States. I remember, too, a mentor of mine who, as a refugee, arrived in America in 1965 aged seventeen, with less than a hundred dollars and unable to speak but a few words of English. Yet he went on to earn an MBA degree, became a board member and major equity holder in a banking start-up that now has $22 billion in assets, and started a scholarship fund aged twenty-four that has awarded over $1 million to 300 deserving college students. Perhaps most amazing of all, he learned to speak English so eloquently that he became one of the highest rated corporate speakers in America.

Which examples do you recall of the exceptional people you've met and known? By reflecting on memories such as these, we begin to appreciate, perhaps for the first time, the actual depth of emotional honesty and inner commitment that many of the most memorable people in our lives brought to whatever they did. This is an act of becoming real, of taking responsibility for who we are, for our own experience, and listening to the *felt* voice of the human heart.

Consider the story of Galileo Galilei, the Italian astronomer and physicist, who was summoned to Rome during the Inquisition in 1632, where his work was examined and pronounced as heresy. He was threatened with torture and imprisonment for the remainder of his life. Having risen from his knees after making a renunciation of his principles, he was heard to mutter, 'Eppur si muove.' ('But they still move.') Galileo was making the point that, whether denied or ignored, what we *feel* as the truth *still moves us* from within; it does not go away.

The Language of Emotions

The common view is that emotions are things that *happen* to us. Yet, in large part, this is not true. Emotions are an inner source of energy, influence, and information. They are inherently neither good nor bad. It is what we *do* with the information and energy they produce that makes the difference. Learning to distinguish your deeper feelings from the other whirring of stimuli and information that bombards you all day is a fundamental requirement for personal growth as a leader. When you are conscious of your emotional states, you gain valuable *flexibility of response*.

A simple question to rely on is, *Where, in your body, do you feel the sensations of emotion?* For many people, an effective way clearly to recognize feelings – and distinguish one from another – is to begin by identifying where in the body they are located. Feeling your emotions as *body sensations* can take much of the confusion or resistance out of getting in touch with them.

It is with the heart that one sees rightly; what is essential is invisible to the eye.

Antoine de Saint-Exupery, The Little Prince

Each emotion is located somewhere: for example, a heaviness in the chest, a lump in the throat, a tightness or trembling in the abdomen, a weight on the shoulders, a knot in your back, or a hint of tension in the neck or jaw. As soon as you locate a feeling in time and space it becomes less threatening and more accessible. When you describe emotions as body sensations, you free yourself from judgments or criticisms of yourself or others: you are simply reporting what *is*. The emotion *feels* this way in my body. And because you can locate it, you can work with it – and guide its inherent energy – more directly. Anger that is experienced in the throat, for example, may well require a different response from anger that stiffens your shoulders and knots up your fists.

With some practice, you can begin to distinguish between the many different emotions and feelings. You may be quite surprised at the range and energy of these sensations, which keep us feeling real and alive. Close your eyes and scan your body. Notice how you are feeling. Then feel your feeling free of any thoughts about it – sense the pure energy, or power, in the emotion. Do you notice that the energy of your feelings has a vibration? Feel it resonating through your body. Notice the intensity of this sensation. As we practise feeling our feelings just as they are, we increase not only our awareness of ourselves but also our trust in ourselves. We recognize that every feeling is real. We feel, through our hearts and bodies, the vibrancy and power of life itself – in ourselves and others.

EQ Map Connections: Emotional Honesty
You may want to refer to the following scales of the *EQ Map* as points of reflection related to this chapter: emotional self-awareness, emotional expression, intentionality, constructive discontent, and personal power

---

EQ IN ACTION: *A CHECK IN*

Throughout this book you'll find a series of EQ-building tools selected from those that I share with executives, professionals, and management teams. This is the first such tool. It's a simple, practical way to build better rapport, increase clarity and empathy, save time, and help reduce faulty presumptions and mindreading during meetings. I call it the *check in*. Some executives call it 'numerical empathy'. It requires only about ten seconds per person at the start of a discussion or meeting:

Ask, 'On a scale of one to ten, give an honest personal rating of your *energy*, *openness*, and *focus*. If ten is the highest energy level you've ever felt at work, and one means you're on the verge of collapsing in a heap from exhaustion, what is your *energy level* right now? Next, what is your level of open-mindedness and open-heartedness today, right now? And, finally, how would you rate your level of *focus* – your ability to place your full attention on the tasks at hand for this meeting?'

Right now:	*Level: 1 (lowest) to 10 (highest)*
Energy	———
Openness	———
Focus	———

Many managers are surprised at how useful these three ratings can be; both individual and group EQ can be enhanced, for example, by raising the awareness and empathy of each participant in a meeting or interaction. In essence, we stop being faces at a boardroom table. We become real, distinctive, and present. By using a *check in*, you help prevent many common misunderstandings. For example, what do you typically assume if you notice another group member doodling or looking away when you speak? Do you give him or her the benefit of the doubt, presuming that he or she is just tired and perhaps has a peak stress-load today, or a headache, stiff neck, or pressing family problem to cope with? Or perhaps you just reacted strongly to this person's unintentional use of a 'trigger word' that irritates you and brings up old memories? Do you weigh such possibilities before making a judgment? Most of us do not. Instead, we automatically assume that what we're seeing in others is disinterest or a deliberate devaluing of our comments or ideas. However, research shows that only in rare cases is such a negative assumption about another person's motives true.[8]

Remarkably, the value of the *check in* does not depend on needing to know any follow-up details, such as specifically *why* a person's energy may be low, perhaps due to an illness, overwork, lack of sleep or a skipped meal. And neither do you need to know *why* he or she is distracted, perhaps by problems in workload, friction with co-workers, marriage or with children, career demands, or finances.

You might also experiment with using a *check in* at the end of a discussion. Ask, 'On a scale of one to ten, how *committed* and *prepared* do you feel – in information, time, confidence, and resources – *to follow through effectively* on the priorities from this meeting?' A low rating number gives you instant insight, and encourages an honest collaborative follow-up question, 'How, specifically, might I/we help you best accomplish these things?'

On a personal note: if you presently are unable to implement a *check in* during group meetings, you can learn to accomplish many of the same objectives privately and intuitively. What you want to do is create your own one to ten scales for *energy, openness*, and *focus* levels. Make it a point to pay several careful moments of attention to each person at the meeting. By this I mean don't just look at them, *see* them, and *sense what they seem to be feeling*. Notice their eyes and posture, their gestures and tension level. Listen to them talk. Is their voice relaxed and natural, or does it seem tight and on edge? If you know them, when they talk, is it faster or slower than usual? Are they concentrating on the task at hand, or doodling or staring off in the distance?

Once you've created three hypothetical scores – many executives I know learn to note their gut hunches on this for eight or ten different people within the first five minutes of a meeting – you can then take these deepened perceptions into account when you interact with each group member. If someone is uptight and defensive, give them the benefit of the doubt and some extra patience rather than getting defensive yourself. If someone seems withdrawn and distracted, gently try to draw them into dialogue and observe the results.

Moment by moment, does the interaction seem to become more humanized? You may notice yourself treating each individual *as* an individual, rather than primarily just a face, name, title, or vote. You begin to see more clearly the group as a collection of unique assets, talents and vulnerabilities, not just bodies sitting around a table checking items off a list. And be sure to ask open, honest questions to clarify your hunches about other people's intentions, thoughts and feelings. For example, when you suspect that someone is ignoring, rejecting or misleading you, or is feeling overloaded, lost, or distracted, for example, gently and firmly ask them if what you're sensing is true. Sometimes, it is not.

EQ IN ACTION: *EQ MORNING NOTES*

How emotionally honest can you be with yourself, in private? One of the best ways to raise this aspect of your EQ may be by spending two or three minutes every morning clearing away the frustrating, trivial stuff that echoes in your head and plants the seeds of confusion or doubt in your heart. How? With *EQ Morning Notes;*[9] you get up five minutes earlier than usual, find your favourite well-lit spot, sit quietly, listen deeply, and get out of your head and into your heart, openly reflecting on your life and work as you write a few pages a day, no matter how random or rough. With emotionally honest writing – there's no 'wrong' way to do this – you help to bypass what Michael Ray of Stanford Business School calls the 'voice of judgment', the mind's censor and inner critic.[10] The key is just to write. Whatever you feel. Tired, anxious about an upcoming meeting or the work day ahead, excited about something you or your loved ones are doing, or hopeful about a new project? Write it down – by hand. Holding a pen or pencil, you will more readily get at the truth inside you than when you type or dictate your thoughts and feelings. It's an amazing thing: the writing hand seems tied to the heart, and finds it hard to lie.

In most cases, these notes are for your eyes only. They are a good way to become keenly aware that your thoughts and feelings are deep and valuable, and they are *your* truth, rather than *the* truth. I've found that in this way the EQ Morning Notes have, over time, enabled me better to make full and passionate presentations of how I see and feel about a given possibility or situation in my work or life, while keenly realizing – and openly acknowledging – that others may see or feel very differently, and just as passionately, about things. In light of this, I find myself dis-appointed less often. I trust more readily, and instinctively value the differences between us, instead of resenting them, or feeling compelled to try to change you, to get your sense of truth and purpose in line with my own.

A few reminders: when jotting in this morning journal, don't judge yourself or worry what others might think, feel, or say if they knew what you were expressing. Furthermore, these pages are designed as a straightforward means of eliciting emotional honesty, and its related wisdom, bringing it to the fore so you can begin using it more effectively. Chances are, if you just start writing, and don't worry about form or grammar, a lot of what gets expressed will be pet peeves and nagging frustrations. Great. Write them down. Or you may find yourself intuitively exploring old resentments or new opportunities. Whatever comes up, it's real. And, according to researchers, it can offer more meaning to your long days, and to your life in general.[11] From time to time, you may get at creative breakthroughs, or some deep insight about yourself and others. Or get clearer about what questions to ask.

I encourage you to commit to trying this EQ-development technique for a minimum of twenty-one days – three weeks.[12] Five minutes each morning. I believe you'll be amazed at two things: one, how initially strong your mental critic is, the little voice in your head that says, 'What a dumb idea!' 'What a waste of time!' 'Emotional honesty? Hah!' And second, that by the end of the first week you start to feel a bit lighter and more energized when you finish writing, and that you are, in fact, more prepared to be open, honest, and creative throughout the day.

You may also want to experiment with keeping an *EQ Log*, or daily journal, at hand throughout the day as a convenient place to jot down observations about your emotional reactions to various situations and opportunities. This is an awareness-building technique used successfully with many leaders and professionals by Deborah Kiley, PhD, director of executive development at Arthur Andersen and Andersen Consulting. At day's end, you can refer to your notes for a few minutes of valuable reflection, identifying the 'hot spots' to approach differently the next time, and exploring key ways to increase your emotional intelligence in the days to come.

Whether or not your emotional honesty will have the space to grow and serve as a source of personal power in your life and work depends largely on your level of energy. This energy is in great measure generative, ignited and sustained by your passions, by what you care about and live for. This may sound quite simple on the surface, yet there are pitfalls to learn about here. In the next chapter, we explore a variety of documented ways to get a better grip on many of your life's continuing pressures and incessant work cycles, and to learn ways to begin shaping a healthy space of lasting energy in your heart, no matter what comes.

CHAPTER 2

Emotional Energy

I was in a boardroom at 3M World Headquarters in St Paul, Minnesota, when the global benefits director rose from his chair, asked for my marking pen, and began sketching a figure on the large pad of paper supported by an easel. Around the conference table, the handful of executives watched the illustration taking shape, and murmured their assent. You could feel the intensity in the room. This session happened to follow by less than a month the biggest restructuring in 3M's 93-year history. In the fourth quarter of 1995, 3M took a $600 million charge against earnings, equivalent to 27 per cent of operating income, spinning off a new company and electing to put an end to $650 million worth of its magnetic-storage business, which includes computer diskette, video-tape, and audiotape manufacturing.[13] The decision was a traumatic one for this paragon of corporate consistency which, for years, has set and met its own annual goal of 10 per cent growth in earnings per share, 20 to 25 per cent return on equity, and 27 per cent return on capital employed.

Your first and foremost job as a leader is to take charge of your own energy and then to help orchestrate the energy of those around you.

Peter F. Drucker, pre-eminent American management scholar

In the boardroom, the benefits director drew an iceberg. Inside the tip, the part exposed above the water, he wrote absenteeism, medical expenses, technology, facilities, technical training, quality control, and bench-marking. Below the water line – on the submerged 90 per cent of the iceberg – he wrote tensions, energy, stress, personal wellness and lifestyle, interpersonal skills, creativity, and ??? Across the top of the chart, he scrawled: *Unimpaired work days*. And he sat back down.

We stared at the image. It was obvious he had struck a deep chord; we were all jotting down notes. It made sense: how many of us in any company are at our best every hour of every day? What's holding us back? Why do surveys report that more than half of all American workers believe they could 'double their productivity'?[14] What's holding them back?

Nearly two years of study at 3M had revealed that many of the factors that restrict or impair the work achievements of managers and employees are submerged and unmeasured. But they are there. And it is high time to start learning about, and taking charge of, them.

The first two words beneath the surface, energy and tension, are a good place to start. That's because, in truth, there *is* one time, in particular, when it may be wise *not* to trust what you feel: when you're tense and tired from long hours at work. No book or programme on emotional intelligence should be without such considerations.[15] As fatigue and muscle tightness mount, for example, many of us get trapped in down moods and we lose our pep and resilience. You know the feeling: small hassles loom up as major obstacles; a delay of a minute feels like an hour; a perfunctory comment can feel like a stinging rebuke. Unless you learn to understand and effectively guide your daily energy and tension patterns, you will lose alertness, which automatically interferes with your ability to pay careful, extended attention, to anything or anyone. This causes a fall-off in both your intellectual and emotional intelligence, and can sabotage close relationships, despite having the best intentions not to do so.

The Energy–Success Relationship

Think about it: on days when you've felt tired out or tense, yet have needed to keep working, how open and adaptable, how curious and empathetic, how truthful and trusting, were you? Have you lashed out at others in fatigue-driven frustration – researchers call this 'negative spillover' – or walled yourself off, becoming distant from colleagues, constituents, customers, or loved ones? If so, you have experienced losing touch with your emotional intelligence and creative edge. To prevent this common dilemma, it takes some systematic self-observation and action. To every success-oriented enterprise this matters more each day.

In the traditional hierarchical organization, weak individual commitment or contribution often went unnoticed, or didn't really seem to matter, amidst the overall ineffectual performance of the company or industry as a whole. Times have changed. In today's lean or re-engineered enterprises, every leader and team member is personally on the line for the result. Not once in a while, but all the time. Sloppy or half-hearted contributions by any individual show up in the results for all to see. There's no place to hide. And this can put a major strain on the spirit and body. Working almost non-stop on substantive pursuits burns up huge amounts of emotional and mental energy, which must be replenished or we'll burn out.

In the so-called information age, a list of individual attributes providing power and influence is more likely to begin with great genius or intellect than with such characteristics as energy, strength, and endurance. But such emphasis would be misplaced ... The top characteristic for acquiring and holding great power in organizations is energy, endurance, and stamina.

Jeffrey Pfeffer, Stanford Graduate School of Business

Let's begin our discussion by creating a simple mental image of moods as background feelings – influenced by energy and tension – that persist over time. Usually they are subtle but sometimes they can intensify and overwhelm us. Whether we are conscious of them or not, mood shifts can motivate us, and may prompt us to take action to regulate or change them. With a lowered mood, we may feel compelled to seek out a friend, reach for something to eat, sip a soda or cup of coffee, or go for a walk. When you feel tired or a sense of being depressed, for example, it can become difficult to separate what your body feels (run down, hungry, physically exhausted, or in need of rest) from your mind (edgy, distracted) and emotions (frustrated, impatient, anxious, burdened). A number of exceptional leaders and creative pioneers have found ways to capture and focus their emotional energy. Take Albert Einstein, for instance, who warned us that, 'Problems cannot be solved with the same kind of intelligence which created them.'

Einstein also acknowledged that, like many of us, he got some of his best intuitive bursts of creative intelligence when walking or conversing, daydreaming, or even showering.[16] He told how, for example, he arrived at some of his best insights through a 'combinatory play' of feelings and visual sensations – imagining, for example, what it might feel like to ride a beam of light and look back at a clock, or what it would feel like if he dropped a coin while standing in a plummeting elevator. In short, Einstein possessed remarkable energy.

And, according to a new study, so do the executives and leaders of the 'hidden champions', five hundred of the world's best least-known companies, each of which is number one or two in world market share or number one in its European market. Hermann Simon, CEO of Simon, Kucher & Partners Strategy and Marketing Consultants in Bonn, Germany, who headed the study, says, 'If I had to choose one common, outstanding characteristic of the hidden champions, it would be the leaders, or more specifically, the incessant energy and drive of those leaders. They are as different as people in general, but all are imbued with the power and enthusiasm that move their companies forward ... and they appear to possess nearly inexhaustible energy, stamina, and perseverance.'[17]

This link between core energy and leadership is evident in every field of endeavour. I recall the nearly inexhaustible vigour and stamina that were the mark of Robert F. Kennedy, and helped him overcome his limitations as a communicator. It was obvious that he did not possess the natural grace or oratorical prowess of his brother John. Yet, as communication researcher and consultant Bert Decker observes, after serving as film director on the 1968 Kennedy campaign, 'There was *something* about Bobby that worked. When he spoke, he made contact with his audience. He had *energy* – and he used it.'[18] Decker saw Kennedy on his gruelling jet-tour as he repeatedly faced all the pressures and frustrations of the campaign trail, including hostile questioners, malfunctioning sound systems, schedule changes, and staff conflicts.

One instance in particular stands out in Decker's memory. It was a sweltering night when Kennedy approached the podium in front of the California State Capitol in Sacramento. He appeared exhausted, at the end of a non-stop month of campaigning. Yet his dream was on the line. As the cameras rolled, Decker thought to himself, 'There's no way he can make it. He can hardly stay on his feet.' But as soon as he was introduced, something happened to him. He engaged the eyes of his audience, and rose up, standing tall, springing forward with enthusiasm. He gave one of the most effective speeches of his life, filled with passion, power, and energy. 'I can clearly understand why this man consistently got to the heart of his listeners,' say Decker. 'His sheer use of personal energy enabled him to connect with the emotions of his listeners. There was energy in his voice and even more in his face, and body language. The vocal and visual power of this man conveyed to the millions who saw him in person and on TV that *here is a man who believes what he says.*'

This kind of passionate, heart-driven energy is also being given considerable attention by those in charge of leading highly creative and entrepreneurial pursuits. Professor Michael Ray and his colleagues at the Stanford Graduate School of Business have been researching and teaching this as part of their acclaimed Creativity in Business courses for nearly twenty years.[19] At Harvard Business School, John Kao describes working with a group of people charged with designing a new advertising campaign for the Hong Kong subway.[20] At first, upon his arrival, he elicits nothing much of interest. The group of people was engaged in sombre methodical work, the harbinger of technical rationality and linear, reductionist reasoning.

Kao decides it's time to shift gears, and he tells the group to think of a favourite scene from a movie, mentioning that his own favourite was the jump-to-light-speed scene from *Star Wars*, which in turn, he tells them, reminded him of sitting on an airplane, which reminds him that he flew into Hong Kong yesterday and is jet-lagged, and he'd prefer a midnight snack to the lunch sandwich about to be consumed. He begins animatedly to map his free associations on the white board. Almost immediately, the rest of the group begins imagining favourite movie scenes, and everyone joins in adding recollections and sensations that move them, beginning to make surprising connections to the subject of the meeting: the Hong Kong subway. By now, the group is electrified, and people are excitedly interrupting each other and finishing one another's sentences, creatively interacting. This is a classic example of energy and tension influencing mood and creative collaboration.

The Energy–Emotion Connection

In the business world most of us experience every day, there are times when what matters most, such as our important personal goals, sense of purpose, or humanity, gets swallowed up in the rush and roar of organizational busywork. According to research by Robert E. Thayer, professor at California State University, Long Beach, there are four primary human energy states, two of which draw this veil over our capacities and priorities – and can skew emotional intelligence. These are *tense-energy* and *tense-tiredness*. The other two states are largely beneficial, and serve to clarify and enhance emotional intelligence: *calm-energy* and *calm-tiredness*. Unfortunately, many of us experience these states infrequently, if at all. And most current theories on emotional intelligence ignore this energy-EQ connection altogether, which is a costly oversight. In brief:

> **Tense-Energy** (high tension and high energy) is a stress-driven mood characterized by an almost pleasant sense of excitement and power. Your physical energy feels high, even though you may face a high level of stresses and strains from long hours on a hectic work schedule. In a tense-energy state, you tend to push yourself impatiently towards one objective after another, rarely pausing to rest or reflect. Your

efforts are infused with a moderate to severe level of physical tension which, after a while, may be imperceptible to you. Without realizing it, by allowing this tense-energy state to persist, you blunt your ability to pay deep, genuine attention to your own needs, other people, or projects, and can suddenly wake up to find yourself at the edge of burnout and exhaustion.

Calm-Energy (low tension and high energy) is a mood state that few of us experience often enough. Calm-energy feels remarkably serene and under control. It replaces tense-energy with an alert, more optimistic presence of mind, peaceful and pleasurable body feelings, and a deep sense of physical stamina and wellbeing. Your mental and physical reserves are high and, when you are in calm-energy, you have the best combination of healthy vitality and increased creative intelligence. You might think of calm-energy as a kind of flow state of relaxed alertness, or mental and emotional overdrive – an extra gear that allows you to do just as much, even more, but with less struggle, less wear and tear.

Tense-Tiredness (high tension and low energy) is a mood state characterized by feeling tired all over. When you collapse in the chair or on the sofa at night after dinner, you are genuinely tired. TV can make the daze worse, or the fatigue is mixed with nervousness, tension, or anxiety. It's not pleasant, and often there is a sense of low self-esteem and of life being a burden, sometimes with what seem to be insurmountable problems. During the afternoon, a stretch of tense-tiredness may be manageable – with a work break, a light snack, some physical activity, extra light, or other brief interventions – but, if you toss and turn at night, you're familiar with how hard it can be to shake a state of tense-tiredness. Depression may also be triggered by, or worsened by, this state of heightened tension and tiredness. 'Much evidence,' says Dr Thayer, 'indicates that tense-tiredness helps create the most undesirable moods and probably underlies depression, low self-esteem, negative thoughts of all sorts, and many kinds of dysfunctional behaviour, including the use of drugs and alcohol to alter mood.'[21]

Calm-Tiredness (low tension and low energy) is a generally pleasant state characterized by the sensation of letting go and winding down. You are comfortably awake and at ease, perhaps reading a book or listening to some quiet music, and your thoughts are generally free from the major, and even minor, problems of work and life. After a while you might become drowsy or sleepy, but calmness prevails and you still feel good. Calm-tiredness, says Dr Thayer, is the healthy state for winding down from a challenging work deadline or at the end of the day, yet for many of us the last time we felt calm-tiredness might have been our favourite vacation years ago.

When you're in a prolonged state of tense-energy or tense-tiredness, your emotional intelligence suffers, and obstacles and difficulties in your life and work may seem overwhelming, even though the same problems would appear much more manageable when you are feeling calm and alert. Chronically low levels of energy appear to increase one's vulnerability to tension, anxiety, and fearfulness.

It is instructive to note, however, that tense-energy and tense-tiredness – which affect the body, mood, and mind – are not the same as *creative tension*, the exhilarating pull of energy you feel when you are whole-heartedly engaged in an invigorating disagreement, for instance, or working towards achieving a clear, compelling goal despite a challenging set of current circumstances.[22] The main point to remember is that, in general, when you feel highly energetic, and at the same time relatively calm, your perception of both yourself and the world are distinctly different from when you are tired and at the same time tense. Not only are memories of past successes and failures likely to be different, but perceived likelihoods of future successes and failures are also different. In order to develop your emotional intelligence most effectively, it's important to manage the energy-EQ connection.

$$(C \times E) - (T \times F) = M$$
(Calmness × Energy) – (Tension × Fatigue) = Motivation

This is the first in a series of simple, symbolic equations that my executive clients and professional teams have found useful in exploring and developing emotional intelligence. Each element is rated on a scale of one (lowest) to ten (highest). In the above equation, *C* stands for your current degree of *calmness* and *E* is *energy* level; the *T* is your present level of emotional-physical-mental *tension* and the *F* is a composite ratio of emotional-physical-mental *fatigue*. M stands for *motivation*, a basic representation of how fully capable you are right now to interact effectively with ideas and/or people in an open, attentive, and vigorous way. Not all motivation is based on emotion of course, but it's a central driving force (the executive development director at a large corporation where I regularly consult uses the expression 'emotivation'). The highest score – which tends to occur during the peak hours of your very best days – is 100. The lowest is –100. This score is of particular importance whenever you face a new challenge, problem, or opportunity. When M is low, molehills loom up as mountains, and you're likely to waste precious emotional energy wrestling with magnified doubts and imaginary obstacles.

Here's an example: let's say it's late afternoon and your *energy* (E) level is a seven (you're feeling a bit of a 'second wind' as you hurry to get things done by the end of the day) and your *calmness* (C) level is a two (right now you feel a typical stomach ache as you scramble to complete two important projects at once). At the same time, your *tension* (T) level is an eight (it's 4 p.m., and you've got your usual settling of frustrations into your body in the form of a stiff neck and tight shoulders) and your *fatigue* (F) level is a mild three (you were feeling more tired an hour ago but you drank two cups of coffee and the feeling of fatigue lessened). Right now, your M rating is a -10. Translation: you'll likely make it to the end of another work day but you're not in very good shape to face any new workplace changes or challenges. Enter the ratings in the equation: (*Calmness x Energy*) – (*Tension x Fatigue*) = *Motivation*.

In this case, $M = -10$. With this relatively low score, you may want to make some immediate choices. You might, for example, take the simple, direct action of tightening and consciously releasing the knot in your stomach associated with the nagging late-day feeling of struggling to finish things up. You might also choose to recall the feeling – and image – of *flowing* more effectively with challenges rather than resisting them. Such choices will raise your *calm-energy* (C) rating and, in turn, your level of available motivation and involvement. You might also reduce your tension level by stepping back from your desk or work station and heading over to a sunny window for some fresh air, eating a bite or two of a small snack, and loosening your shoulders. Such actions, as you will see in the upcoming section of this chapter, may quickly raise your inner drive and ability to focus.

You get the idea. I encourage you to use this equation to rate yourself just before important phone calls, presentations, or inter-actions with other people. Afterwards, note how well things seemed to go. Over time, you'll become more aware of how high, in general, your M needs to be to get more of the results you want. One of the

> other benefits my clients and I have found is that this equation also provides us with an internal cue, or reminder, to manage energy and tension levels throughout the day, not just once in a while.

When you detect a challenge or criticism, for example, your nervous system detects it – so rapidly you may scarcely be aware of this process happening – through the sensory 'filter' of your energy and tension levels. Thousands of times a day you may be confronted with dialogues and tasks that require mental, emotional, and physical resources to accomplish them, and in each case there is a momentary, often unconscious, evaluation of the task in relation to your resources to meet it, summed up in the basic question, 'Do I have the energy and flexibility to engage in this dialogue or the emotional strength to complete this task, no matter what difficulties arise?'

EQ Map Connections: Emotional Energy
You may want to refer to the following scales of the *EQ Map* as points of reflection related to this chapter: pressures and satisfactions, intentionality, and personal power

---

EQ IN ACTION: *MANAGING THE EQ-ENERGY CONNECTION USING BRAIN 'SWITCHES'*

In the early 1990s, I designed professional development programmes for a Fortune 100 company, and they were implemented by a number of divisions and teams. The emphasis was on personal and interpersonal effectiveness under pressure. I preceded some of the sessions with a needs analysis survey in order to identify the group's specific priorities. I remember one in particular in which every member of a department, from support staff to directors, attended the programme. Over a three-day period, we explored many of the scientific insights and practical applications for increasing creativity, energy, intuition, collaboration, and emotional intelligence. What emerged from our dialogues was an action list tailored to the department and its members. At the top of this list was managing energy and tension. Soon after the completion of the programme, one of the directors called to let me know the managers had taken a vote and decided to 'renovate' an area of their office building, converting it into a space for productivity-enhancing work breaks, open communication, and creativity. It quickly became one of the favourite areas for managers and employees to frequent during the work day.

There is mounting evidence that how you feel about yourself and your work and how open you are to engage in dialogue, to value others, to share ideas, and to make the most of informal, creative collaboration, depends on how effectively you manage energy and tension. This, in turn, is influenced by your work space – the environment where you happen to be. If it is a zone of square cubicles and dark, narrow hallways, you are, in effect, at a serious disadvantage – in access to IQ, EQ and other forms of intelligence – and so is your enterprise. Poor lighting, noise, and prison-like quarters bring virtually everyone's mood and effectiveness down, and seem to promote isolationism, fatigue, tension, and mistrust.[23] We feel embattled and weary by the unconscious, constant effort of suppressing environmental work space stressors.

And new isn't necessarily better, unless you plan it to be. Take the example of Lloyds of London.[24] Their new head office building was one of the most expensive ever built in Europe. Yet, within a year after it was occupied, the building manager estimated that $50 million in renovations were needed, ranging from more elevators and cable capacity to new wall and ceiling finishes and surfaces. These flaws in the initial design were significantly affecting the nature of business processes for Lloyds, since so much of the collaboration and selling in the customized insurance market depends on face-to-face interactions. Slow elevators and sterile meeting areas that *felt* uncomfortable undermined in a thousand small but crucial ways the fragile social processes that determined business success, or the lack thereof. This turned out not to be about spending money versus not spending money. The flaws here were in the original design process – and not tailoring it to the unique needs of the organization and its people.

Conversely, we accomplish more 'real work', and enjoy doing it, when we have a say about, and can build some variety and flexibility into, our work environments. We increase the probability that new ideas and connections will arise, and that we'll have the chance to do productive things with them once they do arise. Beyond technological linkages – computer networking, teleconferencing, and the like – we must not forget that face-to-face dialogues, both preplanned and spontaneous, are essential. Leon Royer, head of organizational learning at 3M, sums up the opinion of most executives there: 'We manage an environment to free up your imagination – that's the whole idea.'[25]

This is a theme embraced by Yhtyneet Kuvalehdet Oy, a large magazine publisher in Finland, which has created a central lounge on each floor where writers, editors, and other personnel can gather to watch late-breaking world news.[26] The people in this space readily get into creative discussions, which often carry over into the central courtyard inside the building which is open to all floors, and includes eating areas and beverages. Everyone must pass through these areas to get to the elevator and stairs, encouraging interaction.

The place in which we conduct our work is, in effect, a force field of energy, to use the description from physics. Whenever we are in that field, it affects how we think, feel, interact, create, and perform. Therefore, when we're focusing on freeing up human emotional energy, we cannot disregard the influence of the environment. Among the many features found by researchers to raise the environmental side of workplace energy and encourage creative collaboration are:[27]

- Few arbitrary rules on what 'real work' should look like (bolt-upright posture in front of a computer or desk, for example, or constant motion so you always 'look' busy, whether or not your mind and heart are engaged with your work).
- A setting in which you are encouraged to try new things, build collaborative relationships, and advance new ideas.
- A sense of personal controllability over distractions and interruptions.
- Ready access to central 'magnet spots' designed to draw people together, such as beverage or food centres with fresh, high-quality items; great lighting and natural views; an exuberant variety of interesting, idea-generating things to look at; and with comfortable stand-up counter space and seating arrangements that encourage brief, natural interaction rather than forced interaction as at a meeting room conference table.
- Demonstration of leadership by not only encouraging people to use 'magnet spots' but by setting a personal example by using them yourself, so that managers and employees won't feel they will pay a price for talking to others during work hours. It is up to you to help them feel that this *is* part of their job.

Additional ideas for workscape elements that encourage communication and creative collaboration are limited only by our ingenuity and degree of commitment. This is not to say that unending workplace interaction is desirable. For most of us, it is not. We also need access to, for example, private retreat spaces, quiet hideaways and whatever natural settings promote brief stretches of relaxed concentration, reflection and contemplation.

One interesting twist on the above idea was put to the test by the Chiat/Day advertising agency in Venice, California. The executives there declared that their headquarters would become a virtual office, with nearly all of the creative and account management professionals no longer having dedicated assigned spaces in the central office. Instead, they were expected consciously to choose where they should be each hour of the work day, with a strong encouragement from top executives to spend a large share of their time in the clients' territories or at home. Laurie Coots, senior vice-president for business development and project director for implementing the new 'Team Architecture,' described it this way:[28]

Our new operating philosophy has less to do with working at home than it does with not letting our work become 'geographically relevant'. We want to make sure the value an employee can bring to the client is not limited by his or her need to be in an office. Therefore we have invested heavily in technology in order to bring the tools and collective intelligence of the office to the employee, regardless of their location. Conversely, the contribution an employee can make to the company is not dependent on 'keeping a chair warm' in headquarters.

Not a simple or easy transformation, that's for sure – but imagine the possibilities for free-flowing competitive and collaborative advantage.

What follows is a condensed executive briefing on what I consider some of the most practical, scientifically based ways to enhance your EQ by reducing tense-energy and tense-tiredness and promoting the calm-energy that builds and sustains your emotional intelligence in general and promotes a wide range of EQ-related competencies in particular, including enhanced creativity and collaboration.

According to Martin Moore-Ede MD, PhD, professor of physiology at Harvard Medical School:

Fatigue makes cowards of us all.

Vince Lombardi, US Championship Coach, GreenBay Packers

Fatigued people make errors, which create an enormous detrimental effect. Fatigued people also work more slowly and less effectively. They do things the long and routine way, and fail to see efficient shortcuts.... Without alertness, there can be no attentiveness, and without attentiveness no performance. All the selection, training and motivation in the world does no good unless the human brain is alert and attentive.... A person's alertness is triggered by ... internal and external factors that can be considered the switches on the control panel of intelligence. Understanding how to manipulate them is the secret of gaining power over one of the most important attributes of the human brain.[29]

Each of the following strategies for individual and collaborative human performance enhancement has been well documented, and I encourage you to begin testing each of them, and creating your own action plan based upon the results you experience:

Sense of Genuine Interest, Involvement, or Opportunity

Research indicates that a strong sense of creative involvement in a job, a stimulating project, an exciting debate or discussion, or a new opportunity triggers increased alertness, emotional energy, and performance.[30] In contrast, a too familiar or boring task reduces alertness and puts you in danger of increased mistakes, diminished creativity, and poor performance.

Ten- to Sixty-second *Strategic Pauses*

Laboratory experiments show that if you work too long at mental tasks, your problem-solving time can increase by up to 500 per cent.[31] A strategic pause is a brief conscious disengagement from work every twenty to thirty minutes for a chance to change your mental focus, shift your gaze (look outside, for example, if you've been doing close work), loosen up your neck and shoulders, and invite a few moments of creative lightheartedness. When planned pauses are *not* taken, the human brain unplugs anyway by taking what work physiologists[32] call 'spontaneous pauses': from sheer fatigue, we space out, doze off, or fail to pay attention to our task, listening, or linking with others. In short, we make mistakes, damage relationships, and fall behind.

Two-minute *Work Breaks* at Mid-morning and Mid-afternoon

Numerous experiments on work productivity have demonstrated that rest pauses and work breaks should amount to at least 15 per cent of working time – and this actually speeds up the work, more than making up for time spent on breaks.[33] For each work break, the key points are to change your physical position, move around for a minute or so of exercise, uplift your posture, sip some cold water or other healthy beverage, eat a few bites of a low-fat snack, step outside into some natural light or turn up the room lights, look at a natural scene and relax your eyes, get some fresh air, shift your mind away from the work at hand to something else that's emotionally engaging and creatively exciting.

Frequent *Physical Activity* throughout the Day

Light physical activity is one of the best ways to raise energy and reduce tension,[34] increase creativity,[35] and promote *hardiness* – the ability to stay healthy while embracing hectic schedules rather than cursing them.[36] One of the new priorities here is not only to follow a regular exercise plan but to spend a few key minutes being active *after* meals, and in pauses and breaks throughout the day. Get up and get moving again, go for a brief walk, take a flight of stairs, step outside, do a few muscle-toning exercises or easy, enjoyable flexible movements. The foundation of mental and emotional fitness is grounded in the physical. The abdominal muscles support the body's internal architecture, including your posture and respiratory system. That is what enables executives to stride with confidence, hold themselves tall, and activate the emotions that will carry them through. The midsection also supports the lower back, one of the core places where many professionals hold stress and anger. Basic advice: 100 abdominal crunches a day.[37]

Nutrient-rich *Meals and Snacks*

Eating five or six times daily – three moderate meals and a mid-morning, mid-afternoon, and evening snack – is highly recommended for both health and work efficiency.[38] Research suggests that moderate-sized meals plus small between-meals snacks may help lower blood cholesterol levels and increase your energy and metabolism.[39] For maximized alertness and energy, and reduced tension, plan – and eat – breakfast, lunch, dinner, and a mid-morning and mid-afternoon snack. First, make it a point to skip traditional fat- and sugar-loaded snack foods and other forms of 'empty calorie' munching. Instead, each meal and snack should be low in fat, high in fibre, and great tasting. List your favourites. A low-fat whole-grain cookie or crackers, a bagel or muffin may help you relax, whereas snacks higher in protein – a cup of yoghurt, half a turkey, tuna, or chicken sandwich, a bagel with low-fat cream cheese, or even a handful of peanuts – may boost alertness for up to three hours. How? By prompting natural changes in brain neurotransmitters.[40]

Lightheartedness and *Humour*

This is a universal wellspring for boosting energy and busting tension.

According to scientists, humour may be the most significant behaviour of the human mind.[41] Research suggests that humour can enhance workplace productivity. For example, when we're feeling lighthearted or in a good mood, we tend to be more emotionally open and energized, helpful and generous towards others and we experience improved work processes such as judgment, problem solving, and decision making.[42] Above all, spontaneous mirth is something you *allow* to happen naturally, through a sense of relaxation and fun. Start looking for more of the ridiculous, incongruous events that go on around you all the time. Point them out to others. Remember short stories about the funniest things you see or hear, and use them to spice up the work day and family discussions after hours.

Workscape Adjustments for Productivity

Amazing payoffs can come from enhancing various aspects of your work environment.[43] Examples include: turning up the lights (which, according to Harvard research, can immediately increase alertness and attentiveness), paying attention to posture and ergonomics, choosing some emotionally expansive background music, accentuating positive colours and scents, and doing whatever else promotes your creativity and sense of health and safety, and makes your personal work environment more relaxing *and* energizing.[44]

Deep *Sleep*

On any given day 25 per cent of people with no clinical sleep problems did not get enough sleep the night before and are not alert.[45] And research shows that negative mood states are inevitable consequences of sleep deficits.[46] Here are several key options for action: keep business out of the bedroom; get some light evening exercise and/or a hot bath or shower (according to the director of the Mayo Clinic Sleep Research Center, these measurably deepen sleep[47]); create a more relaxing and restful bedroom environment (which is usually dark, has good ventilation and fresh air, with a comfortable bed and temperature); and awake at approximately the same time each day (sleeping in more than an extra hour throws off brain-body 'clocks', increasing tension and tiredness, much like jet lag).

Studies at Harvard Medical School and other research institutions indicate that when we increase our energy and alertness levels, we enable the brain and senses to be more *attentive* – to pay significantly closer attention to our environment and the people in it, as well as to our own feelings and thoughts.[48] Just as important, when we're fully attentive, the insights and information we receive tend to be more accurate, creative, or constructive than when we are in a tense and tired state. Scientists have also discovered that emotions can serve as a vital source of accurate information about our character, relationships, growth and success. Which brings us to the subject of the next chapter – attending to emotional feedback.

CHAPTER 3

Emotional Feedback

Every feeling is a signal. It signifies that something you value is being called into question or there is an opportunity to be seized – to strengthen a relationship, for example, or to make a change and create something new. Every emotion is a wake-up call to capture your attention. By design, it's supposed to *move* you – to ask a question, to clarify things, to learn and stretch your capabilities, to take action or a stand.

Anger, for example, is, in essence, a fuel. It arises and we want to do something. To speak up, intercede, run, confront, or resolve something. But what many of us do with our anger is muffle it, stuff it, bury it, deny it, medicate it, or ignore it. We do everything but *value* and *listen* to it. Anger is an inner voice that shouts, pleads, compels, and demands. It is a map that shows us our boundaries and aspirations. Anger is meant to be respected and acted upon, not acted out or escalated into rage and hostility.

If we happen to overreact to anger or any other feelings, we are being driven by impulse. When this happens, we find ourselves doing and saying things – they may be petty or they may be downright frightening or dangerous – that are inappropriate and sometimes dead wrong. Or if, for instance, we've conditioned ourselves to ignore the call of feelings – in an attempt to keep all emotion out of our work – the energy of these intuitive feelings does not vanish. It simmers; it builds up. And then, frequently at the most inopportune moment, it takes over. We blow up; we 'lose it', often over something petty. And then, in many cases, we're consumed with damage control, spending large amounts of time trying to mend fences, make apologies, wrestle with guilt and regret. It wastes energy. It distracts us. Usually, we all lose.

Managing Emotional Impulsivity

We all feel emotional impulses, including irritations and frustrations. In many situations, these wake-up calls can serve as valuable intuitive nudges. At other times, especially when we are tense and tired, emotional energy, and a compulsion to speak or act in inappropriate or hurtful ways must be managed – first by feeling the first surge of impulse and then managing your response by redirecting your attention in some productive or constructive direction.

In this usage, I favour the word *managing* over controlling. To me, it's more than semantics, since attempting to constrict feelings by sheer wilfulness or attempted suppression often does little good, and may even backfire, magnifying the impulse even more.[49] When we manage impulses, we can get in clearer touch with the real reasons we're feeling angry or – upset – and we learn to keep closer tabs on our energy and tension levels so that we're more alert and resilient, better able to face challenges and difficulties *without* getting tossed about so often – or overwhelmed – by the storms of impulse.

Nearly thirty years ago, while I was serving in the US Marine Corps during the Vietnam War, I remember a fellow marine who constantly struggled to control his angry outbursts. They kept building up and, as the weeks passed, he refused help from any of us, and faced disciplinary action. One night, in his upper bunk in the large tent barracks where we were stationed, he doused himself with lighter fluid and set himself on fire. I was among the first to reach him. I'll never forget his screams or the look of desperation in his eyes, with his entire face and torso on fire, while we fought to put out the flames. He was hospitalized and then discharged from service.

Following that incident, I learned to be more aware of managing my own patterns of impulsivity, and over the years I have come to realize that managing these sudden waves of feeling is one of the keys to emotional literacy. While we may not set ourselves on fire when angry or frustrated, in the work world there are many other ways that impulsivity can undermine our relationships and success. Here's an example:

Late in a planning conference I was attending, the CEO of a manufacturing and service company flew into a tirade and shut everything down. His behaviour erupted. He screamed and swore, bellowing criticism at the top of his lungs. Four vice-presidents, seven board members, and fourteen managers cringed, sitting in awkward, rigid silence in their leather-backed chairs. No one said anything. Not then. You could feel this coming on, we each sensed, in hindsight. And none of us had a clue how to stop it.

Think back on your own work experiences. We all have personal limits and pet peeves. And nearly all of us detest bureaucracy and hate to waste time. Think of a difficult work situation when things began to go awry. Recall how quickly you felt the first promptings of emotion. And why such gut-level feedback matters. What might you have done differently, to manage that specific situation better?

It's evident that habitual impulsiveness gets in the way of trusting relationships and undermines top performance.[50] One of the signs of emotional literacy is, in fact, the ability to transcend impulsivity and appropriately guide the way you respond to emotion. Yet, paradoxically, it's also unacceptable – and time wasting, if not irresponsible – to ignore or repress your strong feelings while a discussion or meeting gets bogged down or headed astray. By being in that place in time, hearing that conversation, you *are* involved; you are a participant with an influence on the outcome. Reflect for a minute: how do you shut down a discussion when you've had it? We all have our ways. Angry tirades are one; sulking and sabotage are others. A related question, just as important, is what can others do to help you come back into the conversation or meeting once you feel blocked out or shut down?

In several of the companies I have worked with, members of executive, management, and process-centred teams have begun openly to clarify each team member's *personal overload pattern* and *dialogue interruption pattern*.[51] These habits and tendencies, which we all have, can now be made explicit. In the process, these individuals and teams are building closer connections, experiencing each other as more real and uniquely human, which changes the way we relate to and support each other. Let's consider the preceding case: the CEO had an intolerance, he told us, for what he saw as hidden agendas on the part of senior management. He tried to ignore it but sooner or later he couldn't, and the blow-up would come. His problem, he said, was that

> *Most executives have a notoriously underdeveloped capacity for understanding and dealing with emotions.*
>
> Manfred F. R. Kets de Vries, INSEAD, France

he couldn't put into words *what* these hidden agendas might be, or why they were occurring. That embarrassed him because, he said, as a CEO he was supposed to know precisely what was happening. He agreed to catch his emotional signals early on and voice his concerns, even if he couldn't put his finger on what, precisely, was bothering him. This was fine with the others, who acknowledged that the CEO's intuitions were often right on target. It was the blow-ups that bothered them.

The second action step involved the whole group. 'If you *do* happen to lose it,' I asked the executive, 'what can we do to bring you back?' The CEO reflected for a few moments and said, 'Just don't get mad at me or say, "What's wrong with you?" I can't stand that. Ask me something like, "What are you feeling so intensely about?" That way, we can talk about what my intuition's telling me, even if I can't put it in words.'

In the next heated discussion that comes your way, ask, What *needs* are not being met here? What *values* are being infringed upon here? What *assumptions* are causing me to react this way? What *feelings* or *memories* are being activated – and why?

Taking Responsibility for Your Emotions

Look around you: many people have learned to use mood as a smokescreen rationale to explain away recurring fits of iciness, sharp criticism, and periodic blasts of abrasive behaviour. As ethics researcher Joshua Halberstam points out, we often rely on such excuses as:[52]

1. Yes, I shouldn't have said what I did, but you know how jealous I am.
2. Yes, I shouldn't have said what I did, but you know what a temper I have.
3. Yes, I should have answered back, but I'm a coward.

We pin emotional labels on ourselves and then use them to justify our behaviour. We defend ourselves by saying, 'What else can you expect from me?' Emotions, however, are not excuses. You *choose* to lose your temper *each* time you do. You *choose* to act in a fit of jealousy *each* time you do. While it's undeniably more difficult for some people to govern their tempers or jealous rages than it is for others, everyone can exercise control.

This raises the issue of emotional self-guidance, which hinges in part on the ability to transcend impulsivity in the service of a worthy goal based on personal principles. Such goals might include forming a partnership with another person or firm and resisting a sudden urge to withhold a piece of new information that would put the others at an unfair disadvantage. Or, after losing a big account, or experiencing some other setback, you might experience a call for vengeance, a desire to get back at your competitors; but with emotional responsibility you can *choose* to let these impulses pass, and respond, instead, with empathy and credibility. Or you might be faced with the goal of building a high-integrity work relationship with a person to whom you feel sexually attracted, or an accomplished group of people who elicit in you feelings of envy or inadequacy; however, with emotional responsibility, you do not turn such impulses into hurtful or inappropriate actions.

A one-two-three strategy for learning to manage emotional energy can be seen as follows:

1. *Acknowledge* and *feel* the emotion – rather than denying or minimizing it.
2. *Listen* to the information or feedback the emotion is giving you. Ask yourself, for example, 'Which of my principles, values, or goals is at stake here?'
3. *Guide*, or channel, the emotional energy into an appropriate, constructive response.

When I first began using this approach, it was helpful for me to recall that one of the enduring character traits that enabled George Washington to accomplish what he did was his ability to manage emotional energy, in particular his red-hot anger and temper.[53] These challenges were a lifelong issue for him, both in war and peace. Thomas Jefferson and Alexander Hamilton, who served four years on Washington's staff, wrote of this, and noted, as did many other observers, that each of Washington's surges of anger – which were felt by others but usually well-controlled by Washington himself – and his occasional outbursts, came to a quick and definite end. Almost immediately, he would forgive himself and others, apologize to those affected, and take steps to heal any breach that had been made.

It's true that an emotional storm can sometimes clear the air, and anger can serve as a keystone of courage. Yet if such fiery spirit is to manifest itself as such, and not be wasted in useless gestures and eruptions, it must be recognized and guided, which is what Washington took pains to do. With few exceptions, he was renowned for his bravery in battle, and was fearless about speaking out openly and honestly. Yet, as he poignantly realized at a relatively early age, his frustration and anger could rise up so intensely as to produce fear, rather than instil courage, in others, and this would defeat him. And so he had committed himself to developing various skills – and drawing on all aspects of his character and emotional intelligence – constructively to channel and control such impulses toward outbursts and rage.

It is worth noting that anything that produces strong feelings of fear tends to kill ideas. This includes fear of criticism, of ridicule or failure, of yelling bosses, of being fired. Over time, this fear undermines confidence and erodes allegiance, creating a climate of uncertainty, suspicion, and sabotage.

In response to a similar awareness, at the age of sixteen Washington copied by hand a set of precepts: *Rules of Civility and Decent Behavior in Company and Conversation*. The guidelines – 110 in all – outline a constellation of virtues and a map of character, based on a set first composed by French Jesuits in 1595. Throughout his lifetime, these precepts enjoined Washington not only to value himself but to be courteous and forthright, keenly alert to the feelings and needs of others. The overall focus was summed up in the very first rule: 'Every action done in company ought to be done with some sign of respect to those that are present.' This commitment served him well throughout his life.

Emotions are a 'Signal System' and Source of Information and Energy

One of the points to be noticed in Washington's story is that anger, like other emotions, is primarily an energy. It is neither good nor bad; how you respond to its message determines the effect it has. Emotions are our 'signal system', acting as on-the-spot wake-up calls that give us information we need and directing us towards various questions or openings, actions or changes, at any given moment. Washington's temperament, for example, was uniquely his; yours and mine are uniquely our own. If we were to lose our signal system, we become prone to aggression, withdrawal, and other maladaptive behaviour. The emotional 'signal system' is designed to help free us to be the best person possible.

The point is, each of us lives in a stream of emotional information and impulses; some of these are brilliant and appropriate, others are not. To be successful, we must channel and control such surges of energy, and whenever possible direct them towards something constructive. Think about it. All emotions have their place. There are times, for example, when we each need to feel angry or sad, because that is the inner truth we are experiencing right then. And there are times when it is right to feel anxious, concerned, joyful, or jealous. *Unlike the mind, the heart finds it difficult to lie.*

Anger appropriately appears, for example, whenever human worthiness or rights seem violated, when integrity is assailed, or when the spirit is threatened. Anger can also be a source of commitment and passionate motivation, as expressed by William Sloane Coffin:[54]

> A *capacity* for anger is very important because if you don't have anger, you will begin to tolerate the intolerable.... If you do not get angry, you are probably a cynic. And if you lower your quotient of anger at oppression, you lower your quotient of compassion for the oppressed.

In the spectrum of human feelings, each emotion is imbued with its own 'signal' or intelligence. It does not simply *happen* to us; our inner self *generates* it, always for a reason, always to communicate something. And emotions move across a range, and realm, of intensities. The ability to experience the heights of enthusiasm and passion, for example, is commensurate with your capacity for experiencing – for feeling, rather than necessarily *acting out* – frustration and fury. To increase your awareness of this effect, take a piece of paper and sketch the following: first, imagine a continuum of related emotions. Just to the right of centre is the feeling of becoming emotionally involved, or being actively *engaged*, in a challenging problem or meaningful pursuit. This feeling can grow – expansively – into *enthusiasm*, a sense of *flow*, and even *passion* for your work. Contrast this on the opposite side of the same emotional continuum, beginning just to the left of centre with the feeling of *frustration* that may arise when you're faced with an irritating problem or feel stuck carrying out seemingly pointless tasks. If chronic, unacknowledged and ignored over time, this feeling may intensify – constricting – into *anger*, which in turn, and if ignored or unattended, may escalate into *resentment*, even *rage*. Cut off either side of this continuum of feelings, and your range shrinks at the other end equally, leaving you trapped in a murky, relatively bland middle.

Consider a second example: on the expansive side, a feeling of *curiosity* might lead to *openness*, *acceptance of responsibility*, *faith*, *trust*, and *creativity*. On the constrictive side of the emotional spectrum, begin with a feeling of *blame*, *envy* or *jealousy* which may then lead to *mistrust*, and on to such debilitating feelings as *self-pity* and *martyrdom*.

Here's one more example: the *ability to be concerned* may expand into feelings of *empathy*, *compassion*, and *respect*. Moving into the opposite direction on the continuum of emotions, a chronic sense of *fear* may grow into *anxiety*, *dread*, or *panic*.

You get the idea. One of the insights that many of my executive clients and I have learned from this exercise is that a key to emotional intelligence is catching the rising intensity of constrictive emotions early on. When we fail to do that – when we ignore the early emotional signals and find ourselves caught up later on in the throes of resentment, for example, or dread or a tirade tied to martyrdom – we realize that we're going to have to devote precious time, energy and focus trying to recover from the downside.

Therefore, one of the fundamental insights of emotional literacy is that constructive or limiting emotions are a wake-up call. With practice, they can be transformed into expansive or enabling energy, as we'll be discussing in Chapter 7. We can learn not to let such feelings overwhelm us or block us for very long in accomplishing what we want to do. Basically, we must learn to stop, feel the emotion, consider its message and meaning, and respond with appropriate energy and action, pursuing a bit of deep reflection or moving on. Emotional feedback helps guide us in *how* to move, *when* to move, *where* to move, and *why*. Each time, we experience emotions in a constructive way, we reshape our brain circuitry. For example, if you were raised in a home where the first response to anger was to scream and blame, that may be your default option for your entire life, the natural reaction you have to feeling angry. But you may learn to feel the anger and talk things out and extend empathy instead of blame. Not every time, perhaps, but you can change.

It is through the voice of emotions, rather than thoughts alone, that we are prompted to:

- Listen
- Clarify
- Value
- Stand up and step forward
- Learn and innovate
- Consider
- Remember
- Empathize
- Change and motivate

These are among the aspects of emotional intelligence that are being embraced by the American Quality Foundation,[55] for example, and leading companies around the world. Even EDS, the computer outsourcing giant with nearly $13 billion in sales, is deeply committed to the initiative called for by CEO Les Alberthal – to create a radically new identity as the world's most sensitive services company.[56] 'The leaders who advance at EDS,' he insists, 'will be the ones who have seen the light. Our business is about making the customer successful and not having all the assets under my control, so leaders are going to have to do other things than shout orders. The old command-and-control mindset is not how we will be successful.'

This highlights a dramatic shift for this hard-driving culture. Starting in 1994, Alberthal began putting every EDS manager, starting with himself, through a series of transformational training sessions that delve deeply into the realm of feelings, to stimulate new ideas and greater sensitivity to colleagues, employees, and customers.

> **EQ Map Connections: Emotional Feedback**
> You may want to refer to the following scales of the *EQ Map* as points of reflection related to this chapter: life events, constructive discontent, and compassion

EQ IN ACTION: *'IF I TOOK RESPONSIBILITY FOR...'*

To begin with, in many cases when we feel a sudden, strong surge of emotion that compels us to behave in a certain way, it makes sense to take an *explicit* pause. It is not necessarily an escape from conflict but a provider of emotional and mental context and possibilities. Recent studies affirm the value and importance of such a pause.[57] When confronted with a stressful or changing environment, the brain has an inherent tendency to do more of the same, only harder, to react blindly. We can consciously override this shortfall by slowing down for a moment or two in the sped-up world. Such pauses can be productive in unexpectedly vital ways and enable us to listen better to the inner promptings of the heart and spirit.

Beyond the use of an explicit pause, here's an application exercise that I've found very insightful:[58] Ask yourself, *'If I took responsibility for every feeling I experience and for every word I utter, ———.'* What was your answer?

When I have used this exercise with corporate clients, here are some of the endings people have given:

I'd have to be more alert and aware.
I would probably be taken more seriously.
I'd be more accountable.
I'd have to put all my values into practice.
I'd make fewer snap judgments that end up being wrong.
I'd have to be more emotionally honest.
I'd have to pay more attention.
I wouldn't do or say hurtful or short-sighted things.

In one case, an executive protested, 'But I would have to be so *attentive* and *focused.*' Exactly. This underscores the fact that responsibility is not merely a state of mind but, as Gandhi reminded us, a wholehearted willingness to pay careful attention, no matter how busy we are, and to step forward and assume responsibility as needed. Whenever we can reasonably be expected to bear some responsibility, we must be responsible.

Even if we are *given* responsibility in work or life, nothing happens unless we *feel* this responsibility – as an inner-guided *felt sense*, not merely an idea – and then *take* it, voluntarily. Through emotional literacy, we personally take responsibility for the respect or disrespect we bring to discussions and interactions, the kindness or unkindness, the generosity or cruelty, the fairness or lack of fairness. Without emotional literacy, we may try to avoid feelings of responsibility when we say, 'They *made* me do it.' We declare justification for disrespect and cruelty: 'She was getting on my nerves.' 'They drive me crazy.' 'He's to blame for this —' 'Of course I wouldn't have *had* to do it if he didn't —' Who is responsible? If you hear such excuses and do not openly contest them, you are.

Nordstrom, the department store chain noted for its exemplary customer service and consistent profitability, has condensed its employee handbook into a single sentence:

Use your best judgment.

By definition, a *professional* is a person capable of doing the right things even when he or she might not initially *feel* like doing them. This is a mix of self-discipline, inner guidance, and emotional drive. Emotional literacy requires us to acknowledge and respect our feelings while having the awareness and discipline to not be blown about by the emotional winds of the moment; instead, we actively direct our emotional energy into doing more of the right things.

This brings us to the next chapter, which, in essence, is about *sensing* what more of these 'right things' may be. In truth, we do that not only through what we feel from the five traditional senses, but also from our intuitive 'sixth sense' and enteric 'gut feelings' (a seventh sense?), and likely from many other, uncharted sensory dimensions as well. Once you've learned to acknowledge your gut feelings, to be emotionally honest with yourself, to shape and manage your energy, and to transcend impulsivity and actively value emotional feedback, you are ready to call upon your intuition, and begin to trust it in helping to guide your work and life. This is our focus in the pages ahead as we complete our exploration of this first cornerstone of EQ.

CHAPTER 4

Emotional Connection and Intuition

Seeing with the heart. That's what my great-grandfather, Wendell Downing, a medical doctor and surgeon trained at the Mayo Clinic, called it. That's what his father, William Downing, called it, too, when he graduated from Rush Medical College in Chicago not long after the US Civil War and devoted himself to a career as a general practitioner despite the fact that, due to an injury he had lost the use of one of his hands. What enabled both of them to excel in their profession was, I believe, more than academic or technical brilliance alone, but emotional intelligence. In particular, they developed their powers of intuition and empathy best to relate to, and connect with, each patient, family and community need, from the heart as well as the head. This was a hallmark of their lives.

Neuroscientists have identified an enteric nervous system – a network of neurons, neurotransmitters, and proteins – in the human gut, and are confirming that intelligence is not housed in the brain alone. In fact, there's a whole class of neurotransmitters, brain chemical messengers known as peptides, which were first discovered in the gut. They're matched to brain-cell receptors, which tells us that what's happening in the brain is also active in the gut, and the central nervous system is connecting the two together. So emotion influences and activates key reasoning processes in the brain. My grandfather and great-grandfather knew this intuitively and based upon years of experience. They listened to reason and, at the same time, heeded their inner voice.

This is one of the challenges we face in today's careers and organizations: doing both of these things, together.

Shoshana Zuboff, professor at Harvard Business School, says organizations that don't trust intuition are making a mistake: 'So many people go awry because they (only) use sterile analytical tools.[59] The Institute of HeartMath, in Boulder Creek, California,[60] has devoted more than a decade of scientific research to understanding how the physical heart – beating approximately 40,000 to 100,000 times a day and powered by up to 2.5

watts of electrical energy – is forty to sixty times stronger in amplitude than the brain. The institute's researchers point to scientific experiments showing how the heart's electromagnetic signals are transmitted to every cell of your body and then emanate outwards from you; these electromagnetic signals have been detected up to five feet away. Some of the institute's research, recently published in the *American Journal of Cardiology*, indicates that feelings of care and appreciation are actually good for the heart.[61] (We've long known they're good for the soul and spirit.) The concept of heart intelligence is being implemented in the workplaces of such companies as Motorola to boost productivity, rapport, teamwork, and effectiveness.

The Inner Side of Business

To rationalize and reason makes sense to executives and managers, of course. But to value our gut hunches and intuition? Can this, too, be profitable in business? The short answer, backed by scientific studies and empirical evidence, is yes.[62] Intuition is perception beyond the physical senses. It is closely tied to emotional intelligence and includes aspects of intelligence as well. Intuition serves creativity: it is the sense that an idea that has never been tried might work. It unveils hidden possibilities. Intuition also serves inspiration: it is the sudden answer to a question. It draws us to others and helps dispel confusion about what matters most, and what we may yet become.

> *People with high levels of personal mastery ... cannot afford to choose between reason and intuition, or head and heart, any more than they would choose to walk on one leg or see with one eye.*
>
> Peter Senge, Director, Centre for Organizational Learning, Massachusetts Institute of Technology

Many leading organizations – both large and small – have turned intuition into successful innovation, time and again. In one classic case, researchers tested business executives for precognition, the ability to sense or anticipate the future.[63] The CEOs were divided into two groups: those whose firms were losing money at the time of the testing and those whose companies were earning profits. CEOs of successful firms were, on average, able to use intuition to anticipate the future at a rate that significantly exceeded chance expectations. Executives whose companies were losing money scored below average and deviated significantly from chance levels.

There are a number of possible explanations, including the rationale that the intuitive skills of the successful executives were what initially enabled their firms to get ahead in the marketplace and then to stay there; and perhaps the executives who ignored their intuition contributed to their company's poor performance.

Ralph Waldo Emerson distinguished two principal 'tuitions', or ways of knowing.[64] To Emerson, extuition was the voice of the ego and came from outside one's self. In contrast, the source of intuition was the inner self's wisdom guiding and expressing itself. You have to quiet the voice of ego to hear your intuition. It is intuition which involves 'feeling out' a problem, 'getting a feeling' for a project or process, and trusting your 'gut feeling'.[65]

In a recent study, eighty-two of the ninety-three winners of the Nobel Prize over a sixteen-year period agreed that intuition plays an important role in creative and scientific discoveries.[66] It turns out that, rather than avoiding intuition, and related forms of emotional intelligence, more and more companies that excel are seeking them out. Listening to your gut feelings can prove valuable, especially when it comes to important decisions.

Consider the following experiment: in your next meeting or proposal for a new product, process, project, or service, make it a point to determine the strongest feelings beneath the words and gestures of the participants. You might ask, for example, 'How does everyone *feel* about this plan or process?' If people answer, 'Fine', dig deeper by asking a question such as, 'Is anyone concerned about going forward with this? Does anyone have a sense we might be missing anything here?' To keep learning more about the unspoken emotional intelligence in a meeting, keep asking why – 'Why is that?' – and probe further until you feel you understand what is needed to advance or suspend the idea or plan. Throughout this book, I'll be using the expression 'to sense' to go beyond the traditional five basic senses to include what you feel in your gut or heart, and what your sixth sense, intuition, tells you.

An executive at FedEx once remarked to me that, in the shared view at that entrepreneurial and consistently successful company, intuition – or gut hunches – frequently matter more to managers than rigorous analysis. From CEO Fred Smith down, FedEx champions intuitive hunches to conduct its business, and considers all sensed – i.e., achievable – opportunities to be *responsibilities*.[67] FedEx was the first service company to win the Malcolm Baldridge Quality Award. This is all the more remarkable when you consider Smith's days at Yale, when none of his professors thought his ideas would amount to anything, and when you realize how many obstacles and setbacks he had to overcome to turn his dream into reality. Of course, as with any leader or enterprise, certain hunches will turn out to be wrong, yet FedEx has a company-wide determination to let practical intuition overrule the financial experts, which FedEx refers to as 'quantoids'.

In distinctly different industries, but with a similar depth of commitment, 3M champions intuition, too. Every time I have worked with 3M executives, management teams, or divisions, I have come away with new stories of unconventional approaches to solving 'unsolvable' problems, and examples of technological breakthroughs and market successes from ideas that began as gut hunches. At 3M, respect for individual intuition and creative initiative is so great that it has become a permanent part of its way of doing business – and all technical employees can spend 15 per cent of their time on any project of their own choosing.

It's this drive for progress that has infused 3M with the spirit continually to sense opportunities and solve problems that no other company has yet recognized as either an opportunity or a problem, resulting in such overwhelmingly successful innovations as – to name only three – waterproof sandpaper, Scotch tape, and Post-It notes. Each began not with a thorough plan or rigorous analysis, but with a gut hunch, with emotional intelligence. At 3M, all managers and employees are taught, among other things, to be willing to follow their intuition and defy their bosses. They hear stories of many such victories, including that of how current CEO, L.D. 'Desi' DeSimone, five times tried and failed to kill the project that became the wildly successful Thinsulate.[68]

Intuition, especially when followed by thorough analysis and planning, has sparked many successful business changes around the world. Consider the following example:[69] In 1988, Japan's sixth-largest pharmaceutical firm, the Eisai Company, faced a turning point. Haruo Naito, who had recently became CEO and President, gathered together his most trusted advisors and asked for an emotionally honest appraisal of where the company was headed. There was a shared concern that failure was imminent if things kept going the way they were, since the managers and employees were working hard at all times without having any idea who Eisai's end users, the actual customers, were. And the company had no best-selling products.

Hearing this, and feeling the intensity of the concern expressed by his advisors, Naito vowed that he would change the company from one driven by its existing customers – doctors and pharmacists – to one driven by its entire customer base, including patients and their families. Eisai managers, he decided, had to become experts in customer emotions and behaviour, in their desires, anxieties, and perspectives, and then infuse that expertise throughout the enterprise. It was a revolutionary concept for Eisai and almost unheard of in the pharmaceutical industry in general. But Naito believed it could give his company not only a new source of competitive advantage but, at the same time, would provide its 4,500 employees with a reason to care more deeply about their work and thrive creatively.

'It's not enough to tell employees that if they do something the company will grow this much or their salary will increase this much. That's just not enough incentive,' says Naito. 'You have to show them how what they are doing is connected to society, or exactly how it will help a patient.' Naito made the decision to begin with about 100 managers, whom he enrolled in what he called a 'nurturing programme'. 'From the standpoint of making drugs, we certainly knew a lot about diseases and how they developed and spread, but we didn't know about their relations with their family or whether they were in need of specialized care in addition to customary pharmaceutical therapy. My question was, how can we really be producing life-saving drugs if we didn't ever encounter death outside our own families?'

His response: let the Eisai managers do just that. Naito formulated a programme that included a seven-day seminar, three days of nursing home training, and three days of medical care observation in urban hospitals, in distant mountain villages, and on remote islands. 'These managers experienced the difficulties involved in daily care with the elderly, ... and they had to see people who died during their care,' says Naito. 'They also cared for people who were in very severe and critical condition, both emotionally and physically.' After the launch of the nurturing programme, field programmes were established in almost every Eisai division, and involved more than 1,000 employees. Each programme was responsible for communicating the company's new goal of expanded customer focus. At the same time, many of Eisai's staff members – in particular, secretaries and laboratory support personnel – began to get out from behind their desks and meet regularly with pharmacists, both at drugstores and in hospitals.

'Getting them out of the office was a way to activate human relationships,' says Naito. Several other systems have been implemented in this regard, including a seven-days-a-week customer hotline, which has generated many ideas thus far. As a tangible result, many new Eisai drugs will be coming into the global market in the next few years, and now Eisai is a company with $2.7 billion in revenues and $190 million in earnings. It is currently developing one of the most promising drugs to treat Alzheimer's disease and other ailments of the elderly, taking into account cost as well as quality.

All of this because one executive followed not only his business intellect but his intuition, asked emotionally honest questions, and created a radically different approach to successfully competing for the future.

Intuitive Feelings *Fuel* Reasoning

Beyond a host of other values to business, gut hunches and flashes of intuition can prove to be time-savers in many situations. Consider the following example:[70] Imagine yourself as the owner of a growing multinational enterprise. You are faced with a request to meet with a potential customer who can bring you valuable new contacts and business leads, but who also happens to be mistrusted, and even hated, by your best friend. The central question at hand is whether or not to proceed with a meeting about a particular deal. The brain of an intelligent, educated adult with a background in technical rationality will likely react to the situation by immediately showering the imagination with scenarios of possible responses and subsequent outcomes.

Examples of such images include meeting the prospective customer; being seen in the customer's company by your best friend and placing the friendship in jeopardy; not meeting the customer in person; not meeting the customer at all; engaging a business associate to handle the meeting rather than doing it yourself; saying no to a meeting altogether and losing good business but safeguarding your friendship, and so on. In this example, you will notice the essence of quandaries we face every business day. How do you sort through all the possible responses and outcomes and choose the wisest one?

There are several possibilities. One of them is based on the technical rationality view of decision making, which is intellect-dominant, or IQ-driven; another is centred on EQ backed by IQ. Technical rationality, which is the conventionally accepted practice in management and most professions, assumes that formal logic provides us, by itself, with the best possible solution for any problem. Emotions must be kept out of the process. Rational, reductionist reasoning is the key. Different scenarios are listed and dissected, using cost-benefit analysis and other forms of linear-sequential comparison. You consider the probable consequence of each option at major points along a timeline or expense curve, and compare the resulting gains and losses.

Even with only two alternatives – you meet the prospective customer or don't meet – the analysis is far from easy. Gaining a major new customer may produce immediate profit and even greater future revenue. But the exact profit is unknown. You can estimate its magnitude and rate, across time and as connected with changing markets, demands, cost margins, and so forth. You must weigh all this against the potential losses, including the loss of, or potential damage to, your friendship. Since such damage or loss would vary over time, you must also factor in the depreciation rate of the lost or decayed friendship, which may or may not impact on your personal effectiveness, other business relationships, and revenues.

Perhaps the most irrational assumption we can make is assuming that people should behave rationally and unemotionally.

Dean Tvosjold, Simon Fraser University Business School

The process of logical inference must next be pushed through a deepening maze of factors, extrapolated imaginary scenarios, number crunching, and continued generation of a thousand lines of linear thought and reductionist comparison. If this strategy of logical inference and technical rationality is the only one you have, it's not going to work: at best, it will take an inordinately long time, far more than acceptable if you hope to get anything else done today. At worst, you may wind up with a decision at all because you'll get lost in the byways of calculations and give up, in frustration.

But now imagine that before you apply your technical rationality and cost-benefit analysis to the problem, something instantaneous and quite vital occurs: when one particularly unacceptable or bad outcome comes into mind – as the key components unfold in a matter of moments, sketchily, virtually simultaneously, too fast for the rational mind to follow all the details – you experience an unpleasant gut feeling, or, for an acceptable or promising outcome, a sense of excitement in your chest or abdomen. In truth, all of the experiences you've acquired in your life and work are not sterile facts stacked on shelves, but are emotionally laden memories that are stored in the brain. The sum total of those experiences, your life wisdom, doesn't present itself to you as a clean, edited list of 'important things that matter' but instead as instantaneous hunches, as the sum total of gut feelings.[71]

This intuitive, emotion-generated 'felt sense' can often dramatically increase the accuracy and efficiency of the decision process. First, it sifts through the entire wealth of detail and operates covertly (below the level of consciousness), utilizing what may be described as 'as if' loops tied to

EQ, and draws your attention to the outcomes to which given actions may lead, and functions as an *automated alarm signal* – which may lead you to reject, immediately, and prompts you to choose among other alternatives – or as a *beacon of incentive*, which draws you towards beneficial outcomes. This signal helps protect you against future losses and choose among fewer options, streamlining and clarifying decision making. It is *then* that cost-benefit analysis and other aspects of deductive reasoning prove most valuable.

This same practical intuition can be accessed in everyday interactions of all kinds. I recall a story about James Thurber, the late US cartoonist, short-story writer and long-time contributor to the *New Yorker*. He had lost his sight in middle age, and sometime afterwards attended a friend's party. As a certain couple departed, he remarked to his host, 'They're going to break up.'

'That's not possible!' exclaimed his friend. 'I've never seen such friendliness and smiling.'

'Yes,' said Thurber, 'you *saw* them. I *heard* them. I *feel* what's beneath the words.'

A few months later, the couple separated.

Leading with Empathy

It is from the whispers of intuition that we are first called to care, to have empathy. Treating people with empathy is the root of compassion – which literally means 'to feel with' – and is tied to controlling impulses and taking personal responsibility. Taken together, these are among the great ethical codes that most religions are based on. Empathy and compassion connect us with others through the shared language of feelings and experience, one heart to the next, beneath the words, behind the posturing and gestures.

Through feelings of empathy and compassion we not only help ourselves learn and grown, we also enable others to begin to feel safe enough to talk about what is really going on in their lives – to tell their stories – without fear of being judged, criticized, or abandoned. It is then that we begin to empathize *with them*, and extend compassion and support *to them*, rather than remaining distant or unaffected, or sympathizing *about them*. And, more often than not, such empathy and compassion are, sooner or later, returned to us in kind. It begins with intuition, learning to perceive other people's feelings beneath the words.

Nelson Mandela writes in *Mandela: An Autobiography* of his twenty-seven years as a political prisoner: 'It was during those long and lonely years that my hunger for the freedom of my people became a hunger for the freedom of all people, white and black. I knew as well as I knew anything that the oppressor must be liberated just as surely as the oppressed.... The oppressor and oppressed alike are robbed of their freedom.'

Consider, too, this simple story told by Irving Cramer, executive director of MAZON: A Response to Hunger, an organization that collects and distributes funding to feed hungry people:[72]

> *Dad once looked down at an assembly line of women and thought, 'These are all like my own mom – they have kids, homes to take care of, people who need them.' It motivated him to work hard to give them a better life because he saw his mom in all of them. That's how it all begins – with fundamental respect and empathy.*
>
> Bob Galvin, CEO, speaking of his father, founder
> of Motorola

In a kindergarten classroom in northern Minnesota, the teacher asked the children, 'How many of you have breakfast this morning?'

About half the students raised their hands.

The teacher then asked those who did not raise their hands, 'Why didn't you eat breakfast today?'

Some said they got up too late and didn't have time to eat. Some said that they weren't hungry this morning. A few said that they didn't like any of the food that had been served to them.

All of the little students gave an answer – except one little boy.

'And why didn't you have breakfast this morning?' the teacher asked him.

'Because,' he replied, 'it wasn't my turn.'

'It wasn't your turn?' asked the teacher. 'What does that mean?'

'Well,' said the boy, 'there are five kids in my family. But we don't have enough money to buy enough food so that everybody can eat breakfast every day. We take turns eating breakfast, and today, it wasn't my turn.'

What did you feel when you read this story?

In life as well as in business, the threads of emotion that connect us with an experience, such as the one recounted above, have the power to move us, to inspire and activate our involvement. These two emotions in particular, empathy and compassion, are indispensable to the bond that holds relationships, communities and, ultimately, all of humanity, together. Contrary to popular thinking, these emotions require a keen sense of responsibility. There are times, for example, when the greatest kindness to another is to hold them responsible and accountable, accepting no excuses, encouraging them to stand fast or step up to the line and face a difficult situation.

However, in many cases when we turn away from empathy, we ignore human feelings, and in doing so we inevitably ignore the human being who's experiencing them. That strategy is likely to result in a friend, co-worker or employee who stops being authentic, stops bringing talent and energy into the workplace, and stops using feelings to support personal work-related goals as well as the corporate vision. What you do does not always have to be right the first time, but it always has to be real. When you remove posturing, pretension, and false communication, people are free to feel, to be themselves, and to connect on an emotional level with each other and with their organization's core purpose.

Taking Responsibility for Emotional Connections

It is from empathy, especially when there is an environment of trust, that connection comes, one person to another. In terms of corporate and career achievements, it can be said that almost everything begins and ends in the emotions – rather than surface motions – of relationships, in human interconnections. Nationwide surveys[73] indicate that people are made to feel more worthy and valued as a result of interactions with leaders

46% of those who quit their jobs last year did so because they felt unappreciated.

US Department of Labor

they admire and respect. Unfortunately, some researchers report that 90 per cent of employee comments are negative. 'Pay attention to me,' they seem to be screaming at us. 'I'm human too. Value me and include me. Believe in me.'

Consider that the words *credit* and *credibility* share the same root origin, *credo*, meaning 'I trust or believe.' It's a feeling, not just a good idea. And it feels remarkable to be able to speak with executives and employees alike and say, 'I'm feeling concerned about . . . I'm not sure *why*, but what worries me is ...' even if your strong feelings are not yet backed by hard supportive data. Remember the point we made in the introduction: neuroscience research shows that emotional insights, or gut feelings, are an indispensable part of problem solving and reasoning, and provide you with creative, intuitive business intelligence and a desire for rapport and connection.

Companies such as Hewlett-Packard (HP) are proof, for example, that organizations can maintain a high level of emotional connection, even as they grow. The key, according to Lewis E. Platt, HP's Chairman, President, and CEO, is to use every possible way to keep the feeling of connectedness alive. In a recent interview, he said:[74]

> I do a lot of travelling, close to two-thirds of my time, and I spend a lot of time in front of HP people. I do this in fairly informal ways – like wandering around one-on-one, just talking to people. Other times, it's what we call coffee talk – the coffee talk is pretty famous here at HP. We get everybody at the site together and have a half-hour where we talk about what's going on in the company, what's important, what's ahead, and then take some questions from the audience. I usually tack a half-hour or an hour at the end to do some mingling with the people. These things are very important.

Platt's coffee talks are filled with emotional straight talk, intuition and empathy, and they create a feeling of connection that permeates the entire organization. Each talk is a deep-down dialogue centred on carefully listening to people, and then he follows through by trying to incorporate the ideas into HP's ongoing innovation and operations.

Emotional connection centres around shared, or common, good, in which both, or all, benefit, prosper, flourish, and grow. The recognition of this bond opens us to new learning and differing feelings and views, which increase creativity and encourage us to seek the highest good for all, not just ourselves.

No matter how we look at it, emotional relationships are the lifeblood of any business. University of Texas marketing professor Robert Peterson is a specialist on customer satisfaction who has more than 100 technical research articles to his credit. Not long ago, he discovered the determining connection between customer satisfaction and repeat business: an *emotional link* must develop between the consumer and the product or service.[75] Not just by you, but between the customer and everyone he or she comes into contact with at your company. Again: the centre-most key to customer satisfaction and repeat business is not quality, competitive pricing, and a service department – these have become entry requirements just to stay in the game. No, the central key is an emotional link, a feeling of connection.

It's much the same when it comes to the alignment between a business manager and his workforce. 'I don't think of leadership as a position,' says Phil Quigley, CEO of Pacific Bell. 'I don't think of leadership as a skill. I think of leadership as a relationship.'

A relationship.

'You don't care about someone because of who they are; you care about them because of the way they make you *feel*,' observes Irwin Federman, venture capitalist and former President of Monolithic Memories, which was recently acquired by Advance Micro Devices. 'I contend, that all things being equal, we will work harder and more effectively for people we like. And we will like them in direct proportion to how they make us *feel*.'[76] Conversely, as Will Schultz, faculty member at Harvard, points out, 'My relationships with others depend largely on how I *feel* about myself.'[77]

Researchers at the Center for Creative Leadership have discovered that 'insensitivity to others' is the most cited reason that executives and leaders fail.[78] The studies showed that the ability to extend empathy – to understand other people's perspectives – was the most pronounced difference between those who succeed and those who fail.

Once we take responsibility for seeing not only from the neck up but also with the heart, we start to view political correctness and workplace power plays for what they usually are: a sham. Consider the following rejoinders:

'You've got to be careful on that subject.'
'You can never be completely honest around here.'
'In this company, you just never know how anyone really feels about
    things.'
'Tell us something that sounds like it's coming from the boss's heart
    and not from the ledger.'

Comments such as these are but a sampling of the undercurrent that pervades many of today's corporate offices and corridors. There's a common fear in many executives and managers that if we get too close to other people it will ruin our objectivity. Therefore, there's no way to be real and truthful with others; they couldn't handle it. So, face to face, we don't say what we really feel, primarily out of fear that we'll upset someone. And, who knows, someday we may have to fire them, or work for them. So we manoeuvre around issues and relationships by saying things we don't really mean, or withholding feelings by justifying, 'I don't want to hurt them by being open about it.' But, in nearly every case, these are acts of mistrust, and sometimes cruelty, even when not intended as such. Sooner or later, the real feelings surface. And, in most cases, if later, the damage is exponentially higher than if sooner.

Let's take an example of the benefits of taking responsibility for emotional connections. Chances are, listening to and respecting feelings is not a leadership quality that springs to your mind when thinking of the Big Three automakers in Detroit. For years, Chrysler and ex-Chairman Lee Iacocca – who, on the surface may seem to have high EQ but, in truth, had a management style that was often regal and autocratic – were certainly not seen as examples of what could be called a high EQ corporate culture. But times have changed. Iacocca is gone, and Chrysler has transformed itself into what some consider the hottest US car company, even managing recently to out-earn both General Motors and Ford.[79]

In Iacocca's place, the Chrysler board hired Robert Eaton, a man in his early fifties who had run GM Europe from 1988 to 1992. He took charge in January 1993. Almost immediately, Chrysler employees realized they now had a very different leader at the top. Eaton is widely considered continually accessible, intuitive, and an empathetic listener and coach, often answering his own phone and dropping in periodically for informal talks with Chrysler managers and employees.

'I don't think I'll have any less impact on Chrysler than Lee Iacocca did,' he says. 'It'll just be dramatically different because I'll come at it from an inside, teamwork standpoint as opposed to the approach he had.'[80] The first or second time a leader asks people to be honest about how they feel, they may hesitate to give real, honest answers. But if the leader keeps asking, and demonstrating his or her own willingness to engage in honest emotional expression, eventually they will come to believe that the leader truly wants to understand their feelings, not only their thoughts, and will open up.

Among his first initiatives, Eaton implemented a 'Senior Management Behavior Team' designed to teach his senior officers to be more approachable, to encourage subordinates to speak up, to listen when they did, and to make eye contact with people.[81] All of this occurred as new cross-functional 'platform teams' were being formed, bringing together at a single site everyone involved with a vehicle from concept to market. This move at once enhanced communication, streamlined development, reduced costs, and accelerated production.

This led, for example, to the Chrysler Neon. In its early development stages, team leaders enlisted aid and advice from non-traditional allies and suppliers, such as the United Auto Workers Union. It was the line workers who contributed over 4000 concerns and proposed changes to the project. The results shocked the auto industry, with the Neon successfully challenging the Japanese manufacturers in the small car US market. Toyota even recently announced one of the most rigorous exams it has ever carried out on a competitor's automobile. The Toyota report noted that the Chrysler Neon incorporated 'designed-in cost savings unprecedented in an American car'.[82]

Chrysler's goal is, of course, to keep this momentum going and expand upon it, actively involving all of its workers, managers, suppliers and other stakeholders in creating one of the smartest, and most intuitive and emotionally genuine, team efforts in any industry. For men and women at any level of a company to be able to ask each other, 'What's *really* bothering you about ——?' Or 'What's your intuition telling you about solving this problem?' – and to ask such questions without fear of embarrassment or reprisal – is becoming one of the hallmarks of successful enterprises like Chrysler, which was chosen as Company of the Year in January 1997 by *Forbes* magazine for being 'smart, disciplined, and intuitive'.

(A + Q) C = PI
(Attentiveness + Questioning) × Curiosity = Practical Intuition

This is one of the simple equations I've used with management groups to spark some deepened considerations of intuition and ways to use it. Each item on the left of the equation is rated on a scale of one (lowest) to ten (highest). *A* represents *attentiveness*. Without being alert and attentive to our inner voice, we usually have little genuine connection to a person, problem, or possibility, and our intuition will likely be far less reliable. *Q* is for *questioning*, through which we attempt to clarify what we and others are actually thinking, feeling, and intending. *C* is for active *curiosity*, including the extent of your current perception and ability to sense beneath the words and posturing – in yourself and others – to get at the heart of what's really happening in this situation or circumstance, what really matters. The sum of $A + Q$ is multiplied by C and results in a rough estimation of *PI*, or your present capacity for *practical intuition*. The highest score is 200. The lowest is one.

Let's consider the practical use of this equation in several ways. Let's say you're entering a post-lunchtime discussion with a new co-worker or colleague, someone you don't yet know well, and towards whom you feel a bit competitive. At the start of the conversation, your overall alertness and *attentiveness* (A) is a four, and your gut-

---

level inclination for *questioning* (Q) is almost nil, a two (you're feeling turned off by his or her first comments). Your *curiosity* (C), including the outreach of your senses to probe beneath the words, is presently about a four. Thus your current level of *practical intuition* (PI) is 24 out of a possible 200. One translation: you can go through the motions just fine, and may make it through this interaction without a problem, but it's doubtful you're primed for a creative breakthrough or that you will gain many insights into the motivations or character of your colleague.

However, let's say that, as you begin to converse, you feel a flash of resistance or defensiveness. Your *curiosity* (C) is conveying to you a perception that something you care about – your seniority, perhaps, or some favoured project or initiative – is about to be attacked. Some people would say such hunches are intuition at work, but in many cases I'd disagree. Your initial reaction might be to get defensive or to break off the conversation or, in the extreme, to attack the other person first. But let's say you forestall such reactions and, instead, raise the level of various factors in the equation: (*Attentiveness* + *Questioning*) × *Curiosity* = *Practical Intuition*. Let's see what might happen.

Let's say that, at the first flash of resistance or defensiveness, you lean forward, straighten your posture, and begin to pay even closer *attention* (A) to what's being said, and *how* it's being said, which raises your *A* rating from a four to an eight. At the same time, you make it a point consciously to deepen your *curiosity* (C) including your perception of the feelings the other person is transmitting. Within moments, as your perception sharpens, this rating goes up from a four to an eight. Almost immediately, one of the things you notice is that the other person seems unfocused in his or her criticisms, as if grouchy, almost off balance while snapping during the conversation. From here, you raise your level of *questioning* (Q), from a two to a five or six, which raises your *PI* score from 24 to over 100. You might ask, for example, 'What's caused you to feel this way?' One possible answer: 'All those damned delays, that's what! And the piles of paperwork. What a waste!' Or: 'I've hardly been sleeping for the past few days. My kids keep getting sick at school, and I'm fed up with it.'

What you learn is that the adversarial mood had little or nothing to do with you. If you didn't clarify this using emotional intelligence and intuition, and if you reacted blindly and emotionally, an argument would likely have resulted and this would have hurt your work relationship with this person, not to mention wasting time and energy.

But what if, on the other hand, the co-worker or colleague had answered your question, 'What's caused you to feel this way?' with an evasive question: 'Why, what have you heard?' Or what if the reply had been something shallow and insincere such as, 'What? Oh, nothing to worry about. Things are great, as always.' Or perhaps you get hit with a complaint, such as, 'You did! And now I'm stuck doing the work of ten people instead of one.'

While it may be natural to feel a surge of dismay or anger at hearing such answers, if you're aware of the simple *PI* equation, you delay bristling up or lashing out and, instead, take action to raise your attentiveness, perception, and openness to questioning. Which means you're primed to dig deeper and it's actually easier to *shift* your feelings into something creative or constructive than it is try to *stop* yourself from getting more defensive or angry.

In other words, you can choose *consciously to guide* your intuitive feelings, and related sense, towards seeking solutions. You might shift into being more *attentive* and *perceptive*, for example, taking into account the environmental context of the interaction, for example, instead of just the people involved. In other words, to reduce overreacting emotionally, you might, for example, channel the first surge of emotions – anger, impatience, rejection, or resistance, to name a few common feelings – into *listening harder*. That's one of the things that Bob Eaton does at Chrysler. Ask yourself, 'I wonder what I can discover in this conversation?' And then search for what's *unique* in this situation, whatever you can learn from it, instead of getting defensive, making snap judgments, or losing control.

When feelings of not being understood come out as anger, *hearing them –* not shutting your ears or lashing back – can be one of the best ways to help guide the anger constructively, into understanding instead of a fight. You might also ask a simple *question* that shows you are paying attention and that you respect and value the other person's perspective and feelings, whether or not you agree with them. Why blame the other person for starting to upset you? Once you listen harder, perceive beneath the words, and believe that the other person feels heard and understood, then you might *respond* by expressing your feelings as *your own feelings*, not as something the other person has done to you or is doing to you.

One of the ways that I've seen executives respond effectively is with comments such as: 'I can see this is really upsetting you. What, specifically, can we do to turn things around, or to help make sure this doesn't happen again?' Or 'I realize you're feeling strongly about this. Please tell me more.' A leader with a high EQ knows that two of the most persistent barriers to effective teamwork are interpersonal *reactivity*, on the one extreme, and emotional *indifference* on the other. The power is in the middle, where one person actively chooses to break the spiral of reactivity and, instead, to be real to another, to see with the heart, not just the head. As Chrysler, Hewlett-Packard, and other leading edge organizations, both large and small, have already found, it's not only the responsible thing to do, it also pays off – big time.

> **EQ Map Connections: Emotional Connection and Intuition**
> You may want to refer to the following scales of the *EQ Map* as points of reflection related to this chapter: emotional self-awareness, emotional awareness of others, compassion, and intuition.

EQ IN ACTION: *VALUING EMOTIONAL CONNECTIONS AND INTUITION*

Here are several practical considerations that may help enhance your intuitive powers and contribute to clearer emotional connections:

Champion 'moments of silence.'
There are times when it's hard to hear your inner voice when you, and those around you, are talking. In many cases, our noisy high-technology environment bombards us with stimuli and we miss the intuitive creative wisdom that, as neurologists have shown, can be communicated in an instant through the emotions that activate your intuition and reasoning powers.[83] I'm continually amazed to find that many executives and managers have a hard time with *quiet*, even for a minute or two. We all want more breathing space, but the truth is we're not used to it. We get anxious. We plan. We fidget.

Don't.

It's here, when taking a longer-than-usual pause in dialogue, for example, or during a relatively silent stretch of road on a daily commute, that you can consciously listen to your gut instincts and ask inner questions to sharpen your intuition. A work day suggestion:

experiment with a conversational *pause*, a few extra moments of silence after you speak. It's a remarkable communication tool. It projects a strong sense of confidence, and serves to elicit more information and honesty from others. Another good place to savour some quiet time is by spending several *silent minutes* each day, perhaps while you're getting ready to make your EQ Morning Notes (introduced in Chapter 1) which are designed to clear away the nagging 'static' of your mental critic which interferes with the ability to sense, value and interpret intuitive signals. When applying this throughout your work day, the goal is not to be aware of everything, but to be aware more *deeply*. With practice, you can work in the midst of diverse and constant stimuli and this 'noise' will recede somewhat from your consciousness, and you can more readily gather essential intuitive information.

Begin developing insight.
Because intuition is often portrayed as the opposite of analytical thought, many people mistakenly assume that using intuition means rejecting common sense and logic. As you will notice during moments of quiet, these dimensions of intelligence are interrelated. We have an intuitive breakthrough and then we reason, gather facts, and analyze, and then listen to our intuition again, and so on. Other considerations include to:

Respect the language of intuition.
Many of us dismiss intuition because it rarely speaks to us in complete sentences. It presents information as images, symbols, impressions, and sensations. These usually don't 'make logical sense', at least not at first, especially when it's signalling us about the future, and so we ignore it. Yes, intuition can be cloudy, but teach yourself to acknowledge that. Pay closer attention to the deeper information it can convey.

Suspend the voice of judgment.
Intuition adds to good judgment; it does not replace it. Yet, as Stanford Business School professor Michael Ray reminds us, if we let the 'voice of judgment' intercede too soon it obliterates almost any creative or intuitive insight.[84] The point here is that the analytical, logical mind will keep telling you how silly this is to pay attention to impressions about things the 'facts' can't reveal. Your mental critic may whisper, 'This doesn't make any sense,' or 'It's only your imagination,' or 'That

can't possibly be right.' Don't ignore such messages. Acknowledge and make a note of them – of *every* impression – for future consideration. And then move on. Wait to judge until *after* you sense the full range of your gut feelings and intuitive signals. If, for example, your first impression is about another person's intentions, feelings, or thoughts, be certain to seek clarification to know if you're right.

Ask clear questions.

There is an old saying that a question well phrased is half answered, which, when eliciting your intuitive impressions, can prove true. Therefore, be as precise as possible. Let's say you've just had a facilities tour and interview with a company called Galactic Telecom. As you're heading home at the end of the day, you might ask yourself a corporate question, for example, such as, 'Would Galactic Telecom be a good strategic partner?' Or perhaps a more personal query like, 'Would this be a good place to work?' In the first case, what you may actually want to know is whether Galactic Telecom would be a good *investment* over the next five years, or would its reputation enhance the *value* or *market position* of your own company right away, or could their *innovative style* jump-start your own R&D team within a year. Probing deeper, what you may actually want to know is would Galactic Telecom keep growing fast enough to give you plenty of income opportunities, such as a chance for profit sharing or equity, or would employment here add value to your resumé when you're ready to move on or start your own company?

Feel the inevitable moments of fear – and move through them.

In many organizations, where politics is the norm and the status quo is vigorously defended, the only way to get somewhere is to have the guts constructively to debate tough issues, which can trigger the twinges of fear in you. Remember, the voice of judgment is criticism, and can make you afraid of the obstacles thrown up by your own mind. Unlike *chronic* fear, which is debilitating, these *momentary* fears – which can also arise about the latest market threats, for example, or with a concern about pushing beyond limits and out-innovating the competition – can prove to be activating and valuable. You might see these feelings as the opposite of complacency and use them constructively. If you are a senior manager, keep in mind that it's up to you to demonstrate consistently that open, honest debate, where people can speak up about their hunches, worries, and ideas without fear of punishment for doing so, can be vital to your organization's future (we'll discuss this in Chapter 7). If you're not a senior manager, the best advice may be to take small steps. Raise one specific point or issue at a time, not four or five. Get a clear sense of who else on your team tends to use or champion intuition; there is usually at least one. Gather facts to support your hunches before you reveal them to your boss or the group as a whole. Enlist support.

Expand your empathy.

Ask yourself, In the past week, what has stirred my soul? Seriously. And if you answered 'nothing', then what *would* stir your soul? In most cases, when you cannot feel what *moves* you, you're simultaneously blocked from feeling what moves others. One of the reasons this EQ Cornerstone begins with emotional honesty (Chapter 1) and emotional feedback (Chapter 3) is that if you are out of touch with your own feelings, then you will likely have a hard time accurately reading the feelings of others, because you don't know the emotional language well enough. But with heightened self-awareness, when you 'read' someone else's feelings, you're sensing their emotional state even without them telling you what their feelings are.

Mahatma Gandhi knew what had to be done to assist the villagers of India in improving their conditions. However, he felt he still did not empathize fully with the difficulties of living in a village. He had been 'talking and giving advice on village work without personally coming to grips with the difficulties of village work'.[85] Therefore, in 1936, at the age of sixty-five, Gandhi – who, at the time, was India's most prominent leader – went to live in a typical Indian village with no running water, electricity, or paved roads. This was more than a gesture; it was a search to deepen his empathy and commitment.

In many situations, other people will hesitate to say what they truly feel; but they'll usually convey it to you in their tone of voice, rate and pitch of speech, their eyes, facial expressions, and posture. Therefore, especially in many business settings, you should make an effort to understand how people feel without their having to tell you in words. Ask direct, kind questions to clarify what your intuition tells you. 'I'm certainly frustrated about this issue, and it appears to me that you're very angry about it. Is that right?' In applying empathy, you want to sense other people's emotional and mental perspectives without taking on their constrictive emotions. We'll discuss this further in Chapter 12.

Make clearer emotional connections.

It's alarming how one individual – a leader, manager, or professional – can undermine an entire enterprise simply by being out of touch with intuition and empathy. I've found that one of the most overlooked yet common ways that we fail, albeit unintentionally, is to express appropriately, candidly, and consistently what we *feel* as well as what we *think*. This pitfall is known to researchers as *unintentionally ambiguous behaviour*, which gives mixed messages. Next to aggressive or abrasive behaviour, ambiguous behaviour can cause the most tension for managers and employees alike.[86]

Here's what happens: whenever a person in your company behaves ambiguously, it's not just a no-win situation; it's a loss. This is due to the fact that the brain's reticular activating system (RAS) has been primed throughout evolution to amplify *negative* presumptions and minimize the positive.[87] Think about it: when in doubt, most people seem naturally to assume the worst. They see the boss, a co-worker or an employee behaving in what appears to be an ambiguous or secretive way, and try to interpret this unclear or insufficient information. They instantly begin to wonder about this person's intentions or ethics, about hidden agendas, and whether they are viewed as competent or trusted. In the absence of additional information, they quickly begin to make assumptions, usually giving negative explanations for the ambiguous behaviour. They become anxious about what this behaviour *might* mean, what is *really* expected, or what *could* happen. In such cases, people frequently don't have any idea what to do. They curse the darkness and worry about what will befall them. And this leads to speculation and worst-case thinking, which drives a wedge into key relationships and undermines productivity and creativity.

Typical reactions to ambiguous behaviour include:

Secretive decision-making.

When managers, for example, seem to be hiding their decisions from others, or fail to explain fully how and why decisions have been made, it provokes swirls of second-guessing and fear in many workplaces, and fuels other related problems. Secretive, closed-door, behind-the-scenes decision-making is regarded as a put-down. Not being included sends the unspoken emotional message that you don't know enough or your feelings and thoughts aren't valued. In addition, since you were not part of the decision, and were given no opportunity to help, you do not know what to expect; you may feel tentative and uptight, or distracted and on edge.

Lack of responsiveness to feelings, feedback, or suggestions.
When people do not hear back from you after expressing strong feelings or suggestions, they often assume the worst – that their ideas, feelings and input were disregarded or dismissed – and this triggers a destructive combination of mistrust and a sense of powerlessness and resentment.

Mixed messages.
When bosses send a double message or conflicting signals – writing or saying one thing, for example, but expressing the opposite through body language or emotional tone of voice – people worry, and can become paranoid, wondering, 'What are you hiding from me?' Or 'Are you playing favourites?' Or 'Whose ideas was this, really?'

Lack of, or indirect, communication.
This pertains to feedback and constructive information that is necessary to be part of the organization and effectively perform your work. This can be as simple as another person ignoring you when you pass each other in the hallway. Reflect on what it feels like when someone you know passes you at work and this person fails to acknowledge you with a kind word of greeting or even to make eye contact. Do you assume, 'Sure, he's probably busy and distracted right now and he just didn't happen to notice me'? Not likely. Instead, you probably begin to wonder what's wrong: did you do something stupid, or forget something, or are you being deliberately ignored, or does he know something bad about one of your projects or accounts, or are you about to be reprimanded or even fired?

Such worries are common – and usually unfounded – yet we believe them anyway. This is not your fault: the brain's RAS primes you to do it, and therefore you must learn to overcome this tendency by going deeper and overriding the urge to assume the worst. In most cases, he truly *was* just distracted. But herein seethes the problem: executives cannot afford to have people jumping to the wrong conclusions, getting angry for no real reason, and worrying about things that aren't true.

One of the things I've found is that many of us assume that if other people really cared about us, then we shouldn't have to ask for what we want or need, they will automatically know! Seldom is this true. I've found that two emotionally honest statements can prove very useful:

1. This is what I *experienced* and *felt* . . . and
2. This is what I *want* or *need*.

Beyond this, start with a simple action: make it a point to look people in the eye in greeting as you pass them in the workplace. This is common courtesy, of course, and everyone of us has an inherent need for simple *valuing* in others' eyes. 'These looks,' explains Ruthellen Josselson, professor of psychology at Towson State University in Maryland, 'are far beyond words: eyes speak more profoundly than language the tenor of relatedness. They express, surely and absolutely, how much and in what way we matter to the Other. Words may lie; eyes cannot.'[89] In short, *saying* words – 'I care,' 'You can trust me,' 'Great to see you,' 'How are you?' – is essential, of course, but too often rings hollow when you fail to confirm these feelings eye to eye. Think of the look in the eyes of people in an airport or bus terminal greeting an arriving family member or bidding farewell to someone who is departing. No words need to be spoken; the eyes convey the feeling.

Discipline: the Bridge to the Second Cornerstone of EQ

In this first cornerstone of EQ, each of the four competencies – emotional honesty, energy, feedback, and connection/intuition – contributes to emotional literacy and builds an inner locus of confidence. This generates a heightened sense of self-efficacy, or personal power, which includes increased self-awareness, self-guidance, self-respect, responsibility, and connection. These are among the key qualities that increase your capacity to approach difficult tasks as challenges to be mastered rather than as threats to be avoided.[90] On a final note, to put emotional literacy into effective daily practice requires discipline, which can be seen as the connecting trait, or 'bridge', between the first two EQ cornerstones.

THE SECOND CORNERSTONE:

Emotional Fitness

Being clear and *getting along*:
Builds *inspiration* – of self and others – including
authenticity, resilience, and trusting relationships

J ust as physical fitness builds strength, stamina, and flexibility of the body, emotional fitness builds corresponding qualities of the heart. It enables you to put the skills of emotional literacy into practice, developing greater authenticity and believability. These, in turn, enable you to expand your circle of trust, or 'trust radius', which has been positively correlated to profitability and success.[1] It is also through emotional fitness that you are inspired to stretch your capabilities and, when mistakes happen, to forgive more readily yourself and others. Emotional fitness promotes enthusiasm, resilience, and a highly constructive 'toughness' in facing challenges and changes, and this contributes to what is known as 'hardiness',[2] your emotional and mental adaptability in handling pressures and problems in healthier, more open and honest ways.[3]

It is through emotional fitness that we begin to illuminate our core personal values and character, and the feelings which enliven and drive them. We live and work in the ever-shifting moral climate of the dawning twenty-first century, and the temptation to give in, to go along with what others expect or want, can feel overwhelming. In this second cornerstone of Executive EQ, you begin to clarify and forge your unique presence, your authentic place in the greater scope of your life and work. Few things matter more to a successful professional or leader.

CHAPTER 5

Authentic Presence

O f late, authenticity has become an admired and sought-after trait among business leaders and managers. In my view and experience, it's a natural extension of the first EQ cornerstone characteristic of self-efficacy, or personal power, and calls upon us to develop what can be considered a *field of power*. In essence, you might think of it as a silent sphere of energy that emanates not only from the mind and physical form but from your heart, which conveys, moment by moment, the emotional truth of who you really are, deep down, and what you stand for, care about, and believe.

Understanding and developing this field of power – your authentic presence – is a vital first step into the second EQ cornerstone, emotional fitness, through which you bring more of your best self into listening and dialogue, and set the stage for building trust and an openness to change and creative risk. Authentic presence is not something I learned about in academia or management circles, although it's being talked about there today. Instead, as you already know from the story in the prologue in this book, it was something I learned about in the most unexpected way and place. As I write these words I remember a related experience that, for me, deepened the meaning of authentic presence.

It was early autumn many years ago, and I was standing beside an old rutted road at the foot of a mountain in Tibet. I had descended from the summit and was gazing across the rolling meadows towards a sparkling river that ran through the centre of the valley. I watched a family approaching me on foot, and nodded in greeting at a man, his wife, and seven children, who walked past me on the road. 'Pilgrims,' said my guide, an older Tibetan who was accompanying me that morning. After talking with the man, he told me the family had walked for close to 500 miles through the mountains from eastern Tibet to visit the historic landmark set high on the mountain slope above us. In Tibet, it is considered a blessing to make such journeys as a family. At last they had arrived. But then, as I watched in dismay, they were turned away by the Chinese guards at the gate along the road. Curious and concerned, I walked up the hillside road and approached them in time to hear the family being told that Tibetans were no longer allowed to visit this landmark.

In hearing this, I got angry. 'No discussion,' said the officer, abruptly turning to face me, sensing my intensity as I stared into his eyes. He took a step backwards and patted his holstered pistol, gesturing to the nearby guards armed with assault rifles. I offered to pay the entrance fee – the Army's 'toll', which I assumed, based on my experiences in other parts of Tibet, the soldiers would pocket themselves – with my Chinese currency; that same morning I had been allowed to visit the landmark, one of the most sacred in Tibet. 'No,' said the officer. 'New policy. Tibetans cannot come here.'

The family had been watching me during this interaction. They clearly did not understand what either I or the Chinese Army officer was saying. But they were watching us very closely, sensing beneath the words. Now they peered again up the mountainside before slowly turning away. I watched their faces. After weeks of hard travel, I knew their hopes must have been dashed, yet they were talking to each other very openly and honestly. There was an air of anger and disappointment, to be sure, but it seemed to ease, or be consciously released, as they walked together down the slope. The father turned and motioned for me to come with them.

Near the river, the man and his wife spread quilts on the grass and prepared a meagre picnic lunch, asking me to join them. I shared the food I had in my pack. As we ate, I noticed that from time to time each of us turned to look up at the ancient landmark, its golden roof glittering in the sunlight. I found myself thinking of how many times in business and life people arrive at their destination only to find the passage changed or barred, because of the 'wrong' currency, the wrong preparation, the wrong expectations. And, when that happens, how openly do we acknowledge our bitter disappointment and, instead of getting stuck in it, transcend it, moving on? Rarely. After the meal, I thanked the family and rose to leave.

'Wait,' said the father. 'My son wishes to teach you a phrase in Tibetan.' He motioned to one of the boys, who was about five years old. The little one stepped forward and looked me straight in the eyes. He said happily, 'Tashi deley.'

I nodded, understanding, repeating the phrase. He smiled from ear to ear. 'In Kham, in eastern Tibet,' said the boy's father to me, 'we greet all people this way. For several years now, it is again allowed.' I felt my chest tighten, remembering my experiences with the elder who, fifteen years before, had lost his entire family for saying such a greeting, a prayer, aloud. The man brought his palms together in front of his chest and his wife and children repeated the gesture. 'It means,' he said, 'I honour the greatness in you. I honour the place in your heart where lives your courage, honour, love, hope, and dreams. I honour the place in you where, if you are at that place in you and I am that place in me, there is only one of us. Tashi deley.'

Wordlessly, I brought my palms together in front of my heart and looked into the eyes of this family, people who, only an hour before, had been total strangers to me.

'Tashi deley,' I said.

'Now, teach my children a word in English, please,' asked the father in Tibetan.

I thought for a moment and said, 'In America, when we greet each other we say "Hello".' I remembered a professor once telling me it was Thomas Edison who had popularized the use of the word.

'Hello!' shouted the children, beaming. 'Hello! Hello!'

I grinned at them. And then something happened that I will never forget. One of the youngest boys came up to me and tugged on my sleeve. 'In America,' he asked expectantly, 'when people say "Hello," do they honour the greatness in each other?'

His question struck a chord in me. At once I felt tears brimming up in my eyes as I looked into his earnest, bright face. 'No,' I said, and then I added, 'but I wish they did.'

Think about it. When you greet other people at work, in your travels, and at home, what – exactly – do you feel? Do you look everyone in the eye? Without a word, do you honour the greatness in them, even if they are strangers? Or has greeting other human beings become, more often than not, a rote formality, something shallow and distant, going through the motions? It took a journey to Tibet to make me realize that, by and large, it had for me. It was then and there that I made a promise to myself that I would do all I could not to let it happen again.

Becoming Real – and Connecting through Dialogue

Of all the words I've read from the work of Irish novelist James Joyce, I remember most vividly the phrase: 'Mr Duffy lived a short distance away from his body.' There are times when, numb from the daily toil, many of us feel somehow separated from ourselves, out of touch from the core intelligence of our heart. Looking back on it, there have been many times over the years when this could have been an apt description of me. Why do so many of us chuckle when cartoonist Gary Trudeau says, 'I am trying to cultivate a life-style that does not require my presence.' Great humour, but a haunting message.

Because life is characterized by open-ended, reciprocal interactions, dialogue ... is the closest that human beings can come to ... life force.

Robert Grundin, On Dialogue

It is from valuing each other that true dialogue – rather than empty, polite conversation – begins. Dialogue is a word derived from the ancient Greek *dia-logos*, which means the free flowing of meaning between people. It's something every business needs more of, and soon. The challenge is that genuine dialogue is impossible – you can talk, you can hold a discussion, a chat, or a pleasant conversation, but not be in dialogue – without first being emotionally literate. Unless I can come to know what is real about you – something of your life story, what you care about and stand for, what you feel as well as what you know – you do not actually exist for me beyond your name, job title, and appearance. I cannot know or have a dialogue which, by definition, sets for us as its implicit goal *shared meaning*.

It's instructive to note that when people are asked about the impact of situations in which they wanted to speak up but did not, they talk much more about what they *felt* than what they *thought*.[4] Studies suggest that leaders with high EQ do not hide their feelings, even their painful hurts fears, angers, and griefs.[5] They can acknowledge them openly and express them with the same straightforward clarity with which they tell you the weather or the time of day. 'Leaders who garner the greatest future support will increase their capacity for *emotional expressiveness*, a key ingredient in purpose, persuasion and inspiration,' says Jay Conger, a professor at Harvard Business School.[6]

Ordinarily, we think of speech as words projected out, directed at others. Yet the opposite is true for real speech, for genuine dialogue. In these interactions, you are actually inviting the other person to come inside your world, into your mind and heart. National surveys tell us that 70 per cent of employees, nearly three out of every four, are afraid to speak up at work.[7]

'But I don't have any time to greet everyone I see or for *real* dialogue,' complained one top executive I know. 'I *want* to,' he added, 'but I don't have a single spare minute.' That was certainly how things seemed to him. Yet what I observed, beneath the surface, was a leader drowning in paperwork and struggling with the aftermath of ongoing mis-understandings that came from his avoidance of genuine dialogue. It was a vicious cycle, and of late, his business profits – despite all attempts at command and control – were taking a nosedive while his staff and customers complained about relationships disintegrating. Through it all, he felt powerless to do anything about it.

He was too busy.

But was he? Every time we ignore our instincts – our intuition and gut hunches – and miss the opportunity to ask a question, express a concern, or seek clarification, we pay for it, if not now, then later. Whether we consciously acknowledge it or not, we get *busier*, forced to commit time, energy, and other precious resources downstream, attempting to redo mistakes, correct misperceptions and hurt feelings – if they *can* be corrected – and to live with unexpressed and unsolved problems.

$(A \times C) - (U \times E) = AP$

(Attentiveness x Concern) – (Ulterior Motive × Entitlement) = Authentic Presence

Here's a short, symbolic equation that I've used with groups of executives and managers to initiate discussion and reflection about authentic presence. Each element on the left is rated on a scale of one (lowest) to ten (highest). *A* is *attentiveness*, your level of applied alertness, the measure (none to all) of your deepest and most complete attention that you are willing to devote to this specific person, problem, situation, or opportunity. *C* is *concern*, the level of honest, genuine caring, or interest, you have in learning something new from this experience or interaction, and being open to the needs of others as well as your own (authentic presence requires a full personal involvement with each new circumstance, rather than just 'showing up'). When we act from pure concern we avoid the labyrinths of gossip and behind-the-back criticisms that haunt so many relationships and businesses, and deal with others directly when we have a concern or issue to raise with them. *U* is *ulterior motive*, a rating of your ego assertiveness – desire or willingness to use coercion to impose your will or agenda on others, for example, or to feign friendship while acting to see them harmed out of spite – rather than being open to new or differing ideas and to change. *E* stands for your current state of *entitlement* as to what, or how much, you feel you deserve to get from this interaction in return for minimal effort on

---

your part. *AP* is your present level of *authentic presence*. The highest rating is 100. The lowest is – 100.

Let's say you're facing an apparently angry member of one of your business teams. In other examples, it could be your boss, a supplier, a new employee, or customer. You can tell from this person's voice tone and expression that something has gone wrong. It's early morning and you've just arrived at work. Great way to begin the day, you find yourself thinking sarcastically. Your *attentiveness* (A) level is a seven but, the truth be told, your level of genuine *concern* (C) is a three, tops. You have a long list of things to do, and this wasn't on it. Your *ulterior motive* (U) is a desire to get this over with, and to sting the other person so it won't be likely to happen again. This feeling is rising by the second; it's a seven at the moment; you want this over with as quickly as possible and you're primed to smile while secretly manoeuvring to impose your views and strengthen your position. Your sense of *entitlement* (E) is a modest three or four for now; but your hunch is that the longer this drags on the higher that number will go. Enter each rating in the equation: (*Attentiveness x Concern*) – (*Ulterior Motive x Entitlement*) = *Authentic Presence*. In this case, as you begin the conversation, your *AP* rating is a zero to minus seven, and your gut tells you it's downhill from here. Which means, in essence, that you're standing there, faking a smile, but your mind is already scheming.

Let's pause the scene right there. What if your complaining team member, whom you outrank, is criticizing the direction of your recent test project, and is insisting he or she has been up half the night pondering a radically different approach? Do you squelch this criticism and potentially time-wasting shift of direction on the spot? If you answered yes, you've got lots of company. But not at organizations such as 3M. That's because the managers and directors I have worked with at 3M have learned that heated interactions like this one have ultimately led to highly profitable product ideas and have driven their organization from near bankruptcy at the turn of the century to its leadership position today with nearly $14 billion in revenues. One of the reasons I believe authentic presence is so vital to emotional intelligence is that it requires that you commit to wholehearted attentiveness, genuine concern, and creative curiosity rather than politics, evasiveness, spite, manipulation, dominance or entitlement, as the equation suggests. With a high level of authentic presence, when someone criticizes you out of pure concern, you let it in to your heart as well as your head, and try to learn from it.

(We'll discuss this further in Chapter 7).

Using this premise, let's go in the other direction. Let's say you're working to face difficulties and opportunities straight on, and assume that profitable new ideas *can* crop up anytime, anywhere, and when you hear the team member's first complaint and contrary suggestion, instead of squelching it or wielding rank or ego to dominate the discussion, you go the other way. For a few minutes, at least, you get more attentive, curious, interested, involved, open, and creative. Your first numbers for A and C shoot up to eight and nine, while the D and E fade to a two and one. Suddenly, your AP score is up from a minus seven to seventy. Within five minutes you learn something you'd overlooked about the test project, which prompts you to suggest a variation on the team member's idea, and then you begin to realize something good – a better, more open and trusting relationship, if not a profitable product or service – will come from this unexpected, initially angry interaction.

I encourage you to use this simple equation as one means to increase your authentic presence by giving yourself an AP rating just prior to important face-to-face dialogues, telephone calls, and presentations over the next few weeks. After each interaction, note how well, or poorly, things seemed to go. Over time, you may be able to gauge how high your personal AP threshold needs to be to achieve more consistently the level of meaningful interaction that matters to you and that promotes success.

One of the things I've realized is that in almost every part of the world, when we get inspired and motivated it is by real people, the ones with a good head on their shoulders, of course, but always with a heart. No one expects a leader to be perfect, only genuine and honest. And so it is with the notable men and women who have the courage to find themselves, to tell the truth about who they are, the mistakes they have made, the dreams they hold, and what they're most concerned about, and excited about, in growing the business or in growing their life. This is the bedrock for open dialogue and trust. And upon it is based a rare kind of bond within a team or organization, a bond felt outside the company, too, by customers, clients, suppliers, competitors, and families of employees.

One of the best ways to initiate this process is 'for executives to use communication patterns that lead from the heart and follow with the head', advises David M. Noer of the Center for Creative Leadership. 'The change from head to heart is a low-risk, high-leverage change; a small amount of effort will lead to a large gain in authenticity and empathy. Heart-head communication liberates the sender as well as the receiver. Organizational leaders who share their feelings before retreating to analysis experience the cathartic effect of authenticity.'[8]

Consider the Coca-Cola executive who began a meeting by asking all of the participants to imagine – and really *feel* – that they had just been laid off. Better still, to imagine *why* they had been laid off. This triggered serious discussions that led to deepened dialogue and a surge of new ideas. Shake things up. Probe, prod, enquire, advocate. Be real, receptive, and honest. Watch the results. This is emotional fitness in action.

It is through authentic presence that we can more readily face such challenges with greater openness and curiosity, which encourages us to question and apply what we are learning, and what we have come to know. Malcolm Forbes, the executive whose magazine bears his family name, was frequently asked how he decided where to invest his own fortune, estimated at $250 million. His answer was consistently the same: 'I don't need to know what industry the company is in, or what its financials are. All I need to know is, deep-down, what kind of person the CEO is.

'I bet on the jockey, never the horse,' Forbes liked to add, referring to how he applied the essence of what he'd learned over the years about investing. He understood a fundamental element of authentic presence and emotional fitness: the character and values of an organization are established, demonstrated, and *put into continual practice* by its leaders and how they listen and engage in dialogue and reflection.

On a number of occasions I've experienced this principle in action. I also recall an experience that happened to a friend of mine, Norman Carlson, a senior managing partner at Arthur Andersen LLP. He tells the story of going with one of his young managers-in-training to a prospective client's office and hearing this man, the CEO, speak for the first hour of a scheduled three-hour meeting about his company and its needs. For many years, Norm has valued intuition and emotional intelligence in business, knowing that, when combined with technical expertise and experience, they have helped win many new clients to his firm over the years.

In this case, Norm's gut instinct during the discussion kept telling him something wasn't right with this CEO or his company. Norm stood up at the hour mark and said plainly, 'I have two questions before we go any further. First, I sense that you're at the edge of some kind of downturn or fundamental problem which you haven't told us about. Second, I have the feeling that you have us here for reasons other than hiring us to do your historical financial audits. I'd like to hear how you believe our firm could help you sail through whatever rough waters you're facing and, in the next several years, accomplish your greater purpose, whatever that is.'

Norm sat down and waited.

The CEO appeared thunderstruck. At last he said quietly, 'How could you possibly know that this morning we received news that our company is bracing to take two major financial hits in the next year, and our management team is at war within itself?'

'I *didn't* know for sure,' replied Norm. 'But I could sense it. I had a strong hunch something like that was happening.'

The CEO shook his head. 'As for our purpose, or vision, I'm still trying to define that. We want help. A traditional audit *was* the reason I first called you, but to tell you the truth, today that's the least of my concerns. Close friends tell me I can trust you. I want the best possible advice I can get. I want to meet our difficulties straight on and come out a winner.'

Norm was a US Army officer during the Vietnam War. He has a sharp mind and a very strong heart. Over the years, he has learned to go beyond intellect and technical analysis, and to combine emotional intelligence with his extensive business experience to sense beneath the surface of things and ask straight questions, drawing people into dialogue and listening carefully to what he discovers. Again and again, he has found that it saves time and gets results. In this case, due to Norm's initiative, Arthur Andersen won not only the audit but a lucrative series of consulting jobs as well.

This leads to a key point. In business, it seems to me that we all have an ethical responsibility – or is it a spiritual or moral responsibility? – to respect the power of language.

Taking Inquiry and Dialogue Seriously

Whether it is to lead or succeed, life demands that we stretch ourselves to *learn*, and actively to come to understand what others feel and perceive, beneath the surface, beneath the words. Many sales and leadership programmes hold aloft the phrase 'active listening', telling us that this is the key to winning friends and influencing people. That's sensible, of course: listening makes any of us a better companion and more effective worker. But I contend that many 'active listening' seminars are, in actuality, little more than a shallow theatrical exercise in *appearing* like you're paying attention to another person. The requirements: lean forward, make eye contact, nod, grunt or murmur to demonstrate you're awake and paying attention, and paraphrase something back every thirty seconds or so. As one executive I know wryly observed, many inhabitants of the local zoo could be trained to go through these motions, minus the paraphrasing.

There's a big difference between showing interest and really taking interest.

Michael P. Nichols, *The Lost Art of Listening*

What's missing in all this is the fact that listening is a matter of paying deep, genuine attention, with eyes open and *seeing*, mind open and *learning*, heart open and *feeling*. This is how we pay fundamental respect to our conversation partner and to the dialogue itself. It may be the most significant step some managers can take to increase productivity and innovation. According to a survey in *Management Review*, executives and professionals spend an average of 94 per cent of their time each day communicating, primarily listening and speaking, with some writing thrown in. If you spend even a quarter of your time communicating, then competency in open, honest dialogue is a must, which positions you to speak up and speak out effectively.

Courageous speech is indeed one mark of a leader, and it has long held people in awe. While some politicians and managers still fake it – and somehow manage to win elections and keep their jobs – the men and women with authentic presence do no such thing. They are as comfortable with silence as they are in speaking. And when they speak, they have something worth saying, and they say it in a voice that emerges from deep inside them. And in their tone and presence we hear their distinctive emotional resonance as it represents their inner world and convictions. Without explanation, but in a split-second through sound, the human voice clearly tells us *who* is speaking and, in business, who is deeply committed to the work of the Who organization, and who is merely going through the motions.

Who among us doesn't want to *give voice* to heartfelt ideas and perspectives, and to *have our voice heard* by the powers that be? To look a leader in the eye and credibly deliver a sharply differing opinion or question requires a strong, inward sense of equal human worth – and emotional fitness.

Sometimes what holds us back from engaging in authentic dialogue is fear: fear of revealing our true feelings, or exposing our own vulnerabilities or putting ourselves at risk. Sometimes this fear is due to tension and tiredness. If so, correct the cause and the fear will diminish. If it is due to inexperience with emotionally honest dialogues, then commit yourself to practice. In this case, it's a good idea to begin with people you know and trust, building confidence as you gain experience. As W. Edwards Deming puts it, 'No one can put in his best performance unless he or she feels secure. *Se* comes from the Latin, meaning without, *cure* means fear. *Secure* means without fear, not afraid to express ideas, not afraid to ask questions.'[9]

> *I am not always bound to win but I am bound to be true. I am not always bound to succeed but I am bound to live up to what light I have.*
>
> Abraham Lincoln, 1809–65, 16th President of the USA

Having the Courage to Forgive Yourself and Others

Many of us stubbornly hold on to bitterness and resentment about our life and work, not because we are bad or unloving people but because we do not know how to forgive. The more caring we are, the more painful and debilitating it is not to forgive. One of the common causes of fear – and the resulting hesitancy to engage in open, honest dialogue – is holding on to past anger and resentments about perceived inadequacies, affronts or wrongs at work. To drive out this anger and fear, in Deming's words, requires forgiveness, which is a quality of emotional fitness. 'It is through being wounded,' wrote Fredrich Nietzsche, 'that ... power grows and can, in the end, become tremendous.'

While feelings of anger can be an appropriate short-term response to hurt, if we hold on to that anger, we become hurt for a second time, by the anger itself. Through forgiveness, we convert the suffering caused by our own mistakes and from being hurt by others into new energy to move forward. In part, forgiveness depends on choice, and in part on compassion. In the act of compassion, we can at last move out of the role of victim and see beyond the fear, hurt, blame, jealousy, or envy. These old emotional injuries cannot be erased or undone, but they can become the seeds of transcendence and transformation. It is important to understand that forgiving is something you do to free the piece of you that is tied up with regret and anger, even hatred. To forgive is to release trapped energy that could be doing good work elsewhere.

In many cases, it's a mistake to let wrongs done – by yourself or others – go into hiding. They start to fester and grow. Instead, get at them. Face them squarely. Perhaps, for you, this might mean being prepared to admit honestly and readily, 'When you did/said ——, I felt it as an attack or put-down, and I was getting even for that. How can we fix this?' Or perhaps you want to call a time out, saying something like, 'There is so much anger between us that I believe we need to take a break for a while, and work to make peace with this so we can move on.' In other cases, it's useful honestly to tell the other person who hurt you that, even though you were hurt or took offence at something said or done, you've made a decision to forgive him or her.

If we could reach the secret heart and history of our 'enemies', we should find, in each one's life, sorrow and suffering enough to disarm all hostility.

Henry Wadsworth Longfellow, 1807–82, US Poet

Another way to help yourself and others move beyond resistance and fear is through gratitude. Every one of us has overlooked others and has been overlooked ourselves, yet we often have the attitude of gratitude backwards: we are only willing to express it after something good happens to us.

It's largely a matter of choice and habit. Have an extra minute waiting for a meeting or a plane? Carry some note cards to dash out an expression of your gratitude for someone who warrants it. How often have you said to a co-worker or employee, 'Things are a real headache right now, but *thank you* for being a friend through it all'?

What I've found is that exceptional leaders *lead* with gratitude, they express it first, because they have discovered that this is an essential way to improve organizational life, and they know that the feeling of appreciation will come back to them twofold.

That sense of aliveness is crucial to authentic dialogue. We need to be present, to care, to share meaning. And this can prove profitable in many ways in our business endeavours. Heath Herber, President of the Herber Company, describes one example of how this has worked for him:[10]

I would say that listening to other people's emotions may be the most important thing I've learned in twenty years in business. What I do is tune in to what's underneath the other person's words. It might be doubt. It might be irritation or nervousness. Then I just name it matter-of-factly. I say something like, 'It sounds like you have some doubt, and I can sure understand why you might.' I never try to talk them out of it. If I can name it, they start to talk themselves out of it. I caught onto this one time when I was trying to sell a major contract to a car dealer. Things were bogged down and I couldn't figure out why. I knew I had the numbers that made sense to him, but he was stalling around. I saw that he was distracted about something, so I named it: 'You seem distracted, Charlie.' He blinked and shifted gears. 'Yeah, I guess I am. My daughter's getting married Saturday, and I'm having a lot of feelings about it.' It turned out that our daughters were about the same age, but neither of us until that moment even knew we had kids. Five minutes later he had a signed contract and a new friend.

EQ Map Connections: Authentic Presence

You may want to refer to the following scales of the *EQ Map* as points of reflection related to this chapter: emotional self-awareness, emotional expression, emotional awareness of others, intentionality, intuition, and personal power

---

EQ IN ACTION: *GETTING TO THE HEART OF THE MATTER*

Developing authentic presence begins wherever you are. You work on it at home, in each business interaction, in every work project and meeting. Before long, you notice that

Without credible communication, and a lot of it, the hearts and minds of others are never captured.

John P. Kotter, Harvard Business School

going through the surface motions just doesn't cut it any more. It feels off, wrong. Instead, you find yourself seeking out purpose and clarity, and being rebuffed by fluff and jabber. It becomes easier to get clear and get along, which saves you time and helps you get ahead. Here are several considerations.

When you enter a discussion or meeting, listen intently and get clear about purpose.

In Chapters 1 and 3, we explored emotional honesty and the value of getting to the heart of things early on. In most situations, it builds stronger relationships, and saves time. In group settings, it's crucial to extend your intuition and gather a sense of what others are feeling and intending, and then ask clarifying questions to see if you're on target. Are things focused on gossip or on deeper purpose and meaning? Is this interaction about politics or real dialogue? Remain open, empathic, and alert. Keep your eyes engaged with the speaker. You already know how to listen well: now add your heart to it.

All of us can get lulled into a false sense of security or complacency by the tendency to deny what we don't want to hear. We have more than enough challenges to keep us busy. We don't need more work. So when the first signs of an emerging problem pop up, if we can get away with discounting or ignoring it, we often will. We lapse into management *happy talk*: 'Sure we have challenges, but look at all we've accomplished.' During the 1960s, those of us in the United States, and especially those of us serving in the military, experienced a horrifying example of this: the continual stream of reports on how the US and its allies were winning the war in Vietnam, even though, in truth, we lacked the highest-level commitment to do so and were losing thousands of lives.[11]

Next consideration: what if you can't be present at the beginning of a group setting, and walk into a situation that already appears embattled, gridlocked or rife with hidden agendas? Research suggests that it's the first minute or so of empathic listening that is most crucial and, once you've begun a dialogue, within moments after you begin to speak your listeners may have already formed firm judgments and opinions about you and whatever issue or possibility is at hand. Here are several of the strategies I've found useful:

If you're hearing strong views being expressed without any clear reasoning or rationale, you might open by asking, 'You may be right, but I'd like to understand more about this. What, specifically, leads you to feel that . . .?'

If someone has abruptly headed off on a tangent, you might ask, 'Would you please help me understand how this new direction you've taken connects with our original problem or primary purpose of this meeting?'

When you detect resistance or animosity in others, consider asking, 'I'm sensing that there are some intense feelings about this. To help me get clear, when I said (give an example) I had the impression you were feeling (state the specific emotion). If that's the case, would you please help me understand what upset you or how this triggered something that concerns you?'

If you perceive a strong negative or constrictive reaction in others, you might respond by saying, 'This may be more *my* perception than yours, but when you said —— (give a specific example or description), I felt —— (describe the emotion) or I had the impression you were feeling —— (describe the emotion). If so, I'd like to understand what's concerning you about it.'

What if you're beginning an important team dialogue or sitting in a meeting while others are forcefully expressing their opinions, which you quickly sense are uninfluenceable? You might speak up to clarify things and save everyone time by asking, 'Now that I've heard such strong statements, there's one thing I need to ask: is there anything – anything at all – that I can bring up or do that might convince you to consider other options here?' If the answer is no, this may be a good time to excuse yourself and get on with something where you *can* make a real difference. One point to remember is that teamwork breakdowns and corporate turf wars – which plague most organizations and result in monumental losses of time, energy, money, and creative spirit – can, more often than not, be sensed at the outset and headed off with five or ten dedicated minutes of empathic listening and authentic dialogue.

Consider what it *feels* like when other people, especially ones you care about or those who are important to your career, aren't listening to what you have to say. The sense that you are not being heard or understood is both painful and discouraging. That's why an attentive ear and open heart are, when applied together, such a powerful force in business relationships. Consider several phrases that executives I work with have found useful in empathic listening and dialogue:

> 'Please help me understand. Tell me more.'
> 'What are your feelings and ideas about ——?'
> 'What matters the most to you about ——?'
> 'How would you handle this?'

Value congruency and speak up when it's not present.
When beginning an interaction with a team member, customer, or your boss, you might ask yourself, 'Is the "body language" here consistent with the words I'm hearing?' If there is inconsistency, you might then ask yourself, 'Why is he telling me *this* ... *now* ... *here*?' And then, '*How* is he telling me?' If things seem even less clear after this stage of strategic enquiry, be honest with yourself by asking '*Can I admit I don't understand this*?' If yes, then ask yourself clarifying questions such as:

'What are my *feelings* about . . .?'

'What is my frustration or anger revealing to me? What's at risk here?'

'Is any *truth* not being revealed here?'

Adopt group shorthand codes for shared feelings and clarity.

One of the simplest and most useful ways I've found for members of a team, department or enterprise to acknowledge shared feelings in a meeting or open discussion is with a code or sign. That's right. In my company we make it a point to either nod clearly or use 'Ditto' as shorthand to mean, 'I share the same feeling about that; I agree.' I learned this from Kenneth Grant at Hyde School in Connecticut. Example: when you are in a group setting listening to others, whenever a feeling is expressed by another person or a point gets raised that resonates with your own feelings, you simply speak up and say, 'Ditto.' Once you get past some initial awkwardness and chuckles, it can be an amazingly effective way to enable an entire group better to sense the emotional, as well as cognitive, intelligence in the room, and use this to shape the direction of the dialogue, to get clear and save time.

We also use the short-hand expression 'Again please' – spoken clearly but kindly – whenever a participant cannot hear a speaker and wishes to have something repeated or spoken more clearly or loudly. With a bit of practice, these have become comfortable, intuitively clarifying phrases for all of us to use. No one feigns understanding to save face or look good. We've learned that doing this only leads to future problems. Remember, unless you have a hearing impairment, not being able to hear someone is not an acceptable excuse for misunderstanding them.

Respond with care to new ideas.

If there's a vein of gold in your company's future, it is probably found and explored through new ideas. At 3M and other organizations famed for innovative spirit, I've worked with executives and leadership groups discussing the way ideas are generated and received by managers. What happens, for example, if your first mental reaction to someone's new idea is, 'That's the dumbest thing I've heard in a long time, and it'll never work here'? You may or may not be right. It actually doesn't matter. If you say anything like that, you'll never get another idea from others.

But what if, instead, you shifted your intuitive feelings away from

judgment and into open concern and curiosity, reminding yourself
just how many 3M products, for example, have been runaway successes despite early resistance, or at least raised eyebrows, of management. You might ask, 'In what way do you feel this idea would be
profitable to the company?' And then, help the person with the idea
to determine the answer. You might offer to provide resources or
contacts with someone in R&D, marketing, or production. Without
creating animosity, you have used your EQ to offer a way for the
person to assess his or her own idea, identify its strengths and weaknesses, and make an independent judgment. With this approach, you
help preserve, and even enhance, the feelings of pride and enthusiasm
that are so vital if you want yourself, and the others who work with
you, to keep coming up with new ideas. And what professional or
enterprise doesn't?

Write a letter from your private-self to your public-self.
One of the development exercises I've found helpful in exploring
authentic presence centres on setting up a written dialogue between
your inner and outer self. I first learned this thirty years ago in a
martial arts class, in which I was asked, 'What part of you will decide
when, and how much, force to use in a confrontation?' The truth is,
unless such a choice is made clear in advance, the human nervous
system may react blindly, or the mind can trap us into doing what
others seem to want, rather than what is right to us, to our inner
sense of truth. I've used the exercise numerous times, and I have
always found it valuable. One reason is that authentic presence
depends on getting in touch with the deepest part of yourself, and
then letting this voice lead you. It's all too easy to get caught up
reacting to others and circumstances, running our lives from a superficial, and largely inflexible, place of intellect, rather than heart, and
getting work done by going through the motions with our 'public
self.' Yet, sooner or later, we sense something's missing or amiss. Take
out a piece of paper and write an emotionally honest letter from your
inner, 'private' self to your outer, 'public' self. When you finish,
carefully re-read the letter. What did you discover? What questions or
insights warrant further reflection? And in what ways might you
better align with the guidance of your inner truth, and authentic
presence?

One of the points here is, when we ask good questions and are authentic,
we usually *save* time and get clear. Because of this, we're less likely to

ignore our intuition, and we generally get along better with others, which sets the stage for building and extending your 'trust radius', which is a key EQ trait for building and sustaining meaningful and, in business, profitable relationships the world around. And that is the focus of our next chapter.

CHAPTER 6

Trust Radius

It had been several hours since the morning light crossed in front of the stars that were light years in the distance, and it began to snow. Clouds were settling all around like a thick blanket in the central valley among the summits, and the trail was lost from sight beyond a few steps ahead. For several hours it was slow going until the sky lifted and began to clear as we arrived at the ruins of an ancient fortress. My guide and I approached a gap between the crumbling walls and towering outcroppings that could only be traversed along a narrow ledge, a time-worn foot bridge carved long ago into the near-vertical rock face. As we drew closer, I saw through the muted light that a section of the ledge was cracked and parts of it had broken away. The guide took several tentative steps onto it, retreating at once.

There seemed no other way across, not without retracing our path for many hours. I felt the cold air swirling off the rocks as I kept staring at the foot bridge. I found myself growing more uncomfortable by the moment, becoming tense and uncertain, afraid and angry, all at the same time, knowing that this was the passage that took us to our destination, and now it was useless. As I cursed into the icy air, I managed a brief grin however, thinking to myself that this was precisely why a part of so many of us – including me, at that moment – would rather be sitting in an easy chair watching a movie channel or the 'All-Sports Network' than testing ourselves on the mountains – and bridges – of life.

I turned away, pacing anxiously about, waiting.

Within moments, I saw her. From out of the cloud-haze that had settled about the trail came a young Tibetan woman. At her side was a small girl, not more than three or four years old.

The woman walked right up to us and said, 'Tashi deley' as she brought her hands together in front of her heart in traditional greeting. Staring into my eyes, she turned to glance at the treacherous passage and bridge; then she smiled, reaching into the folds of her cloak and then pressing something into my hand. I saw that it was a small piece of Tibetan turquoise, pure blue. 'Kailas,' she said simply, indicating the stone had been found near the famous Himalayan peak by that name. Like many Tibetan pilgrims, both young and old, she carried a small sack of such amulets for energy and good fortune, and symbolic connections to the spirit of our existence.

I looked up to see the little girl scrambling onto her mother's back, firmly wedging her small hands into the folds of the woman's cloak. For a long moment, the girl turned to stare at me, her head tilted with intense childish curiosity. I'll never forget that radiant face and those innocent eyes. And then, without a flicker of hesitation, the woman and girl were scurrying the crumbling ledge, leaning towards the rock wall and keeping a steadying hand lightly against it as they went. And then they were gone into the deep-shadowed trails beyond. Without hesitating any longer to think about it, the guide and I quickly followed them.

I still have that piece of turquoise. It reminds me of the power of emotional trust. The poet, David Whyte, author of *The Heart Aroused*, tells audiences of a very similar experience that happened to him when crossing a mountain pass in the Himalayas.

What bridges of trust have you crossed from time to time in your own life and work? Take a few moments right now to recall one or two such experiences. I believe that every one of us comes to daily chasms of doubt and change in which the passage depends on a broken or untested bridge. On the job, this may occur when we are poised to take a step in the right direction, or a new direction, to speak up, create something unexpected, confront a difficult issue, or initiate a crucial dialogue. Whenever we ready ourselves to head into unknown territory, our hidden fears and weaknesses of confidence loom up to meet us, and then the mind takes over; we begin to *think* about it, to analyze the risks, a very logical thing to do, except that far too often we feel the gap is no longer just difficult to cross, it's unsurmountable, the risk too great, that we should not attempt it, and we must retrace our steps and leave our hopes behind.

What do such decisions cost us? We must be aware of the risks, of course, but we must trust with our hearts, too. Without that, we are lost, and end up going in circles, repeating what we know, listening to the voices in our minds telling us to pull back and wait, to doubt and complain. Throughout my descent from the mountains I remember mulling over the idea of bridges of trust.

Beyond the Bridges of Trust

Trust can be envisioned, metaphorically, not only as a bridge but as a cup. I heard a story about Santana, the composer and musician, who was being interviewed on the National Public Radio programme 'Fresh Air'.[12] The interviewer was reported to say, 'You write songs of your own, yet when giving concerts you also perform the music of many other artists. There are those who suggest this may show your lack of trust in your own work as an artist. Is that true?'

Santana thought for a few moments and replied, 'There are many beautiful and meaningful songs that move me, not just my own compositions. A song is a cup. It's what you pour into it that counts.'

If you view your life as a cup, how much of your emotional trust – and yourself – are you pouring into it? How about your business relationships? Your family?

And then ask yourself, how strong – or weak or leaking – are each of these cups? What kind of trust will it take to repair the cracks, leave old habits behind, and replenish each cup with new ideas and deeper bonds? When we trust enough to pour our hearts into the cups of life, we inspire ourselves and others. We reach out to strangers, and acknowledge or value them in some way, without expecting anything in return. Ironically, or perhaps not, over time this extension of trust usually pays off in one way or another. At the very least, our daily efforts feel more connected to humanity and therefore worthwhile.

Trust does that. Throughout history, notable men and women have known this, applying it to building worthy endeavours. I was reminded of just how important this is while on a transcontinental flight not long ago. I was sitting next to an executive who turned to me and asked, 'How do you become one of the wealthiest people in the world?'

I shrugged my shoulders and peered into her eyes, waiting for a sales pitch, guessing she was in the field of insurance or investment.

'One way,' she said, 'is to trust yourself and those around you so much that you give away 70 per cent of what you own and, in the process, make thousands of your managers and employees millionaires. That's what Bill Gates did with Microsoft. And Sam Walton did the same thing at Wal-Mart.'

'And how,' she went on, 'could your business become the top rated Fortune Service 500 company for profit growth, with nearly $10 billion in revenue within a decade of being formed?'

I looked at her inquisitively again. 'One way,' she said, 'is to trust yourself and those around you so much that you help many of your managers and employees accumulate over a million dollars' worth of stock, some before the age of thirty and starting as shelf stockers. The company I'm talking about is Home Depot.'

She pointed out that there are hundreds of other examples in businesses of every size and description. And she was right. I remembered hearing Minoru Makihara, president of Mitsubishi Corporation – the Japanese trading company with about $176 billion in annual revenues – point out the immense value of 'trust networks.'[13] Trust is an emotional strength that begins with the feeling of self-worth and purpose that we're called to extend outward to others, like the radius of a circle, eventually reaching everyone on their team, in their department, division, or entire company. The warm, solid gut feeling you get from trust – from counting on yourself and in trusting and being trusted by others – is one of the great enablers of life. With it, we have the inner room to grow, to become emotionally fit, and to exercise and expand our sense of trust in building bridges from one issue to another, one idea to another, one person to another. Such character-istics enable us to keep criticism in better perspective, for example, and handle critics more openly, with quiet confidence, and perhaps a smile.

This reminds me of the story of Albert Einstein, after he had gone into exile during World War II, when a hundred Nazi professors published a book condemning his theory of relativity. 'If I were wrong,' he said, 'one professor would have been enough.' That's self-trust, and a dash of humour in the face of adversity.

One of the essential points of this chapter is that trust is more than a good idea or attitude. It's an emotional trait, something we must feel and act upon. When we trust ourselves and can extend this trust to others, and receive it in return, it becomes the glue that holds relationships together, and frees up honest dialogue. Lack of trust, on the other hand, prompts us to spend as much time and effort protecting, doubting, checking, weighing, and inspecting as in doing real – that is, creative, collaborative, and value-adding – work.

As business strategist Michael Hammer observes, 'The overheads of distrusting or wary relationships are enormous.'[14] At Arthur Anderson LLP, partners strive to achieve the highest ratings in their work as 'trusted business advisors'. It's a short phrase but an immense responsibility to fulfil, since *trust* is of paramount concern to their many clients world-wide.

In a recent survey of multinational corporations, *The Economist* concluded that firms are beginning to resemble networks of far-flung alliances, and trust is becoming more of an issue. Charles Handy asks us, 'How do you manage people whom you do not see?' And whom you cannot control or fire, because they may not be your employees. Handy's answer: 'By trusting them.'[15]

Technique and technology are important. But adding trust is the issue of the decade.

Tom Peters, management analyst, USA

Trust Survey

But where do you start? When you're serious about it, one good place is with a trust questionnaire, which you and your team members honestly complete and compare. Start there, and ways to build trust become clear. Of all the questionnaires I've seen and used over the years, the following is my favourite. It was developed by Charlotte M. Roberts, executive consultant and co-author of *The Fifth Discipline Fieldbook*, as she worked with her clients to create organizational learning as a core competency. The Trust Survey is reprinted with permission:

Below are listed 21 aspects of trust.
Place a (+) if the person meets the criteria and a (−) if the person does not.

1. I have a good idea how my team member will act; he/she is consistent.
2. I believe my team member is dependable; he/she keeps agreements, commitments and promises.
3. I feel my team member would not intentionally hurt me in any way; he/she demonstrates caring for others.
4. I have faith that my team member will act in my best interest even if I am not present; we share common values and goals.
5. I know my team member can do the work we have identified; he/she does high quality work.
6. I think my team member's words are true; he/she is honest.
7. I hear my team member's words as authentic; he/she says what he/she means.

8. I know my team member will admit mistakes and fears; he/she is open.

9. I can share my crazy ideas and deep feelings with my team member; he/she is non-judgmental.

10. I am comfortable with the investment (social, emotional, psychological, etc.) I have made in this relationship; my team member respects the relationship.

11. I am not afraid of uncertainty in the future; my team member and I can figure out most anything.

12. I don't mind asking my team member for help in understanding a new process, a new equation, etc.; he/she is a good coach.

13. I openly receive feedback from my team member; his/her feedback is direct, specific and non-punishing.

14. I am willing to suspend my position to understand my team member's point of view; he/she can make a valuable contribution.

15. I know my team member suspends his/her position to understand me; he/she believes I can make a valuable contribution.

16. I can freely disagree with my team member; he/she is equally committed to uncovering the truth and the best solution.

17. I listen to criticism from my team member; he/she accepts me as I am and does not demand that I play a particular role.

18. I feel confirmed by my team member; he/she accepts me as I am and does not demand that I play a particular role.

19. I enjoy a free-flowing dialogue with my team member; we blend our thoughts well together for better understanding.

20. I have fun with my team member; he/she shares a common spirit.

21. My fellow team member has told me that I can trust him/her.

22. Other (please describe your criteria).

What did you learn from this questionnaire?

One of the things I've learned from using it is that there are many dimensions to building and sustaining trust. And they all matter.

The more I trust myself and others, and my environment, the more creative and effective I will likely be, and the more chances I'll have to be successful. Studies suggest that chronic mistrust, and accompanying feelings of hostility, may even damage the human heart and can lead to a fatal heart attack.[16] Redford Williams, director of behavioral research at Duke University Medical Center, is one of a growing number of experts studying the relationship between hostility, lack of trust, and heart risk.

The more limited a person's circle of trust, says Williams, the more he or she may tend to stay angry, annoyed, irritated, or cynical, and to blame others. For a segment of the population, this is 'like taking a small dose of a slow-acting poison – arsenic, for example – every day of your life. And the result is often the same: not tomorrow, perhaps, or even the day after, but sooner than most of us would wish, your hostility is likely to harm your health.'[17] One of Williams' core prevention strategies: build more trust in your life and work relationships.[18]

Other research indicates that trust has a significant influence on group effectiveness, enabling members openly to express feelings and differences, and avoid typical sabotage and defensiveness.[19] When people don't trust each other, they ignore feelings and alter facts and ideas that they anticipate may increase their vulnerability; under these conditions the chances for misunderstandings and erroneous assumptions increase dramatically. Trust has also been shown to be the most significant predictor of an individual professional's satisfaction with the company he or she works for.[20]

Your trustworthiness is built and sustained on a foundation of honest and appropriate disclosure, believability and credibility. There is evidence that business trust depends, first and foremost, on making *emotional* contact with the listener.[21]

> *If there is no sense of trust in the organization, if people are preoccupied with protecting their backs ... creativity will be one of the first casualties.*
>
> Manfred F. R. Kets de Vries, INSEAD, France

Whether it's a product, service, or relationship, nearly all people buy in based on emotion, and then, afterwards, justify with fact. But in case you're assuming that these EQ qualities of success require a high-profile charismatic personality or leadership style, that assumption would be wrong – they don't.[22]

The *internal costs of mistrust* result in inefficient entanglements of hierarchy, communication, misperception, anger, blame, and cynicism that waste time, energy, goodwill, and money. We feel compelled to draw up procedures in great detail, often hundreds of pages, even for simple agreements and transactions – unlike the way some companies in Japan, for example, use trust to ensure that agreements are limited to one or two pages, with phrases such as 'details to be worked out later, if the need arises', knowing that working out such things would be win-win for all parties involved. Without such trust, we not only waste time and often surround ourselves with attorneys, but this also prompts management to assume erroneously that employees need even more rigid supervision, tighter controls, and that they really cannot successfully work without continual monitoring. This plays right into Frederick Taylor's outmoded and insubstantiated contention that workers cannot be trusted and layers of management are essential for supervising their behaviour.

The *external costs of mistrust* can be just as damaging over time, imposing a kind of steep tax on all forms of economic activity. When customers lose faith or confidence in an organization, for example, they are quick to give their allegiance to competing firms they trust, or at least don't mistrust.

Right now, this month, this quarter, what would you estimate to be the costs of mistrust in your career or business? And how might this affect your future employability, opportunities for growth, alliances, creative breakthroughs, and profitability?

Consider the following pair of examples of trust-in-action: the Ritz-Carlton hotel chain, one of the few service-sector winners of the Malcolm Baldrige Quality Award, actively promotes trust as the core of its organizational culture. Every Ritz-Carlton employee, including junior bellhops, can spend up to $2,000 on the spot to fix a guest's problem. No questions asked.

At Southwest Airlines, the USA's eighth largest airline, trust has played a key role in making it the most consistently profitable carrier, repeatedly capturing the US Department of Transportation's top rankings for on-time flights, best baggage handling, and fewest complaints. At Southwest, customers come second (employees are number one), and CEO Herb Kelleher continually emphasizes trust as a driving force – extending it to everyone at Southwest. 'We've tried to create an environment where people are able to, in effect, bypass even the fairly lean structures that we have so that they don't have to convene a meeting of the sages in order to get something done,' he explains. 'In many cases they can go ahead and do it on their own. They can take individual responsibility and know they will not be crucified if it doesn't work out.'[23]

One day, Gary Baron, Executive Vice-President at Southwest, caught Kelleher in a hallway after a Front Line Forum, the regular meetings in which Kelleher gets together with senior employees to focus on how to improve the company. Barron told Kelleher he wanted to talk about the complete reorganization of the management structure of Southwest's $700 million maintenance department. He handed Kelleher a three-page summary of the plan. The CEO read it on the spot, and raised only one concern. Barron said that it was something he was concerned about too, and was dealing with it. 'Then it's fine by me,' replied Kelleher. 'Go ahead.' The entire conversation took about four minutes. Kelleher is trusted. He has credibility with his employees. So do a number of other exceptional leaders, entrepreneurs, and executives, which is what it takes to engender and encourage trust, and then grow and sustain it.

There's Little Trust Without Believability

The word *trust* is defined as an 'absolute certainty in the trustworthiness of self or another'. In our interactions with others, *trust* and *believability* are often nearly synonymous. We need both together; neither alone will do. What few managers realize is that intuition, emotional contact, influence, trust, and believability are all processed in the preconscious areas of the brain – in particular, the limbic system, which serves not only as a gateway to the sites where cognition, or thinking, takes place, but as the brain's emotional centre. Whereas the cognitive brain centres devote their time to sifting through words, concepts, and analysis, the emotional brain continually scans for meaning and judgment from thousands of subtle nuances in voice tone, gestures, eye contact, and a wide range of other behaviour that the cognitive brain centres scarcely register or understand.[25] The limbic system works approximately 80,000 times faster than the conscious cerebral cortex.[26] The conscious mind can process only 126 bits of information per second and only 40 bits of human speech, yet our senses can receive up to 10 million bits of input per second.[27] The limbic system gives us an instantaneous 'reading' on believability and trustworthiness during each of our interactions with others. In short: without believability, we are neither heard nor trusted.[28]

Professor Albert Mehrabian of UCLA has conducted studies indicating that, unless a speaker is highly believable – excited, enthused, confident, and congruent in voice, words, and body language – the listener or viewer makes a rapid and lasting judgment as to the speaker's trustworthiness.[29] In this case, only 7 per cent of the decision about whether to believe or trust someone hinges on the words or content, and 93 per cent depends on the voice tone and body language (eyes, gestures, posture, and related factors). Conversely, with believable and trusted leaders, there is no such inconsistency in the words, voice, and body language – the message and communicator are one. Mehrabian's research also shows that your voice – its auditory resonance and intonation – counts for as much as 84 per cent of your emotional influence, believability and trust when people can hear you but not see you, such as when you are talking on the telephone.

Getting Past Broken Trust

It's fine to work hard at increasing your believability and at building trusting relationships, you may be thinking to yourself, but what about the times when people break your trust? All of us have had our trust betrayed, and many of us have felt so hurt by the experience that we say, 'I'll never trust again.' Indeed, when trust is broken, we may feel isolated and become cynical for a while.

You may be deceived if you trust too much, but you will live in torment if you don't trust enough.

Frank Crane, historian and sociologist

Yet emotional fitness depends, in part, on finding effective ways to bounce back from such experiences and to build new lines of trust. In many companies, people are looking over their shoulders, feeling more vulnerable than ever, not trusting, not excelling, but simply trying to protect themselves and hold on to their jobs. Even in the absence of an atmosphere of trust in your company, on an individual level you can begin building your trust resilience by being straightforward and emotionally honest about your mistakes (which increases believability), standing behind your word, and consciously accepting that times of broken trust are as much a part of shaping lasting trust as doubt is a part of believing. The point is to keep moving, extending trust to others in a new direction, for example, and seeking their trust in return.

On an organizational level, it's up to top executives to stand behind their statements of trust, no matter what. Example: moments after Bob Montgomery, then Southwest Airlines' manager of properties, made a commitment to the city of Austin, Texas, he realized it was a mistake, and knew it could cost his employer $400,000.[30] When CEO Herb Kelleher heard about it, he asked if the deal had been signed. 'No,' the manager said, 'but Bob told them we would.' Kelleher did not hesitate before saying, 'If Bob represented that we would sign it, then that's what we're going to do.' Montgomery, who expected to be fired or lose his dignity, wasn't and didn't. A year later, he approached the CEO and said once more that it was a stupid mistake and should never have happened. Kelleher responded, 'Bob, I'm glad you finally learned from it.' From that point on, the issue was dead. Montgomery has since been promoted to director of properties.

One of the important ways we all learn to build and sustain trust, say researchers and many executives alike, is through sharing stories about it.[31] In this light, consider the following three tales that are among my favourite on the power of trust at all levels of work.

David M. Armstrong, Vice-President of Armstrong International, a manufacturing firm with offices throughout the world, also sees it as he tells one of his favourite stories about trust:[32]

At 11.55 a.m. every work day a whistle blows. It's lunchtime. And as you enter the Armstrong cafeteria, nothing – at first – appears out of the ordinary. There are picnic tables, refrigerators filled with sandwiches and soft drinks for sale, coffee machines, microwaves, and candy machines ... but wait a minute! The vending machines are unlocked and there is no cash register. There is no one watching either the food or the money.

The cafeteria is run completely on the honour system. Employees pay for their food or beverages by putting their money into an open coin box. On a typical day the box will be filled with well over $100. This system works just fine.

Either you trust your employees or you don't. If you trust them, you don't need locked cash registers, time clocks, and scores of supervisors. If you don't trust them, get rid of them.

Think of the message it sends. By getting rid of locked cash boxes and needless supervision, you're showing people you believe in them. We've found that faith is rewarded a thousandfold in higher productivity and new ideas.

That depth of trust and faith was what William Peace had to count on when he became general manager of the Synthetic Fuels Division at Westinghouse in the early 1980s.[33] The entire unit faced termination due to falling oil prices unless Peace could find some way to make it attractive to potential investors. After thorough review, he decided he had to cut fifteen of the division's 130 jobs, and had no choice but to lay off these people despite their good to outstanding performance ratings. Peace and his department heads spent a long, emotional meeting selecting the names of the fifteen, and then the senior managers rose to go to deliver the bad news. He stopped them. Peace intuitively felt he should communicate the decision himself, and wanted to stem any rumours of massive layoffs at the same time he personally faced each man and woman with the terrible news.

The meeting with the fifteen was held first thing the next morning. People wept openly or stared out of the window or at the floor in stony silence. Their world was disintegrating. Peace insisted that the layoffs were based solely on job descriptions, not performance, and he took them through his reasoning in making the difficult choices. He asked them to try to understand why, if not forgive him for, sacrificing fifteen jobs to save more than a hundred others. Peace recalls that it was the most painful meeting he ever participated in. They argued, shouted, pleaded, and accused him of being heartless and ungrateful. Peace empathized, accepted their criticism, and committed himself to trusting his decision and the intentions of those gathered around him. He took all of the heat and did his best to answer each question in frank detail. By late morning, the mood shifted: the range and anger gave way to resignation, and a few of the people expressed grudging understanding and aroused interest in the prospects for the sale of the plant. They shook hands when the meeting ended and he wished them luck in their future.

Many managers in similar circumstances would have avoided delivering the news of the layoffs themselves. But not Peace. And his courage in meeting with these fifteen face to face, and respecting them throughout that long, painful morning, paid off in several key ways. A buyer had been found for the division, and Peace had been kept on as general manager. Months later, the new owners were investing money in the plant. All at once, Peace was in a position to rehire a number of the people he had laid off. Every one of them came back to work for him, even those for whom it meant giving up good jobs found elsewhere. That's one of the long-term results of trust in the face of what at first appears to be betrayal. Peace committed himself to trusting his own instincts and then personally respected – and trusted – the worth and dignity of those he had to lay off, face to face, never shirking from taking on the heat of his decision.

It's natural, of course, that when people perceive that trust has been broken they will respond with anger, and even outrage. Could you face a similar situation, either large or small, open-heartedly, being clear and standing firm, extending your trust and support in a new direction, engaging in honest dialogue – even when it's wrapped in contention – and stay the course without animosity or vengeance?

Ricardo Semler did. When he first took the helm of Semco, his family's business in Sao Paulo, Brazil, his company was enmeshed in hierarchy, regulations, and mistrust. Productivity and morale were low, quality was poor, there were few new contracts, and the signs of financial ruin were looming on the horizon.[34] Semco's five factories manufactured, among many other things, marine pumps, commercial appliances, and mixing equipment for rocket fuel. Over the years, Semco managers had thoroughly analyzed every aspect of the businesses and had created intricate rules for everything from equipment manifest to travel expenses, which included ceilings on airfare, hotel expenses, phone calls home, and an insistence on submitting original receipts. Factory workers were generally treated like delinquents or prisoners, and were required to ask permission to go to the bathroom, and underwent daily theft-prevention checks.

Semler decided that, to compete for the future, he must begin by demonstrating a strong new sense of trust, and extending this throughout his organization. At once, he cut the hierarchy to three levels, set up a profit-sharing plan, replaced the thick rule book with what he called the rule of common sense, instituted collaborative decision-making among management, and decided to submit many company decisions – such as key acquisitions and factory relocations – to democratic company-wide votes. He also decided that he had to demonstrate a strong sense of trust in those he sent around the world to represent his company, and therefore he eliminated expense accounting and announced that payments would be made for whatever travel expenses people claimed to have. Then he opened the company's financial records to everyone on the payroll, put factory workers on monthly salaries rather than hourly wages, ended security checks, took down time clocks, and let people on the plant floors decide their work goals, schedules, and methods. He trusted that people whose bonuses depended on performance and profits were not going to want to waste the company's money or squander opportunities.

He was right. Quality and morale soared, sales doubled in the first year alone, eight new products lost in R&D for years were launched within months, costs and inventory declined, and productivity increased so dramatically that within a few years the company was able to reduce the workforce by one-third through natural attrition and early retirement incentives.

One of the things I've learned from many other executives around the world is that David Armstrong, William Peace, and Ricardo Semler are right and, beneath the media headlines, rumours, and hooplah, trust and believability must be built and sustained through consistently demonstrating them in our choices and actions. One at a time. Which has been, in fact, the only way that some people have survived as leaders, and why some of them have gone on to join the ranks of the most admired men and women in history.

Extending Your Trust Radius

In those rare circumstances when followers are asked to risk their freedom, and sometimes their lives, we learn a lot about the stuff of a leader. I've witnessed such leadership during my travels in Tibet. I've seen men and women trust so much that they were willing to risk everything to do what they believed was right. And some of them died doing it.

Harriet Tubman was this kind of leader, a person of great trust, devotion, and self-sacrifice. In essence, she had to break out of jail, rather than go to jail, for principle.[35] She was born in 1825 into the social prison of slavery. As a teenager, she tried to intercede in the beating of a fellow slave and was knocked unconscious by a two-pound weight. The blow broke her skull and she hovered near death for weeks. Later, through her ingenuity, she escaped north from Maryland and, against all odds, went back south again and again to rescue other slaves.

Her first followers were those with great courage, yet as the word of her trustworthiness and credibility in the face of authority spread, she instilled trust and hope in slaves who had never met her. She also won converts in the north who began to believe, as they saw Tubman outwit posse after posse (she had learned the pass systems, the allowable excuses for blacks to be seen abroad, the secret routes through areas where no excuses were acceptable), that African-Americans had the capacity to conduct their own affairs in a free society. She had no love of violence, although she was prepared to defend herself and her charges. She prayed for her enemies and did not take sides with any of her feuding allies. She could be trusted by one and all to do what she set out to do – she never lost a slave she took into her care. After the war she set up a home in New York for homeless blacks. She had a mission to her people. And she had the believability and trust to accomplish it. She went on to become one of the most admired women in US history.

From Harriet Tubman's life, we learn of another, less known, dimension of trust: the ability to win readily, and sustain, the confidence of strangers. In modern business, this could include business competitors, potential partners, board members, suppliers or customers, as well as the fastest-growing segment of the American workforce: temporary workers. How we treat them, and how, exactly, they rate our believability and trustworthiness, has much to do with our present and future success.

Francis Fukuyama, senior analyst for the Rand Corporation, calls this the 'radius of trust'.[36] It expands based, in part, on a combination of believability and *spontaneous sociability*, an aspect of emotional intelligence indicative of your ease in talking with strangers and in embracing differences and disagreements with openness instead of rigidity, perceiving them as sources of possible connections and ideas that may prove constructive and valuable.

> **EQ Map Connections: Trust Radius**
> You may want to refer to the following scales of the *EQ Map* as points of reflection related to this chapter: emotional self-awareness, emotional awareness of others, interpersonal connection, compassion, outlook, and trust radius

EQ IN ACTION: *EXPANDING YOUR CIRCLE OF TRUST, ONE STEP AT A TIME*

Ask yourself, What is the size of the circle within which I am willing to extend my trust? In business? In my personal life? This is your present *trust radius*. To be more specific, on the job what is your trust radius within management, or your work team or department? How do you treat temporary workers? Like temps? Or, from the start, do you show them respect and trust, give them real responsibilities, and hold them to high standards?

It's easy to say, 'I trust you,' but it pays to ask your heart how much it truly *feels* that trust. As I reflect for a moment on this statement, I remember several lines of C. S. Lewis's writings: 'It is easy to believe a rope to be strong and sound so long as you are merely using it to cord a box. But suppose you had to hang by the rope over a precipice. Wouldn't you then first discover how much you really trusted it?'

In this spirit, take out a piece of paper and draw this circle, and put the names of the people you wholeheartedly trust inside the circle. Pause for a few moments after writing each name to ask your inner voice if you trust this person absolutely. You either trust or do not; on an emotional level, there is nothing partial or conditional about trust. When you finish this self-evaluation, put a star beside the names of those people inside the circle who work with you. How might you benefit if more people from your team or organization were inside this trust radius? I encourage you to seek 360-degree feedback from those you live with, work with, and work for. Explain this simple exercise and ask each of these people, 'Am I one of the people you trust completely?' If not, why not? And how, specifically, do they suggest you might increase your trustworthiness in their eyes? Conversely, is this person inside your trust radius? If not, why not? Unless we can know and respond to such honest insights, there's little chance we will grow our ability to trust, and with it, our trust radius.

If, right now, it feels that your overall trust radius or some of your specific circles of trust are small, begin to look for opportunities to expand them – to *practise* trust – through being more trusting of yourself and others in those situations where, if it doesn't work out, no harm is done. For example, when you're booking an airline flight, trust the ticket agent to give you a good seat, rather than viewing the seat selection as something adversarial and jumping in with a demanding tone, not trusting that this person would give you the best available seat or talk to you about your preferences.

Or trust the person in charge of the produce department at your favourite market to save you time by advising you on what's freshest, rather than assuming that you're being tricked by some hidden ghoul in the market whose sole purpose is to hide the best produce from you, leaving you feeling you have to handle and examine every single apple, tomato, and head of lettuce. Another trust-builder is to become more aware each time when you delegate a basic task – photocopying, mail handling, ordering lunch, resource gathering, you get the idea – and, if the other person seems alert and attentive, remind yourself to let go of trying to over-organize the task.

Make it a point not to hover around. Instead, imagine that things will be handled expeditiously and well, and act accordingly. Move on to your next priority. This frees you from the common nagging sense of micro-management that dogs those of us who are prone to 'delegate' with mistrust and, beneath the surface, rarely actually give up authority and control. Try this with your children, as well.

In large part, it's in circumstances like these that we can most safely and progressively open our heart and condition our gut readily – even instinctively – to extend trust, rather than blindly throwing up the walls of mistrust, in each new interaction. With practice, it becomes easier. And you'll find it easier to take in stride those specific occasions when others betray your trust or when you let yourself, or others, down.

Let's also consider your *accessibility* as a factor in how easily and exten-sively you trust others, and they trust you. In nearly every organization I work with, I hear people complaining that managers and executives are becoming less trusting. Why? In part, because they seem less accessible. And why is that? Due to a widespread perception that leaders are always rushing through interactions with employees, clients, and customers. The main point here is that this is, first and foremost, a perception. I advise executives that, beyond practising the habits of good listening, there are two very important things you can do right away to make time spent with you *feel* longer and more valuable:

1. *Sit down* while you are interacting with other people.
2. Don't make any *time-urgent movements* (such as watch watching) that indicate you are overly concerned about how much time has passed.

It turns out that few things damage trust more quickly or seem to shorten the perceived time a colleague, client or employee gets to spend with you than watching you stand at a door with your hand on it – or any other 'exit' positions – as if poised to flee. If you have only two minutes to spare, that posture will make those two minutes feel like ten seconds to the person you're speaking with, and you have thereby inadvertently cancelled out 90 per cent of this potentially valuable time.

To prove this to yourself, think about standing beside someone who is poised to flee, and trying to have a brief conversation with him or her. No matter what words are spoken, what does it *feel* like? Devaluing? A rejection? You are feeling an ancient instinct in the brain responding to posture of another person. The thing to remember is, we all feel it; and it matters.

Whether you are dealing with a co-worker, boss, or employee, there are certain things you can say – and not say – that may help each person feel that you've given him or her extra time and value. First, when you state how much time you have, say it in a tone of voice that shows you're delighted to be fortunate to have two minutes, or ten minutes, or half an hour. And be certain to eliminate the word *only* and any other negative presuppositions from your statement. Begin your announcement by saying, 'I have ten minutes to spend with you,' instead of, 'I have *only* ten minutes.' This subtle change makes a marked difference in how the other person feels about the interaction.

Next, complete the statement by adding, '... and if you need more time than that, just say so, and I will stay (or schedule another meeting).' When I first tried this, I was concerned that my schedule would get jammed with appointments from people taking me up on the offer. What I found was what researchers had reported: in most cases, the opposite is true – people usually won't take you up on the offer; in fact, they'll often be *more effective* in using the minutes they have with you. And, just as important, they'll start to *feel* – and, in turn, genuinely trust and believe – that you stand out from the management crowd by offering them ample time to communicate. This is the emotional *perception* that's so crucial for good-listening, high-performance leaders to earn. The alternative is a relentless undercurrent of resentment, and even sabotage, which makes both sides stressed, mistrustful, and less productive.

Here are several additional considerations for times when you're getting angry with someone and you're about to lose trust. Consider the following story: from the moment the disagreement began, I could feel it escalating from twenty feet away where I was sitting at lunch in the cafeteria of a major medical centre. Two managers were seated across from each other at a small table by the window. They were arguing, in subdued voices so as not to disturb those seated around them, but arguing nonetheless.

> *It is impossible to estimate how many good ideas are abandoned every day as a result of difficult-to-manage relationships.*
>
> John P. Kotter, Harvard Business School

I recognized these two men from a senior management council I'd attended as consultant at this institution. I noticed that one of the managers held a bound set of papers in his fist and was shaking it in the air. The other was shaking his head, no. Both were red faced and tense. I could tell they were getting entrenched in their positions.

And then something amazing happened. All at once, one of the managers relaxed his shoulders and reached into his suit coat pocket, pulling out a felt tip pen. He picked up a napkin and scooted his chair around the table to sit at a right-angle to, rather than across from, the other manager. For ten or fifteen seconds, he said nothing as he drew a simple diagram of some kind with the pen on the napkin. Then he pointed the tip of the pen at one spot. 'There!' I heard him say. '*That's* where I'm feeling confused. How can we make *that* work?'

The other manager looked at him in complete astonishment, setting down the two-hundred page report and pushing it aside. 'There?' he exclaimed, pointing and reaching for the pen. He proceeded to draw something else on the napkin. 'But don't you see, *there's* how we'll work around it. No wonder it felt wrong to you. You were right.'

A minute later, both leaders were chatting amiably as they left the cafeteria.

What happened? It was a turning point: the first of the managers, realizing he was about to lose trust and enter what could become a destructive argument, paid attention to his 'gut feeling' that it might not be the other manager, or the proposal itself, that was the problem, but some hidden difference in *perception*. There was something other than the 'facts' that was giving him an emotional signal of a misunderstanding or barrier.

No matter what the circumstance, we rarely feel about things in exactly the same way others do. That may now seem obvious. We also don't *see* things the same way others do, which is a lot less obvious. As Stanford psychology professor Robert Ornstein explains, 'The human eye, the most developed and intricate of the senses, conveys to the brain but *one-trillionth* of the information that reaches its surface.'[38]

As I watched the managers sharing the felt tip pen and marking points of confusion or difference on the cafeteria napkin, I was reminded of a series of lectures I attended by Karl Pribram, the neurosurgeon who, for a quarter of a century, was head of the Stanford Neuropsychology Laboratory. Following one of the lectures, he and I talked about the damage caused by heated arguments among scientists when minds and hearts are closed. Disagreements are magical, he said. But we can't lose trust. We must keep valuing and including each other in the dialogue. We must remain open. He quoted MIT's Warren McCulloch, who had once exclaimed, in bitter frustration at the loss of trust and breakdown in a key dialogue, 'Stop! Do not bite my finger. Look where I am pointing!'[39]

With a felt tip pen, one manager helped the other stop biting and instead to begin looking where he was pointing, with his emotional intelligence, with his gut feeling about the proposal – something he could not find in the computer-graphics-laden document but with a simple illustration on a napkin. We must remember that looking is not only with the eyes; it's with intuition and the heart.

In order to uphold trust, we must make certain we're engaged in dialogues that exchange meaning – which is, in truth, shared in different ways. Scientists have discovered that we each have a unique *language instinct*, an inherent preferred style of perceiving new ideas and interacting with others.[40] In order to assure the greatest chances of building and sustaining trust, and sharing meaning through dialogue, we must learn to recognize and adapt our message to several differing sensory modes.

For example, when making a presentation to a group you don't know, you might provide a written summary, oral summary, a diagram, a hands-on demonstration, and time for questions and personalized interactions. Under ordinary circum-

> *People learn in different ways: reading, listening, pictures, watching.*
>
> W. Edwards Deming, management and business process analyst

stances people can shift from one sensory mode to another with little difficulty. But when they are tense or tired, when they are under stress, there's a drastic change: they tend to become locked in their preferred sensory mode. The greater the pressure, the tighter the lock.[41] Therefore, it's up to each of us to use our intuition and knowledge to try to reach other people in the way that *they* prefer learning and talking about things that matter.

Research[42] also suggests that many of us have an inherent, and perhaps largely inherited, need for *getting to the point*, for knowing the bottom line. We need context and we want to feel we know where an issue or conversation is headed. We quickly grow impatient, even intolerant, when faced with someone embarking on a long, detailed discussion that it seems might lead anywhere. In contrast, others of us are put off by this cut-to-the-chase style of communicating. We crave the details. Then we'll make our own judgment as to whether the main point or conclusion seems right. We savour long stories and surprise endings, and when we say, 'Tell me what happened,' we are prepared to invest our time hearing about it.

There is little evidence that we can actually change such inherent tendencies as these. But we can recognize them in our relationships with others, and become more flexible. If it's your habit, for example, to open a discussion with a bottom line summary or to distribute one-page memos, you might also choose to offer everyone else access to the detailed resources, such as documents or key personnel, that helped you reach your perspective or decision. If, on the other hand, you happen to enjoy telling stories, you might build more trust with main-point-first colleagues or customers by beginning with the context, the reason you're telling the story. This helps keep bottom-liners engaged with your message, rather than breaking away. The point is, to build and sustain trust, we must understand, and make allowances for, the way *others* instinctively prefer to interact.

Trust is the foundation from which we begin more fully to value the creative possibilities of human diversity and conflict. The longer the trust radius, the greater are your chances of succeeding amidst the hue and cry of modern work life. It is through advancing this aspect of our emotional fitness that we arrive at the opportunity to get along and get ahead despite, and in part *because*, of everyday disagreements and conflicts. This brings us to the next chapter, which focuses on what I call constructive discontent.

CHAPTER 7

Constructive Discontent

Once Alfred Sloan, head of General Motors, was in a board meeting, about to make an important decision. He said, 'I take it that everyone is in basic agreement with this decision.' And everyone nodded their heads in assent. Sloan looked around and said, 'Then I suggest we postpone the decision. Until we have some disagreement, we don't understand the problem.'

Aristotle said, 'Time does not exist except for change.' The word *change* comes from the Old English *cambium*, which means 'becoming'. One of the questions I pose to busi-

Have you learned lessons only of those who admired you, and were tender with you, and stood aside for you? Have you not learned great lessons from those who brace themselves against you, and dispute the passage with you?

Walt Whitman, 1819–1982, US Poet

ness groups I work with is, Amidst all of today's changes, what are you, as an individual and as a company, choosing, one decision after another, to *become*? More than anything else, the answer to this question gets revealed to one and all by how you respond to everyday conflict.

When we dig in our heels and attempt to deny or resist change, rationalizing and railing against it, we often get passed by or fall, feeling wounded and angry, or fearful and reactionary. On the other hand, when we discover ways to anticipate and embrace change – which requires emotional intelligence, rather than technical rationality, as the primary guide – we may fall, too, but the spirit of the experience of change *enlivens* us. We grow instead of die. As William Blake reminded us, 'Without Contraries there is no progression.'

Not long ago I was asked to consult with an engagement team at an international services firm working on a proposal for a contract with a multi-billion dollar company. The managing partner who hired me confided, 'Right now we're dead last among the four firms asked to bid for this account. I'd love to win. Do what you can to make the team more creative. Keep them open to more of the possibilities. If nothing else, let's see if we can start redesigning the way we come at our proposals for winning future work.'

The engagement team, nineteen members strong, included specialists in various disciplines and experts from across the country. They had already been meeting for over a month. The team leader sent me a thick binder detailing the prospective client's worldwide industry plus articles and reports on the latest analysis strategies and measurement approaches in managing business risk. I read the materials overnight and got up three hours before my 6 a.m. flight to reflect on what my intuition was telling me. I sat down at the computer and, for my own creative purposes, designed a 'possibilities map' for a company that I envisioned had the goal of transforming its industry and becoming the No. 1 provider in every imaginable category of its current and potential markets.

It's your job as leader to create an atmosphere that ... transforms antagonism into creative energy.

John Kao, Harvard Business School

I arrived for the 8 a.m. engagement team meeting and listened for the next hour to the group progress report. Two of the managers had already begun asking the composition specialist – the writer who was present – to finish drafting the team's written proposal, even though we had nearly a month before it was to be presented. There were murmurs of agreement around the table and people began to relax. The group was heading towards early closure.

Finally, the engagement leader asked for any initial questions I might have. I said, 'I have been asked to join this team as an outside catalyst, as a source of what could be called "constructive discontent". It is anticipated that, in some small but significant way, my questions or ideas might help advance the way this firm comes at creating customized proposals in the future.' Several of the managers were staring at me. They were frowning. I could feel tension in the room now. 'I'm not an expert in the client's specific industry,' I admitted, 'or in your exact methods of service. And, for my role on the team, I believe that this may be an asset. My first question to all of you is, What is the largest and most compelling goal for this potential client in the next several years?'

While some of the team members grumbled beneath their breath, I passed out copies of my possibilities map. Eyebrows were raised. Jaws dropped. Shoulders tightened. 'We're not sure,' said one of the partners in answer to my question. 'I think they want to be the national leader,' said another. 'I have a hunch they'll be buying out another company, soon,' added a third. But no one really knew.

I said, 'My gut instinct tells me that, politics aside, the winning proposal for this account will be one closely aligned with the client's vision of the future. Do you agree?'

Heads nodded. 'Let's find out,' I suggested. 'How can we do that?' In short order, the team came up with a plan.

Next I asked, 'Who are the client's decision makers on this proposal?' The marketing director stood up and listed them on a flip-chart as names were mentioned. Twelve in all. 'Now, how many of these people really have a vote?' I asked. It came down to four, plus the CEO. 'And who are these five key people leaning towards right now – you, or a competitor – and why?' That prompted a lot of gut feelings and outright guessing. It quickly became clear that we needed greater certainty about this. Two group members were assigned to the task.

'What's the ultimate prize for your firm if you win this account?' I asked.

'This job,' snapped a partner impatiently. 'What else?'

'No,' countered the team leader, after a moment's reflection. 'The bigger prize will actually be winning the consulting jobs with the client in the next few years. That's where we would generate the most revenues. We might even have to take a loss to get this initial contract. But if we can position ourselves to win the consulting jobs . . .' Everyone began nodding and discussing how that might be possible.

My last question to the group was, 'In light of our discussion this morning, how long can you wait before finalizing your written proposal?'

Many of the team members appeared incredulous. 'Wait? Why? We're almost ready right now,' said one.

'Well, you may be right,' I replied. 'But from what I've observed here today, I'm not so sure, and here's why.' I briefly recapped several key questions that I felt needed answers and explained the Zeigarnick Effect, which indicates that when we finish an important initiative early, when we push for closure, the creative process all but shuts down. It stops. No more insights or changes. But if we can keep issues and possibilities open as long as possible, there is a significantly greater chance to innovate and succeed. Granted, such an approach goes against the existing mindset in many companies. But it can be amazingly effective.

By then it was nearly noon, and time for the team members to critique the Saturday session. To put it bluntly, I got blasted. 'I have the feeling we're wasting time,' said one manager in frustration. 'We could have had things wrapped up by now,' said another angrily, staring at the possibilities map in front of him. 'Of course it's always good to have an outside consultant here,' said one of the partners, making an obvious effort to appear courteous, 'but clearly we've got to get back on track now, and soon.' The team leader, who knew me and my work, explained once more why I had been added to the team, and asked the group to hold the course and stay open.

The meeting was adjourned. I wished the group members well and left a rather subdued conference room behind as I headed for the airport. I had no idea what would happen next. Sometimes in cases like this the group resistance is so great that nothing really changes. And that bothers me. Still, I had learned to trust the process; in my experience, more often than not, something unexpected happens in the business environment, or a single team member starts digging deeper into things and begins to question openly – and perhaps change – the way the group comes at problems and opportunities.

The following Wednesday, I received a call from the senior partner in charge of the team. Since our Saturday meeting, many events had transpired that affected the proposal. On Monday morning, he had learned that a key vice-president had resigned from the leadership of the prospective client company. On Monday afternoon, the front-running, most serious competitor among the services firm bidding for the contract had been disqualified for a conflict of interest. On Tuesday, a major operational dilemma surfaced in the client company, and the CEO was reportedly enraged. On Wednesday afternoon, just prior to my call, the engagement team met once more. The tone of the group shifted dramatically. Now, the leader told me, I had lots of credibility. The team members were voluntarily committing to staying open as long as possible in creating and delivering the revised proposal. There was a sense of excitement and possibility. Whatever work it took, it would be worth it. That was the new conclusion of the team.

The month that followed was hectic and enlightening. Much of what happened occurred because of constructive discontent and other aspects of emotional intelligence. The outcome? Eleventh-hour politics shifted things so that the auditing job went to the incumbent firm. But my client was assured a lion's share of future consulting engagements, which had been the bigger prize all along.

This is but one of the many times I've experienced how constructive discontent can pay off. Executives at Ford, Levi Strauss, Sun Microsystems, Honda, Motorola, Chrysler, 3M, Hewlett-Packard, and a growing list of other companies, large and small, have found this to be true – and, in many cases, immensely profitable. As Peter Senge, of MIT's Center for Organizational Learning, puts it, 'The key to unlocking openness at work is to teach people to give up having to be in agreement. We think agreement is so important. Who cares? You have to bring paradoxes, conflicts, and dilemmas out in the open, so collectively we can be more intelligent that we can be individually.'[43]

I believe that high EQ culture of successful organizations in the twenty-first century will encourage people to accept the inevitability of disagreements and discontent,[44] and learn new ways to tap the creative energies that arise when we give up having to be in agreement. Look around: how often do some people, before they even hear what you have to say, get defensive, even hostile, and voice their disapproval and doubts, scepticism and criticism? Groucho Marx once said, 'Whatever it is – I'm against it.' Was he speaking about organizational life? Paradoxically, most attempts to 'overcome' resistance end up making it worse.

Leaders of the future are already advancing in the opposite direction. They extend respect and trust. They stay open – curious, empathetic, and constantly learning – in the face of resistance and criticism. They welcome contention as a stimulus to quality and innovation. Because of this, many managers are exploring various ways to legitimize conflict as a natural and healthy part of an enterprise's culture. Intel has its 'push back' norm, in which everyone is encouraged – in responsible ways – to push back (testing assumptions and validity of innovation) against any new idea until it has proved its reliability, consistency, and relevance. Motorola executives talk with pride about their company's 'debate culture'. Scott McNealy, CEO of Sun Microsystems, has publicly praised dissent over consensus.

Open, vigorous, emotionally charged dialogue has also become a hallmark of Levi Strauss, where workers and managers champion the free flow of ideas, feelings, and suggestions.[45] In the early 1990s, Levi was losing millions of dollars in revenue to competitors who were quicker in producing new product lines and replenishing retailers' inventories. Chairman and CEO Robert Haas decided to get more serious about empowerment, and he began systematically to tap over 6,000 of his 36,000 employees for their ideas on how the company's operations could be improved. Their input is having a dramatic influence on the $500 million reinvention of Levi's manufacturing, marketing and distribution systems that is underway. 'We're not doing this because it makes us feel good – although it does. We are not doing this because it is politically correct. We are doing this because we believe in the interconnection between liberating the talents of our people and business success.'[46] Haas believes that a diverse, empowered and constructively discontent workforce is a rich source of innovation and commitment.

The Constructive Value of Discontent[47]

For all its unsettling nature, discontent can prove to be a hotbed of creative ideas and opportunities to build deepened trust and connection. At the same time, it's one of the most reliable access points to those ubiquitous human frustrations that, if ignored and unresolved, so often block or undermine success. By learning to value discontent rather than denigrating or shying away from it, it can pay off in a number of specific ways for your career, customers and company:

Awareness.
Discontent and conflict heighten recognition of what really matters to you and other people, and what you and they care about, are sensitive about, and are willing to fight for.

Problem exposure.
Dialogue about areas of frustration and irritation can identify relationship blocks, excessive costs, wasted timed, injustices, poor quality, and under-efficient projects and processes.

Applied empathy.
The feeling of empathy has meaning only when it is *applied*, and it's at times of difficulty and conflict at work that our sense of empathy is put to the test. Can you stretch to understand the value of diversity and differences in others, and draw upon this as an aid, rather than feel it as a detriment, to progress?

Trust.
Only in an environment where we can be real – open and honest, and in a situation in which we feel free to disagree – can we fully accept and value ourselves and others, and thereby build and sustain genuine trust.

Inclusion and participation.
Morton Deutsch, a pioneering social psychologist, argued that discovering how people believe their values and goals are related is a highly useful way to understand how they work best together.[48] It's one thing to talk about empowerment and partnership in running an enterprise. It's another to demonstrate it and live it by welcoming the full range of differing ideas and feelings into everyday interactions

and dialogue, and to integrate the needs of people – for respect, to be heard, to contribute – and the requirements of successful work.

Creative Collaboration.
Compliance and consent do little, if anything, for innovation and advancement. Constructive discontent, on the other hand, can be an effective catalyst for sparking, shaping, reflecting on, and advancing new ideas, especially when people begin to realize that they can be open and trusting, that their leaders are actively encouraging them to take a stand, to speak up, and to be involved.

Better solutions.
Debating divergent feelings and opposing views compels us to get beneath the surface of issues and generate insights, producing more relevant and integrated solutions to problems.

Learning in action.
There's justifiable interest in companies becoming 'learning organizations'. And debate and conflict are among the long-valued catalysts required in an effective learning laboratory, whether inside or outside corporate walls. As Mark Twain joked, 'The person who grabs the cat by the tail learns about 44 per cent faster than the one just watching.'

Challenge and engagement; even fun.
Research from the Institute for Circadian Physiology at Harvard Medical School[49] indicates that the brain's alertness is raised by a sense of passionate involvement – that is, *genuine* interest, rather than routine interest – in work. Constructive discontent keeps work more enlivened and meaningful, with a heightened sense that your ideas and input are helping to shape something worthwhile.

Saves time; increases opportunities for doing 'real work'.
Many managers spend more time and energy avoiding and attempting to smooth over differences than they would if they talked about them directly. When guided and valued, constructive discontent reduces the time wasted by destructive arguing, hidden agendas, office politics, backstabbing, turf protection, erroneous assumptions, ambiguous behaviour, misunderstandings and redoing tasks and assignments, and other common pitfalls.

In many organizations I've found that management's avoidance of disagreement is based on either a lack of experience in handling heated dialogues or on the worry that we – managers and professionals – will lose control if the opposition becomes vocal and the conversation intense. We're afraid we'll say things we don't mean, which often is a euphemism for worrying we'll say what we really feel and really mean.

All of us know people – and most of us have counted ourselves among them from time to time – who take it upon themselves to smooth things over, to 'keep harmony' so that everything appears just fine and going along according to plan. We bury discontent, at all costs.

What we fail to realize is that high-level cooperation can emerge naturally even in teams and firms with many independently thinking individuals in far-flung places without dominant central authority. Robert Axelrod, professor of political science at the University of Michigan and winner of the MacArthur Foundation Fellowship, the so-called 'genius' award, researched universal principles of cooperation studying a broad range of egoists in collaborative and competitive situations.[50] What emerged in his findings were some consistent principles that people seemed to adopt naturally: avoid unnecessary conflict, respond in the case of uncalled-for provocation, forgive after that response, and be clear about your actions so that the other side knows exactly where you stand at all times. This sounds like a description of EQ in action.

It is important to note that there's more to this than simply venting feelings, which will rarely, by itself, lead to profitable outcomes. Stanley Kalms, founder and Chairman of Dixon's, the United Kingdom retail conglomerate that includes electronics, photo equipment, home appliance outlets, Currys and PC World, observes another side to the dilemma.[51] He recalls noticing a display in one of his stores and, turning to the young buyer in charge, saying, 'I don't think much of that.' Kalms was hoping the buyer would say, 'It's terrific, and here's why.' But the next thing the Chairman knew, the buyer had withdrawn the product. 'I didn't mean him to *withdraw* it,' explains Kalms. 'I just wanted to stimulate him to defend it. It's a pity that the boss's word does that, but that is how it happened.'

During heated discussions, executives find it hard to impose compromise or compel a consensus. This reminds me of Ambrose Bierce's definition of *compromise* as the resolution of a conflict that leaves all parties equally *dis*satisfied. What's required here is help from leadership in enabling people to channel their feelings into practical, constructive actions. This requires two principal qualities: first, you must be gutsy enough to clarify or challenge assumptions – your own and those of others. This doesn't mean being right; it means using your emotion to spark a shift in attention and then getting out of the way – letting the learners, all of you together, find the answers, rather than you feeling the need to try to *tell* others the answers, which you may indeed not even know.

D × D × M > S
Discontent × Direction × Movement > Status Quo

Here's a basic equation for effective change that has helped a number of executives and organizations clarify the power of constructive discontent.* If, as an individual or as a group or organization, you want to initiate and produce effective change, you must have D, which represents *discontent* about how things are right now. This is the immediate *value* of discontent: without it, there's an unconscious sense of being on autopilot or going through the motions, often accompanied by complacency or inattention, and no lasting change progress can occur. This first D is multiplied by a second D, which stands for *direction* – a clear path, or open direction, along which something new or different could be done which would feel rewarding and produce a desired change. Without sensing the precise direction in which to move, feelings of discontent are not channelled constructively and, instead, begin to fester, producing a growing sense of frustration, cynicism, and doubt.

Discontent x Direction is then multiplied by M, for *movement*, which represents the specific steps, or actions, which act like 'emotional magnets', drawing you forward, or setting you in motion, towards the desired change. Without this initiation of movement, we get wishful thinking that usually ends up leading nowhere. If you have *discontent* and *direction*, but no *movement*, you're caught in the quick-fix approach to management that yields little significant or lasting change. The product of $D \times D \times M$ must be greater than S, the current *status quo*, which represents the firmly established beliefs, rigid attitudes, and strongly held mindsets of your group or organization – in short, its resistance to change. This is consistently one of the most obstinate and substantial barriers that we must overcome or transcend. It takes $D \times D \times M$ to do it.

---

* My associates and I have been working with this D x D x M > S model for several years, but I owe a special debt of gratitude to Kathleen Dannemiller and the partners of Dannemiller-Tyson Associates, Inc., of Ann Arbor, Michigan, whose related model, adapted from Dick Beckhard at MIT, was a forerunner of mine and helped shape and clarify my thinking on this subject.

> Imagine one specific, compelling change you'd like to make personally or with your team or organization. Assess it using the $D \times D \times M > S$ formula. Where, specifically, should you focus your attention and leadership in order best to ensure the change will be successful?

Nearly all of us feel an instinctive urge to use force to overcome resistance, and in many cases it doesn't work.[52] Jean-Paul Sartre may have been partly correct when he wrote that 'hell is other people'. Actually, hell is other people who are vehemently disagreeing with us if we are among those who recoil from discord and view a leader's role as 'overcoming resistance'. Not so when we develop our emotional fitness, which includes the flexibility to welcome disagreement and draw creative benefits from the respectful but honest and open conflict of perspectives and feelings. Consider the following:

Jan Timmer, CEO of the Holland-based electronics giant Philips, took the helm amidst a recent crisis and now Philips is back on top, with $34 billion in sales.[53] In facing a rigid culture that was fast losing market share, Timmer designed Operation Centurion to change the way people related to one another at Philips, with the goal of increasing honesty and openly sharing information, feelings and ideas. The programme brings together professionals of all ranks, products, functions, and countries for discussion and debate of strategic plans, product and service ideas, and processes. Every voice is heard with equal attention. Personal attacks and power games are not allowed but open disagreement is encouraged, even with senior management. Two years into Operation Centurion, Timmer says: 'The relationships are different now. If you sit ... through sometimes very emotional discussions on very difficult issues, then you get to know each other, you get to respect each other. That is the most important fact that has contributed to our success.'

Operation Centurion has been expanded into what executives at Philips call the new way of life. It encompasses impromptu free-ranging discussions and 'town meetings' held at plants, where managers must stand before employees and answer questions – any questions posed – and includes the posting of blank pieces of paper throughout offices and factories for people to write their comments, criticisms, and ideas. 'This was really tough stuff,' says Timmer, 'but the best of the managers went through it very well, and the advantage was, we really began to get the best out of our people. Managers began to listen to the shop floor, where there is so much knowledge. It took the managers deflating themselves a little – deflating their importance – but it had to be done.'

Creating contention is also a hallmark of Honda Motor Company. 'Listen, Ask, and Speak Up' is one of the operating principles of this innovative, quality-driven firm, which has been called the best-managed company in the world. At Honda, the constant questioning of ideas, decisions, and processes is

In great teams conflict becomes productive. The free flow of conflicting ideas and feelings is critical for creative thinking, for discovering new solutions no one individual would have come to on his own.

Peter Senge

encouraged, even demanded of each employee. In fact, Honda has become one of the world's exemplary practitioners of what has been called the art of 'constructive contention'.[54] Honda cofounder Takeo Fujisawa says, 'There are discordant sounds within a company. As President, you must orchestrate the discordant sounds into a kind of harmony. But you never want too much harmony. One must cultivate a taste for finding harmony within discord, or you will drift away from the forces that keep a company alive.'[65] Honda's culture of self-critique and creative diversity stands apart from many large Japanese firms, which, in the past, have emphasized conformity and compliance.[56]

Yet Honda's performance – rising to prominence in twenty-five years from a small, local motorcycle shop to a premier auto maker – is centred on creative discontent. Differing ideas, feelings, and perspectives among Honda's various functional departments are actively encouraged, with the view that such contention sharpens and improves the end products. Design and development teams, for example, are purposely staffed with engineers from peripheral disciplines who are unfamiliar with the core technology under development. Company-wide Idea Contests – open to all employees – are regularly held, and the most promising receive organizational support, time, and funding. Few, if any, of these ideas would have emerged from traditional product development channels. Another telling insight: Honda's forty senior executives work in a common area and share six desks – so they are encouraged to remain uncomfortable and creative. Most work side by side at conference tables, which encourages open interaction, and constructive contention. Young engineers are given exceptional levels of responsibility and are encouraged to question their superiors sharply in regular dialogue and debate sessions. This arose from the experience of a young engineer shortly after the company was founded.[57]

Companies that create the future are rebels. They're subversives. They break the rules. They're filled with people who take the other side of an issue just to spark a debate. In fact, they're probably filled with people who didn't mind being sent to the principal's office once in a while.

Gary Hamel and C. K. Prahalad, Seeing the Future First

One starting-level bench engineer at Honda, hearing that management was open to new ideas, believed so passionately in an innovation concept that he got into a heated debate with the company cofounder Soichiro Honda over the relative merits of water and air-cooled engines. So determined was this young man that when Mr Honda did not seem to grasp his creative point, the young engineer decided to go on strike for a month, withdrawing to a Zen monastery. Impressed by the young man's passionate courage to pursue a new idea, Mr Honda reconsidered. Before long, he changed his mind, to the company's lasting benefit. The young engineer who convinced him was Tadashi Kume, and today he is Honda's CEO.

EQ Map Connections: Constructive Discontent
You may want to refer to the following scales of the *EQ Map* as points of reflection related to this chapter: emotional expression, emotional awareness of others, interpersonal connection, intentionality, constructive discontent, and intuition

---

EQ IN ACTION: *CONSTRUCTIVE DISCONTENT – AN APPLICATIONS STARTING POINT*

When two people in business always agree, one of them is unnecessary.

William Wrigley, Jr., 1861–1932, US executive

Profiting from constructive discontent takes practice. It is a dimension of emotional fitness that grows stronger and more valuable with regular use over time. Here are several practical suggestions for ways you might begin developing this aspect of emotional intelligence in business:

Use the power of entrainment.
Entrainment is a process, discovered in 1665 by the Dutch scientist Christian Huygens, by which rhythms of voice and emotion are drawn

into productive balance with each other. It is a well-accepted principle in modern science,[58] and Frederick Erickson of the Interaction Laboratory at the University of Pennsylvania has shown that entrainment takes place in conversations, too.[59] One way to apply this principle is to join a dialogue by *talking slowly and calmly*, not denying any of the emotions present, but not getting battered about by them either. As a meeting or discussion heats up, change the rhythm by speaking calmly and more slowly, which draws everyone into great awareness of the dialogue process, and can begin to open minds and hearts. The leaders who do this demonstrate enormous presence in allowing discord to continue, but disarming it, inviting disagreement as a catalyst to stimulate dialogue and engage the creative energies of the group *without* permitting any of the individuals involved attacking each other. You are entraining the group, holding the centre. It's one of the rare skills that will set you apart from, and, paradoxically, bring you into greater collaboration with, teams and partnerships at every level and in every shape, within an enterprise.

Stay open when things heat up.
Remember what happened to me with the Big Six engagement team critique. Adversaries and sceptics will tell you exactly what's bothering them. Their words will sting. At first, you may feel like dismissing their comments. But don't. These people are conveying the truth as they see or feel it. Since few others

It is possible to fashion various mechanisms for coping with conflict. Better yet would be for the organization to fashion a culture that appreciates the creative power of conflict and seeks to harness it.

Michael Hammer, author of Beyond Reengineering

may respect them, you may be tempted to lash out at them or put them 'in their place' with a brutal barrage of words. Don't do it. What happens is symbolic. As soon as you lash out, you make it unsafe for others to speak up honestly and openly, which kills collaboration and fans the flames of mistrust and cynicism. Instead, when a barbed comment comes your way, acknowledge your instinctive surge of anger or resistance. But then *use* the energy for learning instead of protecting. How? By heightening your curiosity, for example, and extending some extra empathy. By saying to yourself, 'He's not really yelling *at* me, he's yelling *for* himself – and it's great he can get this out in the open.' Then ask yourself, 'I wonder what I can discover from this?'

'Ditto' – engage the EQ of the whole group.

Acknowledging what others believe and feel does not mean you *agree* with them; it means, that whatever these views and feelings are, they are real, and, at least in this sense, the person is entitled to them. Sincerely saying, 'I appreciate how you feel' or 'I can sense how strongly you feel about this approach' or 'If I were in your shoes, I'd probably be just as angry' confirms that the other person is being heard. Consider adopting non-threatening shorthand expressions as clarifiers. Examples, as explained in Chapter 5: use something like 'Again please' whenever you, or someone else in your group, cannot hear what someone is saying and wishes the person to raise his or her voice and speak more clearly. In my firm, in large groups and settings we use 'Ditto' as shorthand to mean 'I share the same feeling about that; I agree.'

Go with the flow to increase understanding and opportunity.

Extend your senses during each dialogue. If someone pushes against your feelings or position, listen for understanding, welcome the push, and learn. Keep reminding yourself that, by and large, the others in the group care or they wouldn't be disagreeing – they'd be gone. In some cases, resistance stems from a reluctance to choose. In what ways could you support something the other person feels strongly about? Do you sense any points of alignment between your own purpose and theirs? It pays to remember that *feelings are facts to the person experiencing them.* In many situations, a single calm comment can help defuse emotional *over*reaction and promote creative solution-finding. Therefore, *don't rush to respond. Instead, listen harder.* It's rarely helpful, for example, to tell angry people to calm down. Doing this can make them feel like you're denying their right to feel upset.

Balance advocacy and enquiry.

The priority here is to make your feelings and thinking process *visible* – bring them out in the open during dialogue – and ask others to do the same. Organizational learning consultants Charlotte Roberts and Rick Ross, suggest building trust and clarity in the midst of discord with such statements as:[60]

> 'Here's how I feel about this...'
> 'Here's what I think, and here's how I got there...'
> 'I assumed that...'
> 'I came to this conclusion because...'

'To get a clearer picture of what I'm talking about, imagine that you're the customer who will be affected...'

'What can you add to this idea?'

'What leads you to conclude that...?'

'Can you help me understand your thoughts and feelings about this?'

'Have you considered...?'

'When you say such-and-such, I worry that it means...'

'What do we feel is right or true, even if we have no data for it yet?'

'Are we starting from very different assumptions here?'

Identify cooperative possibilities.

You might pause periodically during a heated dialogue to ask – and answer – the question, 'What am I learning thus far?' Identify concrete ways you and the others will be further ahead by cooperating than by working against each other. You are committing to using the energy of conflict to create better solutions for everyone involved. 'What do you believe will happen if we don't find ways to work together?' is a question that can loosen viewpoints and raise alternatives.

Bypass defensiveness; speak from your own experience.

One of the most effective ways to build a bridge of trust in a heated discussion is by avoiding getting defensive or lecturing other people with accusatory 'you' statements and advice-giving lines such as, 'If you were smart, you would ...', or 'If you really understood things the way I do, you would ...' Instead, make a conscious effort to speak from your own experience: 'I'm really aware of the difficulty we're having in coming to grips with this issue and finding a solution. One of the things I'm considering is my own struggles to learn ways to ... I wanted to put this out on the table as a related experience that might have some value.' Encourage others to do the same. I've experienced how a clear, gutsy approach like this can interrupt cycles of arguing, finger-pointing and blaming, and helps bring to an end the posturing and turf battles that characterize adversarial business meetings. Whether others acknowledge your ideas or not is not the point; your empathy and your emotionally honest *presence* are being felt by everyone in the room and, right or wrong, you'll likely find people listening more openly to the next things you say.

121

Say no when you mean no.

It's up to you to let others know where you stand. Instead of hemming and hedging for fear of being disapproved of or rejected – and ending up wasting valuable time and energy because of it – say no when you mean no, and say you don't know when you don't know. As Peter Block reminds us: 'Our role models should be six-year-olds. They talk straight. They agree, disagree, they like, they hate, they say yes, they say no. Period. . . . If we feel that we cannot say no, then our yes's don't mean anything.'[61] Great point. What we're seeking is a way to be firm without being overbearing, saying no without walling off, and being self-respecting while respecting the rights, views, and feelings of others.

Nine times out of ten, vague statements, assumptions and rumour prove more damaging to relationships and enterprises than the truth would. Practise telling people in unmistakable terms where you stand, what the problem is, and why we need to discuss what we're discussing, and why we must decide on the actions we must take. Whether it's good news or bad, speaking plainly makes us more real, more trustworthy, and more effective in finding the creative value of disagreement.

Follow through on outcomes.

As strategist Gary Hamel reminds us, 'If nervous executives open up dialogue and then ignore the outcome, they will poison the well.' We must each be clear about commitments we make during dialogue. And then keep them.

Deal productively with anger.

In expressing honest opinions, many of us expect protection from other people's anger. But is this *really* what we want? As we've already seen, irritation, passion, discord, and even brief flashes of anger are part of most active – translation: caring – dialogues. They are an emotional investment in conversation. They make it alive, creative, and real. There's no doubt that frustration and anger must be respected and guided; venting anger carelessly can magnify it into rage or aggression, and may crystallize hostile beliefs, attitudes, and perceptions, leading to heart and health problems.[62] Yet it's a form of manipulation or victimization to view 'hot' emotions as punishment and struggle to stifle them completely, or to assume they are always a personal attack. In many cases, they aren't. And often they confirm how deeply we care about things.

In *The Nicomachean Ethics*, Aristotle writes about the importance of character, will, and mastering the emotions. He reflects on how difficult it can be to be an emotionally intelligent person, expressing feelings appropriately: 'Anyone can become angry – that is easy. But to be angry with the right person, to the right degree, at the right time, for the right purpose, and in the right way – this is not easy.' The challenge has changed little from the time of the ancient Greeks to the modern day.

When used early on and constructively, anger can be transformational: it sparks courage and creativity, draws us towards correcting perceived injustices, prompts us to speak out, and stimulates progress. It keeps us from getting too comfortable or compliant. It *moves* us. Appropriately expressed anger generates tremendous amounts of productive energy. Here are several considerations for capturing the *constructiveness* of anger, and keeping it from escalating into rage, hatred, hostility, or aggression:

Ask yourself: what am I disappointed in? It might be that another person let you down, or that you let yourself down. If so, then this is what you need to talk about, and take steps so it doesn't happen again. Once you've identified the source of your disappointment, let the appropriate people know you are disappointed and that you, or they, are not meeting your expectations:

> 'I am disappointed that I didn't get the chance to be part of that creative team.'
> 'I feel upset at the way you just spoke to me.'
> 'I'm feeling angry about being ignored in the meeting.'
> 'I'm angry at myself for letting the department down on this deadline.'

Sweeping statements, such as 'You always let me down', or 'I got screwed on this one', or 'Here we go again with jerks running the show' slam the brakes on the productive expression of anger, and can bury everyone in a cloud of negativity or pessimism.[63] By being more specific about being disappointed in an unmet expectation, you are acting to promote a clearer, more trusting relationship, one that is both dependable and resilient.

Unfortunately, many of today's corporate cultures try to block disappointment and anger in an attempt to keep everyone calm and happy. Worse, we even lie to each other: 'Oh, there's no reason to be so upset, you did a *great* job.' Many times, even if we can rationalize it, such statements are emotionally dishonest. Talking you out of your feelings doesn't make things OK, doesn't make the emotional energy disappear. Many managers have been conditioned to assume that if people feel angry or disappointed they will stop contributing to the company. Not true. Employees can be at least as capable as managers in expressing disappointment or anger, and then getting on with their work. It's the inability to experience or express it in a healthy way that gets people stuck and creates an ongoing state of turmoil and payback.

Be willing to acknowledge that there are cynics who, no matter how hard you try to reach them, don't want to be constructive, no matter what the issue.

When someone criticizes us openly and with genuine concern, the emotionally intelligent person takes this message to heart as well as the head, and reflects on it, searching for the value within it, to see in what ways, if any, 'the shoe fits'; if not, little or no harm is done, and in fact, a stronger and more authentic relationship may be formed with the other person. In contrast, when someone criticizes out of spite (or with ulterior motives and emotional dishonesty, often through behind-the-back gossip and sabotage), the person with high EQ has learned to acknowledge this and to ponder the barbs intellectually but to deter them from getting into – and numbing or poisoning – the heart. It's worth remembering that for a relatively small percentage of people, it doesn't matter what the situation or circumstance, they are bound to deny, resist, blame, and act out of spite, rather than genuine concern. For reasons known or unknown, they don't want to be part of an open dialogue, and won't willingly contribute to the betterment of any enterprise or community. Face this attitude straight on by acknowledging it. Offer these individuals resources if you sense it may give them something to ponder or chew on, but do not caretake them. In addition, make it a point *not* to set up their support as a requirement to anything that matters to you. If they work for you, consider arranging for them to find other work that better fits or inspires them; or let them go.

Capture the value of golden gripes.

One aspect of constructive discontent has to do with seeking to get everyone's pet peeves out in the open. No kidding. According to several studies,[64] this can turn out to be one of the healthiest and most overlooked ways to increase productivity and profitability. Example:

'Care about golden gripes' was one of the central themes in a pro-gramme instituted by William Arnold, President of Centennial Medical Center, the flagship operation of Hospital Corporation of America. Over a four-year period from 1989 to 1993, cash flow (before debt service) increased from $11 million to $30 million, bad debt decreased to less than $\frac{1}{2}$ per cent, accounts receivable days decreased from 78 to 44, staff turnover decreased by more than 50 per cent, and earnings increased by over 33 per cent.[65] Arnold tested and developed his approach with the help of Jeanne Plas, professor of psychology at Vanderbilt University.

Their findings suggest, among other things, that millions of people are robbed of energy by chronic gripes every day of their working lives. Most managers pay very little attention to them, but employees' pet peeves can be deadly. They're the most important cause of the death of personal initiative in corporations. Ask disaffected workers in any kind of job in any organization why they have stopped putting personal initiative into their work. Their story will likely be one of unresolved frustration: something wasn't right. They complained about it. The complaint was ignored. Maybe they griped a second time. Nothing happened. They responded by unplugging their personal energies, feelings, and creativity from the organization. They turned off.

People don't stop complaining just because management has brushed off the problem, say Arnold and Plas, co-authors of *The Human Touch*. They gave up griping, perhaps, but they didn't give up the gripe. The truth is, most personal peeves need to be tracked down and brought out into the open rather than stifled, contained, or ignored. In companies that lack vitality and growth potential, man-agers often are provided with an arsenal of pet peeve repellents. They ask the irritated employee to 'put it in a memo'. They roll their eyes heavenward as if to say, 'I agree with you, but we both know the top brass doesn't want to hear this kind of thing.' Some managers may play dumb, asking the employee to describe the issue in a half a dozen ways because they 'really have no idea what you're talking about'. Sometime the complainer gets a subtle but clear communication that maybe it's time for a rest – or a transfer. But no matter what strategy it used, the message is that griping and complaining have no legit-imate place in the organization.

When people feel their gripes and concerns are being addressed, the constrictive energy bottled up in discontent gets released to be used for constructive purposes. In the UK's NatWest Life, staff in one section were highly critical of their manager, contending he didn't manage his time well and failed to give clear leadership. Yet as soon as the manager responded to feedback and was clearly committed to change the way he managed and communicated, 'there was a rush of energy from the staff [who realized] the change process had become real, and they were keen to participate. From a feeling of gloom, the atmosphere shifted and the staff became much more helpful and self-confident.'[66]

When managers start to listen, the typical tendency is to discriminate quickly between the gripes that are product or service oriented and those that reflect self-interest. In the early stages, most people find themselves thinking that the golden gripes are the ones that reflect direct interest in work performance. They are wrong. The ones that reflect frustrations over personal concerns are every bit as important as the quality improvement issues. Energy that gets bound up by complaints over late reimbursement cheques, poor quality food, broken vending machines, narrow parking spaces, not enough pay telephones in meeting and conference areas, poorly ventilated (or poorly heated or cooled) offices, dull and drab staff rooms, and low-quality paper towels is energy that is not devoted to the job. More important, these issues profoundly affect the sense of wellbeing of a corporation's employees.

What if no one seems to be paying attention to your concerns? We all experience times, of course, when legitimate complaints aren't heard or heeded. And times when the hand of fate throws a barrier in our path or knocks the wind out of our sails. These are the days we need a deep and ready capacity for emotional adaptability and resilience. In addition, sooner or later, virtually all of us come face to face with the fact that doing more of the same, only faster and harder and longer, isn't the best way to accomplish more. Numb from struggle and overwork, we become blind to better pathways and start producing less and less. Our spirit begins to wane. These are the times we need emotional renewal. And it's these three characteristics of emotional fitness – adaptability, resilience, and renewal – that are the subject of the next chapter.

CHAPTER 8

Resilience and Renewal

On 10 March 1986, an airliner crashed into the side of a mountain. Everyone on board was killed. Among the dead were my brother-in-law's sister, Patricia, a physician, her husband, Rafael, a business executive, and their three children, aged four, six and eight. They were travelling on their first vacation as a family. Searchers at the crash site discovered Patricia and Rafael's bodies with their arms wrapped around the children. They died together. From the moment the rest of the family – and everyone who had ever been touched by the presence of these five people – learned of the crash, our own lives were altered.

We rise to great heights by a winding staircase.

Sir Francis Bacon, 1561–1626

I remember thinking on that day about how many different ways human beings get changed over a lifetime. If we're fortunate, a lot of these changes are by intention and choice. Yet, inevitably, we are shaped, too, by how we feel and respond to turns of fate and shifts in circumstance. For most of us, these are the deeper changes, the ones that last longest. Always, they are emotional. They anchor us and liberate us.

As I write these words, I recall another experience, a quarter of a century ago: it was late summer and the electric utility company had dispatched a crew to connect a new power line to my small home and adjoining business. I was teaching classes at night, and attending the university with a full course load, and using my military benefits – the G.I. Bill – to pay for tuition. I had built my home and the business building by hand, on a limited budget, to save money, to get a start. But while I was away on a work project that day, something went wrong with the new powerline, and it started a fire.

By afternoon, when I returned, everything was burned to the ground. Everything I owned was gone: my personal books, journals and plans, photo albums, high school, military, and college awards. Everything. I stared far into the night at the smouldering ruins, all that was left. It was an emotion-charged image, one I will always remember. Fortunately, no one was hurt. I realized how much worse it could have been. I also knew I was not alone. Millions of people face fires, tornadoes, and floods. I am curious about you, my reader: what have you faced? As I sifted through the ruins, in tears, I reached down into my heart and vowed I would bounce back. That night I started over, building a new future.

My wife, Leslie, has a saying above her desk: adversity builds character. Of course, there are other ways to build character, too. But adversity always rears its head. I remember my grandmother saying that God never gives us a burden our shoulders and heart cannot bear. I suggest to my executive clients that they find a quiet place where there's a piece of sunlight and spend some time recalling three or four of their own stories of emotional fitness being summoned and shaped. According to ancient seekers and modern brain scientists, this is how we learn, *really* learn, through the stories of our human experience.[67] Of crises tamed, tragedies faced or averted, help arriving at the last moment or not arriving at all, great intentions and foolish undertakings alike.[68] As Charles Handy reminds us:[69]

> Ask people … to recall two or three of the most important learning experiences in their lives, and they will never tell you of courses taken or degrees obtained, but of brushes with death, of crises encountered, of new and unexpected challenges and confrontations. They will tell you, in other words, of times when continuity ran out on them, when they had no past experience to fall back on, no rules or handbook. They survived, however, and came back stronger and more adaptable in mind and heart.

I encourage you to take a few minutes to write down a brief synopsis of one or two such stories in your experience and then to reflect on some of the specific ways your life and work have benefited from them.

The Stuff Great People Are Made Of

History reminds us that, over the course of a lifetime, most notable men and women have encountered periods of rough going. Time and again they've had to face daunting obstacles and endure failures or setbacks. How they handled these experiences shaped the person they became.

Their ultimate triumphs were often due, in large measure, to their refusal to succumb to their mistakes and defeats. All of us experience times of travail in our work and lives. How we respond to these challenges – with gut instinct and creative intuition, and then afterwards, with reflection – transforms a piece of our heart and shapes our future, and that of the people around us.

Only those who dare to fail greatly can ever achieve greatly.

President John F. Kennedy

During informal conversation, most of us readily admit that almost nothing worthwhile is achieved without mistakes and setbacks. But most of us dread such experiences. We anxiously anticipate them. Murphy's Law, we call it off-handedly: if something can go wrong, it will. Lost luck, the stars, bad fortune. But there's more to it than that. Difficult challenges are the 'living laboratory' of emotional intelligence. Adversity, not comfort, is the test of our core and character, both public and private. Winston Churchill said, 'Success is going from failure to failure without loss of enthusiasm.'

This is rare, and a quality of achievement that is widely admired. The word enthusiasm is derived from the Greek *entheos*, meaning 'from the spirit within'. Adaptability is, in effect, about how well, and readily, you can keep your enthusiasm alive. 'It's also about how well you flow with changing circumstances, rules, regulations, and needs. While there are many situations in which we can't control what is happening, we can always change how we're relating to it. This is adaptability, which in turn promotes resilience.

It's why William Kennedy persevered through rejections from forty-nine publishers of his eventual bestselling and critically acclaimed novel *Ironweed*.[70] It's why Mary Kay Cosmetics, for example, was able to carve a niche in the entrenched and lucrative cosmetics field by using women in the marketing force. Prior to this time, the industry practice had been to use men almost exclusively. Mary Kay Ash had a gut feeling[71] that women who could acknowledge their self-worth could indeed become very successful marketers and entrepreneurs, helping each other. She relied on the adaptability of her individual consultant-marketers to create sales staffs capable of regulating their own work hours and devising ways to balance family, work, and faith. This adaptability has characterized the company since its inception and has contributed to exceptional success for her employees and organization.

It was also a strong sense of adaptability and emotional resilience that enabled Elizabeth Blackwell, daughter of British emigrants from Bristol, England, to be accepted by Geneva (later Hobart) College in New York as a medical student in 1847.[72] She had already been rejected by twenty-eight medical schools. In actuality, the administrators at Geneva didn't want to admit a woman but were persuaded to consider her application seriously by eminent Philadelphia physician Joseph Warrington, who had taken a professional interest in the young woman, whose family – after losing its sugar refinery business in a fire in England – was nearly destitute. (Elizabeth's father had died of malaria shortly after arriving in the States).

Hoping not to offend Warrington, the administrators struck upon the idea of leaving the decision up to the students, believing they would vote against her. They did not – they voted to accept her, as a joke. The decision was final, and the hilarity short-lived. Blackwell graduated at the head of her class in 1849, the first American woman to receive a medical degree. She joined the anti-slavery society in Cincinnati and, at the invitation of Harriet Beecher Stowe, became a member of the Semi-Colon Club, a literary association.

Blackwell's work in medicine, however, continued to be uphill all the way. In the hospitals she attended during medical school, she was the only woman doctor, and was bitterly resented by the male physicians. Upon graduation, she served an internship at the only medical institution that would accept a woman doctor, La Maternité Hospital in Paris. While there, she contracted an eye disease. This led to the loss of her left eye, which ended her hopes of becoming a surgeon. In 1850 she began a year's internship at St Bartholomew's Hospital in London, and met Florence Nightingale, who became a lifelong friend. She returned to the USA in 1851 but no hospitals would hire a woman doctor. She opened a small clinic, the New York Dispensary for Poor Women and Children, in the slums of lower Manhattan. Here the poor could receive treatment and medicines at little or no cost. Successful fundraising enabled her to expand the clinic and take in two associates, her sister Emily, and Marie Zakrzewska, new graduates of the medical school at Western Reserve College (now Case Western), where they had been admitted with Blackwell's help. The New York Infirmary for Women and Children (now New York Infirmary – Beekman Downtown Hospital) opened in Greenwich Village in 1857.

After returning to England in 1869, Blackwell helped found the British National Health Society, and taught at the newly chartered London School of Medicine for Women. She retired in 1884 and a year later published her autobiography, *Pioneer Work in Opening the Medical Profession to Women.* Elizabeth Blackwell was indeed a pathfinder, and as much as her keen intellect was essential, it was her emotional intelligence – of sensing ways around obstacles, for example, and calling again and again upon her adaptability and resilience – that enabled her to succeed.

Adaptability-in-Action

Over the years I have come to appreciate the various ways that emotional adaptability activates and expands physical and mental adaptability. This coordination of capabilities happens *in action*, giving you a kind of flexibility-in-motion which can be seen as a forerunner of *flow*, which we'll be discussing later in this book. These are learned aspects of emotional fitness that improve with practice, and assist you whenever you sense a sudden change in circumstances or find obstacles in your path. That said, for contrast here's a short story of what creative adaptability *isn't*, as told by Jack Kornfield:[73]

In response to your request for additional information in block number three of your report form, I put 'poor planning' as the cause of my accident. Here are the relevant details:

I'm a bricklayer by trade. On the day of the accident, I was working alone on the roof of a new three-story building. When I completed my work, I had five hundred pounds of bricks left over. Rather than carry them down by hand, I decided to lower them in a barrel using the pulley on the side of the building. Securing the rope at ground level, I went up to the roof, swung the barrel out, and loaded the bricks into it. Then I went back to the ground and untied the rope, holding it tightly to ensure the slow descent of the five hundred pounds of bricks.

You will note in block number eleven of this report form that I weigh one hundred fifty-five pounds. Due to my surprise at being jerked off the ground so suddenly, I forgot to let go of the rope. Needless to say I proceeded at a rather rapid rate up the side of the building. In the vicinity of the second floor, I met the barrel coming down. This explains the fractured collar bone.

Slowed only slightly, I continued my ascent, not stopping until the knuckles of my right hand were deep in the pulley. High up in the air, I had the presence of mind to be able to remember and hold on tightly to the rope. However, the barrel of bricks hit the ground and unfortunately the bottom fell out. Devoid of the weight of the bricks, the barrel now weighed approximately fifty pounds. I again refer you to my weight in block number 11. As you might imagine, I began a rapid descent down the side of the building...

A rapid descent. There's no evidence of adaptability-in-action here, but there are signs of emerging wisdom and adaptability *after* action. In this regard, a dose of humour can certainly help. I'm reminded of a story of Charles de Gaulle, French statesman and general, when an assassination attempt was made on him and Madame de Gaulle in August 1962 when being driven through the outskirts of Paris. Bullets punctured the car tyres, it swerved violently, and the bodyguard in the front seat shouted for the de Gaulles to get down. Neither moved. When the car came to a screeching halt they got out, brushing the glass from a shattered rear window out of their clothing. 'They are really bad shots,' observed the general calmly.

Madame de Gaulle, asked later if she had been frightened, replied, 'Frightened of what? We'd have died together, and no old age.' This is a good story about emotional resilience, which is characterized by a strong sense of flexible optimism and the ability to bounce back after things go wrong.

Some people feel they can do no wrong and instinctively blame others or circumstances for every misstep and misfortune. Other people blame themselves for everything, even when they were only slightly responsible. Either of these habits can prove to be a serious problem in business and life. Emotionally intelligent people accept fair blame for their part in mistakes and setbacks. In the preceding case, Madame de Gaulle was in no way at fault, and did not blame herself or lash out at her security guards or circumstances, even though, within hours after this incident, French government security was reviewed and tightened. Emotionally intelligent people also reject chronic feelings of self-pity and martyrdom, which we mentioned in Chapter 3. When things go wrong, it's natural to feel sorry for ourselves, at least briefly. But when such feelings are chronic or constant, it's unhealthy and causes us, and those around us, problems.

> *No one can make you feel inferior without your consent.*
>
> Eleanor Roosevelt, 1884–1962, US diplomat and wife of Franklin D. Roosevelt

Wal-Mart CEO David Glass has said that the number-one thing that stood out about Sam Walton was his ability to admit yesterday's mistakes and leave them behind, getting on with today's work. He was a flexible optimist. 'He trusted others and he simply wasn't afraid to fail,' says Glass. The feeling of optimism, like hope and trust, means having a strong and durable sense that things will turn out all right in your work and life, despite setbacks and losses, difficulties and frustrations. 'My advice is find "fuel" in failure,' says sports superstar Michael Jordan, reflecting on his life. 'Sometimes failure gets you closer to where you want to be.... It doesn't matter if you win as long as you give everything in your heart. I can accept failure. Everyone fails at something. But I can't accept not trying.'[74]

To date, some of the most compelling proofs of the power of emotional adaptability and resilience – in particular, flexible optimism – in producing business success come from University of Pennsylvania psychologist Martin Seligman's studies of insurance salesmen with the MetLife Company.[75] Being able to handle rejection with grace is essential in sales of all kinds. This is especially true with a product like insurance, where the ratio of no's to yes's can be dauntingly high. Because of this, three-quarters of all insurance sales professionals quit in the first three years on the job.

However, Seligman found that new salesmen who were by nature, or training, optimists – and who were, in a sense, emotionally resilient –

Success is 99 per cent failure.

Soichiro Honda, founder of the Honda Motor Company

sold 37 per cent more insurance in the first two years on the job than did pessimists. And during the first year, pessimists quit at twice the rate of optimists. This is not to say that there is no worthiness in caution, and at times, pessimism. The cynic or pessimist in most groups adds value by holding up the 'wait a minute' flag, prompting us to listen to our gut hunches and go deeper, to take into account many factors. Credible leaders are hopeful about the future yet open enough always to consider – and, if right, to heed – words of caution. They also have an enduring belief that they can always learn something from others.[76]

A Persistent Sense of Curiosity and Resilience

In this light, I recall how Albert Einstein is almost as well known for his humility and compassion as for his scientific genius. Although he recognized that he was regarded as the foremost physicist of his generation, this comparative judgment meant very little to him. He felt his personal challenge was to understand the universe and how it worked, and against that vastness, his reputation meant little. It was in this way that he maintained his humility and persistent sense of curiosity.

This is something many exceptional business leaders do, as well.

Take Dian Owen, for example. She used a combination of grit, humility, resilience, and intelligence to bring Owen Healthcare, a Houston-based hospital pharmacy management company, back from the brink of failure and the throes of personal tragedy.[77] Her company was founded in 1969 by her husband Jean, a hospital pharmacist, on the unheard of notion of providing complete hospital pharmacy services under outside contract. The company supplies everything required: the inventory of drugs and supplies, computer systems to keep track of them, and the pharmacists and staff to run it. When she met Jean Owen, Dian worked to oversee an oil company's relations with government agencies regulating that industry. They were married in 1969 and she joined her husband in running his new business. Jean had obtained capital for the business, Pharmacy Management, from some accountants, who soon figured out that profitability would improve if they got rid of him. He came home the day before Christmas, three months after they'd got married, and said to Dian, 'I got fired today!'

Rather than panic and retreat to the safety of salaried jobs, they considered starting a new company to compete with Pharmacy Management. 'We got a phone call at home one night,' recalls Dian, 'from a guy we were negotiating with at the time Jean was fired. He wanted to tell us he was ready to sign a contract. Jean had to say he couldn't sign with him because he was no longer with the company, but he also told him we were thinking of starting our own company. The guy said, "Fine, I'll wait till you do it." This gave us the confidence to go forward, and that was the beginning of Owen Healthcare.' Dian and Jean spent the next seven years growing the company, and then, in 1976, disaster struck.

While flying himself and two employees back to Texas, Jean encountered an unexpected thunderstorm and crashed. All were killed. Jean had never insured himself, and they were millions of dollars in debt. Many people expected Dian to sell the company, and the misfortune attracted many aggressive buyers. When she refused to sell out at a loss to one hospital management firm which held twenty-three of the Owen Healthcare contracts, the firm cancelled all of the contracts, which represented 75 per cent of Owen's business. Jean had left no operational systems in place – he micromanaged everything himself. 'People called me at home,' Dian remembers. 'They'd ask, "What's going to happen?" "Do I still have a job?" "Is there still going to be an Owen Healthcare?" With so much confusion on all sides, I could see that if I didn't want to lose this company, I'd better get out there immediately and lead it.'

She did, selecting a core of trusted advisors and building a renewed organization that combines formal structure and free-form interaction. Managers and employees have flexibility in how they perform their jobs; relationships are open and honest; paperwork and formal reporting are minimized. In recent years, contract renewal rates have maintained an unprecedented 100 per cent. Owen Healthcare now employs 2,100 people and generates revenues of over $320 million per year.

As this story illustrates, few among us have failed to experience the fear of disapproval or rejection at the hands of associates or an audience we consider important. It's not a question of whether we care about what other people think. We care. But we need the emotional adaptability and resilience to make the right choices despite this, to seek counsel from those we trust most, realizing that some people won't like what we're going to say or do, but it's important that we say or do it anyway.

Consider the emotional resilience of John Tu and David Sun, co-founders of Kingston Technology, which makes computer memory products.[78] Tu, a Chinese immigrant educated in Germany, recalls how he and Sun lost $2 million – all their savings – in the stock market crash of October 1987. 'Had we not lost all our money we very possibly would not have Kingston. That's how things work out ...' Nine years later, in October, 1996, Sun and Tu sold 80 per cent of their new company to Softbank Corp. of Japan for $1.5 billion. Two months later, they gave their 523 employees a $100 million Christmas bonus.

Another case in point: in the 1950s, W. Edwards Deming's ideas on quality leadership was overwhelmingly rejected in the United States. He left and went to Japan, where, in all the subsequent years, he had a major influence. In fact, Japan's highest award for quality in business is the Deming Award. By the 1980s, American business began to follow, adopting Deming's 'Fourteen Points to Achieve Quality' as corporate guidelines. At the age of ninety, Deming worked a heavy schedule and his optimistic credo was continual learning and growth. He believed that each person and organization is gifted with a unique potential which defines a destiny. He ended letters to young aspirants with: 'I'm sure I have a lot to learn from you.' Deming, a resilient man and a flexible optimist, acted from the heart.[79]

This brings us to an issue that many business people have long scoffed at or ignored: renewal. Emotional renewal. And, as a core dimension of this, off-the-job renewal – or what's commonly called work-family balance. As Mary Catherine Bateson pointedly reminds us, 'Until you are at home somewhere, you cannot be at home anywhere.'[80]

> **EQ Map Connections: Resilience & Renewal**
> You may want to refer to the following scales of the *EQ Map* as points of reflection related to this chapter: life events, pressures and satisfactions, intentionality, resilience, constructive discontent, outlook, personal power, and integrity

EQ IN ACTION: *BUILDING RESILIENCE THROUGH BREATHING SPACE AND RENEWAL*

Let's return to Einstein's story for a moment. One of the things he learned over the years was that renewal mattered. He believed it not only kept him healthy but it made him more receptive to new ideas – and more ingenious in implementing them. He was right. Einstein loved to play the violin and relax on his sailboat or drift aimlessly about in his canoe on the waters near Princeton University. While it was well known that he committed himself to the passions of his work, what is less known is that, with almost equal verve, he pursued the passions of his non-work life. These included, we are told, such diversions as boating, going for long walks in the city and countryside, standing barefoot on the university lawn, and pursuing mundane family tasks or child-like adventures. He valued what this did for him in terms of emotional and mental renewal, and he kept at it, even when fame came to him. There's a lesson here for all of us.

To make a living is no longer enough. Work also has to make a life.

Peter F. Drucker, preeminent management scholar, USA

Sceptics take note: strategies for work-family renewal and balance have not only entered the corporate mainstream, they've become a source of competitive advantage.[81] Leading organizations are already recognizing that work and family – and personal renewal both on and off the job – are not discrete phenomena. They interconnect, often profoundly. Consideration of the individual and family must be built into job design, work processes, and organizational structures. It's already happening and a first-ever *Business Week* rating of work and family strategies acknowledged Motorola, DuPont, Hewlett-Packard, Marriott International, Eli Lilly, First Tennessee Bank, MBNA America Bank, Unum Life Insurance, and Merrill Lynch, among others.

Before we delve into renewing ourselves, I want to acknowledge that on a bad day resilience can fail any of us, and periodically does. During such times, we must find our own best way to bounce back and renew. Perhaps it takes a run or a hug, a talk with a trusted friend, a few minutes of fresh air or sunshine, a healthy snack, some hot tea or your favourite music, or a rerun of *M*A*S*H* or *I Love Lucy*. Whatever options work for you, learn to choose the most appropriate one on the spot to catch and turn around downsliding energy or mood. It's up to each of us to identify practical skills to stay more adaptable when we get our backs up or start feeling tense or tired, and to renew ourselves regularly along the way.

In truth, the crucial measure of successful living is less about money than about breathing space. Breathing space is the ability to create 'islands of peace' in the midst of your weekly array of tasks, problems, and the rest of the full-scale web of demands competing for your attention and energy.[82] How often have you said, 'If only I could get a little breathing space'? Now's the time to find it – even just five or ten minutes here and there – and to write it in ink on your calendar and capture the benefits, beginning with the best *feeling* of being home.

When I work with management teams and groups of professionals, I hear people complaining that it's harder than ever to feel 'at home' when they're at home. With so many hours on the job, they just can't seem to shake the feelings of *being* at work. Gallup surveys report that 'Americans feel fractured, scattered, torn in pieces by the competing demands of work and home.'[83] And there's considerable evidence that the quality of non-work relationships influences job productivity and disease resistance.[84] For many of us, when we arrive at home to face the people we love – and who love us – there's something missing, a piece of ourselves. Despite our best intentions, we feel numb and disconnected. Our jobs have devoured so much of our time and energy, we have little, if any, left to give.

To begin with, no matter what our job, research indicates that there is a certain intensity – a rhythm you can feel – when you're at work, and it's considerably different and probably more intense than the rhythm you experience when you feel 'at home'.[85] It's essential that leaders and managers find new ways to break away from work *at work*, and savour even a few minutes' reprieve from the rush and roar of the daily grind. This is one way to begin bringing a revitalized sense of being home – in your heart and imagination – for a few minutes wherever you happen to be, even at work.

One of the simplest and most useful ways I've found to help people achieve this recovery spell, is to downshift away the rhythm of your job with a brief *transition time*. By this I mean devoting the final minutes of your work day to some of your least-pressured tasks, which might include such things as returning selected phone calls – to people you enjoy talking with, for example – or clearing your work space, finalizing tomorrow's schedule, and organizing upcoming projects.

Removing limits on what people can achieve can be a perverse invitation to burnout. It's exhilarating to be stretched to your limit, but after a while you need a break before you break.

Michael Hammer, US business strategist

What about days when you find your thoughts and intuition ablaze with uncompleted business? Put pen to paper. Or fingers to keyboard. Otherwise, if you tell yourself, 'I won't forget – I'll just keep it in mind for tomorrow,' chances are your subconscious will do just that, and keep your mind distracted and emotions agitated well into evening.

For many of us, this late-day transition is also a good time to replenish nutrients. Researchers have found that many a needless family argument has been triggered or exacerbated by hunger-related tensions.[85] Experiment. See if your emotional balance improves – and you're more relaxed and adaptable at home – when you eat a late day snack. Brain scientists have found it can make a significant difference.[87] If you're feeling highly stimulated by work, and perhaps somewhat tense, reach for a snack that is low in fat and protein but high in carbohydrates. Examples include some wholegrain crackers or some fresh fruit. This kind of carbohydrate-rich snack helps produce a surge of tryptophan, an amino acid that activates the brain neurotransmitter (messenger chemical) serotonin, which promotes a healthy relaxation response.

If, on the other hand, as the work day winds to a close you tend to feel emotionally drained or even drowsy, choose a snack low in fat and high in protein, such as a cup of yoghurt, a handful of peanuts, a 'high-protein snack bar' from your health food store, or a small sandwich with turkey, tuna, chicken, or low-fat cream cheese. When you eat something with enough protein, you naturally alter the chemical structure of the amino acid tyrosine and stimulate the group of brain neurotransmitters known as catecholamines, which promote increased emotional energy and alertness lasting up to three hours.

Now let's consider a few of the other ways you might increase your emotional fitness when leaving work and heading home, which needs to happen symbolically even if you work at home. I recommend a simple 'transition audit.' Does great music boost your spirits or help you unwind, buffering the noise of traffic? How do you feel when you listen to a book on audiotape? Or talk with a loved one or good friend on your cellular phone? Or use a note-recorder to engage yourself in creative dialogue about a future project or opportunity? Select whatever works best for you. This mental disengagement and emotional shift can be so powerful[88] that it readily draws you towards the slower rhythms of home and you arrive more adaptable and energized.

Right up to when you walk in the door, which is a key time to pay extra attention to your feelings. Few of us realize that the first fifteen minutes or so at home can be a danger zone for relationships, a prime time for dumping complaints on each other and the time during which up to half of all family arguments are started or worsened.[89] Consider an alternative: arrange in advance with family members for a different kind of greeting. When you each walk in the door, you warmly acknowledge others who are home but limit your first comments to half a minute or so, such as : 'What a hectic day! It's great to be home, sweetheart!'; or 'Things were *crazy* at work, but I'm really glad to finally be here!' Now take a ten-or fifteen-minute timeout. Delay talking about your day (or hearing about your partner's day, or what the children argued about, which household appliances broke, who needs money, and so on).

This kind of transitional 'buffer zone' can help you regain emotional balance and renew your spirit in finally being home. You might use this brief interlude to get some brief exercise, take a shower, change into

Happiness is having a large, loving, caring, close-knit family in another city.

George Burns, comedian, USA

loose, comfortable clothes, switch on some music, or enjoy a relaxing cup of tea or a glass of wine. You get the idea. *Then* talk about the day with your loved ones.

Make it a point to add as much humour as you can. Come up with the funniest event of the day. Share it with others, and encourage them to do the same. I know many executives and managers who seem afraid of fun. For certain stretches of my professional life, I've been one of them. If I laugh too much, if I let go too much, I might lose my edge. Or so the voice in my mind rationalizes. Which, according to research, is not true.[90]

Learning Alliances: Creating a Larger Field of Emotional Intelligence in Your Life

As you broaden and deepen the feeling of balance between work and home, you build for yourself a foundation from which to relate, and adapt, not only to your own growth – and your family's changing needs – but to your future. It is through emotional fitness that we strengthen our spirits and condition the sensory essence of our heart to extend a feeling of care and support to others.

This brings us to an important point: emotional intelligence doesn't flourish in a vacuum. It's one thing if, for now, you're forced by an unenlightened employer to work solo on your business-related EQ. But your life *off* the job is another thing. In my experience, the executives, managers, and professionals who've made the greatest progress in developing their emotional intelligence are those who have made it a point to bring the exploration and development of EQ home and to their neighbourhoods, religious and civic groups, and communities. They form what I call 'learning alliances', informed partnerships and organized groups dedicated to studying and discussing subjects of interest. The participants interact to stretch and deepen the learning process, sharing personal experiences and support, and building truer friendships along the way.

In this light, I encourage you to share ideas from this book with your loved ones and friends, and with everyone in your sphere of influence, including your co-workers, top customers, and boss, the local schoolteachers, and community leaders. Consider starting an EQ study group. Circulate some copies of *Emotional Intelligence* by Daniel Goleman, as well as *Executive EQ*. Other favourites from our reading list at the back of this book are *Descartes' Error* by neurologist Antonio Damasio, *The Heart of Parenting* by psychologist John Gottman, and *The Passions: Emotions and the Meaning of Life* by philosopher Robert Solomon. As Harvard Medical School professor Robert Coles reminds us in *The Moral Intelligence of Children*, the shared, daily experience between emotionally connected adults seems to be the crucial factor in instilling a well-developed moral sense of character in family members of every age. As Coles reminds us, 'moral intelligence isn't only acquired by memorization of rules and regulations, by dint of abstract classroom discussion or kitchen compliance. We grow morally as a consequence of learning how to be with others, how to behave in this world, a learning prompted *by taking to heart* what we have seen and heard.'

One of the leading clearing houses on emotional intelligence for children, families, schools, and communities is the Foundation for Education in Emotional Literacy (F.E.E.L., 1623 Stanford St., Santa Monica, CA 90404; website:http:/www.eq.org)). Consider adding your name to their mailing list. My young daughters have already enjoyed several of the children's books recommended by F.E.E.L., and these reading experiences have helped open up family discussions about the values of emotional intelligence in the home, at school, and in life in general.

Intentionality: the Bridge to the Third Cornerstone of EQ

In this second cornerstone of EQ, each of the four competencies – authentic presence, trust radius, constructive discontent, and emotional resilience and renewal – contributes to emotional fitness and builds an increased sense of inspiration, of self and others. The word inspiration means 'to breathe deeply; to fill with an animating sense of enthusiasm and innermost confidence'. On a final note, to put emotional fitness into practice requires intentionality, which can be seen as the connecting trait, or 'bridge', between the second and third EQ cornerstones. Derived from the Latin words *intentus* and *inten(dere)*, intention means 'to stretch forward'.

THE THIRD CORNERSTONE:

Emotional Depth

Reaching down and *stepping up:*
Builds *core character* and calls forth
your potential, integrity, and purpose

One of my business mentors, a man who over his lifetime had risen from abject poverty and ridicule in school to the top of his chosen profession, once said to me that life and work seem to flow much like a river. At times they can be swirling high against the banks, and at times, free from wind and storm, they can move in relative silence, steadily onwards, drawn by hidden currents. From the shoreline, he said, we can admire the water's glass-like, ever-changing appearance, or in a boat or on a swim we can skim across its surface, although, in either case, we learn little about it beneath the façade. On the other hand, mused my mentor, by choice or storm or circumstance, we may end up plunging to the river's depths, and, from that point on, because of what we experience and learn, we are never the same. He was silent for a while, lost in thought, and then he turned to me and asked, 'What about you: do you live only on the surface of your life? Or do you dive to the depths?'

I've kept pondering those questions ever since. Whenever we live or work on an emotionally superficial level, things can feel relatively easy, or comfortable, but there's no foundation there, nothing to draw upon. And, in one way or another, at one time or another, we end up feeling shallow and lost. Emotional intelligence cannot thrive or expand without emotional depth, this third cornerstone of Executive EQ.

When you live from the depths of the heart, you walk your talk, heed your conscience, and don't hesitate to take a stand. Your voice rings true and gets heard. It is through emotional depth that we begin, for example, to discover, and commit to, the unique potential which defines our destiny and leads us to the fulfilment of our larger purpose in life.

Consider an example:[1] John Shad, Chairman of the Securities and Exchange Commission during President Reagan's administration, made good on his promise to crack down on insider trading. He then became Ambassador to the Netherlands. While this transition was occurring, he awarded a grant of $20 million from his own estate to Harvard Business School to establish a teaching programme in ethics. Amazingly, Harvard's faculty expressed apparent bewilderment at such a request. 'Ethics? How on earth do we blend that into a business curriculum?' they seemed to be asking. *Business Week* quoted a professor who said, 'They [the administration] still have to sell this to 100 tenured faculty who think the whole discipline [ethics] is garbage.'

144

John Shad happens to be a member of Harvard Business School's heralded class of 1949. It includes such accomplished executives as C. Peter McColough, retired CEO of Xerox, and James Burke, CEO of Johnson & Johnson, who won admiration for his leadership integrity in handling his organization's Tylenol crisis in the 1980s. By specifying that Harvard Business School devote every dollar of his personal grant to a teaching programme on ethics, Shad was giving voice to what he felt was right and worth taking action on. He acted from his depth of character, and, by doing so, forced Harvard to look deeply, too, and to change. The faculty ending up grudgingly approving the course, and then struggled to create it. It quickly became one of the most sought-after courses at Harvard. It is being taught today, to much acclaim.

Sooner or later, every leader stops to wonder about what breadth, depth, and height the human heart, mind, and soul can reach, to paraphrase the eloquent words of Elizabeth Barrett Browning. The first two cornerstones of Executive EQ can be seen as dealing with emotional breadth, and the fourth will venture into the heights. But this third cornerstone is the one devoted to journeying beneath the surface of who you are and what may yet become.

CHAPTER 9

Unique Potential and Purpose

O ne of my favourite stories about unique potential and inner purpose is from China in the third century BC.[2] It is the story of Sun Bin, who as a young man was known as Master Sun, or Sun Tzu II. He was a descendant of General Sun Tzu who wrote the strategy classic *The Art of War*. Sun Bin's teachings, entitled *The Lost Art of War*, were lost for nearly 2000 years until a nearly complete version, recorded on 232 small bamboo tablets, was discovered in 1972 in an ancient tomb in Shangdong Province.

The bravest are surely those who have the clearest purpose ... and go out to meet it.

Thucydides

Sun Bin's Era of the Warring States was a time of chaos and brutal competition, not so unlike today in many areas of the world. According to the traditional anthology known as *Strategies of the Warring States*:[3]

Usurpers set themselves up as lords and kings; states that were run by pretenders and plotters established armies to make themselves into major powers. They imitated each other at this more and more, and those who came after them also followed their example. Eventually they overwhelmed and destroyed one another, conspiring with larger domains to annex smaller domains, spending years at violent military operations, filling the fields with blood.

Fathers and sons were alienated, brothers were at odds, husbands and wives were estranged. No one could safeguard his or her life. Integrity disappeared. Eventually this reached the extreme where seven large states and five smaller states contested each other for power. This all happened because the warring states were shameless greedy, struggling insatiably to get ahead.

According to ancient documents, the young Master Sun studied warfare and strategy along with a certain Pang Juan, who later became a high-ranking military commander. Their teacher was the mysterious sage Wang

Li, author of one of the most intricate and sophisticated of strategic classics.[4] After completing tactical studies with Wang Li, Master Sun's classmate Pang Juan was hired by the court of the state of Wei, where he was given the rank of general. Concerned that his own abilities as strategist were not equal to those of Master Sun, Pang Juan conspired to eliminate him.

To ensure his rival's downfall, Pang Juan had Master Sun invited to Wei as if to consult with him. When Master Sun arrived, Pang Juan had him arrested as a criminal and condemned him to the severest torture. Both of young Master Sun's feet were cut off and his face was horribly disfigured – a punishment designed to reduce a person to the status of a permanent outcast. This was why, from that day onwards, he became known as Sun Bin, 'Sun the Mutilated'.

However the story was far from over. Sun Bin had long possessed a deep, abiding sense of his own unique worthiness as a person. He believed that, despite this terrible setback, he could still pursue his calling in life. Perhaps this purpose was to create the strategies that would ultimately unify the Warring States. Perhaps it was to devise a new means to win battles – in life or war – with the least damage done and fewest lives lost. Whatever it was, this calling or purpose gave him the drive to transcend his torture. And, while still imprisoned, he managed to gain a brief, private audience with an emissary of the state of Qi.

Although maimed and in excruciating pain, Sun Bin quickly astounded the envoy not only with his courage but with his obvious wisdom about strategy and warfare. The emissary sensed a solidity to this man, not as much from the strength of his body – with its layered maze of hideous purple-grey scars where once had been his handsome face, head, and neck – as from the sureness of his heart and ideas. Recognizing the tremendous value of such an ally, the emissary smuggled Sun Bin out of Wei into his own state of Qi.

From that day on, Sun Bin's drive and discipline enabled him to move beyond his grotesque physical form. He learned every way to expand and extend his inner capabilities. He was soon appointed strategist and military consultant to the famed general Tian Ji, who greatly admired Sun Bin's piercing intuition and field counsel. Many years later, Sun Bin's strategic prowess was immortalized in the popular *Extraordinary Strategies of a Hundred Battles* by the great Ming Dynasty warrior-scholar Liu Ji.[5]

The tactics of Sun Bin were centred on securing victory with minimal harm and at minimal cost. If possible, both sides would end the conflict without humiliation. His metaphors can be applied to many life events other than warfare. If we wish to remedy oppressive conditions, for example, we must understand these conditions and how they affect us. We must know ourselves, know our challenges, and know where we are and what is going on. This applies not only to battle but to all fields of contention and competition.

Identifying Your Unique Potential

As Sun Bin knew, there is a longing in each of us to find and invest ourselves in our life purpose, in things that matter, that are deep. This requires, first and foremost, coming to know our talents and aligning them in service of our calling in life. It's what some leaders – and, in particular, Joseph W. Gauld author of *Character First*[6] – call *unique potential*.

> *It's never too late to be what you might have been.*
>
> George Eliot (Mary Ann Evans), 1819–80

It's something rarely acknowledged or actively explored in business. In fact, it's usually ignored altogether. In many companies there's an unwritten rule: let's try to fix what's wrong and let our strengths take care of themselves. The theory is that if you work on fixing weaknesses in an individual or team, then the individual or team will become stronger. This is similar to assuming that if you write an error-free paper – no typos or grammatical errors – it will automatically be an outstanding one. Not so. Similarly, success is *not* the opposite of failure. Everyone *cannot* do whatever they set their minds to. Of course, it's great to aspire. But then, as Sun Bin and other leaders have shown us, the aspiration must be *directly linked* to one's unique potential and purpose. Only then can you rise to meet the challenges of success, no matter what comes.

If a person's unique potential is based on strengths rather than weaknesses, what would happen if we studied what was *right* with people instead of what's *wrong* with them? That question prompted more than forty years of ongoing research into the thoughts, feelings, and behaviours of successful people. The firm conducting the studies is SRI Gallup, a research and consulting firm which has reviewed in depth more than 250,000 successful salespeople, managers, leaders, executives, teachers, and other professionals.

This research suggests that executives and managers should ask themselves the following question: what, specifically, are my greatest strengths and talents? In truth, every one of us can do one or two things better than any other ten thousand people.[7] How do you define such strengths, from which you begin to discover your reason for living, your unique potential and purpose? Consider these characteristics:[8]

1. *It's a yearning.* You'll feel it – it pulls or attracts you toward one activity over another like an inner magnet, although it's not tied to glamour or arrogance.
2. *It's something that deeply satisfies you.* You get a 'kick out of doing it'. This kind of satisfaction is rarely present when your talents or strengths are not.
3. *The learning is easy.* You catch on quickly and it feels exciting to learn.
4. *You sense moments of flow.* You feel this is something natural for you and you catch glimpses of yourself performing well in this talent area.

It pays to be aware of personal vulnerabilities, of course, but principally because they must be acknowledged and *managed*, not because we can necessarily 'fix' them. Abraham Maslow reminded us that many of us 'tend to evade personal growth because this ... can bring a kind of fear, of awe.... And so we find another kind of resistance, a denying of our best side, of our talents, of our finest impulses, of our highest potentialities, of our creativeness.'[9] One of the ways to move beyond such resistance is through developing our emotional intelligence and coming to *value* deeply and *apply* our strengths and talents while improving our ability to *manage* our vulnerabilities. Don Clifton, Chairman and CEO of SRI Gallup, and Paula Nelson tell the following story:[10]

David Brown, a New York securities broker, earned more than $500,000 in commissions in 1989, making him one of the top one per cent of securities brokers in the nation. He reasoned that if he could devote 100 per cent of his time to his primary strengths, that of working with customers, he could boost his commissions to $750,000 annually. To accomplish that, he also ... isolated his areas of weakness: specifically paperwork and reports, activities that chewed up more than 30 per cent of his time. Brown adopted new strategies for 'managing the weaknesses' that freed him to exercise his strengths over the following twelve months and realize his goal. Which he did.

Before there was Boeing, there were Wilbur and Orville Wright. Before AT&T, there was Alexander Graham Bell. Before Microsoft, there were Bill Gates and Paul Allen. Before CNN, there was Ted Turner. Before FedEx, there was Fred Smith. Every new

Each of us is meant to have a character all our own, to be what no other can exactly be, and do what no other can exactly do.

William Ellery Channing, 1780–1842, US writer and clergyman

industry, product, service line, and movement has its creative founders, the visionaries who followed their gut feelings, identified their unique potential, committed to a purpose, and led the way in building something successful. Research shows that people do their most creative and effective work when they love – rather than just tolerate, or even pleasantly like – what they do.[11] Far too often, we follow a path not because it's what we care about most passionately but because it's what other people want or expect. We may do efficient or good work on such a path, but it's rarely great work and virtually never creative work.[12] A bit later in this chapter, we'll introduce several ways to explore your talents and identify unique potential. Then, like the needle of a compass, you are drawn onto a path of purpose and calling.

Purpose is the Inner Compass of Your Life and Work

A purpose is far more than a good idea; it's an emotionally charged *path* in your work and life that provides orientation and direction. It's an internal locus of awareness and guidance which defines you by who you are and what you care most about, rather than where you find yourself at the moment. It is from this calling or purpose that you, in the words of Mary Catherine Bateson, begin truly 'composing a life'.[13] Purpose is not a strategy or goal, although it is a

Clarity of purpose exposes the foundation of the inner heart.

M.H. McKee, Forbes

powerful attractor for meaningful strategies and goals; it is the fundamental aim of your existence and your organization's existence.

A purpose, in the broadest and most lasting sense, is what you, and the people on your team or in your company, want to contribute to. The major purpose of work is to build an enterprise of our own choosing and one that we believe in. As Kenichi Ohmae, the Japanese business strategist, describes it, 'Successful business strategies result not from rigorous analysis ... but from a process which is creative and intuitive rather than rational.'[14] And from this we must 'create constancy of purpose', urged W. Edwards Deming in the first of his fourteen points for personal and corporate transformation.[15] He was among those who realized that only by identifying our unique calling – as an individual and organization – can we discover our purpose. And it is only when we wholeheartedly commit to this purpose, and align our daily work with it, that we are enabled to grow and succeed.

Composer Michael Hoppé was routinely scorned by his parents as 'the Dreamer'.[16] He was told from the time he was a child that artists were selfish and irresponsible people, and he was urged to become a businessman instead of a composer. Financial success, his parents and others told him, would yield far greater satisfaction and success than following his musical dreams. An obedient son, he became a senior executive at Poly-Gram, one of the world's largest record companies. Gifted with composer's ears, he brought to his label many fine composers and artists. All the while, he quietly composed his own music, unable to reject completely the calling he had so long felt. Things might have continued this way except for a fateful event.

He was asked to audition his company's talent for a major film producer. Hoppé made a tape of his artists' work and sat through a long meeting as the producer rejected artist after artist. 'No, no! Don't you have anyone who is right for me?'

As the tape was spooling to an end, a short piece of his own music came on. What an embarrassing accident, thought Hoppé, realizing he had dubbed the other artists' work over a tape that had several of his own compositions on it. He reached to turn off the recorder.

'That's it. That's him! That's our composer,' exclaimed the producer. Hoppé was shocked. He *represented* composers; he was not one himself. But the producer was insistent. In that moment, Michael Hoppé's unique potential and purpose were freed. He has since followed the direction of his inner compass to score feature films that have won awards at the New York, Houston, and San Francisco Film Festivals, as well as reaching the Oscar shortlist. His endeavours in the music industry have garnered fifteen gold and four platinum records, and 'The Yearning' was selected by the editors of *CD Review* as CD of the year. When I listen to it, I always pause to recall that, according to others, he was not supposed to compose these melodies.

When we are attuned to our feel ings, we become aware of the many different parts of ourselves, and what we want and need. Some of these things are likely in conflict with each other, and only you can sort them out, sensing what is deepest and matters most.

President John F. Kennedy loved to tell the tale of small boys in Ireland who would have footraces across the lush hills. When they came to a fence they were afraid to cross, they would challenge each other to throw their hats over first so they would feel compelled to go after them. Purpose is about throwing your hat over the fence into the future, so that you are inspired to follow it. There is difficulty here, and magic.

We live in a time in which most people believe there is not much inside them, only what teachers, parents, and others have put there.

Michel Cassou and Stewart Cubley, authors of
Life, Painting and Passion

In many of the time-honoured traditions of building character and leadership, the image of purpose is the deepest one of all, one of going home, of finding your own true home in work and life. But it takes a tremendous commitment and lots of soul-searching to find this home. But it can be done. Great men and women and organizations have done it, and are doing it. It was Frederick Buechner who wrote that purpose – or 'the place God calls you to' – is 'the place where your deep gladness and the world's deep hunger meet'.[17]

In this way, purpose is something that is always worked towards but never fully realized.[18] Until we recognize and live in accord with our unique potential and purpose, life may feel like a puzzle with missing pieces. We're missing our 'deep gladness' and *raison d'être*. We work and sleep, make money and spend it, experience our share of pleasures and difficulties, and may be a whiz at juggling projects and going through the motions, but there's an emptiness inside us as individuals, and inside our organizations.

Sooner or later something sparks a strong feeling which calls us onto a particular path. This is what I must do, it says. This is who I really am. You cannot fake it; it must be authentic to you. Can you give a whole-hearted 'yes' to the statement, 'My life satisfies my deepest needs'? It is towards our deepest sense of purpose that integrity seeks to align itself, with direction of the inner compass of your calling in life and work. For centuries we have searched for the right term for this 'call'. The Romans named it *genius*; the Greeks, your *daimon*; in Middle English, *purpose*. Keats reminded us to find it in the heart, not the head, and Michelangelo's intuitive eye always perceived a unique image in the heart of the person he was sculpting.

It's almost never too late in life or work to discover a calling and to commit yourself to doing those things that matter most to you, to being *on-purpose.* Of course, some people will continue to gamble or win a lottery, or manage to get rich in other ways, without a purpose. Rarely, however, do we hear how fulfilled their life is or how much they have grown and learned deep inside; they simply have a lot of money.

What lies before us and what lies behind us are small matters compared to what lies within us. And when we bring what is within out into the world, miracles happen.

Henry David Thoreau, 1817–62, US author and naturalist

A number of leaders have told me they feel an inner drive to keep growing and learning and frequently check, and recheck, the direction of their life and career. I recall what my friend, James Kackley, a senior managing partner at Arthur Andersen LLP, chose to do during his sabbatical several years ago: he spent the first part of it at the Aspen Institute, working with James O'Toole and a faculty that includes some of the world's leading thinkers on business leadership and purpose, and then spent the last part of his 'work break' trekking across Isle Royale, the remote wilderness island in Lake Superior populated only by packs of wolves and herds of moose. Jim slept under the stars at night and hiked each day, stopping from time to time to observe the wildlife, take in the spectacular views and reflect. He made daily entries in his journal about vision and calling for himself and his highly successful company. He meant to clarify and deepen his personal potential and purpose, and his firm's. Jim has advised the executives at many organizations over his career and, when he had an opportunity to take a break from work, he devoted it to getting in deeper touch with his capacities, responsibilities and direction for the future.

When Jim interviews prospective new managers, he asks the candidate to pull up a chair beside him while he reaches for a small brown leather binder from his briefcase. He opens it and flips through the pages, showing the prospective Arthur Andersen manager the definition he has written of his own unique potential and calling, and reads the description of his personal and leadership purpose, reviewing his specific roles and goals in his business and personal life. He describes how each week he opens this binder and consciously realigns himself with his potential and purpose. Then he turns to the job candidate and says, 'I'm curious to know what you believe is your unique potential and purpose in life and work?' He leans forward and listens carefully to every word. Then he asks, 'And how do you believe you could realize this potential and purpose here at Arthur Andersen?'

In reflecting on the power of purpose, Joseph Campbell wrote, 'You may have success in life, but then ask yourself – what kind of life was it? What good was it if you've never done the thing you wanted to do all your life or went where your heart and soul wanted to go? When you find that feeling, stay with it, and don't let anyone throw you off.'[23] To find that feeling, begin by imagining that you can choose anything you want, whatever you feel is your greatest motivation or dream. This deep-down purpose is larger than needs and desires. It's the heart's inner compass that keeps you 'truing' in the direction of your personal strengths and ultimate contribution to humanity.

One of my favourite methods for discovering unique potential and purpose – or deepening and enlivening an enquiry into potential and purpose – is the *five whys*, a sequence of questions used by our ancient mentors and applied in recent years by business researchers Jim Collins and Jerry Porras.[19] Here's the essence: begin with a descriptive statement, I am drawn to doing X or I am talented at Y, and then ask yourself, why is that important? five times. After a few whys, you'll sense that you're getting down to a fundamental purpose. Then reflect and clarify what you've found. Write it down. Test it. Keep asking, Does it *feel* right – and why or why not? The five whys can help an individual or group approach work in a more creative and meaningful way.

Discovering Your Unique Potential and Purpose

Here is a series of considerations to start the process and to re-visit from time to time for increased clarity and focus.[24]

1.   What do I feel are my greatest strengths and personal talents, those qualities which comprise my *unique potential*? Remember, your purpose is about creating, not fixing, something. List those *capabilities* and *directions* (where your talents *point* you) that are natural and spontaneous, the skills you most enjoy expressing. Describe each in one or two words. Circle the top five strengths or talents you have. Write a summary sentence or two. My unique potential is: _____

2.   If I had unlimited time and resources, what would I choose to do? When I reflect on my personal life, what activities do I consider of greatest worth or value?

3.   What are the most important relationships in my life?

4.   What are my most important roles in life? Much frustration comes from the feeling that we're succeeding in one role – as an executive, specialist, or entrepreneur, for example – at the expense of other important roles, such as that of parent or spouse. Balance in your roles does not mean you must spend equal time in each of them; it means remaining *aware* of all of them, and taking steps to align them in pursuing your purpose. You might begin to notice areas where your passions in life parallel or augment those of other family members, for example, and use this awareness in planning activities in which, instead of feeling you're acting out of familial duty but have little in common, everyone finds an avenue for individual and shared enjoyment and growth. A synergy begins to take place, and although you may be spending the same amount of time in this role as you spend now, you'll likely feel more 'in sync' with your loved ones and connected to them. Name one or two specific things that you feel could make a significant difference in each of your roles. What about as a parent? A spouse? A son or daughter? A friend? A leader or employee? Listen to your intuition.

5.   In what kind of work does my burning passion reside? These are dimensions of myself that I daydream about and wish I could channel more energy (and time) into. When I reflect on my work life, what activities do I consider of greatest worth or value?

6.   Who is the person who has had the greatest positive influence on my life? What was it about this person that was exceptional?

7.   What am I most proud of in my life? Describe how you've made a difference to your business, community, or family. What are the greatest contributions you hope to make? Project this into the future, say 100 years out. Is this the legacy you want to leave, the difference you most want to be remembered for? If not, what is?

8.   Start a page in a notebook. Write a sentence or two in the present tense that evokes the emotional depth of what you care about and most want to do.
   And then enter the heading, 'My personal calling and purpose in life...'

Now begin the *five whys* method. Ask yourself, why is this important? five times. Does a *yes, that's it* sentence about your purpose appear? If not yet, fine – such images often take a

Keep your eyes on the stars but never lose awareness of the flowers at your feet.

Agnew Meek, Vice President, 3M Company

while to shape in the heart and come into focus. Encourage that feeling, and be patient with yourself in understanding and explaining it. When you feel it's right, you'll know it was worth the wait. From there, your behaviour and day-to-day choices will begin to align themselves with this core purpose. You will be able to develop specific short-term and mid-term change goals or visions, images you see in your mind that are desirable, feasible, focused, and communicable, and that are consistent with, and clearly advance, your purpose. In this way, you'll make it easier and less time-consuming to generate new strategies and, as a result, to achieve and celebrate more short-term, meaningful wins – and mistakes, too – as sources of new learning.

Here's a final question as you consider how to bring your purpose into action: what are two specific ways I will stand out from the crowd in the next year by being on-purpose?

EQ Map Connections: Unique Potential & Purpose
You may want to refer to the following scales of the *EQ Map* as points of reflection related this chapter: life events, pressures and satisfactions, emotional self-awareness, intentionality outlook, intuition, personal power, and integrity.

EQ IN ACTION: *INNER COMPASS NOTESTREAM*

This is a simple, portable EQ tool that can provide a host of time-saving and creative payoffs. Once you have discovered your fundamental purpose and are beginning to align your daily schedule and priorities to advance that purpose, take several minutes to do the following:

List the major work projects and specific goals that you feel really matter to you and your company over the next several months. From this list, circle the ones that your intuition tells you will potentially generate the greatest value for you, your company, or key customers.

Put a star next to the top seven of these that depend on, or can be advanced by, your own initiative rather than depending on the initiative of others. Review each priority area, asking, Do I feel confident this is a practical area of development where I can make progress? If not, what resources do I need to ensure this? Be certain that at least several of these priority areas have a long-term connection to your purpose and will stretch your capabilities.

Take a blank piece of paper and put the date in the top corner. Divide the page into seven large regions. You might draw squares, rectangles, triangles or circles, whatever is most appealing to your eye. Vary the sizes as desired. Now enter a brief heading in each of the seven areas to correspond to the seven work priority areas. You might consider generating a template for your own NoteStream using computer graphics software.

When you're finished, make several copies. Fold one up and keep it in your pocket. Place another in your schedule book or agenda. Put a third in the notebook you keep at hand during meetings and phone conversations.

Every time you have a new creative idea or intuitive hunch or concern; enter it in the appropriate priority area(s). Each time you pick up the phone or sit down at a conference or meeting, pull out a copy of this month's NoteStream and keep it next to your notebook. When a meeting starts to drift off course or get bogged down, use your NoteStream as a visual cue to speak up, shift focus, and move things back on track, not only for your benefit but for everyone involved. This helps keep you in touch with your purpose and priorities, not just once in a while but all day long. Use your NoteStream when:

- Your intuition beckons
- Your conscience prods you to stay on-purpose
- You think of a new angle, leverage point, or shortcut to improvement
- You learn something that could benefit a customer or client
- You sense an unexpected way to increase revenue or add value
- You want to transform a boring discussion into something more relevant

In short, the NoteStream is designed to spark connections and collect your ideas, questions, and concerns. If you run out of space in one of the seven areas, simply put a numbered asterisk at the end of that line, flip the page over and continue writing. You can also use the back side of the NoteStream for ideas that fall outside the seven priority areas, and for longer streams of consciousness.

At key times of the day, review your entries. Evaluate your current reality and contrast it with the direction of your inner compass. Take action wherever indicated. Call a colleague with a creative question. Contact a key customer with an innovative idea. In working with executives and professionals in many industries, I've found that just having a NoteStream at hand stimulates staying on-purpose and being creative. It can also save you steps and time. For example, instead of trying to make sense of a pocketful of scraps of paper, napkin corners, crumpled business cards, Post-Its, and other loose notes jotted here and there, your NoteStream offers a place to consolidate key ideas and tie them directly into your priority work flow areas. It's simple. It's intuitive. It's aligned around your purpose.

Once you've begun to clarify the deeper potential and purpose in your life and work, the challenge you face is putting this into action, and aligning more of your daily efforts with the needle of your inner compass. This requires a sense of commitment and courage, which are called forth and guided by the heart's voice of conscience and backed by accountability. These are the traits of emotional depth that form the next chapter's central threads.

CHAPTER 10

Commitment

Rachel Louise Carson grew up along the Allegheny River on a small plot of land purchased by her father, an unsuccessful businessman, near Springdale, Pennsylvania.[25] She developed an early love of nature, and was an avid reader and enthusiastic student who was forced to miss long stretches of school due to illness. At eighteen, she was admitted to the Pennsylvania College for Women (which later became Chatham College) and majored in English, hoping to become an author. However, in her second year, she attended a required course in biology taught by a brilliant teacher, Mary Scott Skinker. That class awakened Carson's unique potential and aroused in her a passionate curiosity about nature and science. She switched her college major.

Future generations are unlikely to condone our lack of prudent concern for the integrity of the natural world that supports all life.

Rachel Carson, Silent Spring

After graduation, she received a summer college fellowship at the US Marine Laboratory in Woods Hole, Massachusetts, and then won a scholarship to Johns Hopkins University in Baltimore. After earning her master's degree, she and her family faced two tragedies: the deaths of her father and sister. To help support her mother and two remaining sisters, Carson took a job at the US Bureau of Fisheries in Washington, DC. Within a year, she passed the civil service exam, garnering the highest possible score, and was made a full-time aquatic biologist with the bureau. She authored *Under the Sea-Wind* in 1941, and followed this *The Sea Around Us* in 1951 and *The Edge of the Sea* in 1959, which provided a vivid account of the physics, chemistry, and biology of the ocean and its shores.

In 1958, Carson received a letter from a friend describing the devastating effects on her private bird sanctuary in Massachusetts after it was sprayed with pesticides used in the state's mosquito control programme. Carson, who had long been aware of the real and potential dangers posed by chemical poisons decided, then and there, that she had to speak out or 'there would be no peace for me'. She knew it would raise a controversy, especially since the agricultural industry had come to depend on chemicals to increase crop yields and that manufacturing companies had a general indifference to the effects of chemical waste. Even the US Department of Agriculture advocated using herbicides and pesticides.

After several years of careful research in America and Europe, Carson wrote *Silent Spring*, which was published in 1962. In it, she called for a new and vigorous debate on the environmental costs to the natural world she loved, and described with tremendous conviction how the fragile existence of all living creatures, including humans, was being imperilled by DDT and other more toxic chemicals. Carson was attacked by the agricultural industry, which mounted a vast and unsuccessful campaign to discredit her warnings. She stuck to her position and purpose. President John F. Kennedy was impressed by the book and demanded a re-evaluation of the Federal Pesticide Policy. In 1963, the president's Science Advisory Committee endorsed Carson's position. It is now generally acknowledged that the modern environmental movement began with the publication of *Silent Spring*. As one editor observed, 'A thousand words from her, and the world took a new direction.' Such is the power of purpose backed by emotional commitment.

One of the things I learned from Rachel Carson's life is that no matter what your endeavour, and no matter what talents or purpose you have, without a strong intrinsic motivation to *use* them, without emotional commitment, you probably won't advance very far. As the German philosopher G. W. F. Hegel wrote, 'Nothing great in the world has ever been accomplished without passion.' Most executives and leaders realize that motivation can prove more vital than intellectual or technical skills. After all, it's not the head that moves us; it's the heart.

Emotion arouses and motivates us, and calls us to commit. This internal drive is essential to the successful implementation of any kind of intelligence or strategy. Some people, for example, are adept at coming up with solutions to the problems of work and life but they seem unable to implement them, stymied at translating these solutions into practical and effective action. We have to *want* to succeed and then *emotionally commit* to succeed, with or without the support of others if possible, or alone if necessary. It's less about sustaining a commitment than it is about being sustained by your commitment. What is the greatest story you know about emotional commitment?

This brings me to a long-lost tale of emotional commitment, a story of quiet courage and inner leadership that runs counter to the glorified 'hero' archetype perpetuated in our culture. In about AD 900 a secret language was created known as *Nu Shu* ('women's script').[26] It soon spread across broad areas of China. Yet its design and code were so effectively concealed that it was detected by not a single one of the powerful rulers in that vast land, men who surely would have banned it. So effective was the concealment that it wasn't until 1950 – 1000 years after its inception – that a team of archaeologists stumbled upon a *Nu Shu* source book in the mountains of Hunan but it took cryptologists and linguists until 1982 successfully to decipher and translate the secret code.

From all indications, this language was devised in response to the voice of conscience among Chinese women, a growing number of whom were convinced, despite millennia of male dominance and condemnation to the contrary, that they were worthy people entitled to educate themselves and communicate with each other. They felt so strongly about this that they created the means to do so, a method of communication from woman to woman, hidden in obscure stories written on the quilts they sewed, the baskets they wove, the pottery they designed, the songs they sang, the poems they created, and in the minds of the families they raised. Had this language and method of education been discovered, there would likely have been mass imprisonments or executions.

But these women were as emotionally committed to secrecy as they were to their purpose, and the *Nu Shu* was not discovered by the rulers. Despite their oppressions – for millennia, China was a society where only men were publicly allowed to read or write – in stark, simple characters, the women communicated and taught the wisdom they had gained. Their writings could be easily recognized by the trained eye, but were virtually insignificant to those who did not know what to look for. The *Nu Shu* would be sketched on the borders and between the lines of traditional Chinese writing, or sewed in handkerchiefs, fans, clothing, and napkins sent as unassuming gifts. Through the *Nu Shu*, many insights are given on what was called the Sacred Way of Living. These teachings were brought into the ebb and flow of everyday life for millions of women whose consciences called them to risk their lives to become educated. By circumstance, they were forced to transcend, in secrecy, their society's harsh inequalities and impoverishments of gender. It was through a shared sense of purpose and conscience – which, in turn, brought forth courage and commitment – that these women, whose names are lost in time, persevered and won an astonishing measure of success for their heartfelt cause.

Such commitment and ingenuity are essential elements of emotional depth. I contend that they inspire, or help activate, what Yale psychologist Robert Sternberg calls *practical intelligence* – the ability to translate hope or theory into meaningful actions and abstract ideas into practical accomplishments.[27] They are also about calling upon the determination to undertake the hard and treacherous task of leading ourselves and others through tough times, choosing to go forward into unchartered territory, and learning when to follow through courageously.

Advancing with Commitment and Courage

It was a Saturday in mid-summer 1960. I was nine years old. My grandfather Downing and my mother had taken my younger sister, brother, and me to go swimming at the community pond, an old gravel pit that had been converted by the town park board into a swim area.

It was early afternoon. Not long after we had all headed in for a swim, the lifeguards began waving their arms and screaming for everyone to get out of the water. Minutes later, we stood shivering on the beach, watching as my grandfather waded out to meet one of the lifeguards who handed him the limp body of a teenage boy. The mass of people backed away from the water's edge as my grandfather, the city's senior physician and surgeon, set the boy on the sand and checked for signs of life. At once he began resuscitation efforts.

Courage . . . is nothing less than the power to overcome danger, misfortune, fear, injustice, while continuing to affirm inwardly that life with all its sorrows is good; that everything is meaningful even if in a sense beyond our understanding; and that there is always tomorrow.

Dorothy Thompson, 1894–1961, US journalist

We squirmed through the crowd to get up close. I wanted to watch him bring the teenager back to life. I was sure that out of the corner of his eye he saw me. For what seemed a very long time, he worked to restore breathing and a heart beat. Many in the crowd were crying as they watched. There was an ambulance siren wailing in the distance, drawing closer.

But it was too late. The boy had drowned. His friends were sobbing, saying they noticed when he didn't return to surface after diving off one of the deep-water rafts, and they signalled a lifeguard who dived to the bottom of the pond and found him there. When my grandfather finally rose to his feet to speak with the boy's parents, who had just arrived, and the ambulance attendants, he looked exhausted. But his voice was quiet and assuring. The parents knew and trusted him. Before long the paramedics were placing the body on a stretcher and covering it with a blanket. My grandfather led the way through the crowd to the ambulance, which left the park area with sirens silenced.

Soon afterwards, the lifeguards reopened the pond for swimming. The large crowd dispersed. About half of the people left the area, heading out on the main road by car or bicycle. Some of the rest headed back into the water, splashing and talking. Others milled around. Not long after that, my grandfather came up beside me on the beach. I was standing off from my brother and sister, who were splashing their feet in the shallow water. Unable to get the image of the dead boy out of my mind. I didn't want to go back in. Grandfather put his hand on my shoulder. 'What are you feeling right now?' he asked me quietly.

'Nothing . . .' I started to say, stammering. 'Afraid,' I admitted at last, 'to go in.'

'Because you might drown like that boy did?'

'Yes.'

'A lot of people are feeling upset or afraid about what happened,' he said. 'They –'

'But I could *die* out there,' I remember blurting out, pointing to the water.

'Yes,' he answered. 'But *out there* in the water is no more dangerous than *out there* on the highway.' He swept his upraised arm toward the two-lane road in the distance. 'The truth is, people can die anywhere. Sooner or later, all of us die. But a lot of us don't ever really *live*.'

'What do you mean?'

'What I mean is not very many of us have the faith and courage to take risks and do things we want to do but which we're afraid of. Faith is what your heart believes is possible, or true, even when your mind can't prove it. When you first learned to swim, Robert, you needed faith to go in the water and to try. And then, when it wasn't easy, when you first went into the deep water, you needed courage to face your fears and listen to your teachers, to stick to it and learn. You began to excel at it. Lots of people who could be great at something in life like swimming, and enjoy it, give it up. Something frightens them and they don't go back into the water. I can tell that right now you feel afraid. That's nothing to be ashamed of. What matters is, how much faith and courage will it take for you to go back into the water?'

'I don't know.'

He looked me straight in the eyes and said softly, 'How are you going to find out?'

Many times since then I've heard that question echoing in my mind and felt it in my chest. He didn't tell me what to do. He asked me how I was going to find out. He was holding me accountable to my own conscience, to my unique potential. What if I had quit then and there or run away? He knew that I would have to face my fears again, sooner or later.

I went back into the water that day in 1960, and years later after my grandfather had faced a long battle with cancer and died, I went on to become an All-America swimmer.

I encourage my professional audiences and executive clients to do some deep reflecting on their lives and work. I ask them to write down highlights of two or three of their

Courage is what it takes to stand up and speak; courage is also what it takes to sit down and listen.

Winston Churchill

most important stories of times when they've called upon faith or courage, or been held accountable to their best effort and have emotionally committed to it, and what the outcome has been. I encourage you to take out a notebook right now and invest several minutes in this simple exercise.

$P \times (C + A) > R$

Purpose × (Commitment + Accountability) > Resistance

Consider that almost every worthwhile accomplishment requires transcending some level of *resistance* to change, represented by the R in the above formula. It may be your own internal resistance that gets in the way, or a determined foe, group mindset, or ingrained organizational attitude. In the simple, symbolic EQ equation above, each element on the left may be rated from zero (lowest) to ten (highest). P gauges the clarity and depth of your *purpose*, either your life purpose in the case of a major career decision, for example, or your specific business purpose in a given situation. The C is your current level of *commitment* to conducting yourself in accordance with that purpose, and A represents the depth of your personal or group *accountability*, that is, how fully you are willing to be held accountable for your adherence – in words and actions – to your purpose and commitment.

In a perfect world, the highest product from multiplying the factors on the left would be 200. The lowest, zero. And how high might the R go? You be the judge. Let's say, for the sake of example, that the peak is 175, meaning there is almost always *some* way to transcend it. Whatever R happens to be in any given circumstance, in order to make progress you must be able to reach a higher number with $P \times (C + A)$. Which is why I believe this simple equation is worth pondering. When we're unclear about our purpose, or dabble at commitment and accountability, or brush off the voice of conscience and hesitate to step forward with courage, we usually lose. And then many of us tend to blame everything and everyone but ourselves – or *only* ourselves, which can be just as demoralizing and counter-productive. That's life, we say. However, as even this simple equation suggests, no it isn't.

As Will Rogers observed, 'Even if you're on the right track, you'll get run over if you just sit there.' It is up to leaders to demonstrate their commitment through sincere personal conviction; by announcing choices openly, for example, and making the subsequent actions visible, we offer tangible, unequivocal evidence of our commitment to purpose. 'People can smell *emotional commitment* (and the absence thereof) from a mile away,' observes Tom Peters,[28] who notes that a leader who is not passionately committed to a cause will not inspire or draw much commitment from others. 'I choose people with my nose ... what else is there?' asks Paul Fentener van Vlissingen, CEO of SHV Holdings, a $11 billion company that sells energy and consumer goods, headquartered in the city of Utrecht, Netherlands. 'I don't read psychological reports. I sit down with them and have a dialogue.'[29]

During the remainder of this chapter, we're going to do some exploring of the *C* and *A* in the preceding EQ equation, beginning with several business examples of commitment and courage at work. The first begins over forty years ago, when a young man graduated from the university and took a job as a starting-level professional in a small department at a Japanese company. He worked hard and attentively, but he did something more.[30] On numerous occasions, he contacted corporate executives to point out flaws in the organization – he always offered specific suggestions on how to correct them – and opportunities for improvement and advancement, with practical ideas on how to seize them.

For a decade, his ideas were virtually ignored, but still he kept communicating what he believed, what he noticed and sensed about the enterprise. But one day, as he was leaving work, a manager from corporate headquarters approached the young man. He was led from one building to another, and one elevator to another, finally being ushered into the president's corner suite. He was told that one of his ideas was about to be implemented. The president said he expected it to save an entire division from bankruptcy. Not long afterwards, it did.

Today that young man is Ryuzaburo Kaku, sixty-nine years old and Chairman of the company that once ignored his phone calls and messages from below. But because of his courage as an advocate of improvement, it is a far different organization, one in which creativity and challenging ideas are welcomed at all levels, and celebrated. Canon, the $19-billion maker of copiers, printers, cameras, fax machines, and office automation, employs 68,000 people and holds the leading market share in almost every industry in which it operates. This organization is considered one of the most successful and innovative enterprises on earth, and still is growing.

So, too, is the Swiss watch maker Swatch, back from the brink of hard times. Chairman Nicholas Hayek observes, 'We are convinced that if each of us could add our passion and commitment to an emotional product, we could beat anybody. Emotions are something nobody can copy.'[31]

This is a guiding theme in another of my favourite stories about emotional commitment, courage and faith. Kye Anderson is Chairman, CEO, and President of Medical Graphics, a rapidly growing St Paul, Minnesota medical technology company she founded on her dining-room table. Through it, she found her own unique way passionately and successfully to express her calling and purpose in life.[32] Since 1977, Medical Graphics has invented and produced the lion's share of what's new in cardiorespiratory diagnostic equipment – the graphic presentation of data, the breath-by-breath technique for immediate results, diffusion by gas chromatography, the first fully computerized plethysmograph, and the first FDA-approved expert system for the diagnosis of lung disease.

It all began when Anderson was thirteen and her father had a massive heart attack. He died several days later. Diagnostics in the late 1950s were more an art than a science because physicians had so little objective information to work with, and they had no way of detecting heart disease early enough to prevent a heart attack. Her father's death left her numb for several years and ended up shaping the rest of her life. There were nine children in Anderson's family, and Kye worked her way through school with jobs in hospital laboratories. 'Whenever you do a medical test,' one of her first mentors, a lab director, told her, 'I want you to pretend you're doing it on your father.'

At the time, Anderson thought it was a cruel thing for someone to say, since the lab director know how close she had been to her father. 'But it's something I still say to Medical Graphics employees,' she says now. 'Suppose you bring a parent or a child to an emergency room. Suppose it's your daughter, and she's having trouble breathing. Suppose the nurse wheels up a piece of Medical Graphics equipment to test her with and find out why. What is it you want to feel at that moment? A sense of relief – because you helped build the best equipment in the world, because you know it gives meaningful, accurate results, because it can save your child's life.'

That has been her guiding energy in building Medical Graphics, ever since she got a phone call from Dr Stephen at St Paul Children's Hospital in 1979, pleading with her to develop a piece of equipment to save the life of a dying boy with a respiratory disorder. She had two weeks. She put in calls to suppliers in the Netherlands, Kansas City and Seattle. By overnight express, they shipped her transducers, analyzers, computers, calibrators, pumps, a pneumatachograph for measuring the rate of respiration. 'I put them all together Rube Goldberg-style on my dining-room table,' she remembers. 'What this collection of equipment had to do was measure oxygen and carbon dioxide accurately in each small mass of expired air, translate the results into digital information, feed these data into a computer, and render the combined results precisely, sequentially, instantly, and in a graphic form that a doctor, nurse, or technician could quickly read and understand.' No one had ever done it before. Designing the software alone kept her up until four in the morning ten nights in a row. Using the new equipment, Dr Boros and his staff were able to stabilize the boy's breathing at an adequate, sustainable level. His name was Colin. He lived.

And Medical Graphics was born.

Since 1979, there have been ups and downs, of course, and times when Anderson struggled to learn effective new ways to manage her company as demand rose and sales soared. One of the ways she has managed to keep her organization in a strong leadership position is by seeking out – and winning over to her cause – exceptional advisors and mentors, including Earl Bakken, who developed the first wearable, external, battery-powered transistorized pacemaker in 1957, founded Medtronic, Inc., to produce it, and then took the company from a garage start-up to $1 billion in sales.

I remember when my paternal grandfather died in 1968 of his fifth heart attack. For years, my family and I felt helpless as we watched him deteriorate, and felt his frustration at facing increasing debility and paralysis, with his doctors saying there was nothing they could do. One heart attack after another. There were no Medical Graphics instruments then. I can personally appreciate the passion of purpose with which Anderson approaches her life's work. With incredible intensity of purpose and commitment, she invented a technology, sold her ideas to doctors and investors, and built a corporation with 130 employees and $24 million in sales.

Anderson's and Kaku's stories remind me that it was Albert Einstein who, throughout his writings, encouraged us to take the business of making progress into our own hands; to insist on thinking and feelings our own thoughts and feelings, even if they are not blessed by consent from the crowd; and to rebel against the presumed inevitability or orthodoxy of ideas that do not meet the test of an original mind and heart.

From time to time, stop and ask yourself: am I an *advocate* of improvement, of unconventional ideas that serve the best interests of others as well as myself? Am I not just *in favour* of these, but am I *openly* passionately committed to their realization, speaking out, jotting notes, making calls, and engaging others in dialogue about them?

Courage emboldens such capabilities as the willingness to take a stand, to raise your voice, to face pain and rejection, to act with honour and grace under pressure, to maintain your values in the face of opposition and fear. It also means having the courage to be vulnerable and authentic in ways such as risking failure, making – and admitting – mistakes, asking for help, acknowledging that you don't know something and then having the gumption to go learn it. This is not to overlook the fact that in life and work there *are* things that warrant a healthy dose of fear, times when the voice of caution delays an inappropriate reactionary comment, for example, or tempers foolish courage.

Most managers are, by tradition and training, experts at caution, which in many situations is indeed an asset. We're skilled critics and cynics, trained to go after every weakness and we can shoot holes in virtually any idea or initiative, and have fun doing it. But, more often than not, what enables us to create a successful future is courage, not caution. And we could all do some soul-searching on what, exactly, we believe in enough to advocate, to reach down in our heart and step up to the line, to identify and seize opportunities, and have the guts to learn through what we feel as well as what we think, and through our stumbles and setbacks as well as our successes. In the words of Deborah Smithart, Brinker International's Executive Vice-President, 'Making a mistake used to mean you were fired or ostracized. Today it's more like if you don't see a person making mistakes, they're probably not pushing hard enough for new opportunities.'[33]

Transformational Change Begins One Person at a Time

There is a long-standing theory that says organizations can only be changed from the top down. It's a strongly supported theory and, in many respects, appears to be valid. Yet there's a contrasting theory that says the world, and organizations, can be changed from the bottom up, by a courageous individual advocate of change, or a small, dedicated group.

Wisdom is knowing what to do, virtue is doing it.

David Starr Jordan, Forbes

Recall the stories of Rachel Carson and Harriet Tubman. Consider, as well, the story of John Woolman,[34] a man whom I first learned about in middle school thirty-five years ago and again from Robert Greenleaf a decade ago.[35] Woolman lived in the United States in the 1700s and his literary journals are still studied in many classrooms. Yet this is not what he became best known for.

During his life, many wealthy, conservative Quakers were slave owners. Woolman found the idea of slavery intolerable and, based on a strong sense of conscience and purpose, he committed his entire adult life to eliminating the practice of slavery among members of his religion. He set about accomplishing this through the art of kind yet persistent persuasion. Over a twenty-year period, he visited thousands of Quakers along the East Coast. He did not criticize or infuriate them. Instead he asked questions, such as 'What does it mean to be a person of good, strong character, a moral person? What does it mean to own a slave? What does it mean to give a slave to one's children?' He persisted courageously, advocating reflection through questions, believing it would lead others to make their own clear choices and changes, and trusting that a wrong could be righted by individual voluntary action. He visited valley after valley, and farm after farm.

By 1770, prior to the Revolutionary War and a full century before the Civil War, not a single Quaker owned a slave. In fact, the Quakers were the first group to step up and publicly renounce slavery. John Woolman, a purposeful man with a vision and courage, transformed his church. What might have been possible if there had been ten John Woolmans, or a hundred, journeying across the colonies in the 1700s, persuading people, one by one, through non-judgmental questions and heart-felt advocacy?

We know now from the perspective of history that a small shift in tensions might have prevented the Civil War, with its 600,000 lost lives, and lasting trauma that can be linked across time to social problems today. Since first learning of his story, I have believed there must have been John

Woolmans in America at the time. But they did not have the courage he did to follow their conscience and purpose, to find every possible way to help right a wrong and shape a better future.

EQ Map Connections: Commitment
You may want to refer to the following scales of the *EQ Map* as points of reflection related to this chapter: pressures and satisfactions, emotional expression, emotional awareness of other intentionality, interpersonal connection, compassion, outlook, trust radius, and integrity.

Holding Yourself Accountable to Your Best, and Others to Theirs

John Woolman spent his life working courageously to hold himself and others accountable to their inner truth. Instead of giving advice, he opened his heart and lived by it, sharing his own direct experience with others, and asking questions that made them stop and reflect – and eventually prompted many of them to change their attitude and actions. He made a dif-

When there is not wind, row.

Portuguese proverb

ference and left a legacy, but what if others had felt as deeply as he did – and had, in turn, held more of those around them accountable? If we do not hold ourselves accountable for what we experience, we attempt to hold someone else, or circumstances, accountable. And if we are not satisfied with what we experience, we seek to change it by manipulating the other person. Blaming and complaining, for example, are usually an attempt, or ploy, to make someone else responsible for what we experience and to fix things for us.

The problem, of course, is that we cannot know what another person will do. Whether on or off the job, we cannot depend upon another person for the experiences we believe are vital to our wellbeing and success. To commit emotionally to a purpose and be accountable for our experiences along the way requires that we 'take into account' unique talents and passions, our own and those of others. This also requires that we put an end to 'happy talk' in which we lull ourselves into a false sense of security about our job or our company's future. We must step up to question those who keep reminding us, 'Sure we've got some tough challenges, but it'll all work out – look at everything we've accomplished.' Almost always it's better to be specific and accountable.

There's a phrase in West Africa called 'deep talk'. When a person is informed about a situation, an older person will often share a parable or axiom, and then add to the end of it, 'Take that as deep talk.' Meaning you may never find the answer. You continue to go down deeper and deeper.

Maya Angelou, US Poet

What important experiences in your life have been shaped by a deep sense of emotional commitment and accountability, or a clear lack of these driving forces? Reflect on this for several minutes and write down your perspective. How does this affect the way you emotionally commit – or resist committing – to the things you feel are most important in your current life and work?

In what specific ways do you hold yourself and others accountable? For example, do you have a *confidant*, a close, trusted friend or colleague with whom you regularly – perhaps once a week – openly share your toughest challenges and innermost dilemmas? There is evidence that engaging in this kind of dialogue may improve your health and advance your career.[36] The best *confidants* are drawn from among the people you highly respect, and who value – and have a clear and at least basic understanding of – your work. They are good listeners and are unafraid to be emotionally honest with you, asking hard questions of character and growth, encouraging you to pay attention to things you may be too busy to notice on your own, challenging you to step up, and holding you to your best. Whether on your own or with a trusted *confidant*, you might begin to monitor one yardstick of personal progress by regularly noticing where you stand in four broad categories of emotional commitment and accountability:[37]

- off track
- going through the motions
- putting forth best effort
- transformational growth

One of the simplest and most effective ways I know to educate or strengthen our accountability is to make and keep promises; to learn what we are capable of doing with our unique potential, and what others are capable of doing with theirs, and then openly saying what we will commit to and committing to what we say. Along the way, we stay aware of how deep our continuing emotional commitment is, and that of others as well. If we find ourselves getting *off track* or just *going through the motions*, we stop to reassess where we are. The dark side of commitment is blind perseverance and martyrdom. Yet if we're acting on-purpose, and in alignment with our unique potential, then we find it feels right to recommit, day after day, to *putting forth our best effort* and, whenever possible, reaching for the stars by breaking out of daily routines, stretching ourselves, accepting the challenge to learn and excel in new ways, and thereby generating *transformational growth* – not just repeating past habits but effectively changing who you are as you create the future.

It is this kind of emotional drive – from none to all, from stop-and-go to continual – that largely determines how closely and consistently we align with the inner compass of our unique potential and purpose. It calls us forward to stay the course with courage and advocacy. This, in turn, could elicit in us a sense of responsibility and, more specifically, accountability – we are willing to be emotionally honest with ourselves about where we are and how we are doing, and to empathize with others and be honest enough to hold them to their best, too. This does not mean *telling* others what they should do, which nearly all of us instinctively resent and reject. It's about caring enough better to understand others and relate to them by sharing *our own direct experience* of struggling, searching, committing, falling, and climbing upwards again.

When Mahatma Gandhi left the scene of India's political power in 1946 to visit riot-torn states, he was seventy-seven years old. His schedule was brutal and packed with appointments. He worked fifteen to eighteen hours a day and walked 116 miles in sixty days to meet with victims in forty-six villages. In the midst of terrible savagery walked a man with the courage to fulfil his commitment to truth and non-violence.[38] That's accountability. And without a word of advice – instead, simply through the power of his presence and example – others stepped up to hold themselves accountable, too, and joined him.

Emotional commitment is not only a barometer in personal initiative, accountability, and successful hiring, it's also one of the underlying forces that helps see us through hard times. Horst Schulze, President of the Ritz-Carlton Hotel Company, remembers a stretch of recession that hurt his company and the hotel industry in general: 'The other day, one of my vice-presidents said, "You know, maybe the biggest accomplishment in our ten years is that we're still good friends." He mentioned that I did what I had to do – re-energize them, and keep re-energizing them. What was hardest, however, was to re-energize myself every day. At one point, I put Post-It notes all around to remind myself not to give up, to stay committed and do the right thing, not the convenient short-term thing or what seemed right to others, but to do the right thing.'[39]

Schulze held himself accountable. Some executives I know favour the phrase, 'If it's to be, it's up to me.' They don't mean this as blind faith or martyrdom or an avoidance of delegation; they mean it as a statement of accountability. This is an aspect of emotional depth that invokes a willingness, and an inner drive, to take responsibility for leading the way and being accountable not only to, and for, yourself and your own best effort and principles, but also to hold others accountable to theirs. In some organizations this is known as the Brothers' Keeper principle.[40]

This may have arisen, in part, from Dr Albert Schweitzer's writings on medicine, music and education, which in 1913 had already received much recognition when he went to Gabon, in what was then French Equatorial Africa, in order to build a hospital.[41] In answer to the question he kept asking himself, am I my brother's keeper? he answered: 'How could I not be? I cannot escape my responsibility.' He insisted that all human beings counted as brothers, and his obligation was to respect them, help those in need wherever he found them, and to learn about them and hold them accountable to their own best effort, whatever that was.

Accountability is generated from within your heart; it cannot be 'given' from outside. It prompts you to avoid finger-pointing and blame, and, instead, to sense – and catch – emerging problems and opportunities early on, and accept a role in responding to them.

Working with an Active Conscience

Accountability is principally a call from your conscience, which can be considered, in essence, the deepest voice of your intuition. Its frequent proddings are variously felt as internal nudges, twinges, pushes or, for some people, as 'God's voice in your ear'. Through gut feelings and heart-level intuition, the conscience urges us to attend to our unique potential and stay closely aligned with our purpose and integrity. A trained conscience is developed through personal reflection and exploring emotional depths. But without a commitment to emotional honesty, what some of us 'hear' in our heads as conscience is actually rationalization.

Many of us were raised believing that conscience is about twinges of guilt or shame for not being good enough or not doing something right. That's not what we're talking about here. Instead, conscience inspires and drives us to stay in integrity and find and follow our life's calling with courage and emotional commitment. It's not a guilt trip; it's an asset.

Every human being has work to do and influence to exert, which are peculiarly his, and which no conscience but his own can teach him to attend.

William Ellery Channing, nineteenth-century social reformer and author

Conscience is an inner voice aligned with the compass to our destiny. It calls upon the best of who we are, hidden or lost though that may seem at times, and encourages us to hold others accountable to their best selves, as well. One simple effective way to educate or strengthen our conscience is to make and keep promises; to say what you will commit to and commit to what you say. And then follow through – courageously, and with accountability.

Begin small. You might make and keep a few basic new promises to yourself, for example, such as to get up earlier each morning and exercise, or to forego some television time each night to take a walk with the family or to sit together and talk. Conscience works best when backed with a sense of faith, courage, and accountability. When you happen to fall down in failure or make a mistake, conscience calls on us to face it straight-on, and ask, 'What can I learn from this?'

With important questions, listen to your conscience for answers, not just to your rationalizing mind. In the words of American educator John Sloan Dickey, 'The purpose of education is to see men made whole, both in competence and conscience. For to create the power of competence without creating a corresponding direction to guide the use of that power is bad education. Furthermore, competence will finally disintegrate apart from conscience.'

Today most of us live and work in places inundated with noise, activity, media, and urgency. We lose our conscience. Or, rather, it gets drowned out. It is only when we step back for a moment to commit to searching deeply, and with an honest heart, that we once again begin to feel our conscience and its wisdom.

To help demonstrate the power of conscience, conduct the following experiment.[42] For the next several minutes, find a quiet place. Reflect on the relationships you care most deeply about in your business and life. These could be with a key client, customer, partner, boss, supplier, employee, spouse, parent, child, or friend. Choose one of these relationships that you sense needs to be deepened or improved. As you reflect on that relationship, call upon your conscience and ask yourself the question, what, specifically, could I do to deepen or improve this relationship?

As you consider the question, listen to your deep inner self.

Does an answer come?

When you sense an answer, ask yourself, how confident am I that doing this will deepen or improve the relationship?

I have found with professional audiences and executive teams that nearly everyone has some immediate sense of a practical way to make a change, and they are confident that this change will improve the relationship. Often they can't *explain* precisely why this change could make a real difference. They simply 'know' it's the right thing to do and it would work. That's conscience.

Just to be sure, ask yourself, is this action consistent with my purpose and integrity?

Almost always I find that the answer is yes.

Another way to deepen and activate conscience is to make a list of the things done to you – or that you've done to others – that you have abhorred. Call upon your conscience to help you keep from doing them to others, ever. Make a second list, this one of the things done for you by others which have meant the most in your work or life. Enlist your conscience to help you notice when to do them for others from now on.

From the purpose, conscience, and emotional commitment there naturally arises a sense of integrity. And it is this latter quality of emotional depth that serves as the capstone of character and is essential to self-respect and credibility in business and life. These are among the central themes of the next chapter.

CHAPTER 11

Applied Integrity

One of my first lessons in integrity came the hard way. I was in first grade and my grandfather Cooper had 'hired' me to clean up some brush in his yard. It was a Saturday morning and I was trying to get the task over with. The week before I had promised my grandfather I would help, but had no idea that on this particular morning the children in my neighbourhood would be playing a baseball game, and I wanted to be there, not working.

First we must understand that there can be no life without risk – and when our center is strong, everything else is secondary, even the risks.

Elie Wiesel, Holocaust survivor and Nobel laureate

'It won't take long,' my grandfather promised me. 'This is how you build integrity.'

'What's that?' I asked.

My father's father was a large man, nearly seventy, a former detective, wilderness guide, surveyor, community leader and school superintendent, with a square jaw, vice-like handshake and penetrating blue-grey eyes. He had suffered four heart attacks and was still not fully recovered from having his back broken years earlier when a drunk driver ran a red light and hit his car. He walked with a cane, but he still did hard physical work every day, just more slowly than he used to. He bent down to face me and talked, as he always did, as if I were grown and not a child. 'Robert,' he said, 'integrity is about your character. That's what's inside you, in your heart. You promised me you'd do some work for me. You came here because you knew it was the right thing to do, even though you're missing part of a baseball game. That's integrity. Let's get the job done.'

I nodded and went to work. After a while, he excused himself, saying he had to go into the house to make some business calls on the phone.

I gathered up armfuls of brush and carried them to the pile to be burned.

After about ten minutes or so, all I could think about was how great it would feel to be playing baseball instead of doing this. The brush was scratching my arms and face. My integrity, whatever exactly that was, was less important to me every passing minute. Instead of picking up full armfuls of brush I began tossing some of it back into the shadows of the adjoining woods. Before long, I wasn't carrying anything across the yard to the burn pile. I was scattering it into the woods. At last there was no more brush along the edge of the yard.

I hurried to grandfather's front door and called out, 'There! I'm all finished.'

I'll never forget the look he gave me. 'Before I pay you, come walk with me, Robert,' he said. I followed him as he moved with difficulty across the yard to the woods. 'You didn't do the job you promised me you'd do. Why not?'

'Yes, I did!' I lied.

He said nothing, waiting. It was then that I realized he must have been watching me from the window.

'But it's all cleaned up. That's what you wanted, wasn't it?' I protested.

'No, that's not what I wanted, and you know it.'

I remember rolling up my eyes or grumbling.

He said, 'I hired you to move all the brush I had cleared from the woods over to the pile to be burned. Instead, you scattered a lot of it back into the woods.'

He waited again.

'So what do you want me to do about it, grandfather?'

'The question, Robert, is what are *you* going to do about it? This is about integrity.'

'What do you mean?'

'With integrity, here's what you would volunteer to do. First, you would apologize to me for breaking my trust. And promise me it will not happen again. And then you would go into the woods and clear out not only the brush you threw back in there, but more. When you're finished, you would come and tell me, and then we'll inspect the results together.' He paused. 'And, last, you will refuse to take my money when I offer to pay you.'

Which is exactly how things happened. Fortunately, for my own character development, I was caught. I suffered a humiliating reminder of right and wrong: I had cheated. I had 'finished' only because I had broken my agreement. I missed the entire baseball game. I made no money. But I came face to face with integrity.

Like most of us, there have been many times over the years when I've found myself slipping out of integrity, and making mistakes or damaging relationships because of it. Almost invariably, there comes a sharp twinge in my conscience and a moment when I remember my grandfather – when I feel his presence again – and correct my course.

Virtually all managers believe they behave with integrity, yet in practice many of us struggle with how to *apply* effectively a sense of integrity in our actions and interactions. Some managers and professionals assume that integrity is the same as blind loyalty and discretion, or keeping secrets from others. Some think it requires narrow or rigid consistency, even in a false or damaging cause, while others believe it's honesty, pure and simple, or a ban on outright lies. All of these views miss the mark. In essence, integrity in business means accepting full responsibility, communicating clearly and openly, keeping promises, avoiding hidden agendas, and having the courage to lead yourself and your team or enterprise with honour, which includes knowing, and being consistently honest with, yourself, not only in mind but heart.

Can Integrity Be Developed?

There are many people who say that integrity and ethics sometimes have to take a back seat to expediency and profits. Many others maintain that the purpose of leadership is not to listen and serve but to acquire power and privilege. Many people are wrong. At work, integrity requires a commitment to dialogue and evaluation – involving yourself and others – of what is right not rote. It comes down to being authentic with yourself, being authentic with others, and doing the things you say you will do. According to David Kolb, Chairman of the organizational behaviour department at Case Western University, integrity is a concept describing the highest form of human intelligence.[43] Integrity, asserts Kolb, is a sophisticated integrative consciousness and a deep state of processing experience in the world in ways that encompass creativity, values, intuitive and emotional capabilities, as well as rational-analytic powers. Can integrity be developed? According to researchers, the answer is yes.

Integrity can be seen as a deepening and expansion of emotional honesty. It bespeaks a unifying process. Integrity works. It's not just a good idea, it is a compelling core feeling based on your own set of operating principles rather than a rigid code of behaviour. It is often contended that emotions are without judgment, or at least without *sound* or *good* judgment, but I am among those who believe that, on the contrary, emotions and passions are themselves intuitive judgments of the most important kind, and from which our integrity is born and upheld.[44] Echoing this, philosopher Robert Solomon, whose writings are among my personal favourites of the past two decades, insists that our emotions are *constitutive* judgments according to which our reality – and integrity – is given shape and structure.[45]

I have often thought that the best way to define a man's character would be to seek out the particular ... attitude in which, when it came upon him, he felt himself most deeply and intensively active and alive. At such moments, there is a voice inside which speaks and says, 'This is the real me.'

William James, Letters of William James, 1878

Furthermore, it is through this strongly inward and intuitive sense of integrity that there emerges a resonance, or force field, of energy, creativity, pride and possibility. Integrity is also *interactional*, involving the management of relationships between one individual and the surrounding others, between one group within the context of other groups.[46]

Three Core Characteristics of Personal Integrity

Integrity – or as I prefer to call it, *applied* integrity – can be seen as calling upon a deepened sense of conscience and prompting you to have the courage to act upon it. According to Stephen L. Carter, professor of law at Yale University, integrity requires three central elements:[47]

1. *Discerning* what is right and what is wrong;
2. *Acting* on what you have discerned, even at personal cost; and
3. *Saying openly* that you are acting on your understanding of right from wrong.

The first criterion captures the idea of integrity as requiring what Carter calls a 'degree of moral reflectiveness', in which every dimension of intelligence – IQ, EQ, and others – are coordinated and brought to bear on an issue or problem.

The second criterion brings in the ideal of a person of integrity as steadfast, making clear commitments and keeping them, even at personal risk. We especially admire this forthrightness aspect of integrity in our leaders, trusting them to say what they truly believe and feel, and to be exceedingly clear about what they mean, even at risk to themselves or their career.

The third criterion underscores the fact that a person of integrity is unashamed of doing what he or she believes is true and right and good, and does so by openly acting and speaking on behalf of what he or she believes, showing a steadfast devotion to principle yet being willing to temper this, according to specific circumstances, and with compassion.

One cannot have integrity without being honest, yet one can certainly be honest but have little integrity. By this I mean that a person may be honest without ever engaging in the hard work of discerning right from wrong in each specific situation, or taking into account the context and feelings and timing involved. He may state truthfully an honest belief without ever stopping first to confirm that it is appropriate to *this* unique situation, thereby ascertaining that, indeed, this belief must be stated and acted upon *now* because it is good and right and true in this circumstance. As Carter reminds us, 'The problem may be as simple as someone foolishly saying something that hurts a friend's feelings; a few moments of thought would have revealed the likelihood of the hurt and the lack of necessity for the comment. Or the problem may be more complex, as when a man who is raised from birth in a society that preaches racism states his belief in racial inferiority as a fact, without ever stopping to think that perhaps this deeply held view is wrong. Certainly the racist is being honest – he is telling us what he actually does think – but his honesty does not add up to integrity.'[48]

There is evidence suggesting that only from the depths of integrity are we humans empowered to reach upwards with our finest creative talents.[49] If you sense, for example, that something isn't being said in a conversation, it usually pays to stop things right there and say so. If you're gut hunch is wrong, you'll find out soon enough. But if you don't say something you will likely carry the feeling of doubt or concern away with you, which weighs you down, creatively speaking, because a small portion of your mind and heart will still be occupied with it, the same portions of you that need to be free for creative breakthroughs.

One of the greatest branches of integrity is to tell yourself, 'Only I will know.' Only I will know if I betray my convictions and values. Only I will know if I am unethical with people who trust me. Only I will know that I have no intention of honouring my promise. The implication is that your own judgment is not significant and only the judgment of others matters. But this is not true. Your heart *will* know. Others will sense this, too. And your integrity will be gone.

Consider the following true story told by Jack Hawley:[50]

Patrick, a consultant working with an apparently successful company, senses something is wrong. Despite the outward success, the atmosphere in the executive suite is flat and lifeless. How can this be?

He talks with senior managers throughout the company, trying to get a handle on the vanished energy. Slowly the answer pieces itself together: 'creative bookkeeping'. They have always lived a policy of going right up to the line of legality relative to taxes; recently they have tripped over that line a few times. Finding it so easy, they have taken up residence there, and it's sapping their vitality.

What to do? Patrick knows the motivational project they hired him for won't work while this pall hangs over the place. He takes the weekend to mull it over, listening for directions from his inner truth.

On Monday he walks into the president's office and recommends a full IRS audit. 'A what?!!' Yes. He tells them for their own good to call in the Federal Revenue agents. Is he out of his mind? What is this, Irish chutzpah? The advice all but empties the account of goodwill that he had built up with them.

But this isn't only the story of Patrick's courage. It's about leadership heart, too. After some heavy agonizing and palpitations – and some good, clear planning – the company leaders decide to do it: they request an audit! It ends up costing them a few million dollars in back taxes and penalties. Ouch! But vitality comes home – and creativity comes with it. Their profits soar again.

I once mentioned this story to the president of a large financial firm. His reaction was immediate. 'Yeah, that was a smart move,' his head bobbing forward as he said it, 'not only honest but also practical.' He explained the dreadful drain of money, time and spirit that double-dealing causes – and how all this casts a cloud over everything. His message: be brave, own up to your shortcomings and breathe the fresh air of integrity.

D × (A + V) = I
Discernment × (Action + Voice) = Integrity

Consider this bare-bones EQ equation that I've found to be useful for encouraging executive and management groups to reflect on three core characteristics of integrity. *D* is a measure of the depth and commitment you have right now in *discerning* – in heart and mind – what's right from what's wrong in a given circumstance. This requires paying considerable – and careful – attention to what you're feeling and what's going on around you. *A* represents the depth of your willingness to *act* on whatever personal truth you've felt and discerned about what's right or wrong in this particular circumstance. And, once you've committed yourself to take action, *V* is for the degree to which you're willing to own this inner personal truth and give *voice* to it, sharing your convictions forthrightly with others, not only yourself. The product *I* represents a hypothetical rating for your present level of applied *integrity*. By scoring each factor on a scale of zero (lowest) to ten (highest), the peak score – likely reserved, at least in many cases, for saints and archangels – is 200. The lowest? Zero.

Let's say you're making a decision about calling a customer with some unexpected bad news. A defect has been found in one of your company's products. It's a small thing, probably, nothing that will cause injury or loss of life, although it would be costly if the defect were to show up during a production run or in the middle of some other work process at the customer's company. Chances of this happening? The R&D people say one in a thousand, maybe one in ten thousand. What do you do?

First, consider the *D* in our equation, for discernment. You're at the end of a hell of a long work day, and this is not what you wanted to hear. You know it's a relatively inexpensive product but that on-sight repair or installation costs would be horrendous. And the timing couldn't be much worse for you; this is a tight year, financially speaking, at your company and you are up for performance review in a month, and there are rumours that more layoffs are likely soon. And then there's the fact that the customer happens to be one of your best, whether or not that actually matters in this case. If you call the executive in charge and give her the news, what will happen? No way to know for sure: lost business, perhaps, and a demand to replace all similar products, even those from previous production runs with no known defects? What if you told her the news and explained the nearly non-existent risk to her company, and offered to get a crew of technicians there for a speedy replacement if, at any point, there was a sign of a problem?

You stop yourself, now, and try to stem the chorus of rationalizing voices in your mind. What's really the right thing to do here? Back to the formula: *Discernment × (Action + Voice) = Integrity.* In this vein, dig deeper and, using the preceding hypothetical and admittedly sketchy example, rate yourself on a scale of one to ten for *D*, deep discernment.

Once you've done whatever you're presently going to do to determine right from wrong, how willing are you to *act* on this determination, to do whatever is necessary to see it through? What, for example, are the possible political ramifications of your decision for your job, career and company, and how much would you let such considerations constrain you from taking action? Accordingly, rate yourself from one to ten on the *A* in the equation.

And finally, how committed are you to giving voice – the *V* in this simple formula – to your discernment and action? In other words, you are making a certain level of effort to distinguish right from wrong, and then you are taking some level of action to do what you've determined is right. Consequently, will you then try to get this whole integrity thing out of your mind and heart right away, to go through the motions and, in effect, act with integrity *unconsciously*? Or will you *actively reflect* on what you've discerned and are doing – and will you *clearly and openly share this with others who are affected or involved?* That's the true *V* rating. Now multiply $D \times (A + V)$ to get a rough gauge of your integrity in this situation. Note that for each of the factors there is no clear-cut 'best' answer across the board. Integrity is, by definition, deep and always personal.

No doubt you could come up with a long list of real-life 'test cases' that examine the $D \times (A + V)$ of your personal integrity; probably some of them have occurred within the past hour, or past business day.

Living and working with integrity requires that each of us be willing to do the hard work of discernment, to explore our feelings and perspectives, and those of others, to make the considerable effort to determine what – for each of us as individuals, and for us as groups – is right in every given work circumstance. It's an ongoing process that many people engage in once in a while but seem loathe to commit to as a *way of working*. It requires courage and dialogue, through which we ask hard questions, acknowledging that there are few perfectly clear or easy answers. Ready for some further soul-searching on the subject? Read Stephen Carter's (*integrity*) (yes, that's how he writes the title).

Over the next several weeks, I encourage you to do some quick maths each time you're faced with a choice that calls upon your integrity. How do you score when no one else but you knows whether you're in or out of integrity? Which of the three factors on the left side of the formula tends to be the lowest? That may be a good place to focus on making improvements. Without some kind of simple tool or technique to make integrity more explicit, it remains murky in the minds of many managers, or a mystery, and it's too easy for us to ignore it, even at the highest levels of an organization.

I recall a situation about five years ago when I had flown to New York with two of my business colleagues to meet a wealthy, well-known investor who heads a Wall Street venture capital firm. On the flight with me was the founder of a high-tech healthcare initiative, and beside him was a former CEO who over a decade had taken a media and manufacturing corporation from $6 million a year in revenues to $600 million. I was serving as US consultant for the initiative, which after $4 million in investments for prototypes, patents, and beta testing had, to date, produced a solid success record. We were headed to Wall Street seeking venture capital for a full-scale launch in America. A government-backed technology investment firm had just conducted a due diligence process on the initiative and was offering several million dollars of first-round funding.

In advance of our meeting, we had sent the investor letters of reference, descriptive materials, quotes from medical and healthcare experts involved with the project, and a document building a strong case for our concept, citing hundreds of scientific and medical studies. The day before our arrival, we confirmed the meeting. Yes, he had read our materials and was very interested, said his secretary.

When we arrived, he was not there. He ended up keeping us waiting in his conference room for an hour and a half. I remember his colonial-era oil paintings. And the massive walnut conference table and elaborately decorated chairs. All antiques. For all I know, George Washington sat in this chair, I remember thinking to myself. We spent half an hour talking to his senior aide, explaining our project. His secretary kept stepping into the room and apologizing, 'He knew you were coming.' 'I just phoned him again.' 'Yes, he knows you are waiting.'

At last, he walked into the room. I'm not sure what I had expected, but this wasn't it. With slumped shoulders and distended abdomen, he wore polyester trousers hemmed high above the ankles. The rest of his attire was similarly off kilter. He spoke from the throat, barking at his aides, who were Wall Street bankers. He never looked us in the eye; never acknowledged that we'd been kept waiting or apologized for being late. I tried to get a sense of who he was beneath the surface, his character. But I felt nothing authentic about him, not that day.

'Is there a lot of money in what you're doing?' he asked us point blank, reaching over to the table and tapping his forefinger on our proposal. Before we could reply, he turned to his senior aide and answered his own question. 'I don't believe it. What do you think?'

The aide looked at us and hesitated.

'Well,' he huffed, 'yesterday you agreed it wasn't right for us. Now you're not sure?' He turned back to us. 'I'm not interested. Come talk to me again when you need funding before the IPO. I'll take you public. That's where *I* make money on health companies.'

He reached into his sports jacket pocket and drew out of pack of cigarettes and a lighter. Without a word, three feet away, he lit up and took a long drag. We immediately rose to leave. Enough was enough. He got to his feet and walked over to us. I'll never forget his last words: 'You know, none of this prevention crap' – puff, puff, he blew the smoke directly at us – 'ever works, anyway.'

I walked out of the panelled conference room and never looked back.

Whether or not this man was acting with integrity I cannot say. At the time, it certainly didn't feel like it to me. In hindsight, to give him the benefit of the doubt: perhaps he was dying of some terribly painful disease and, because of this, had grown cantankerous and started smoking as a source of personal comfort in his final days. It's possible, of course, but a long shot, and even if true, he didn't share even a hint of it with us and therefore it wasn't a viable consideration during our interaction.

Bottom line: we never again approached him for funding of the project.

Putting Integrity to Work

It's one thing to discuss and commend integrity – which is something most business people are wont to do. Yet putting it into action requires a keen perception, intuition, and conscience, backed by ongoing reflection. You may know, for instance, that deceiving another person is out of integrity, but may choose to do it anyway to gain a profit or patch up a relationship you don't want to lose. You may know that it is right for you to be compassionate with those less fortunate, yet fail to be because you worry it might cost you prestige or money. Professor William Torbert, of Boston College, teaches self-examination techniques to his business students so that they can grow and develop. The heart of effectiveness, contends Torbert, is building integrity through the constant observation of one's lack of integrity.[51] Integrity is not a personality trait, it's a character trait. It is strong and purposeful. It is deep and reflective.

Take out a piece of paper and jot down short answers to the following five questions related to integrity. Ask yourself honestly the following four questions:

1. What do I stand for?
2. Do I consciously *discern* what is right and what is wrong, *act* on what I have discerned and *say openly* that I am acting on my understanding of right from wrong?
3. What do I hope that we together (a partnership, group or organization) can accomplish – now and in the future?
4. What am I willing – and not willing – to do to achieve this success?

These are the kind of questions used successfully by Robert Webster, a US regional vice-president of sales for SmithKline Beecham, the UK pharmaceutical company that ranks fifth in the world in its industry.[52] Several years ago, I was brought in to design and present a professional development programme for one of the top sales groups at this company just as it was going through a major restructuring and downsizing in its sales force.

The sales leaders responded by committing to clarifying their focus and dealing with 'full integrity' when representing the firm's products to physicians, pharmacists, and the public. They agreed on five core values: integrity, innovation, production, people, and customers. All questionable sales practices that over the years had come to plague the pharmaceutical industry were systematically examined and either rejected or changed to align with the new commitment. One of Webster's goals was to build an expanding trust radius. 'You can count on us,' was the central theme, backed by the mandate for steadfast integrity. It began to pay off almost immediately, and over the next several years sales and profits grew steadily. Webster recently announced the hiring of 400 new sales representatives.

Consider, too, the lessons of Dee Hock, founding CEO of Visa

International, who put integrity first and subsequently produced one of the most impressive success stories in the past thirty years. Since 1970, VISA has grown by approximately 10,000 per cent, continuing to expand at roughly 20 per cent per year, operating with some half a billion clients in over 200 countries around the globe. This year, its annual revenues are expected to crest the $1 trillion mark. Advises Hock: 'Hire and promote first on the basis of integrity; second, motivation; third, capacity; fourth, understanding; fifth, knowledge; and last and least, experience. Without integrity, motivation is dangerous; without motivation, capacity is impotent; without capacity, understanding is limited; without understanding, knowledge is meaningless; without knowledge, experience is blind. Experience is easy to provide and quickly put to good use by people with the other qualities.'[53]

This is something Kathy Masera, President of the *California Job Journal* in Sacramento, learned well. Years ago she had the idea of publishing a newspaper dedicated to job fairs and to providing timely and relevant leads for job seekers and employers.[54] She studied everything she could get her hands on about the industry and invested her own money in launching the company. She had a strong sense of what she needed to do to make a profit on each edition of the journal. She had design, production, and distribution in place. And she was running low on funds. She submitted loan applications to banks and venture capital firms. They turned her down. Masera pursued a number of private investors. Finally, she was able to arrange a meeting with the last investor on her contact list. He listened carefully. He asked some very straightforward questions about her vision for the *California Job Journal* and her skill, management style and integrity in heading the initiative. He offered her a sum far short of the amount she knew was necessary.

At the next meeting, with the investor ready to write her a check, Masera explained that her experience had taught her that underfunding a venture like this would mean failure. She refused his initial offer. After much discussion, they both agreed to the full amount, shook hands and struck a deal. The investor became quiet, opened his desktop drawer and began fumbling for something. Masera watched, a bit uneasy, wondering what was happening. She remained silent while he removed a tattered paper, old and yellowing, and began carefully unfolding it, looking up at her. He cocked his head and smiled, and then cleared his throat to speak. 'Every name on this list, Kathy, has become a millionaire.' He stopped and examined the tattered paper, taking out a pen. 'I'm adding your name to it.' She was the 41st person on the list and the first woman he had ever backed with an investment. She and her husband now run the company and have a thriving business with thirty employees.

Unfortunately, unlike SmithKline Beecham, Visa International, and Kathy Masera's *California Job Journal*, many people and many companies seem to operate under the assumption that integrity is either something you're born with or you have. For the most part, it's not, and that's something Kevin Dolan learned during the time he was a professional and executive with J. Walter Thompson Advertising. One of his favourite integrity stories is about Norman Strauss, Chairman of the agency in the early 1960s:[55]

RCA gave Strauss a new reel-to-reel tape recorder to advertise. Strauss marched into RCA's CEO and announced that the machine chewed up tape and turned it into spaghetti. Strauss said, 'The product doesn't work. We can't advertise it.' The RCA CEO replied, 'If that's your point of view, we'll give some other agency the entire RCA account.' Strauss turned to walk out the door. 'Wait a minute,' shouted the RCA chief. 'If you feel so strongly you're willing to sacrifice the whole account, it must be a bad product. We'll fix it.' So. J. Walter Thomson kept the account. Dolan, who was standing outside the door holding Strauss's bag, said it made an enormous impression on him because his boss's actions represented the integrity of the company.

The Shadow Side of Integrity and Emotional Intelligence

One definition of the word *integrity* is 'adherence to moral and ethical principles; soundness of moral character; honesty'. It also is defined as 'the state of being whole, entire, and undiminished'.

What has no shadow has no strength to live.

Czeslaw Milosz, Nobel laureate

Let's consider this for a moment. To be whole and undiminished in our emotional depth, integrity requires us to face, accept, and integrate the bright and generative side of our nature with the hidden shadow side. This raises a vast and vital subject that, for the most part, is beyond the scope of this book. However, I believe it's important to encourage you to begin some personal reflection on this contrasting area of emotional depth. As Mahatma Gandhi said, 'The only devils in the world are those running around in our own hearts. That is where the battle should be fought.' Gandhi's voice invites us to enter, each in your own way, a necessary battle of growth and learning. You might start by simply reading about the shadow side of human nature and then to discuss it with your loved ones and close friends, and perhaps a trusted co-worker.

To begin with, it's important to acknowledge that most of us share a natural human tendency to want to dwell on our values and virtues, and avoid facing the opposites in our character. Of course, we recognize there are darker elements in ourselves but do our best to skim over them or push them aside, hoping they'll thereby diminish or vanish altogether while we attend to the urgent surface emotions of getting the job done and living our lives. However, sooner or later, we discover that this isn't enough. One way I've come to see this is, just as the *physical* human heart has a collection of chambers that produce blood flow, the *feeling* heart can be seen as having its own collection of chambers – some filled with light and others veiled in shadow – that generate a deeper *life* flow.

All of us in the work world experience times when frustrations mount; when funding is cut, jobs are lost, resistance seems insurmountable, our trust gets betrayed, or we face growing opposition or inertia. If we attempt to deny or ignore such dark moments, they take on an added power, growing larger as obstacles that tend to rear up at the worst times. Paradoxically, if we face these dark moments straight on, their power is immediately depleted and we have fewer constraints in advancing into the future.

The underlying point about this is that light without darkness is neither integrated nor whole; one without the other leaves us, by definition, out of integrity and incomplete. In this state, we create less, worry more, love less, and doubt more. However, this has become such a common way to work and live that it can seem well nigh invisible to us, and therein lies the danger because it's all too easy to say, 'That's just the way life is.'

This presents us with a challenge in developing our fullest emotional intelligence, and was a primary reason why, in designing our professional training programmes, we focused on the *application* of EQ in real work and real life, and engaged Prasad L. Kapia, PhD, CEO of Knowledge Architecture, to help us use a Pyramid-Building Technology™ developed over the past decade by the CPR Group (Tel: 408-866–8511) and used successfully by top executives at such companies as Ford, Boeing, Pacific Bell, the Deming Institute, and Xerox. With permission of the CPR Group and with Kapia's help, we created not only an *EQ-in-Action Pyramid*™ but also an *EQ-in-Action Shadow Pyramid*™. Because the shadow side of our attitudes and emotions is often concealed, most of us have got used to downplaying or ignoring its voice and influence. This can be a mistake, since it periodically intrudes in our daily life.

The truth is, we can learn a lot about our inner selves when we commit to noticing this occur, and in detecting parts of our personal shadow that may be revealed, or reflected, in the critical comments we get from others. We generally have lots of practical deflecting or denying such comments in order to portray ourselves in the most positive light. Think about several of the times you have received comments that others perceive you as ——. Fill in the blank: aloof, self-centred, arrogant, mistrusting, uncaring, always blue, or controlling, perhaps. The point is, when you hear a number of people saying the same thing, or something similar, it may be a good time to explore more deeply what's inside you. This takes courage. And gives many of us a sharp poke in the ribs for having assumed that we build depth of character and integrity by merely leaving behind our vices. There's more to it than that.

This means, essentially, that sooner or later we must investigate our deep, dark side as courageously as we do our deep, bright side. 'Human beings have always employed an enormous amount of clever devices for running away from themselves,' observes John Gardner. 'We can keep ourselves so busy, fill our lives with so many diversions, stuff our heads with so much knowledge, involve ourselves with so many people and cover so much ground that we never have time to probe the fearful and wonderful world within.... By middle life, most of us are accomplished fugitives from ourselves.'[56] This ultimately restricts our emotional intelligence.

Over the years, I've come to believe that most people who lead successful and fulfilling lives sooner or later must come face to face with the areas of darkness or emptiness inside themselves. One of the things that experience teaches us is that whenever we open ourselves up to this side of human nature, we, in effect, not only take away much of its destructive power but free up new sources of energy and passion, creativity and deepened trust. It may, in fact, be in what we at first *don't* accept about ourselves – our frailties, fears, and shadows – that eventually we discover our humanity.

Most of us are prone to think of our shadow side as containing only darkness, yet in Carl Jung's words, the shadow's essence is 'pure gold'. 'There is no light without shadow', he wrote, 'and no psychic wholeness without imperfection. To round itself out, life calls not for perfection but for completeness.... One does not become enlightened by imagining figures of light, but by making the darkness conscious.' In other words, in business we cannot lead others if we cannot first lead ourselves; we can face in others only what we can face in ourselves. 'Loving oneself is no easy matter just because it means loving all of oneself,' says James Hillman, 'including the shadow where one is inferior and socially so unacceptable. The care one gives this humiliating part is also the cure. More: as the cure depends on care, so does caring begin with nothing more than carrying.'[57] This means, I believe, a willingness to accept and *carry* – or own – our inner darkness rather than pretending it does not exist.

Viewed constructively, when we begin to face the shadow side of our human nature, we empower ourselves to:[58]

- Realize more growth on the light side of the EQ spectrum: Emotional intelligence has a wide range; for many feelings, the darker the shadow, the brighter the light.
- Achieve a deeper, more genuine self-acceptance, based on a more complete understanding of who we truly are; in many cases, this is what frees us to change and grow.
- Acknowledge, experience, and guide the darker more constrictive and reactionary parts of ourselves, rather than suppressing them in which case they erupt unexpectedly, often at the worst times.
- Free ourselves of much of the chronic guilt, resentment, remorse, or shame associated with the 'dark side' feelings.
- Improve or help heal our relationships through courageous self-examination and more open, honest dialogue with others.
- We release what some call 'excess emotional baggage', or what Robert Bly refers to as the 'invisible bag we drag behind us'.[59] According to Bly this includes all the things we stuffed in there when, as youngsters, teachers and parents told us to sit still, not to get angry or upset about things, not to argue or complain, ad infinitum. This bag gets very heavy as we hit middle age, and many of us are feeling worn down from lugging it. Sometimes, physical symptoms appear: when you happen to be reflecting on today's dose of aches and pains, angst and aspirations, you might ask yourself:[60]
  – What, right now, can't I *shoulder* or *stand?*
  – What can't I *move, bear,* or *stomach?*

Your power over the shadow side of human emotion rests in not having to *act* on your dark feelings. In this way we may also begin to see, for example, that the shadow-side emotions are, by and large, not something destructive in their creation or essence, but are simply a part of our deeper presence that's usually hidden from us.

Let's turn our attention to the workplace shadow for a few moments. Ask yourself, do certain company policies seem to be forcing me to dominate others, disregard feelings, tell lies 'for the good of the organization's future', or sacrifice my integrity in other ways? in every career and job field, we develop certain competencies and approaches to our job, and feelings about it, while leaving our other capacities and emotions in the shadows. This may seem to work just fine until one day our outer, success-driven *persona* collides with a situation that calls for us to respond from our emotional depths, which we've hidden away out of reach. What then?

> *Preserving the soul means that we come out of hiding at last and bring more of ourselves into the workplace.* Especially *the parts that do not 'belong' to the company.*
>
> David Whyte, The Heart Aroused

Similarly, what is it that stops many of us from achieving all that we actually believe, deep down, would be possible to attempt or achieve? Why does something inside – at the edges of our awareness – reach out faster than the eye to sabotage courageous efforts, undermine hopes and aspirations, or goad us to flee from success? When you commit to taking some quiet time to begin unravelling this mystery, you'll likely sense that many workplaces have stifled the expression of your heart and soul in more ways than you've realized. We can rationalize that this is a necessary part of the push to conform and fit in. But that doesn't make it right, or of integrity.

As you get in touch with the brighter aspects of your emotional depths, encourage yourself to remain open to acknowledging and learning from your personal shadow, including its various currents of impulses, habits, contradictions, and haunting feelings of doubt, self-pity, greed, martyrdom, jealousy, envy, lying, blaming, resentment, and remorse, to name but a few. The more you come to accept your imperfections and faults, you'll also detect voices of genuine caution and wisdom that crop up from time to time out of the darkness.

Consider, too, that each opposing emotional cross-wind or thrust gives life and work a bit more of its magic and richness, its uniquely unfolding diversions, distinctions, and drive. If we let it, that is. Which approach, then, will you choose: stuffer or explorer? In recent years, I've found that asking myself this question from time to time has had a lot to do with my own growth, and my relationship with my work, family, and the world.

Deena Metzger, a Los Angeles poet and psychologist, suggests a sequence of questions that help set a context for the territory in which the shadow self resides, in which we acknowledge that the shadow self is a continuation of ourselves, our other face:[61] 'What are those qualities or attributes in others that you find least like yourself? Remember a time when you felt hate. Are there those who may hate you? What are your most intractable prejudices? With what group do you feel least affinity? Who are the people you could not and would not imagine being because they revolt, offend, terrify, or enrage you or are beneath you, are grotesque? Under what circumstances would you feel too humiliated to continue living? What horror within yourself do you find unbearable?'

Through examining our responses to such questions, we face up to the fact that each of us contains within ourselves the potential to be both destructive and creative, to love and to hate. We can begin to distinguish our moral values and ethical principles from the emotional undercurrents that tug at our senses, without obvious reason, from the shadows. It is from here that we can begin to face and explore the hidden side of our nature, making it more explicit, less volatile and random.

Our ability to feel joy, for example, is commensurate with our capacity to feel grief and sorrow. Like two ends of a long line of related feelings, if we avoid facing and experiencing grief, then we blunt our capacity for joy. In reality, little about ourselves can change unless we face it, accept it, and grant it a place in the reality, rather than background, of our life. It is through working in our emotional depths that we also open the way to much-needed spiritual and creative assets. And slowly, steadily, we begin to integrate the chambers of the heart, and the integral dimensions of our lives.

The truth is, no man or woman standing at the edge of darkest inner shadows is without the urge to pass by this stage of emotional growth, to find a way around it, or over it. But that is not the approach we were born to take. Human existence is half dark and half light.

EQ Map Connections: Applied Integrity
You may want to refer to the following scales of the *EQ Map* as points of reflection related to this chapter: emotional self-awareness, emotional awareness of others, intentionality, resilience, personal power, and integrity

---

EQ IN ACTION: *INTEGRITY TIME AGREEMENT*

One of the tools I've found most useful in working with executives and managers is what I call an Integrity Time Agreement. It's something you write out yourself, in your own words, and commit to it on your weekly schedule, perhaps in conjunction with the *EQ Morning Notes* exercise described in Chapter 1.

> Purpose: I will use Integrity Time to sit quietly and pay close attention to my inner life as it moves me forward into the future. I will open myself to the full range and depth of my feelings and images, both bright and dark. I will seek to learn more about the inner consciousness that shapes what I feel, think, say, and do.

> Commitment: I will schedule at least — minutes (not less than five to ten) each morning for the next — weeks (at least three) before I begin the rest of my daily routine. I commit to using this Integrity Time for self-reflection and exploring my emotional intelligence, both the shadow and light sides of my heart and spirit, knowing that each is integral to who I am and what I become throughout the rest of my life.

Sign and date your agreement, and enter it on your daily schedule.

Imagine, for a few moments, what might be possible if you committed yourself to living with integrity at all times, no matter what comes? What if everyone in your department or organization committed to being a source of integrity, each connected to the others? What would happen if all of the energy typically diverted into cleaning up the fallout from integrity slip-ups and breaches could be used instead for creative collaboration, including discovering every possible way to lead the field, benefit humanity, *and* compete for the future? What might your life and work feel like then?

> *Our deepest fear is not that we are inadequate. Our deepest fear is that we are powerful beyond measure. It is our light, not our darkness, that frightens us.*
>
> Marianne Williamson

It is from a deepened experience of our unique potential and purpose, backed by a commitment to integrity, that our genuine *influence* grows. When used without coercion, it becomes the indispensable source of energy that shapes our dreams and real-world accomplishments alike. It is this influence that enables us to make our presence felt in today's vast interconnecting networked world of people, problems and possibilities, in all of which, in some form and on some level, you are a part. Those who ultimately succeed in life and work learn to exert their influence in creative and respectful ways, without rank, privilege or authority. And that is the subject of the next chapter.

CHAPTER 12

Influence without Authority

Vaclav Havel, the poet-president of Czechoslovakia, observes, 'I never fail to be astonished at how much I am at the mercy of television directors and editors, at how my public image depends far more on them than it does on myself. I know politicians who have learned to see themselves only as the television camera does. Television has thus expropriated their personalities and hearts, and made them into something like television shadows of their former selves. I sometimes wonder whether they even sleep in a way that will look good on television.'

At the heart of each of us, whatever our imperfections, there exists a silent pulse, a complex of wave forms and resonances, which is absolutely individual and unique, and yet which connects us to everything in the universe.

George Leonard, author of The Silent Pulse

That, ironically, is a rising risk not just for leaders and managers but for all of us. As the power and allure of media continue to grow, more work is being conducted at a distance via computers and video-conferencing. Will we resist becoming a media shell, a surface image of our real selves? Or will we abandon emotional intelligence for the sake of the 'face' we portray to the world on camera or in the boardroom or the sound bytes our customers and prospective customers hear? These are questions worth pondering.

For more than 200 years, the typical management concentration has rested squarely on analysis, external power and technical rationality, a shift which can be seen as starting with Voltaire and other thinkers in the eighteenth century. This has largely overshadowed other recognized human characteristics such as spirit, emotion, intuition, and experience. As executive and historian John Ralston Saul reminds us, 'Rationality and reason are no more than structures. And structure is most easily controlled by those who feel themselves to be free of the cumbersome weight represented by common sense and humanism. Structure best suits those whose talents lie in manipulation.'[62]

At its best, emotional intelligence is about influence without manipulation or authority. It's about perceiving, learning, relating, innovating, prioritizing, and acting in ways that take into account *emotional valence*, rather than relying on logic or intellect or technical analysis alone. Our emotions, as much or more than our bodies and minds, contain our histories, every line and verse of every experience, deep understanding, and relationship in our lives. They comprise the feeling of who we are, and enter our systems as an energy that radiates, that resonates. This energy is the transmitter and recorder of all feelings, thoughts, and interactions. In some respects, our biography becomes not only our biology but also our presence in the world.

> *Fields of energy react with each other in a stimulating, equalizing, or sedating way. We can experience this upon entering a room filled with people, quickly sensing whether it is permeated with vibrations that are harmonious or discordant.*
>
> Charles Klotsche, American scientist

Few managers would deny that competition is intensifying everywhere in the world. Yet, in more and more cases, the traditional ways to compete – in offers and markets, in customer-centred focus – are getting subsumed by competition through *influence*. What the old, linear model fails to take into account is the context, the environment, in which more and more new business takes place, which is an environment that integrates conflict and cooperation, chaos and creative collaboration. Strategist James Moore calls these environments *business ecosystems*, a kind of organized chaos and crucial coevolution that parallels what takes place in biological eco-systems.[63] Biologist and leadership researcher George Land first called this to our attention a quarter of a century ago in his classic work *Grow or Die*.[64] Business school professors Adam Brandenburger and Barry Nalebuff have given it a new twist through game theory and call it 'co-opetition'.[65]

Your Sphere of Influence

Just as in biological ecosystems, many businesses today find that traditional industry boundaries are blurring and, in many instances, are disappearing altogether. Executives and managers find themselves scrambling to comprehend and fulfil diverse and changing roles in relationship with each other, person to person and company to company. Consider, on a basic level, the interconnecting case of IBM, Microsoft, and Intel: in some markets, they are fierce competitors; in others, they are suppliers of vital value to each others' profitability; in yet other business settings they are, at the moment, creating the future in what appear to be distinct and separate arenas, or on seemingly unrelated fields. In every industry, from manufacturing to energy, healthcare, telecommunications and media, vast interconnected webs of shared imagination, trust, and influence are extending across product, market and geographic boundaries and, interactively and continually, keep shaping and redefining success for each company and stakeholder.

The passing era of business intelligence was dominated by physics, a mathematical model that treats everything as if it were inanimate and sequential. The new model of business intelligence uses a biological model that treats people, markets, ideas, and organizations as unique and alive, and inherently capable of change, interaction, synergy and growth. In many cases, people who are attuned to intuitive information and the cues of emotional intelligence will find that they have more influence than others under the time pressures of today's workplace.[66] Why? In part, because the more analytical five-sensory human focuses principally on exerting influence through the external pursuit of power and control, manoeuvering and manipulation. In contrast, with high emotional intelligence we tend to be more inner-directed and can access a wider range of competencies than with cognitive power alone, and this is expressed as a form of influence that might best be called *resonance* rather than authority.

It was Dee Hock, the visionary leader who, as a vice-president of an obscure bank in Seattle, vowed that if he ever got to create an organization he would try to conceive it based on biological concepts and metaphors.[67] In June 1970 he had that chance. Following two years of dialogue, arguments, brainstorming and planning, he became CEO of National Bank Americard, Inc. (later renamed Visa International). Visa is one of several sterling examples experts cite to demonstrate how the dynamic principles of how biological models and chaos theory can be applied to business.

Working at the Boundary Between Chaos and Order

Healthy, adaptive systems always seem to exhibit a dynamic tension between chaos and order and, in Visa, Hock encouraged as much competition and initiative as possible throughout the organization – chaos – while building in mechanisms for ethical cooperation, or order. The results weren't easy but they skyrocketed, and the influence is growing still. According to Hock, the heart and soul of leadership is this: 'If you look to lead, invest at least 40% of your time managing yourself – your ethics, character, principles, purpose, motivation, and conduct. Invest at least 30% managing those with authority over you, and 15% managing your peers. Use the remainder to induce those you "work for" to understand and practice [these principles]. I use the term "work for" advisedly, for if you don't understand that you should be working for your mislabelled "subordinates," you haven't understood anything.'

I recall the story of how Gandhi, early on in his career, was in South Africa, where he developed a strong sense of purpose and was working toward his visions.[68] One day, a man arrived from a distant country and volunteered to join Gandhi. The man said, 'Aren't you surprised that I've shown up like this?' 'No,' answered Gandhi. He explained that when a person discovers what is right and purposeful, and begins to pursue it, the necessary people and resources tend to appear, as if attracted to the cause. That's influence, and resonance. Although he never held any official position in government or business, had no wealth, and commanded no armies, Gandhi could mobilize and inspire millions of people.[69]

The more we study the problems and possibilities of our era, the more we realize they cannot be understood in isolation. They are interconnected and interrelated. Each attitude, emotion, and action you have – and that others have – creates an influence, a radiance. This influence, or radiance, is continually alerting our physiology and perceptions; in the process, we also influence the function and growth of the brain and individual cells, and our relationship with life.[70] Unfortunately, we cannot easily recognize that the problems we face are part of the systems in which we play an active role. We are inclined to externalize problems, keeping them 'out there' and insisting it is others who have to change. Our first reaction is to tell them this. Next, we try to force them. Experience teaches us this is not only unsuccessful, it can be disastrous.

Emotional Resonance: Energy, Information and Influence

The point I want to make is that the problem is usually not 'out there' but rather it's 'in here', inside us. The external system that many of us complain so much about actually exists within each of us.[71] We are, in effect, transmitters and receivers of energy and values. Emotions are currents of energy that arise in us, activate our values and shape our behaviours, which emanate outwards, influencing others. We feel this in many daily interactions and must accept responsibility for learning from, and guiding, this source of connection and affect. We experience the unique emotional tone and presence of ourselves and others, and this stays with us – the feeling of each action and interaction lingers. Startling scientific research suggests that not only can the heart's feelings be felt from five to ten feet away,[72] but the human heart responds to every single word spoken[73] and, in dialogue, the person who is listening is not only *reacting* or *responding* to the speaker but is in a sense, *part of* or *one with* the speaker.[74]

Above my desk is a small plaque which reads, 'Give the world the best you have and the best will come back to you.' I have come to believe that when we work from a place of purpose and conscience, and give our best effort, whether we succeed or not, we exert a meaningful influence. By that I mean that even if an initiative happens to end up in failure, our best effort creates another *dimension* of influence – something those around us can feel and value, even in failure.

Do you remember the lone man, an unarmed protestor in Tiananmen Square, stepping in front of the military tank during the Chinese government crackdown? He was doomed to fail, yet those of us watching from halfway around the world felt something. We felt his courage. His commitment and effort *resonated* with us. In some small way, even without him knowing it, his actions changed us, connected us. Here was a man who was giving his best, against all odds, to a cause he believed in. He could be counted upon. That's what we sensed. Not through the intellect but the heart, through resonance.

If you keep to one corner and neglect the myriad aspects of the totality, if you take one thing and discard the rest, then what you attain will be little and what you master will be shallow.

Lao Tzu, *Understanding the Mysteries*, Sixth Century BC

It is in this way that we climb upward on the ladder of purpose. Every feeling and thought influences every fibre of our being, radiating outwards to others. This is resonance. Understanding it, and being accountable for it, is a keystone of emotional depth.

And while it's true that too much emotion can confound the reasoning process, in most business cases the reverse is far more of a problem: too little emotion can thwart or paralyze reasoning.[75] Many leaders and managers do not yet fully grasp the nature of their role as value generators and beacons of, and receptors to, emotional intelligence; or that they can become aware of, and guide, this resonance. They do not fully realize how closely they are observed, even from afar, and how the smallest details of their speech, gestures, and daily behaviours are noted, sensed, interpreted and remembered by virtually everyone who comes in contact with them.

Such was the case with one unexpected leader, Hwa Mu-Lan, in China nearly 500 years ago. Throughout its long history, China as fought in many wars, and her families have traditionally sent their sons off to battle. During one such time, in a small village lived a young woman named Hwa Mu-Lan.[76] Her family had no sons of military age. Her father was feeble and her brother was a little boy. So to protect her father and brother from military service, Hwa Mu-Lan disguised herself as a man, joined the army, and went off to fight. She was strong and intelligent, and served as a courageous leader and effective soldier, and eventually went on to become one of the most respected generals of her era. At first, she enlisted as an act of selfless compassion, to save her father and little brother. Yet from this circumstance she discovered the path of her life and began to exert her influence.

The same is true of many entrepreneurs and leaders of business. Once passionately committed to a deeper purpose, they work wholeheartedly to learn and excel, and then to have influence. Some of them have dreamed of founding or cornering a market. Or of conquering an industry or, lately, the Internet. Of amassing a fortune. Yet few people actually accomplish such things, and virtually no one does so these days by following traditional business school formulae. Ironically, for those who *do* succeed, the accomplishments themselves may feel mysterious, elusive, somehow even magical, as if hingeing on the hand of fate or a gift of luck. Perhaps, to a degree, they do. Yet there is more.

For thirty years one of my persistent curiosities has been, what makes a great leader? In searching for an answer to that question I've delved into historical writings and I've studied a number of modern day leaders. And when it comes to growing an empire against all odds, few leaders have intrigued me more than Songtsen Gampo (SONG-zen GAHM-poh). Let me tell you a bit of his story.

He was born the eldest son of the ruler of a small and isolated land. At the age of twelve, his father was fatally poisoned by rivals and his mother was killed before his eyes. What saved his life was, in a single word, resonance. Even at that young age, there was something about Songtsen that his father's inner circle of advisors and protectors felt was worthy of their respect and support. Instead of killing him and seizing the crown for themselves, they helped him learn to lead and protected him while he grew. This was a monumental challenge: these were dangerous times, violent and unpredictable. Almost every imaginable good was by then available in world trade, and competition was fierce in every marketing route. Rebels and raiders struck without warning. Trade channels were won or lost overnight. Leaders vied for power. Intrigue and assassinations were commonplace.

Yet in the thirty-year period that Songtsen Gampo and his advisors led Tibet prior to his death, they created an empire which grew to nearly twice the size of China. It was an empire where none had been before, arguably grander in size, scope and influence than those of Caesar, Attila or Alexander. Songtsen repeatedly won military encounters in which he was outnumbered by more experienced enemy forces. Through a series of brilliant strategies, he forged lasting alliances with the most powerful neighbouring lands. Although he suffered betrayals and assassination attempts, he committed himself to learning from them, and in many cases adopted the practice of forgiving those who opposed him.

In the early years, he did not speak the various languages – or understand or value the differing beliefs and customs – of the various peoples in his land. He committed himself to learning these, and he did, which helped him become the first leader ever to unify the hundreds of feuding, unruly clans and warlords throughout a region stretching more than 5,000 miles from end to end. And he did it despite the fact that, for centuries, these groups had a long history of violence and had rejected all previous attempts at alliance.

One man, and his inner circle of advisors, changed all that. Beyond innovative strategies, it was the emotional depth of what Songtsen's people called his 'authentic presence' that won and held the trust and loyalty of neighbouring rulers. This feeling radiated outwards to the heads of far-flung kingdoms and cities, whose leaders soon joined him in a shared purpose, which included better trade, peace through unified strength, education, and respect for differing cultures and views. Who Songtsen Gampo was and what he stood for resonated in the hearts of others. Even those who hated outsiders and who wanted no part of his plans came to acknowledge the power of his purpose and commitment, and his strategic brilliance.

Along the way, he gained control of the mountain passes, rivers, and trade routes. He built a major capitol city from scratch and commissioned a unique form of architecture that is recognized and admired around the world. He honoured differing cultural heritages and welcomed people of divergent beliefs and backgrounds, thriving on the creative inspiration he received from far-flung cultures and knowledge, from the Roman Empire, India, China, Persia, and beyond. Over the final decade of his life, his accomplishments included establishing a representative government, expansive worldwide trade, a moral code and advocacy of human rights, commissioning his land's first written language and plan for national literacy, a medical care system based on the finest traditions from Greece, India, and China; and promotion of a culture so egalitarian that his enemies called it 'the kingdom of women'. Then, in the midst of one of the most violent periods in history, he introduced his empire to Dharma, the path of non-violence.

According to historians, here was a man who crossed bloody trade frontiers and won more than a hundred strategic alliances. He transcended jagged intellectual divides and cultural chasms and forged an abiding sense of shared purpose and understanding. He faced long-standing territorial and doctrinal disputes and established the grounds of fairness and honour. He encountered treachery and bitter rivalries yet won a lasting peace.

Songtsen Gampo lived in Tibet from *c.* AD 591 to 650. Little was known about him outside his native land until western scholars discovered a secret storehouse of seventh-century historical documents – concealed in a fashion similar to the Dead Sea Scrolls – buried beneath the desert sand in Central Asia. According to Lee Feigon, Chairman of the East Asian Studies department and professor of history at Colby College, 'In times past, an independent Tibet ruled vast portions of China, India, Nepal, Central Asia, and even the Middle East ... Reams have been written about smaller rival states, but no other great dominion is as little known as the one the first Tibetan kings forged high in the Himalayas ... Songtsen Gampo was not a simple military chieftain. He was a clever, imaginative ruler able to foresee the complex needs of his new empire and to understand the political and cultural structures necessary to build a fresh civilization.'[77]

One of the things I've learned from studying the lives of leaders, including this man who lived in Tibet 1300 years ago, is that every one of them has faced resistance, often for long lengths of time and on all fronts. However, this does not stop them. Some have prevailed through brute force. Others through force of will. Or a stroke of creative genius or right timing. Yet I have come to believe that many of the best of them prevailed, or left their legacy, largely through emotional resonance and its resulting influence. It was this kind of heart-level intensity in Socrates' quest and Martin Luther King, Jr's call to destiny, to mention just two examples, rather than the supremacy of their arguments, that gave them their incandescence – the presence that made so many others leave an encounter with either of them feeling they must change their lives.

A seminal 1976 article in the *Harvard Business Review* entitled 'Power is the Great Motivator', was based on extensive research and defined a leader's true power not as the capacity to destroy but as the ability to *influence* others.[78] And John Kotter, professor of leadership at Harvard, emphasizes that, these days, to accomplish everything that needs to be done, managers need access to kinds of power and influence that go well beyond the ability to hire, fire, and administer budgets. In the twentieth century, there have been a host of business leaders around the world who have marshalled such influence and built empires of industry or ideas. Many of them, it is said by those who knew them, emanated a special kind of feeling, some combination of higher calling and emotional intelligence. It was something that others sensed and respond to. And, even today, such is the power of their stories.

What are Your Life Stories?

One source of building lasting influence comes through our personal stories. The stories about who we are, what we stand for, and what we may yet become. Once told and heard, they resonate within us. We hear and perceive at a deeper level. They touch us in the heart the way no flowchart or rational argument ever can. They change us. In fact, through the emotion of such stories we shape the person we are becoming.[79] Studies show that many of the world's leading companies with an institutionalized capacity for innovation build such capacity through stories.[80] Robert Coles recalls one of his medical mentors telling him, 'The people who come to see us bring their stories. They hope they tell them well enough so that we understand the truth of their lives.'[81]

The physician and poet William Carlos Williams, a close friend of Coles, once prodded him by saying, 'Their story, yours, mine – it's what we all carry with us on this trip we take, and we owe it to each other to respect our stories and learn from them.'[82] David Whyte, the English-born corporate poet, participates in the executive programmes at Boeing and many other companies, encouraging leaders to share their stories as a means to advancing their emotional and creative intelligence.

Throughout his life, Songtsen Gampo sought out other people's stories, and learned from them. And he shared his own stories which, slowly at first, and then exponentially, expanded his leadership influence and responsibility. Similarly, the modern business enterprise is, like each of us who work in it, a transmitter and receiver of energy and values. There is both individual and collective *consciousness* and *conscience*. Even a statement of purpose or vision can create this effect. Example: 'A Coke within arm's reach of everyone in the world.' This phrase generates both an image and a feeling which resonates in thousands of managers and employees at Coca-Cola who, together, form one of the most enthusiastic and successful workforces in any company.

One of the central ideas in Howard Gardner's research on leadership is that leaders are all those 'persons who, by word and/or personal example, markedly influence the behaviors, thoughts, and/or feelings of a significant number of their fellow human beings'.[83] Through its leadership – the fundamental principles by which a company conducts business and the way it treats employees, suppliers, and customers – an organization's presence resonates outwards into our communities and societies like waves. They have an impact on us all, in many more ways than we realize, and on our culture at large. There is no way to be an effective leader or successful professional today without a clear understanding of the diverse network of people around you. This means knowing the unique talents and real concerns of each relevant, involved person, even though there may be hundreds of them.[84] It means understanding their differing perspectives of all relevant individuals and groups – what their *real* interests are, what they care most about, how they look at the world, what makes them feel valued, and what brings out their creative and collaborative spirit. All of this information, much of it tied to emotional intelligence, is vital to effective decision-making. 'There is an energy field between humans,' according to psychologist and philosopher Rollo May. 'A resonance exists between leaders and followers that makes them allies in support of a common cause,' observes Warren Bennis.[85]

If, as a person and a leader, you experience fairly mild resistance to your presence or ideas, then a fresh slant on things or some new information may be all that's required to make progress. However, if resistance is deeper, information alone – facts alone – will never be enough to create such a shift. Most leaders and managers, in seeing their reasoning and list of facts being resisted, soon turn to the Force of Reason, whereby through brute persuasion they try to force people to see the correctness of their picture of reality. It doesn't work.

In business, as in war, we have a tendency to dehumanize our enemy. We insulate ourselves. We suppress our feelings and thwart any chance we'll empathize with an opponent. Not so with Songtsen Gampo. He was known for honest dialogue and forgiving others for their transgressions. This won him respect and lasting alliances. He learned to dispense with trying to convince people that he was on the side of right and goodness, or that all who opposed him were not. Instead, he kept trying to discern his enemies' *humanity*. He wanted them to be human in each other's eyes, and his eyes. He wanted them to align with him in shared purpose, rather than weaken each other through bickering and war. He championed character and resonance as means to win alliances and to advance his dreams of an educated, just and productive empire. Did the hand of fate assist him? Certainly. Would the future he helped shape *last*? He could not have known.

Yet I believe he realized, as we must, that we create the future only when we *grow* ourselves into it through understanding the principles of change and influence without authority. Each of us shapes a part of the future yet we cannot control it – at its heart it's inherently wild and open, part mystery and magic, part evolution and webs of relationships. Great leaders put words to the formless longings and deeply felt needs of others. They create connection through resonance, and build communities of shared vision, practice and influence. They tell stories that capture aspirations and win hearts.

A metaphor that has been used for this since antiquity is that of concentric circles of human connection, with the self at the centre, surrounded by circles for family members, friends, work group, work community, greater community, and the rest of humanity. Hans Ulrich at the St Gallen Business School in Switzerland developed a model known in European management circles as the St Gallen model.[86] It is based on the view of the business organization as a living social system and incorporates many ideas from biology, brain science, ecology, and evolutionary theory. W. Edwards Deming said that the majority of problems in organizations are with systems, not people.[87]

In recent years, a number of the business leaders I believe are most creative and effective have begun to transform the way they lead. They've eased their grip on planning and prediction and are, instead, exploring the workings of dialogue and influence, the anticipation of opportunities and changes, and embracing initiatives of shared responsibility and purpose. These notable men and women are coming to understand that the waves of intelligence – emotional, creative, and practical – have a resonance that continually exerts its influence in all directions, from the self outwards, and from the system, of which we are a part, back to us. We do not weave this web of business and life; we are each a strand in it. Whatever we feel, think or do to ourselves and others, we do to the web.

EQ Map Connections: Influence without Authority

You may want to refer to the following scales of the *EQ Map* as points of reflection related this chapter: emotional expression, emotional awareness of others, resilience, interpersonal connections, constructive discontent, compassion, intuition, and trust radius

---

EQ IN ACTION: *HOW FEELINGS SPREAD FROM PERSON TO PERSON*

Through the principle of resonance, emotions are not only *felt* by others, they can also be *picked up* by others. By that I mean that there is such a thing as emotional contagion.[88] This is usually unconscious, and can happen in a split second. When someone approaches you in a down mood, for example, you may suddenly begin to feel blue. When someone is enthusiastic and vibrant, you may 'catch' some of that emotional state, too. This underscores why one of the foundations of emotional intelligence is managing your energy level (Chapter 2): when you are tense and tired, not only do problems and obstacles appear larger than life, but you may also be more susceptible to being 'infected' by the low moods of others. Conversely, when you renew and sustain your energies and manage to stay relatively calm and alert, this emotional state may give you some natural 'immunity' to the down moods of others,[89] and may also help other people feel less emotionally agitated and may raise their mood.

Think about it: does just being *near* certain people get you down? You may not know why, but you can feel it, even from across the room. These may be people who seem addicted to describing problem after problem, magnifying the smallest frustrations into major dilemmas, often with lots of exaggeration, blaming, and symbols of self-pity or martyrdom (perhaps with whining, sighing, groaning, and looks of tiredness). Several performance researchers[90] have labelled this behaviour *chain-dumping*, noting that it occurs when someone heaps, or dumps, a string of problems first on one person, then on the next, eventually pulling down everyone who will listen. This is distinctly different from 'opening up to others' in which, at appropriate times and in appropriate ways, you honestly express your feelings about a specific issue, idea, circumstance or experience.

In chain-dumping, the person complaining is always the victim of the story being told. The listeners usually first express sympathy and then find themselves becoming distressed by the episode, and distracted from their work tasks. The net result is mental and emotional fatigue, for the complainer and for all the listeners. And when we 'rescue' chain-dumpers through sympathy or by offering to 'help out' by taking over some of their responsibilities, we often only make matters worse, encouraging more draining conversations which turn into arguments and become circular, that is, each of you blames the other for causing problems and provoking bad feelings.[91]

Naturally, there's no denying that we all have down moods and bearish, bad-tempered days. There are a host of reasons for this and no quick-fix solutions. The 'Don't worry, be happy' rhetoric is fool's gold; and there just aren't enough exuberant, positive people for all the rest of us to cluster around them and try to 'catch' *their* emotional uplifts, either. So what's the most realistic thing to do? Here are several considerations:

Recognize and respect emotional distance.
The manager with high EQ usually has some understanding of his or her own struggles with inner demons and doubts. When sensing an emotional downturn in a co-worker, boss, or employee, she does not perceive them as her own. This enables him or her to give other people more room for understanding and allow them to experiment with various ways to move ahead constructively. 'It's simply not possible to solve other people's life problems,' says psychiatrist Ronald M. Podell of UCLA's Neuropsychiatric Institute, 'or give them the self-esteem they lack, or brighten their spirits when they're dark. By trying to do so, you only risk joining them. So what to do? You remain empathetic, and set appropriate limits, not coldly or vindictively, but with wisdom and purpose.'[92]

Whenever you feel an emotional drop, check to see if it's from being in the presence of a complainer. It's important to hold to your own best energy or authentic presence, doing whatever you can to avoid getting pulled down, and positioning yourself to give others a lift by your emotional presence and resonance. If things get really bad, you might put on an imaginary 'emotional raincoat' that creates an image of protecting yourself from the energy-depleting 'rain' of words. Raise clarifying questions such as, 'What do you plan to *do* about this situation right now, anyway?' and then move on. If necessary, break away from the interaction as courteously as you can.

Speak from your own experience; don't lecture or advise.
Most of us resent or reject advice from others, whereas we generally

value the chance to learn about other's experiences that are similar to what we're going through. When you step forward to assist another person, especially one who is presently struggling with a difficult challenge or circumstance, make a conscious commitment to empathize and share something meaningful you've learned in your own life and work. Express it as something to consider, offered in the spirit of friendship. This feels very different from saying, 'You're blowing it. Here's what to do ...', or 'If I were you, I'd ...'

If the shoe fits, wear it; if not, discard it.
Dark cloud verbal outbursts can include sharp criticism, most of which is likely to be irrelevant or false. It pays to remember that when you allow irritating or hurtful words to get inside you and fester, you're torturing yourself needlessly. Practise replacing distressing statements with calmer, more validating ones, such as:

'Easy does it. Let's get some air and start to talk this through.'

'I realize that he/she is upset. I also don't want to forget his/her many great qualities, too.'

'Right now I'm/you're upset, but I believe this is basically a strong and good relationship.'

The idea is to reassure yourself that the other person's mood probably has little if anything to do with you. Remain flexibly optimistic, as discussed in Chapter 8. In this way, you'll be less vulnerable to contagious emotions, according to research by psychologists Chriss Hsee, of Yale University, and Elaine Hatfield of the University of Hawaii.[93]

Be alert not to escalate a problem in the name of 'emotional honesty'.
This is one of the times when saying what you really feel can be counterproductve, to your own mood and energy, that of the other person, and the relationship. When appropriate, you might look for chances to lighten things up with some humour, which can be one of the fastest ways to trigger a burst of creativity and enable us to break out of a low mood.[94] Avoid making statements that *blame* ('If you weren't so gloomy and grouchy, I wouldn't feel so stressed out all the time'), *instil guilt* ('You're so focused on yourself that the rest of the company hardly knows you any more'), *make charges of incompetency or inadequacy* ('Only an idiot would say those things and act that way'), or *threaten abandonment* ('I'm sick of this – I'm ready to quit and never come back').

Keep renewing yourself.
When you build emotional resilience through renewal – discussed in Chapter 8 – it may help you become partially immune to the downside of emotional contagion, and enable you to have greater and more consistent influence over others without requiring or relying on authority, rank, or coercion.

EQ IN ACTION: *FEELINGS OF FAIRNESS – INFLUENCE AND THE 'EQUITY FACTOR'*

In virtually every relationship, both on and off the job, the process of give and take plays an important role in influence.[95] We establish and sustain relationships based on gaining influence through making *exchanges* which promote respect and value to all involved. Those who are skilled at this are ever ready to take the first risk, to extend trust to others, not knowing for certain if it will be returned in kind.

You can buy people's time; you can buy their physical presence at a given place; you can even buy a measured number of muscular motions per hour. But you cannot buy enthusiasm ... you cannot buy loyalty ... you cannot buy the devotion of their hearts. This you must earn.

Clarence Francis, Fortune

'I hate the word *fair*,' says Al Zeien, CEO of Gillette, the $6 billion international firm with 34,000 employees, makers of shaving blades, personal care products, Paper Mate and Waterman pens, Braun electric shavers, and Oral-B toothbrushes.[96] 'Everybody says, "Yeah, I want to be treated fairly." I say, "The world is not fair." I use the word *appropriate*. I think it's important that the company treat people appropriately.' Zeien clearly makes it a point to protect and reward employees who, as he puts it, 'are carrying a torch for something'. 'Lots of times,' he says, 'I will make a trip or a phone call or whatever to support a guy who is carrying a torch, and carrying it right off a cliff. But most of those times, we have asked him to jump off the edge of a cliff. People need to know what failure means, and they need to know that the organization stands behind them. That's the role I play.'

This is certainly not an easy road: identifying and fighting injustice, and making every effort to be fair and appropriate is a gnarly challenge in today's society where prejudice, racism, and discrimination of every description can crop up in almost any conversation or circumstance. If we are to succeed, we must remain vigilant about feelings of fairness.

It's worth noting that envy and resentment can be poison to any initiative or enterprise.[97] The founders of the American republic recognized that most other republics in history had failed because of envy; the envy of one faction or family for another, or of the poor towards the rich.[98] To have a long life, a republic must defeat envy and resentment. The best way to do this, or one of the best ways, is to generate economic growth through diverse industries, initiatives and channels of opportunity, so that every family has the realistic chance to see its economic condition improve tangibly over time. This realistic hope for a better future is essential to all members of society, including the poor. Only then can people feel in their hearts that hard work, trust, faith, goodwill, creativity, and persistence pay off. Without this realistic hope, cynicism and pessimism soon follow, sometimes shadowed by hostility and rage.

Fred Smith, CEO and president of FedEx, knows this principle well. Management at FedEx strives to support its Guaranteed Fair Treatment Procedure (GFTP) in every way it can, with money, time, communication, and continual monitoring. But the most significant show of executive support comes from Smith, who sits on the Appeals Board (one of two adjudicating groups) almost every Tuesday, where meetings sometimes last all day long. Board members report that Smith has the best attendance record.[99]

Any organization that consists of two or more people is certain to have issues of fairness that will arise from time to time. If these issues are not recognized and resolved, they will dissipate the group's energy. Many aspects of fairness revolve around the *equity factor*, a hidden system of balance that guides and influences what people contribute to any relationship. Based on a series of workplace studies, here are several of the discoveries about the equity factor:[100]

Despite constant posturing and rhetoric to the contrary, a basic principle in most work relationship is that people give to get. This does not infer greed or pure selfishness, just a powerful unconscious level of expectancy for fairness and balance. The phrase 'After *all* I've done for you ...' is a simple, outward expression of an inner feeling that what you have given does not equal what you have received in return. Often, it isn't your intentions, your effort, or the amount of time you contribute to a relationship that count most. Instead, it's the other person's *perception* of these.

Leaders and managers want their colleagues and employees to be productive and committed yet are often disappointed when they arrive late for meetings, take extended breaks, pad expense accounts, take company property home for personal use, and call in sick even when we're sure that they're not. And we're frequently dismayed when, all at once, these people quit their jobs and go to work on their own or for our competitors.

Begin with a simple equity-factor audit: select an important work relationship – with a subordinate, your boss, or a key team member. Divide a piece of paper into two columns: label the left side 'What I give' (*Inputs*) and the right side 'What I get' (*Outputs*). Enter all of the contributions you are making to the relationship; these might include pay, time, mentoring, professional development, respect, trust, emotional support, loyalty, advice, and so on. Then, in the right hand column, write down all the benefits that you are receiving from the relationship. Compare the two lists. Do they feel equal?

The perception of inputs/outputs is highly personal. Nationwide surveys have indicated that 53 per cent of managers and 83 per cent of employees in large corporations report feeling under-rewarded and resentful.[101] In many cases, the 'facts' of the matter would likely not confirm this. Which makes little difference. What may actually matter most to many is how they *perceive* and *feel* about things. This constitutes over 90 per cent of their view of reality. Once people begin to feel under-rewarded day after day, they may experience feelings of self-pity or martyrdom, feeling unappreciated, misunderstood, and increasingly burdened because of expectations not met. Remember, the facts may say otherwise, and as a leader you may have actually done nothing to 'cause' this feeling on the part of the other person. Yet the feeling is real. Trying to confront it head-on and deny it or prove it wrong, simply shames the other person and may trigger further anger, resistance, resentment, and even revenge.

When people feel that they give more to a relationship than they get in return, they feel distress, and, according to management professors Richard C. Huseman and John D. Hatfield, they will respond in one of three ways:[102]

1. They *reduce inputs*, cutting back on their contributions to the relationship by one or more of the following: coming late to work, missing meetings, doing less work, doing careless work, complaining, spreading gossip or rumours, calling in sick, taking extended breaks, 'forgetting' to carry out tasks, and sabotaging their work and the work of others.

2. They *increase outcomes*, by trying to change what they receive from the relationship, by asking for one or more of the following: pay raises, bonuses, promotions, increased job security, more benefits, transfers to different jobs, or better working conditions.

3. They *end the relationship*.

One of the most effective ways to restore balance to equity in your relationships – both on and off the job – is to learn about, and then contribute more of, what the other person needs and values most. This is the power of equity, of mutual exchange: getting what you want and giving others what they value and need. You can engage the other person in discussing options *without* challenging his or her position by using one of the most powerful phrases in the English language: 'What if . . .?' If you find out the issue is money, for example, you might ask, '*What if* you were to reduce the magnitude of the project to fit within your budget constraints?' You begin to collaborate on mutually beneficial solutions – to many kinds of issues. You might also ask for this other person's advice, which is likely the last thing he or she expects you to do. You are, in essence, acknowledging the other person's competence and value. Ask, 'What feels fair to you?' 'What would you do if you were in my shoes?'

Here are several key considerations:

- Begin by assuming that the other person is a good person and potential ally.
- Extend your trust and build rapport.
- Check your inner compass: Are you clear about your own goals and priorities in relation to this person?
- Determine your potential ally's talents, concerns, priorities, needs and wants.
- Identify which of your own strengths and resources may be of value to this person.
- Ask for the ally's opinion: 'What if . . .?' 'What would you do if you were in my shoes?' 'What feels fair to you?' Listen to the answers and ideas you receive.
- Take the first step – commit to an action that demonstrates value for the other person.
- Suggest an exchange: offer what you have in return for what you want.

    Carry out a similar equity-balancing process with your co-workers, employees, customers, family members, and friends. What does each want most from you? How do they feel most appreciated and respected? You'll find these answer in the heart, beneath the skin and behind the words. Respond accordingly.

This leaves your boss, who may not feel the obligation to improve the relationship, or may lack the EQ skills to do so. You must use some of the above strategies to determine what *you* can do to improve your alliance with this person. Great bosses are, in a very real sense, made at least in part by the way the rest of us help shape them. It is as much the professional's or employee's responsibility to help make the boss a good leader or manager as it is for the boss to help professionals and employees feel fairly treated, valued, and successful.

EQ IN ACTION: *CORPORATION AS COMMUNITY*

Beyond fairness, there is another dimension of influence of which we are each an integral part: our community. In years past, it was our village or neighbourhood, our town or valley. But for many of us today, the workplace has become our primary source of community. It is where we spend the majority of our waking hours. It is where we seek and respond to many of the challenges in our lives. It is where many of our friendships are made, where we hope to be valued and to belong, and it is where we have a chance to contribute to society. It is also the principal place where we learn and grow, and where we discover, or fail to discover, an essential part of the meaning in our lives.

Communities are the ground-level generators and preservers of character. Character is developed chiefly in settings in which people deal with one another face to face. Important among these is the workplace.

John W. Gardner, author of On Leadership

In 1727, Benjamin Franklin founded the Junto, one of the first US civic clubs.[103] It was chartered by business people having goals of community, fellowship and service. Character and values were of high concern to that organization. The celebrated social philosopher John Dewey suggested that the primary outcome of organizational life was less the production of things than the development of people.

In essence, an organization can be seen as a synergistic reflection of the beliefs, principles, ideas, efforts, feelings, and conduct of the people connected to them. This is the ancient conceptual embodiment known as a community. Michael Dell, CEO of Dell Computers, explains one of the practical ways he has begun to put this concept to work:[104]

Any kind of activity where you can get people together and communicate is very helpful for our business. You have to break down barriers and promote informal communication. You build friendships within the company, and people begin to understand that 'these people aren't out to get me; we're all in this together'. One thing I think has worked particularly well for Dell in Austin is that our workforce is very active in volunteer and community activities. We regularly sponsor volunteer fairs, and the company, through its charitable donations, directs funds at those activities that employees participate in as volunteers. We poll our employees to understand what they're interested in and direct our funds toward those charities.

When you reflect on the word *corporation*, what feelings and images arise?

When you reflect on the word *community*, what do you feel and see?

According to organizational strategists Juanita Brown and David Isaacs,[105] the responses people make to questions such as these are surprisingly consistent: *corporation* elicits feelings and images of authority, bureaucracy, competition, power, rigid rules, machines, and military chain of command. *Community* evokes feelings and visions of volunteers helping others out, barn raisings, cooperation, town meetings, democracy, and personal responsibility, commitment, teamwork, creative magic, and fun. Community gives a richer, more involved sense of people opting to be part of a relationship to a larger whole.

As I write these words on the shared sense of community, I find myself recalling a journal entry by sculptor Jenny Read (1947–76):[106]

It is not more light that is needed
in the world, it is more warmth.
We will not die of darkness but of cold.

Over the past several decades, a number of top executives have begun paying greater attention to this sense of community and the need to bring 'more warmth' as well as light to their companies, especially as we lose many of our face-to-face interactions in the shift towards virtual offices and work through the Internet and corporate intranets. Consider the community-building actions of Wayne Calloway, recently retired CEO of Pepsico. During the years he headed the growth of the $30 billion food and drink company he consistently demonstrated an active interest in the human *beings* behind the human *assets* of his organization.[107] He made it a point to express his concern for families and communities, not just careers, and in personal problems and personalities. Each has its own form of influence or resonance, one connecting to the others, and the more a leader knows about this, says Calloway, the more he can help people achieve the happiness and motivation that keeps what he calls the 'circle of creativity and value' spinning.

'Sometimes we have a person who has the right values,' he explains, 'and it is still not working,' meaning the person's performance is coming up short. 'Then it is time to ask, "What can we do to help you?" Sometimes we find out that his wife had cancer for six months and he hasn't been able to sleep at night, and a three-month leave of absence gets things back on track. Then there are other times when they say, "This job is not what I thought it was going to be, and it's not what I wanted to do, but I've got a lot of bills to pay and I just can't quit." And we say, "Maybe we'll pay your bills for a year. You go out and figure out how to make this more fun." ' Which comes, in large part, from an understanding of connection and resonance – and the power of exerting influence without authority in order to encourage people to embrace the opportunities they claim to want. Adaptability in responding to different individuals and their needs is part of building a sense of community and trust, says Calloway, 'of not saying, "Screw them. They're not performing. Get them out of here." That doesn't work.'

One of the things that does work is creating a spirit of individual and community learning at work. In 1994, the Bank of Montreal built a $50 million residential facility for its Institute for Learning (IFL).[108] Vast hallways feature windowed alcoves designed for informal conversations and a sense of community. The central hall is marked with an 'affinity wall' on which clients write new ideas and connect threads of dialogue. Open Forums are held for hundreds of people at a time, employees and managers from all levels with no planned agenda or presentations. Participants rely on open dialogue to generate innovative ideas and, in turn, to create their own agenda.

Ask yourself: are we the kind of enterprise that draws our people together as a business community, not just a workplace? Do we inspire the greatest motivation and voluntary creative participation from our members? Do we encourage real dialogue, not just within teams but through the organization? Do we actively learn things together that we *care* about, even during times of uncertainty and difficulty? Peter Drucker reminds us that the best and most dedicated people in any enterprise are volunteers, those with the opportunity to do other things with their lives besides showing up for work.

Leaders who use the language of voluntarism and community elicit what Brown and Isaacs call an 'intuitive image of mutual commitment and contribution', as opposed to training people how they *should* behave in a command-and-control workplace. Most of us are willing to commit ourselves to an inspiring organizational purpose. Yet we seek solid evidence that the enterprise, in return, is committed to us, as well. We can share the pain of difficult times. We can flow with challenges and work together to create a better future. Yet we also want to share in the rewards of building that future.

Reflect on what, specifically, you could do today, or this week, to bring an increased sense of community to your work? Will you do it?

A few years ago, a visitor to mother Teresa's Calcutta mission was in awe of the commitment being made to the nearly overwhelming and never-ending task of caring for the sick, starving and indigent.[109] 'How do you possible hope to feed all the hungry people who come to your mission?' asked the visitor. 'One mouth at a time,' came the simple, honest reply. That's what influence, and a sense of community, boil down to. That's how we'll turn our companies into companies, too – one heart at a time. One interaction at a time. This brings us to mentoring.

EQ IN ACTION: *MENTORING AND COMPASSION*

There is no one among us who would deny that the climb to the top is long and gruelling. People become fatigued, distracted, disenchanted, and disappointed. They are tempted to lose heart and give up. It is the role of a leader to encourage the heart of constituents to carry on, to steer according to the deep currents of purpose and vision. This cannot happen without example.

Caring for persons, the more able and the less able serving each other, is the rock upon which a good society is built.

Robert K. Greenleaf, Harvard Business School

Successfully intelligent people can often point to several significant role models in their life. These are people who have helped them understand their unique potential that defines a destiny. In many cases, these individuals have helped make the turn from a path of failure to one of success. It's not enough just to have such people in our lives, however. We must make the most of whatever they offer us. And then, eventually, to make the commitment to serve as role models ourselves.

According to Robert Vanourek, 'The true leader cares about the people. The leader places the well-being of the followers on a par with himself or herself. So, enlightened leadership requires a sense of inclusion and service, not selfishness. And why does a leader care? Because he or she knows the potential that is there in each of us. He or she respects those untapped powers and feelings. ... The leader wants to empower people, to unlock those hidden potentials. People intuitively sense that. They aren't foolish or dumb. They can't be tricked for long. They know in their hearts that a true leader is worthy of their trust. So they commit. Voluntarily. With their whole mind and their whole body and their whole heart. Great victories are won in the hearts of people.'[110]

Chances are, you know that Thomas Edison was granted 1,093 patents and is considered the father of modern research and development. He was inventor of the light bulb, the phonograph, and talking motion pictures. Yet few people realize that he was also credited with the concept of scientific *teamwork*. Edison's laboratories were among the first to promote collaboration among professionals, and, since he was nearly stone deaf, the efforts at collaboration were more challenging, more intuitive, as much from the heart as the head.

Cynics may claim that mentoring is mostly just a cover for the old supervisory role. Not true; in fact, far from it. Mentors don't 'solve' problems; they step forward, when asked, and provide resources and help. They do not hover. They monitor results and measurements, yet serve as a resource to be drawn upon when needed.

We cannot with integrity deny our responsibility for stewardship of every part of the whole.

M. Scott Peck, author of The Road Less Travelled

In recent years, such leaders as Robert Eaton of Chrysler and Lew Platt of Hewlett-Packard have served as mentors. The word *mentor* derives from the Greek roots meaning 'counsel', 'remember', and 'endure'. As a prominent recent article in the *Harvard Business Review* stated, 'Everyone who makes it has a mentor.' Who have your own mentors been? Ask yourself, what, specifically, have I done and am I willing to do to answer the call of mentoring? What, specifically, is my true influence – including my emotional resonance – in the larger communities of which I am a part?

It pays to notice that in many cases, leaders take it upon themselves to bring forth other leaders. William Peace, the Westinghouse general manager mentioned in Chapter 6 on trust, tells the story of Gene Cattabiani, who had been his boss and mentor.[111] In the early 1970s, Cattabiani has just taken over the troubled Westinghouse Steam Turbine Division in Philadelphia. He was forced immediately to reduce costs and raise productivity, with all indicators pointing to the factory floor, where there was deep animosity between labour and management. Several recent union strikes had grown violent, and managers saw labour as lazy and selfish, and in many cases scorned them. Cattabiani believed that Union cooperation was the key to saving the division, and vowed to treat the workforce with honesty and respect. Against the advice of his team of managers, he made the choice to give presentations to the entire labour force on the state of the business, including a question-and-answer period. Due to the size of the workforce, he scheduled several different sessions. The first immediately turned into a firestorm of protests.

Cattabiani tried to help employees see that the division was floundering and that their jobs depended on a transformed labour-management relationship. The workers, however, saw Cattabiani as the enemy and subjected him to heckling and outright verbal abuse. Peace and his other management colleagues were convinced that Cattabiani would see the error of his ways and end the presentations. He did not: with growing dread, he persevered. At each session, he exposed himself to the catcalls and insults of the mass of employees who didn't seem to notice or care about anything he said. He followed the presentations with the first in a series of regular visits to the factory floor, which was something none of his predecessors had ever attempted. He made it a point to speak directly with those who had heckled or insulted him more vehemently and, amidst this open animosity, tried to strike up conversations with them.

A human being is part of the whole, called by us the 'universe'. He experiences himself, his thoughts and feelings, as something separated from the rest – a kind of optical delusion of his consciousness. This delusion is kind of a prison for us, restricting us to our personal desires and to affection for a few persons nearest us. Our task must be to free ourselves from this prison by widening our circle of compassion to embrace all living creatures and the whole of nature in its beauty.

Albert Einstein

Within a month after these visits began, the workers he spoke to began to acknowledge his presence by nodding, and some of them appeared to be listening to what he had to say. A few even began to debate with him. He was making himself difficult to hate and impossible to ignore. Gradually, he ceased to be just a face, a useless manager, the Enemy, and became a real person to them, giving him a human status no other manager had ever had in that division. By the end of the following month, he had acquired a degree of credibility, and a dialogue soon replaced the grim, silent hostility.

In the months that followed, he initiated major changes in how the division was run, and labour-management relations improved significantly. He introduced higher standards of quality and productivity, greater work flexibility, and, where absolutely necessary, laid people off. Each change was a struggle, but Cattabiani persisted, keeping himself accessible and facing anger and dismay straight on. The division's performance improved enough to ensure its financial survival, and with it hundreds of jobs. According to William Peace, who was being mentored by Cattabiani throughout these changes, he became far better prepared to face his own challenges in the future. There is growing evidence that having a mentor and strong peer relationships are two crucial aspects of success.

Who are your current mentors? And for whom are you presently a mentor? Do you spend an hour a week, or several hours each month, in a high-EQ mentoring relationship? What is – or might be – the value of such a commitment to your personal and business life? Consider involving yourself in at least one new mentoring opportunity in the year ahead.

Not long ago, I received a call from a friend, Lynn Sontag, who had just left her post as one of the directors of executive development at 3M to become executive consultant and director of research and development for MenTTium^{SM}, an enterprise that provides expertise in the first US and Canadian mentoring programme for mid-level, high-potential women.[112] It has been cited by the US Department of Labour as the model for mentoring systems nationwide. The programme is designed to match women who aspire to senior management with top-level executives from outside their companies. More than 450 companies already sponsor their emerging female leaders for membership in MenTTium^{SM} while investing their top executives as mentors. Nearly 1,000 pairs have been successfully established, and evaluations indicate that this has been a life-changing – not simply work-changing – process for mentors and mentees alike. By the year 2000, MenTTium^{SM} plans to expand into the twenty largest US markets and begin international operations.

There are many who believe that such initiatives are essential to the larger role of business in shaping and creating the future of our entire populace and planet. If we are not only to succeed in business but also to overcome the most pressing current problems in the world, including unequal opportunities, violence, hunger, homelessness, and despair, it will require work by many mentorship groups and individuals, on many fronts, with as much ingenuity and courage, with as great a feeling of shared *community*, as went into work against segregation, apartheid, and the threat of nuclear war which Martin Luther King, Jr, and many others, rose to face.

In 1964, many were ready to abandon hope of peaceful solutions to such oppression. It was too difficult, some suggested. We're too busy with business, others complained. They were wrong. And today, over three decades later, we have more evidence than ever that we must heed

Every man must decide whether he will walk in the light of creative altruism or in the darkness of destructive selfishness. Life's most persistent and urgent question is, What are you doing for others?

Martin Luther King, Jr., 1928–68

not only our heads but our hearts, that we must reach down and step up. It is in this way that we have the greatest hope of sharing in the successes of the collaborative business empires of the new century and, at the same time, to shift our individual and collective consciousness towards creating the best possible future for humanity, one and all.

Flow: the Bridge to the Fourth Cornerstone of EQ

In this third cornerstone of EQ, each of the four competencies – unique potential and purpose, commitment and accountability, integrity, and influence – builds inner character and generates an increased sense of creativity. We also necessarily begin to integrate our emotional shadow side with our light side. We come to acknowledge readily the voices of fear and doubt that are always with us, along with the urge to live on life's surface instead of knowing its depths.

It is in the forthcoming and final cornerstone of Executive EQ, emotional alchemy, that we expand our capabilities for solution-finding, innovation and transformation, and step forward to create the future. Such competencies cannot be gained through cognition or willpower alone. Rather, they require that we *flow* with our intuition, stop pushing, let go, and *allow* our capacity for emotional alchemy to grow. In this light, *flow* can be seen as the connecting trait, or 'bridge', between the third and fourth EQ cornerstones.

THE FOURTH CORNERSTONE:

Emotional Alchemy

Sensing opportunities and *creating the future:*
Builds *confluence* – including intuitive innovation, integration,
situational transformation, and fluid intelligence

The French philosopher Jean-Paul Sartre wrote that emotions are the source of 'magical transformations of the world'.[1] This fourth cornerstone of Executive EQ initiates an exploratory discussion of several of the ways in which such transformations may be possible in work and life. We call it Emotional Alchemy. *Alchemy* is defined as '... any power or process of transmuting a common substance, thought to be of little value, into something of greater value'.

At the boundary life blossoms.

James Gleick, Chaos

Through heightened awareness and intuitive applications of emotional intelligence, we become, in effect, alchemists. We learn ways to sense, adjust and align the varying emotional frequencies or resonances we feel in ourselves and others, rather than automatically repelling or resisting them. We learn ways to apply our gut hunches, heart-felt aspirations, enthusiasm, discontent, and other emotional energies as catalysts for change and growth, or antidotes to rigidity and stagnation, in ourselves and our organizations. It is here that we begin to experience one of the key outcomes of emotional alchemy – *confluence* – which is a drawing together of disparate intuitions and talents, purposes and competencies, people and possibilities, into a unified whole.

James Autry, former Fortune 500 executive and President of the Meredith Corporation, observes that, in the final analysis, the bottom line must follow everything else, and therefore it's up to each of us as professionals and leaders to establish environments where we, and all those around us, are enabled to be at our unrestricted best in producing the bottom line. Autry refers us to his poem, 'Threads':[2]

> *Listen.*
> *In every office*
> *you hear the threads*
> *of love and joy and fear and guilt,*
> *the cries for celebration and reassurance,*
> *and somehow you know that connecting those threads*
> *is what you are supposed to do ...*

It is in this final cornerstone of EQ that, in continuing our exploration of the maps of life and work, we introduce some of the useful ways that emotional intelligence enables us more effectively to *flow* with challenges, *transform* difficult situations, *sense* opportunities, *explore*

> *Work is an attempt to find an adequate alchemy that both awakens and satisfies the very root of being.*
>
> Thomas Moore, *Care of the Soul*

uncharted territories, *change* the rules, and *create* the future. Throughout, we continue drawing together the threads of our emotional intelligence in ways that advance our work and our lives, our purpose and relationships, our learning and legacy.

CHAPTER 13

Intuitive Flow

When your intuition is highly developed, you don't have to work to turn it on, it stays on. It *flows*. It becomes part of the way your heart and senses relate to every experience and circumstance. From the shifting nature of work, from a thousand details, a hundred discussions, a towering stack of reports, and megabyte after megabyte of computer-displayed data, we call upon some sixth sense to draw us to the precise place at which to act – the one key point in this vast and changing pattern we call work where, right now, we have greatest leverage, interest, and influence. Where our presence can make a difference.

Dwell as near as possible to the channel in which your life flows.

Henry David Thoreau

That sixth sense is intuitive flow. Almost all of us have experienced it from time to time when performing at our peak or stretching beyond our limits. In art, literature, music, athletics, leadership, or when pursuing heart-felt goals in school, relationships, or business. These are often remembered as the best moments of our lives. A composer describes it this way:[3]

> You yourself are in an ecstatic state to such a point that you feel as though you almost don't exist. I've experienced this time and again. My hand seems devoid of myself, and I have nothing to do with what is happening. I just sit there watching in a state of awe and wonderment. And the music just flows out by itself.

That description is similar to hundreds recorded during two decades of research on intuitive flow and creativity by University of Chicago psychologist Mihaly Csikszentmihalyi.[4] Rock climbers, dancers, chess champions, surgeons, scientists, executives, basketball players, engineers, accountants, and even filing clerks tell of flow experiences. The signs of flow include a feeling of spontaneous challenge and elation, and even, on occasion, rapture. You're performing at a very high level of alertness and accomplishment. Because flow feels so integrated and fluid, it's intrinsically rewarding and increases our creative confidence. It drives us to take creative risks and make outstanding achievements. You are transcending daily routine and preoccupations. Intuitive flow gives us a heightened sense of self-worth and satisfaction. And there is evidence we can *choose* to experience this state more often, perhaps even continually, in our lives and work;[5] but most people don't.

At least, not yet.

I've known some exceptional men and women who, on their best days, worked in intuitive flow. And one of the most remarkable examples of flow that I've ever experienced didn't happen to be in business. It was when I had a chance to spend a few days learning from a master at tracking lost children. His name was Ab Taylor, and he was one of the US Border Patrol's most successful trackers. Charles Bronson starred in a movie about his life.

For thirty years, in some of the most dangerous conditions and most daunting terrains, Ab had been called in to find armed fugitives from justice or children who had wandered off from their family at a wilderness campground or had run away from home. His heart went out to them. He was the one who would find them, terrified when their calls for help went unheeded, sometimes for days. These were children trapped in a nightmare. Some of them died. Once local law enforcement and search and rescue teams had exhausted their own best efforts to find the child, Ab was flown in.

To watch Ab at work evoked in me a sense of awe. He could pick up the trail at any point and follow it, for days if need be, through dense forest in day or night. He had learned to read every impression that can be made by a human foot. He knew every subtle marking left when a leg or arm passed through foliage. He knew what the rain or the passage of time did to tracks. In the still of the night or the roar of a storm he could follow 'old' trails, including those all but obliterated beneath the footprints left by groups of eager, untrained searchers before he arrived.

At the start, Ab would reach a point in the trail and swing his gaze from side to side, getting a good sense of the terrain. Usually, he'd been briefed about the person he was to find, and he told me he would always take several moments to imagine: what if he were this person? What would it feel like to be running or lost? Where would he go?

Then he would turn things over to his gut instincts and innermost intuition and begin tracking. Almost immediately he was in a state of intuitive flow. That's one thing researchers have found about this kind of optimal experience: intuitive flow is not something that happens when we are passive or distanced by the mind from an experience; it occurs when we are fully engaged with that experience and stretch ourselves to accomplish something difficult or worthwhile.[6] In other words, it is not something that happens *to* us or is random, it's something we *make* happen.

To walk next to Ab Taylor when he was tracking was to witness a man moving quickly and gracefully, almost noiselessly; he sensed – rather than saw – the signs. From time to time, he would stop and explain how his intuition noticed some nearly invisible signs, combining them so clearly that he could almost *be* the person running or lost. From a million small signs he could sense the fear or panic of the person he was tracking, and their level of tension and fatigue. Ab knew he had not a single moment to spare. He dreaded finding a child who had just died, perhaps only a few hours before Ab arrived. Those images haunted him.

During the time I spent with him, I remember feeling that the complexities that Ab Taylor faced were an apt metaphor for what many of us must deal with in our life and work. We seek something just ahead, in the unknown. The wilderness of business life is ever changing. It is complex and uncertain. We must marshal every asset at our disposal, every instinct, every kind of intelligence to see us through. We can't afford to miss any of the signs, or to drift off the trail and get lost. The rational mind cannot accomplish all of this. Not all at once. No chance. We need the heart to do it. We need the kind of intuitive flow that Ab Taylor had.

Or some other, equally powerful kind. Max Planck, the father of quantum theory in physics, felt that the pioneer scientist and professional must have 'a vivid intuitive imagination for new ideas not generated by deduction'.[7] I remember being in a scientific laboratory at a branch of the Max Planck Institute in Germany. It was first thing in the morning and I was talking with scientists doing research on cellular production of adenosine triphosphate, ATP, the energy of life. I'll never forget the feeling of incredible excitement in that lab. It was contagious. As I met members of the research teams engaged in different aspects of the investigation, I realized that what was taking place was innovative collaboration of the highest order. Times of intuitive flow. From one discovery to the next. One mind and heart to the next. Continually venturing from the edges of the known into the unknown.

The institute's director explained to me that the staff scientists came from more than a dozen different countries. They were charged – individually and as teams – with designing and conducting research that, in most cases, no other scientific institutions in the world were presently conducting. Once an initiative had been advanced to the point were a university or other institution would take on the project, those at Max Planck would wrap up their study and move on to the next frontier of investigation. I was told that each study must hold the promise of providing something of value to humanity or to the healthy future of our planet. Here, in the midst of scientific rigour, creative hunches seemed to be in play at all times. So was good humour. Despite the long hours and modest pay, what seemed to keep these men and women engaged in the combination of intuitive flow backed by meticulous analysis was the excitement of *ongoing* innovation. Not the occasional 'bolt out of the blue' creativity in other institutions. Here, it was something they were living every day. And every year they were publishing hundreds of studies on their findings. Wow.

> *There are always two parties, the party of the past and the party of the future; the establishment and the movement.*
>
> Ralph Waldo Emerson, 1803–82, US essayist and poet

To this day, a decade and a half later, I remember the amazing feeling that place generated. There have been times in working with 3M and few other companies when I've felt something akin to that feeling. But what organization couldn't benefit from more intuitive flow and creative advancement among its leaders and professionals?

I believe it's something within reach of people in every field.

Direct Knowing without the Conscious Use of Reasoning

Thomas Edison had an intuitive way of hiring new engineers.[8] After completing an interview, he'd give the applicant a light bulb and ask, 'How much water will it hold?'

> *The really valuable thing is intuition.*
>
> Albert Einstein

There were two principal ways to determine the answer. The first involved using gauges to measure all the angles of the bulb, plotting the numbers on paper and making advanced mathematical estimates of the bulb's surface area and then, taking into account glass thickness, project the volume. At its best, this was a difficult process – considering the shape of a light bulb – and required up to thirty minutes or more.

The second approach was to fill the bulb with water and then pour the contents into a measuring cup. Total elapsed time: about a minute.

Engineers who met the other requirements but took the first route in the light bulb question, performing their measurements by the book, were thanked politely for their time and sent on their way. If you took the second route, you heard Edison say, 'You're hired.'

During the darkest periods of the Revolutionary War, George Washington turned his deepest challenges over to the creative, intuitive part of himself. By his own testimony,[9] Washington used that kind of insight to guide his decisions during his presidency. So did Abraham Lincoln. According to Willis W. Harman, President of the Institute for Noetic Sciences, the founding fathers thought intuition was so important that they made it a point to remind us on the back of the US dollar bill, where there is an unfinished pyramid with an eye over the top of it. The meaning of this symbol is thousands of years old: 'To light the way.' We do not become whole and successful until our intuition is playing an integral role in guiding our decisions.[10]

Leaders have many different ways to refer to intuition: as an inner way of knowing, their sixth sense, gut feeling, deeper self, or higher instinct, while others speak of inner guidance. The dictionary defines *intuition* as 'direct knowing without the conscious use of reasoning'. As noted in Chapter 4, it's one of the most sought-after qualities in an entrepreneur or leader. Intuition is closely related to, and can transcend, emotional intelligence. It *moves* us and, at an advanced level, we learn to enter intuitive flow by choice rather than chance. It helps us listen to the heart to distinguish opportunity from vulnerability. Truth from politics. Depth from motion. Intuition is a heightened dimension of emotional intelligence. As business school professor Weston Agor puts it, 'intuitive signals are transmitted in the form of *feelings*'.[11]

Throughout history, many of the world's greatest scientists, philosophers, musicians, artists, entrepreneurs, and leaders, including such individuals as Einstein, Churchill, Gandhi, Eleanor Roosevelt, Rachel Carson, Beethoven, and Mozart, have freely admitted that they owed their greatest accomplishments to intuition. No longer the province of a gifted few, intuition is now recognized as a natural human ability, and a key dimension of the creative princess, problem-solving and decision making.

In one classic case set forth by the Newark College of Engineering, researchers tested business executives for precognition – the ability to sense or anticipate the future – and found that CEOs of successful firms were, on average, able to use intuition to anticipate the future at a rate that significantly exceeded chance expectations. Executives whose companies were losing money scored below average and deviated significantly from chance levels.[12]

'When I go into a factory, no matter where in the world, I can sense the atmosphere if I walk around for a half hour with the factory manager,' says Jan Timmer, CEO of the Holland-based electronics giant Philips, with 241,000 employees and $34 billion in sales.[13] 'I can tell you whether that factory works or not; I can tell it from the body language of the employees and the way the people react to the foreman and the answers people give to him and the managers, and how unafraid they are. And I can walk out without looking at the figures, and I can tell you if that factory makes money.' This a clear *feel* for people, trends, and capacities – backed by knowledge, experience and caring.

> *The primary wisdom is intuition. In that deep force, the last fact behind which analysis cannot go, all things find their origin.*
>
> Ralph Waldo Emerson

Think about it. When you first started out in business, what happened if you noticed your boss or a customer looking uncomfortable when discussing last month's sales figures or projecting growth from a new product line. You, sensing you are on to something important, may have said, 'I noticed you looked uncomfortable when talking about those sales figures and growth projections. What's the matter?' If the other person was alone and in a relaxed mood, he or she might have simply looked embarrassed and said, 'It's nothing. There's nothing for you to be concerned about.' But if it happened in front of a group, or if the other person was tense or tired, you might have been blasted, hearing the boss telling you such insubordination is not tolerated in this company, and to worry about your own performance and sales figures, not how things appear to your untrained eye. Sometimes it takes only one experience like this to blunt your innate voice of intuition. The more often this happens, the harder you must work to reclaim it later on.

Type-1 and Type-2 Challenges

Many business people still see management as just one set of circumstances after another, sets which repeat themselves, can often be analyzed in advance, planned for, and solutions decided on prior to their arrival.[14] Such Type-1 situations, as they are called, constitute the core of management training programmes. Yet a survey of fifty of America's top CEOs[15] and related research[16] suggests that today's executives, managers and professionals are constantly confronted with a maze of problems and opportunities beyond the scope of what he or she has learned in school or on the job. Compare the following:[17]

Type-1 business situations	Type-2 business situations
Simple or analyzable	Complex-unanalyzable
Solutions foreseeable	Solutions unforeseeable
Solutions predictable	Solutions unpredictable
Opportunities are obvious	Opportunities are hidden
Unchanging conditions	Changing conditions
Programmable	Unprogrammable
'A' leads to 'B'	'A' may or may not lead to 'B'
May occur routinely	Never routine
Similar to 'XYZ'	Unique
Can be planned for in advance	Cannot be planned for in advance

Due to accelerating social, political, and technological change, the incidence of Type-2 situations is dramatically increasing – and companies will remain successful only if their leaders and professionals can master continually changing conditions, which are *not* treatable with standard management solutions. They require more than technical analysis; they require emotional intelligence and, in particular, intuitive flow.

This, at its best, is not something you turn on and off. With practice, it's both natural and ongoing, enabling you to manage more fluidly Type-2 challenges. At its essence, intuitive flow is about *allowing* your inner senses to guide you rather than trying to *control* or *force* it to happen. Emerson called it the 'blessed impulse' and neurologist Antonio Damasio calls it 'the mysterious mechanism by which we arrive at the solution of a problem *without* reasoning toward it'.[18] It's a valuable kind of knowing that is readily acknowledged and utilized by a growing number of executives.

Two decades ago, Henry Mintzberg reported in the *Harvard Business Review* (HBR) the results of an extensive study of executives.[19] He found that the best manager and leader operating under chaotic and unpredictable conditions is a 'holistic thinker ... constantly relying on hunches to cope with problems far too complex for rational analysis'. Mintzberg concluded that 'organizational effectiveness does not lie in that narrow-minded concept called "rationality"; it lies in a blend of clear-headed logic *and* powerful intuition'.[20]

There is something within you that knows much more than you know.

Rochelle Myers, co-author of Creativity in Business

Mintzberg's findings are echoed in a recent HBR report, which noted: 'The ultimate expression of understanding is highly trained intuition – for example, the insight of a seasoned director who knows instinctively which projects to fund and exactly when to do so.'[21] Or an experienced manager who is hiring, appraising, planning, or interacting. Or an entrepreneur searching for a breakaway idea, or an investment advisor who realizes that the ordinary financial rules of thumb enable us to calculate only 20 to 30 per cent of risk in an investment.[22] Ed McCracken, CEO of Silicon Graphics, explains, 'You have to do all your homework, but then you have to go with your intuition without letting your mind get in the way.'[23]

One company that learned the hard way to champion intuitive flow is 3M. After pulling themselves from the brink of bankruptcy just after the turn of the century, the managers and scientists at 3M vowed to sustain a corporate culture where every new idea was welcomed and considered.

Shortly after the Second World War, 3M introduced a clear cellulose acetate tape, coated on one side with pressure-sensitive adhesive.[24] They called it Scotch Tape, based on the fact that they intended it as a book mending material, and a way of preserving things that would otherwise be thrown away. In the consumers' hands, the product quickly came to be used in hundreds of ways, few of which had anything to do with mending books or torn papers. It was used to wrap packages, decorate surfaces, affix labels, secure posters to walls and photos to album pages, even to curl hair and take lint off clothing.

3M's managers did not regard any of these unexpected uses as a failure of their marketing plan. And neither did they write them off as a stroke of good fortune. They *noticed* them. They *sensed* or *felt* the consumer excitement and linked their intuition with emerging ideas to explore quickly new markets and variations on the product. Every step of the way they stayed open to surprises and possibilities. They became even better at listening. They enjoyed creative dialogues with current and possible customers. They backed each new hunch with rigorous analysis and, wherever they sensed it was right, with investment and development processes.

234

Executives at a handful of other visionary firms adopted a similar approach. Max Palevsky worked as a mathematician at Bendix Corporation, then founded Packard Bell Computer Corporation, next founded Scientific Data Systems Inc., and finally became a member of the board of Xerox after its acquisition of Scientific Data Systems. He learned to count on his intuition because, in his words, 'The decisions I made where I trusted my intuition were far and away better than the ones where I second guessed.'[25]

Consider the following story from Kate Ludeman, an engineer with a doctorate in psychology who is CEO of the Worth Ethic Corporation in Austin, Texas:[26]

Intuitive managers have special skills that are likely to become more valuable in tomorrow's rapidly changing environment. They are the people who dream up the new products. ... They are the people who have a feel for what the consumer wants.

Weston H. Agor, University of Texas

I took January 1991 off for rest and relaxation, as a reward for my first year of billing half a million dollars as a consultant. I spent most of it with my daughter, enjoying the outdoors. For a year I had been toying with the idea of creating proprietary software for conducting personal assessments and other surveys. Every time I thought about this I got the special flurrying feeling in my chest that I get when I have an intuition that I ought to move on rapidly. The glitch was that these developmental projects are costly, and I would have to dig deep into my own pocket to do it. Also, I talked to several companies to assess enthusiasm for 360-degree assessments. It was lukewarm at best, because no one knew that such assessments would become popular until a few years later.

I decided to run the idea past Ken Schroeder, president of KLA Instruments who had been my mentor and coach to me in the mid-eighties. Ken strongly recommended that I go ahead. I mounted some resistance, arguing that my daughter was just starting college and I didn't have extra money to spend. In spite of what my inner critic said, I trusted Ken, and I trusted my own body-sense of intuition. Even though I had little support from my potential customers, I decided to go ahead with the project. I spent $20,000 in 1991 on developing the product. After I had committed my own money and time, Intel gave me $15,000 to customize the software for their company, so in actuality I invested only $5,000 of my own money. To date (autumn, 1995), the product has brought in $3,000,000 in revenue. I'm tremendously grateful to Ken for helping me believe in the project and my own intuition.

If you want to go from here to there in business, no straight line will take you.

William Ahmanson, Chairman, National American Life Insurance Company

That's great, you may be thinking, but isn't there a downside to intuitive flow in business? For the most part, no, although like any other aspect of emotional intelligence, it must be developed with practice and applied with awareness. That said, here's an important caveat to consider: in social psychology, several studies question the trustworthiness of everyday intuitions about the intentions, thoughts, and feelings of other people.[27] In other words, we perceive others through the filter of our own thoughts, habits, and feelings. When you have a hunch that someone is ignoring you or misleading you, for example, ask them if what you're sensing is true. Sometimes it is not.

Remember our discussion in Chapters 1 and 3 about the brain's reticular activating system (RAS), which appears to play a central role in accentuating, or magnifying, criticisms and prompting you to assume the worst when you get ambiguous signals from other people. Example: when someone looks away while you're trying to make a point, it's likely that you're *not* the cause – this person maybe is tense, tired or distracted about something else in their life or work. Unfortunately, we tend to take such gestures personally, and negatively. That's the RAS magnifying worst-case thinking. You have to question such 'intuitions'. When you have a hunch about another person's intentions, thoughts, or feelings, be clear and ask.

EQ Map Connections: Intuitive Flow
You may want to refer to the following scales of the *EQ Map* as points of reflection related this chapter: life events, emotional awareness of others, creativity, intuition, and personal power

---

EQ IN ACTION: *EXERCISING YOUR INTUITIVE FLOW*

One of the main things to remember is that, in most cases, you don't just need *more* intuition, you need *better* intuition, a clearer and more trustworthy inner voice. It needs to be nurtured and observed, questioned, stretched and respected. There is no 'perfect time' to practise and apply it.

So don't wait for one. Start wherever you are and go from there. Kabir said, 'Wherever you are is the entry point.' I have found that this is not only true but can be a remarkable time-saver in my work and life. Here are several documented ways to make it easier to enter intuitive flow:[28]

Immerse yourself in the experience.
Intuitive flow is a natural human capacity, so you don't have to *try* to receive impressions or force it to happen. You *allow* it by immersing yourself in each experience, with your senses tuned. Make it a point to intentionally direct your complete attention on the task or challenge at hand, since a highly attentive state of mind and emotions is essential to intuitive flow.

Stretch your capabilities.
Entry into flow can occur when you engage in tasks you are learning to be proficient at, and then increase the level of challenge so that it moderately taxes your abilities. As Csikszentmihalyi explains: 'People seem able to enter flow best when the demands on them are a bit greater than usual. If there is too little demand on them, people are bored. If there is too much for them to handle, they get anxious. Flow occurs in that delicate zone between boredom and anxiety.'

Stay open to all possibilities and transcend fear.
You can't be intuitive if you're trying to be right. Don't worry about whether your intuitive impressions are 'right' or 'wrong'. Remember that intuitive flow is an inner information-gathering process that can help draw you closer to the truth or success. The first impressions you receive don't have to make sense with one another. They may even seem contradictory. Wait for a few moments or more before allowing your mind to judge what's right for you. You can usually evaluate and modify hunches later on.

In addition, intuitive flow often occurs most readily for those who have become adept at stepping outside rigid beliefs, positions, biases, and opinions about the way things are or should be. Fear cultivates projection – imaginary evils that rarely come to pass. We know, for example, that on any given day, many people – especially those who are tense or tired – in rush hour traffic or racing through an airport have images of their car or plane crashing. However, it's extremely rare when such 'flashes' are valid intuitions. They are, instead, fears projected forwards onto upcoming events. Throughout the work day, practise distinguishing the sensation of fear from the voice of intuition. Learn to distinguish between fear and genuine intuitive hunches. It takes practice to keep ourselves from getting trapped in the predictable. If not, while we're worrying about looking foolish in front of others, our competitors who've moved beyond such fears will be creating new products and services, dreaming up scintillating campaigns, and coming up with ingenious solutions.

To keep your intuition flowing, be sure to notice when the barrier of self-censorship shows up. It's what Michael Ray, the noted creativity professor at Stanford Business School, calls the 'voice of judgment'.[29] One of the ways you'll recognize this inner critic is by a faint sensation of fear, and a voice whispering to you to pull back, to stop sensing and exploring. This voice of negativity and judgment says, 'This is a waste of time,' 'It'll never work,' 'Everyone will think I'm foolish.' What if you are talking to another person who happens to be a prospective customer, and, instead of your usual instinct to fly to his city to follow through, you have the urge *not* to? Is this urge coming from a fear that it will be difficult to make the sale, or is it a genuine intuition that the meeting will be unnecessary or unproductive, or that there is something closer to home that matters more?

Identify, and find ways to move beyond, whatever blocks you from flow.
Some people have a difficult time sustaining intuitive flow when they get interrupted too often by others or the phone. If this is the case with you, do whatever you can to gain a few longer stretches of time – as few as ten or fifteen interruption-free minutes may be enough – here and there throughout the day when you route phone calls to a message board, voice-mail or an answering machine. For other people, what blocks flow may be the sense of confinement or sameness – they need external stimulation to enter flow and may benefit from periodically stepping out the door for a few minutes, for instance, or changing environments more often.

Extend your senses beyond business.
Intuitive flow in any area of life will likely enhance the others as well. I remember how the original theoretician of computer sciences, Norbert Wiener, founder of the scientific field of cybernetics, met Albert Einstein only once, by chance, on a Swiss train traversing Lake Geneva. Weiner recounted that during the entire time they travelled together, they never once spoke of physics or mathematics, but were principally immersed in a state of intuitive flow as they sat side by

side and observed the intricate, shifting light and colours of the clouds, lake, and hills. The world of nature was communicating, and they listened together with gratitude and wonder, which can foster a creative, receptive openness to intuitive flow in other areas of life and work as well.[30] When's the last time something like this outside the job captured *all* of your attention?

Pay extra attention to your *first* response to questions.
Intuitive flow often gets set in motion, or sustained, through good questions – those we ask silently as well as those asked aloud. We lose intuitive flow the instant we're not emotionally honest with ourselves, or try to be clever or to respond in ways we hope will impress others or make us look good. In many daily activities, you'll notice yourself asking questions from moment to moment. How am I doing? What's next? Am I learning anything? Will this pay off? Right now, what do I want? What are the hidden signs that may help me advance? It's a good idea to keep these reflective queries as simple and direct as possible so they can serve as catalysts that generate useful intuitive information and insights.

Notice how your intuition communicates with you.
Intuition seems to come in on three channels: word, picture, and emotional body-sense. Most of us receive all three, but are better on one channel than another. According to researchers Gay Hendricks and Kate Ludeman, it seems that the majority of us get our intuitions in the form of images and gut feelings.[31] Therefore, it can pay to sharpen your ongoing awareness of what you feel and what images arise when you face the next problem or imagine the future. Through self-observation you can learn better to notice when your sense of intuition is conveying a message to you.

Spend several minutes a day on EQ Notes.
In order to active our intuitive flow, we need to take concrete steps to clear away much of the frustrating, trivial stuff that echoes in your head and stands between you and your creative power. The best way to do this is get it down on paper. Seriously. There's excellent research that writing a few pages a day of stream-of-consciousness stuff, no matter how random or rough, can help develop emotional intelligence and heal past hurts.[32] We introduced EQ Morning Notes and a Daily EQ Journal in Chapter 1. Hopefully, you're still doing them. They

activate your inner senses and can directly contribute to your intuitive flow throughout the day.

By getting out of bed every morning and devoting a few minutes to emotionally honest writing – remember, there's no 'wrong' way to do this – you help to bypass the mind's critic that so often belittles and disempowers us. You may hear an inner voice saying, 'This doesn't make sense. Give it up.' Know that your logical mind is acting as censor, trying to blunt intuition. It's good at this. Very good. Don't ignore it, but don't let it dominate you, either. Write it down, and then move on. Acknowledge all of your impressions. Feeling tired, anxious about an upcoming meeting or the work day ahead, or hopeful about that new project? Write it down. It's important to write by hand, rather than type or dictate your thoughts and feelings. Through the hand – slower than the tongue but tied to the heart – we begin to see how we feel. This voice on the page seldom lies.

This is why you must simply write Morning Notes, no matter what mind chatter tries to dissuade or distract you. Enjoy music? Turn some on, in particular, the kind of expansive music that instills a sense of safety and lifts your spirits. See if this helps you sidestep your mental censor. With or without music, jot down whatever things sweep through your consciousness – concerns about the job, that next car you've been wanting, tonight's dinner, or the weird look in someone's eye. Some things may be deeper and more significant, such as:

'I've got to take better care of my health.'

'My gut tells me there's a better opportunity just around the corner.'

'I sense our company is losing its competitive edge, but I don't know why.'

'I feel that (a person's name) is hurting inside, and is trying not to let on.'

The EQ Morning Notes and EQ Journal share a simple purpose: to teach you to stop judging yourself, and your creative capabilities, and just allow yourself, through writing a few pages a day by hand to listen to the voice of your feelings and clear the way for intuitive flow.

Add a range of confidence.

One of the key points to remember is that *intuition adds to good judgment; it does not replace it.* There are many useful ways to clarify intuition. Decision science researchers suggest that every estimate or decision, no matter how intuitive, includes a *level of confidence.*[33] For example, let's say you have a conversation or meeting and give an intuitive estimate, such as 'I believe we can sell between 150,000 and

200,000 widgets next year to market A.' If you add, 'I feel 80 per cent sure,' this gives a different sense of your confidence than 'I'm reasonably sure,' which might mean 10 to 50 per cent certainty. In business, where numbers always matter to some degree and accuracy is vital, adding a level of confidence is a smart way to combine heart and head, and make intuition more explicit.

As you develop intuitive flow, one of the other feelings you may begin to experience – as many leaders and top performers like Ab Taylor do – is that of timelessness, of being wholly absorbed in what you're doing, giving it your complete attention. But what about those occasions, both on and off the job, when you find yourself struggling to complete a dozen disparate tasks and cope with frequent interruptions? In these circumstances, we must call upon another dimension of emotional intelligence which I call reflective time-shifting, the subject of the next chapter.

CHAPTER 14

Reflective Time-Shifting

Whenever any of us in business brings up an unusual creative idea or mentions some unconventional way to boost effectiveness or solve problems, someone invariably asks, 'How, exactly, would you put that into practice at *this* company?' This is a good question. Here's what happened when it was asked of me by a vice-president and senior editor at a one of the world's leading publishing houses.

Time is the substance I am made of. Time is a river that sweeps me along, but I am the river; it is a tiger that rips me apart, but I am the tiger; it is a fire that consumes me, but I am the fire.

Jorge Luis Borges, author of A Personal Anthology

I was in Manhattan for a meeting and had just described some of my experiences with executive teams using a creative principle known as the Zeigarnick Effect,[34] which is about keeping all creative possibilities in play for as long as possible on important projects, rather than hurrying through things or doing something the usual way, just to get it off your list. The moment you reach closure, virtually every bit of creativity on that project, issue, or possibility shuts down. It's over with.

'But that's how we get things done around here,' I hear people say. True, but not your best work. When you do something exceptional, almost always you stop doing your job like an administrator. Something grabs your attention and you start caring about what this project or challenge is *really* all about. You feel energized and you instinctively begin holding yourself and others accountable for creative inputs and best effort. You stretch yourself, exploring new ground until the last possible minute. You likely have more fun than usual even though, towards the finish, you're sweating the time line. In nearly every case, you end up creating something great or learning something valuable.

At the publishing firm, I asked, 'When you think about this year's important projects, name one of them that your intuition tells you could be transformed for greater success.' There came an immediate reply: seasonal sales conferences. These events, which are tied to semi-annual sales catalogues describing new books, are the pivotal way in which a publishing house motivates its sales representatives to hustle up advance orders from booksellers.

'What does your intuition tell you is missing in your catalogues and sales conferences?' I asked.

'We rarely seem to be able to pull together all of our best creative ideas before the catalogues go to press and the sales conferences are held,' said the editor.

The vice-president was nodding, and she added, 'We know that we publish some of the most important and exciting books, books that could sell thousands more copies each year if we could convey everything that's great about them in our catalogue and to the sales reps.'

'For the sake of an example,' I said, 'let's take a look at those books being shipped to stores this season, today. About a year ago you were putting together the catalogue for these books and briefing the reps at the sales conference about them, hoping to get large advance orders from the book stores. If you could go back in time and change anything about that catalogue and sales conference, what feels most important? What was missing?'

The editor said, 'We could have brought in the cover-design and catalogue-layout teams earlier than usual to brainstorm design possibilities for the books we were most excited about.'

'And we might have involved the key sales reps, too,' added the vice-president.

'OK. Let's shift our attention to another season of books,' I suggested. 'Let's take the new books you've just finished editing, the ones that will be in the next catalogue and sales conferences. Let's imagine you had no constraints, either on time or resources. What does your intuition tell you needs to be done right now, this month, to make the new list of books set revenue records? How, exactly, do you feel you could make every one of these books more successful?'

It was the vice-president who spoke first. 'In our weekly meetings, we could refocus some of the time spent on relatively petty details, or on talking about books in stores now, and use it to create more innovative ways to sell future books.'

'It would also make a big difference if we could gain at least two months more lead time for the catalogue and sales conference,' added the editor, tapping his fingers on the conference table.

When you embrace a new idea, a new business, new product . . . – you have to make sure that everyone throughout the company knows about it early enough so that every segment of the business can promote or exploit its potential in every other possible market, product, or context.

Michael Eisner, Chairman and CEO,
The Walt Disney Co.

'Any other ideas?' I asked.

'What if we explored getting everyone together – designers, publicists, marketing people, sales reps, authors, and editors – once every month or two on videoconference, perhaps through the Internet or in some other innovative and efficient way, to advance creative ideas about each new book,' suggested the vice-president.

'Yes,' agreed the editor, 'that's one of the ways we could come up with better promotional and marketing approaches. And with some extra lead time, we might find lots of other ways to make this work.'

Our meeting came to a close and, after we shook hands, one of them left the room saying, 'At next week's board meeting, I'm going to recommend some changes in how we do things around here.'

Freeing Yourself in Time

The preceding story illustrates what I call *reflective time-shifting*.[35] It's based on the fact that we each *feel* a sense of time, and by using this aspect of emotional intelligence we are able at will consciously to direct our feelings, which include creative intuition, from *past*-experience to *future*-experience and then to *present*-experience. In this way we shift perspectives, and can alternately choose to be forward-sensing and alert to new opportunities, or aware of past experiences and lessons learned, or fully attentive to the present. With practice, we can make such sensory adjustments to time in a matter of moments. It makes us more flexible and adaptable to circumstances. We innovate more readily. We get stuck less often. We flow.

Albert Einstein was a champion of such intuitive shifts in reflection. Consider the story, related by the physicist Banesh Hoffmann, Einstein's assistant in 1937, of what it was like when Einstein came to an impassable obstacle in his work, or others came to such an obstacle and would seek his help:[36]

We would all pause and Einstein would stand up quietly and say, in his quaint English, 'I will a little think.' So saying, he would pace up and down and walk around in circles.... At these moments of high drama, [we] would remain completely still, not daring to make a sound, lest we interrupt his intuitive feelings or train of thought.

Minutes would elapse this way and then, all of a sudden, Einstein would visibly relax and a smile would light up his face ... then he would tell us the solution he had sensed to the problem, and almost always the solution worked.... The solution sometimes was so simple we could have kicked ourselves for not having been able to think of it by ourselves. But that magic was performed invisibly in the recesses of Einstein's intelligence.

Reflective time-shifting is about your ability to experience more fully a specific point in time, and to grasp intuitively connections and feelings evoked *during* that time. It's not just the *notion* or *idea* of the future or past. It's about feeling – and thereby imagining, no matter how briefly – actually *being* there, *feeling* the experience, reflecting on it, and positioning yourself to do something more effective, and perhaps innovative, in the present, something based on inner values rather than reaction or expediency.

Reflective time-shifting is a dimension of emotional alchemy because it enables you to face the same thing that others around you are facing but to do it with sharper instincts, or greater creative engagement or involvement, and thereby to respond differently, more wisely and innovatively, because you are not stuck in time with your feelings and thoughts. You also begin to develop an exceptional *tolerance for ambiguity* and can leave things 'in process' or 'in play', creatively speaking. You are still highly effective in accomplishing your objectives. Yet, in doing so, you can stay open and imaginative longer than your competitors do. And you actively encourage such capabilities in others. You bypass the tendency, which is especially strong in Americans, to label possibilities and challenges as either 'right' or 'wrong', 'good' or 'bad'.

Francis Crick and James Watson found some of the missing pieces to their work on the structure of DNA in the published work of Linus Pauling, who missed out on getting credit for the discovery because he couldn't tolerate ambiguity quite long enough and settled for a structure – a helical one – but not quite the right one. Like many of us developing a creative idea, when things get really uncomfortable we become impatient, and may prematurely settle for less than our best possible solution or contribution. Or your boss or partner or customer may be putting all kinds of pressure on you to get this initiative, whatever it is, over with. Time and again, products and services are brought to market that weren't quite right. In many cases this is because a person or company was unwilling to use the Zeigarnick Effect to stay creatively open as long as possible, and to capitalize on the resulting creative 'tension' to gather more insights and produce a better product. What might have been a huge success ends up mediocre, or worse. Or a competitor jumps in and gets it right.

Creative Time-mapping

For the next several pages, I am going to shift our focus from the individual to the group, and review several of the simple tools I have used to help executives, managers, and professionals develop their capacity to time-shift and stay open longer to creative inputs. A number of breakthrough ideas have been sparked by a process known as flow-charting, or creative time-mapping. In some organizations, really sophisticated software is used to display and link new ideas digitally. In other companies, the emphasis is on white boards and large clipboards designed to capture creative inputs across time. Posted in central locations, any group member can walk up and enter ideas to improve the business, note a pet peeve or intuitive concern. It is then management's responsibility to provide clear, insightful responses. It sounds simple, yet it's an effective method to express feelings and capture group creativity.

In other innovation-conscious companies, individuals and teams use traditional large square Post-It notes or, if possible, hexagonal-shaped Post-Its called Keynotes.[37] This kind of flow-charting is similar to the physics departments in many leading laboratories and universities, where hallways are lined with blackboards which facilitate ongoing dialogues between and among physicists and other scientists reaching for insights and break-throughs.

In the business setting, creative time-mapping or flow-charting requires either a flip chart, an oversized pad of paper on the top of a conference table, or a large sheet of white paper (4' × 6' paper, and larger sizes, is available in rolls in many office supply stores) affixed to the wall of a meeting room. You choose a work concern or a creative idea or question, and write this in bold letters in the top of the paper. Then you begin to build a map. On square or hex-sided Post-Its you write various elements of a revamped work process, for example, or time line, or better ways to enter a new market or implement and test a new idea. One by one you

246

stick the Post-Its on the chart, connecting the edge of one to the edge of another.

Almost immediately, it's likely you'll begin to notice unexpected connective relationships, including missing links, areas of vulnerability, or hidden opportunities. The reason for using Post-Its is that they're moveable. They help you get past thinking in lines and boxes. Anyone involved with a project can change the positions of various notes, raising questions and inserting ideas for improvement or breakthrough. The six-sided shape of the Keynotes helps stimulate multi-directional shifts across time and playing out intuitive hunches. As the flow chart expands, you begin visually and emotionally to sense hidden linkages and possibilities, and this brings teams and individuals closer together in shaping future business.

With this flow chart, you can time-shift ahead into the future and imagine what various outcomes would feel like, and then return to present circumstances and concerns, shifting the positions of Post-Its and realigning the present to intersect a better future outcome. The map can end up taking on any shape, eventually involving not only your own enterprise but current and potential markets and customers, suppliers and collaborators, friends and families, today and far into the future. At any time you walk up and rotate, move, or replace any note. You might use different colours for different purposes.

Keep asking yourself, how do I feel about this picture, about the connections? What's missing or possible? The chart encourages being flexible not only in process but in *time*, and sparks unexpected linkages from idea to idea, problem to possibility. When today's meeting ends, you can leave the chart openly unfinished, serving as a visual and gut-level stimulus to generate more ideas, taking advantage of the Zeigarnick Effect. This can really pay off.

At Hughes Technical Management Systems, all proposals are put through a 'wall review' with a Post-It flow chart. 'The comments and comments-on-comments lead to a much better proposal,' says Tom McDaniel, a manager with Hughes.[38]

Mark Morgan, Manager of the Total Quality Program at Grumman Technical Services, engaged his team to create a flow chart which he called a Process Tree.[39] They began by identifying the major operations and processes, business services (accounting and compensation, for example), technical services (equipment and systems, measurements, and so on), and value for existing and potential customers. Work teams got actively involved. According to Morgan:

Everything we did as an organization was illustrated in a 10' by 6' diagram – 850 individual tasks were linked together on this chart. Something unexpected happened when it was all laid out. We posted it in an active conference room – almost everyone came trough the door in the course of the week for one meeting or another. We found people stopping to look at the chart and understand it – they would look for their place on the chart and say, 'Wow, that's what I do – I never really understood how I fit into the whole process.' They gained insight as to their individual role.

People began to leave keynotes to correct language and processes. They got involved with the process map and when the steering committee began to look for improvements, they had a picture of the entire operation. They began to see how changes could ripple through the entire organization.

Prior to that we would charter a team to go look at a piece of the system and they would feel disconnected. When we talked about doing something that impacted profit, they would say, 'We aren't involved with profit' or 'What we do doesn't impact that.' By using this diagram, we could show their connection to cost, research, service, or defect measures that then related to profit.

Our overhead rates have come down by 18 per cent which helped us win a $340 million job. All of our twelve key indicators have shown steady improvements. And our accounting team's ability to report information improved significantly. They consolidated several processes and had an 88 per cent improvement in the cycle time for producing financial reports.

On a more personal note, a number of executives and managers I've worked with have chosen to put up a small white board in a common office area and begin to use creative time-mapping or flow-charting for their priority projects and individual or shared creative ideas. How might such a practice benefit your work?

Extending Your Time Horizon

How we relate to time says a lot about us. There's growing evidence that the farther into the future you can imagine – and feel – yourself or organization functioning, the more competent you'll become right now in handling complexity, managing myriad responsibilities, and integrating tasks.[40]

It was the Soviet neurosurgeon. A R. Luria who discovered that the frontal lobes of the brain are involved in a 'programme which ensures not only that the subject reacts to actual stimuli, but within certain limits foresees the future, sensing the probability that a particular event may happen, will be prepared if it does happen, and, as a result, prepares a programme of behaviour.'[41]

Our time-horizon is a very real thing. It defines the outreach of the world we each live in.

Elliot Jaques, MD, PhD, author of Executive Leadership

This 'time window' is of great significance in human achievement, says Elliott Jaques, a physician and social psychologist who has spent more than three decades studying executive development and the relationship between time and job competence. Jaques' research makes a significant connection between a person's 'time horizon' and the extent of his or her work capacity.[42]

With a limited time horizon – less than a year, for example – the brain appears to be rigid and rule-anchored. The individual tends to overreact – mentally and emotionally – to minor problems and has difficulty sensing the long-term consequences of current behaviour. In contrast with a time horizon of five to ten years or more, a person's ability to function creatively and effectively during periods of chaos, complexity, uncertainty and paradox may be dramatically enhanced.

Consider, for example, that Matsushita, the vast Japanese conglomerate that among its immense holdings owns the Panasonic brand, has a one-hundred-year plan to account for possible business and market trans-formations.[43] It does not matter whether or not the imagined world a century from now will exist; the pay-off comes from stretching our intuition and senses to perceive what might be possible. All Matsushita executives, for example, develop the ability to use reflective time-shifting to bring the imaginary future directly into current creative designs and work processes. In doing so, they are helping to *create* the future.

Reflective time-shifting is distinctly different from what many of us in business have come to call strategic thinking or strategic planning. As corporate strategist Gary Hamel observes, 'It works from today forward, not from the future back, implicitly assuming, whatever the evidence to the contrary, that the future will be more or less like the present.... Only a tiny percentage of an industry's conventions are ever challenged.... An industry's boundaries are taken as a given; thus the question is how to position products and services within those boundaries rather than how to invent new, uncontested competitive space.'[44]

In many enterprises, strategy-making has long been an empty calendar-prompted ritual. We go through the motions. But we don't use emotional intelligence to fire the imagination with feelings of *being* in the future, experiencing various scenarios and sensing a broadly imagined landscape of hidden possibilities (which we'll be talking about in the next chapter). When planning is abstract and limited to *listing* ideas, we can fool ourselves more easily and often than if we extend our intuition and feelings through imagination into the past or future and use our emotional intelligence to *experience* actively and hypothetically *test* such ideas.

EQ Map Connections: Reflective Time-Shifting

You may want to refer to the following scales of the *EQ Map* as points of reflection related this chapter: emotional self-awareness, emotional awareness of others intentionality, creativity, and outlook

---

EQ IN ACTION: *FLASH FORWARD AND REFLECT BACK*

To stretch your capacities in reflective time-shifting, I suggest beginning with the following trio of exercises that I've found effective in working with executives and managers. Sit comfortably with a pad of paper and pencil next to you.

Better for most of us, despite the risks, to leap into the future. And to do so sooner rather than later.

John P. Kotter, *Harvard Business School*

First application exercise: many managers, and companies, describe themselves as 'market leaders'. But being at the head of the pack today does not in any way assure – and, in some respects, may make it harder to be in – that position in tomorrow's world.

Answer the questions on the opposite page, both for *today* and for how you imagine yourself answering them in the *future*, ten to fifteen years from now.[45]

Compare your two sets of answers. Do you have reasonably detailed and substantially different responses to the *future* questions when contrasted with *today*? If not, there's strong reason to believe you'll not fulfil your unique potential, nor will your company be able to attain or sustain a market leadership position.[46] As for why there's a question on improving the human condition, several leading strategy researchers have found that executives and managers who successfully compete for the future are, time and again, those able to empathize with basic human needs and who are constantly striving to better the human condition.[47]

Time-Shifting Questions	Today	10 to 15 Years from Now
1. What are four specific EQ competencies or capacities that make me most valuable as a leader or professional?		
2. Who are my most important business partners and customers?		
3. How well do I really know them as individuals with unique talents, potential, passions and purpose?		
4. In what specific ways do I help them better achieve their priorities?		
5. How many individuals are in my inner circle of complete trust?		
6. How many of them are included in my work?		
7. How many people trust me unconditionally?		
8. Who are my foremost competitors?		
9. In what ways am I striving to better the human condition rather than just make a profit?		
10. What is most unique and valuable about my approach to life and work?		
11. What are two key ways I am positioning myself to capture the most value growth in my career?		

Now for the second time-span exercise: relax, close your eyes, and extend your senses back in time, recalling an experience where you were thinking, feeling, and performing at your best. Perhaps the image of the past was a time you felt exceptionally enthusiastic, or grateful, or deeply confident and calm. Practise seeing how rapidly you can 're-enter' this emotional state, and, in essence, bring it back across time with you to the present. In emotional alchemy, you can develop the ability to conjure up certain expansive or generative emotions at will and use them more fluidly, and consistently, to perform, and learn, at levels most other people cannot.

Before heading into your next interaction with a group of angry customers or savvy competitors, for example, you might pause for moment to recall a feeling of gratitude for a past kindness or an alliance that one or more of the people in the room – or people *much like* the people in the room – once extended to you. Or you might recall a strong feeling of inner confidence or creativity in finding solutions. In this way, you are eliciting and applying emotions at will to help you stay more relaxed and curious, rather than tense and antagonistic if things heat up right away during your dialogue. Can you think of other specific uses for this kind of emotional alchemy?

Here is the third time-shifting exercise: sit in a comfortable chair and relax, imagining that all constraints are removed, including the current limits of finances, logic, science, media, telecommunications, and rationality. Gone. Shift your imagination ahead into the future. Take your pad and pencil in hand. Select several of the following experiences:

- Sketch out or list some of the unexpected design features of highly successful break-out products for the year 2015. Do the same envisioning for a new service. For each of these, ask yourself, what would it *look* like and *feel* like – when you use it, receive it, or benefit from it?
- Jot down design ideas or sketches about a high-EQ notebook computer for the year 2020. Seymour Cray, father of the supercomputer and designer of the fastest computer of every generation since the 1950s, always designs computers using pencil and paper, believing that a computer's overall design should spring from the intuition of an individual.[48]
- Imagine the family healthcare model of 2050.
- Invent some breakthrough design characteristics of the 2025 Chrysler minivan or BMW coupe.

- Imagine everything about an ideal corporate meeting design for the year 2040.
- Start your own stream of ideas in any field or market.

Now return to the present and reflect on your notes or sketches. Which of them are the most intuitively intriguing to you? Which might have some application in your work in the year ahead? Repeat this exercise on a regular basis. 'Flash forward and reflect back' – that's what some of my colleagues call it. Post your ideas in a prominent place (so that they can spark more ideas), or keep them in a special notebook in plain view in your principal work area.

New solutions arise not because we happen to be incrementally more efficient than our competitors, but because we're significantly more unconventional and, because of this, we are willing to extend your senses farther into the future, connect our imaginings with the demands and opportunities of the present. No one can predict the future with certainty. But we can shape it, and through our active involvement, help create it. The action of extending your intuition and senses there progressively enables you to become more creative, adaptable, and inventive. That's the power of reflective time-shifting.

On a final note, it pays to remember that computer keyboards have a 'pause' button. Physician Stephan Rechtschaffen suggests that we each establish one of our own.[49] Whenever you feel anxiety building or sense an opportunity appearing, pause. Make a split-second intuitive choice about where in time to direct your attention. If an issue or possibility seems to lack a future perspective, for example, flash forward for a few seconds – a day, a month, a year, a decade, or whatever intuitively feels appropriate – and then reflect back. Ask an unexpected question. Establish a new sense of work rhythm.

It turns out that our ability to time-shift reflectively may be partly a matter of rhythm.

Consider that Bill Gates rocks.

Literally. The founder of Microsoft and one of the world's richest men, sits in a rocking chair during business meetings, creating his own rhythm and creative flow, entraining others into it.[50] Tom Jackson, President of Equinox, a consulting firm, begins each and every meeting with a one-minute pause, a time of silence and reflection. He uses this approach to break set, to disengage from the work rhythms of distraction and urgency and transition into a more creative and collaborative awareness for the meeting at hand.[51]

As you increase your ability to extend your intuitive emotional intelligence anywhere within your time horizon, one of the first rewards you'll likely notice is a heightened sense of the vast number of hidden and emerging opportunities that are now within your reach. This is the subject of our next chapter.

CHAPTER 15

Opportunity Sensing

There is a principal line of force generated by each and every problem, issue, and possibility. This path of energy is either directed *at* you – as in the case of a problem, personal criticism, or competitor's attack, for example – or is directed *by* you, as in when you are actively pursuing new learning, solutions or opportunities.

Imagine for a moment that you're standing on top of a large compass, facing north. Let's take an aerial view and look down on your position from above. Imagine that a specific criticism is directed straight at you – at heart level – and the line of force is moving from north to south. If you stand – either literally or figuratively – rigidly in place, you'll experience the incoming force straight-on and it may bowl you over, emotionally if not physically or mentally.

> *Most companies have huge repositories of undiscovered gold mines of ideas.*
>
> Hermann Simon, CEO of Simon, Kucher & Partners, Bonn, Germany

Now, imagine that you're wrestling with a new challenge or old problem that's coming from the same direction or person. Your past habits and instincts are likely telling you to get ready to grapple with the 'attack' and hope you can get it under control. Sometimes you can, sometimes you can't. The basic rule is: if the problem pushes against you, you push back. And you keep doing this until you win, lose, give in, or give up. Or until reinforcements arrive, in terms of money, motivation, or personnel.

It's a natural reflex. You perceive you're getting pushed – by your boss, spouse, customers, paperwork, or deadlines – and you resist, you push back. By day's end you may be left feeling tense and tired, or discouraged and resentful, or pessimistic or cynical. Sound familiar? It's a prime reason why many of us feel trapped in the narrow routine of our jobs – and the harder we push, the more we risk burning ourselves out.

Back to our experiment: let's say you're standing, relaxed, on top of the compass and sense the incoming force of an argument or a tough problem. From a geometric perspective, except in the case of receiving genuine, honest personal feedback, the only angle you *don't* want to use is the one you're now facing: in this example, the north-south line. It is here that you take the 'hit' of words or problem-images full force. Just as bad, if you don't budge from this position you can also end up being, or feeling, too close to the issue at hand, and thereby lose emotional and mental context; you can't see the forest for the trees.

Consider an alternative. If you keep your alertness high (Chapter 2) and, where possible, enable yourself to function in a state of intuitive flow (Chapter 13), you will have an effective 'early warning system' to detect many incoming problems and organizational headaches before they're on top of you. And, once you sense them coming, it is easier to loosen your position or attitude and be ready to *move in any direction except the line of force coming at you*. Step off the patch of ground you're on, or let go of the attitude or mindset you happen to be holding, and flow with the challenge. With a single relaxed, well-timed sidestep – of the body, or, metaphorically, of the mind or heart – you shift from being the target to being the guide, turning to move *beside* the line of force and extending your senses to detect every possible way to solve the problem or honestly answer the complaint. If necessary, you might choose to deflect the incoming force, altering its line of movement, perhaps responding with something as simple and unexpected such as a smart question, and shifting the outcome towards new options rather than old entanglements.

Let's build on this picture. Imagine that you're standing inside a three-dimensional sphere – instead of a two-dimensional circle – of energy or influence. You alertly avoid getting caught up in tug-of-war with busywork and head-on collisions with urgent but relatively unimportant issues. Instead, you remain as open, emotionally flexible, and mentally relaxed as you can. You keep moving, acknowledging, rather than denying, the problems that you're facing or about to face. Instead of your senses getting locked up, tunnel-like, around the first description or feeling of the problem, you begin to trust that you're within reach of an almost infinite number of unrestricted angles of sensory, and physical or mental, movement – above you, behind or beside you, obliquely to the left or right, and so on – within which to find alternatives. This is an image of interaction that I first learned about at age twelve in aikido class. Over the ensuing three and a half decades I've found it can be as useful in the boardroom or office as in martial arts.

Allow me to expand a bit more on this theme. Opportunity sensing is about extending your awareness as far into the distance as you can using your traditional five senses, plus incorporating your intuitive 'sixth sense' (Chapter 13) and enteric 'gut feeling' (seventh sense?), along with every other dimension of human perception and intelligence within our reach. In this way you're able to remain fully attentive to the present, but can *sense beyond it*. Of course there is more to opportunity sensing than emotional intelligence alone, yet I believe that our innermost feelings activate or drive the process, enabling us instinctively to scan for hidden possibilities in every setting and circumstance, rather than ending up doing what we usually do: struggling on autopilot with problem number twenty-seven today.

Let's imagine that you're instructed by your boss, or happen to make the decision on your own, to go out to meet some upcoming problem or bottleneck or to forge a crucial alliance or invent a new service or product. You name it. Many of the executives and managers I have worked with tend to approach such challenges in a linear, sequential fashion, much like a Roman legion commander: once you decide on a direction, you put your head down and go after it. Sometimes this works. More often it does not, or, let me rephrase that, most of the time it doesn't provide the best possible solution.[52] And afterwards we end up saying things like, 'I never noticed that possibility', or 'It was all I could do just to handle the problem in the usual way.'

Consider that Jim Clark, who was chairman of Silicon Graphics in 1992, had reached the top of his profession and had no obvious reasons to change jobs or do anything risky. Yet he intuitively sensed a host of

Discovery consists of looking at the same thing as everyone else and perceiving something different.

Albert Szent-Gyorgi, MD, PhD, twice Noble laureate

stunning possibilities that virtually no one else had yet detected. Without delay, he acted on them, following his hunches and investigating a number of future scenarios. He needed a partner and, against all conventional thinking, he listened to his intuition and set his sights on Marc Andreessen, a 21-year-old University of Illinois student with a keen savvy for software design and a rare, expanded sense of future possibilities, something he had fine-tuned while co-writing Mosaic during college.

Clark invited Andreessen to join him and together they co-founded Netscape with an unparalleled vision of the Internet. Since then, they have given away $12 million in versions of its Navigator software, pursuing the unconventional belief that the power of the Internet would increase with the square of the nodes. They responded by giving something away to get something back. Clark recalls, 'Boy, if this doesn't work, people are going to think I'm the stupidest person alive.' They don't, because Netscape now commands 75 per cent of the Web browser market and has placed Navigator on 45 million PCs and reaped tons of mind share, making Clark the first Internet billionaire, and earning Andreessen over $100 million.[53] In a recent interview, Andreessen's teachers and friends observed that he was a good all-around student, especially in the classes he cared about, but the one comment that intrigued me the most was, 'Marc just seemed to have *a broader sense than the rest of us* [emphasis added]. He would talk about [things] in a more complete way, with more than one view. And we'd sit back on our heels and say, "Wow, oh yeah." '[54]

Expanding Your Sensory Field

The truth is, virtually all of us are closer to new opportunities – for learning, growth, innovation and new successes – than we realize. I believe that one of the characteristics of many men and women with high EQ is their capacity to sense farther, deeper, and faster than those who rely on IQ alone. I would argue that the sixth and seventh senses – those of intuition and enteric 'gut' feelings –

Imagination is the secret reservoir of the riches of the human race.

Maude L. Frandsen, Forbes

play a pivotal role in expanding our access to this field of possibilities beyond the obvious routes and routines that fill our everyday lives. My colleagues and I see examples of it in action almost everywhere we work with executives, managers, and entrepreneurs.

Let's consider one unconventional way you might approach expanding your sensory field. It's straight from human biology. Consider that the *fovea* is a tiny area at the centre of the retina of the eye. It's a microscopic spot where light-receptor cells are tightly packed and it is here that the eye's perception of images is crystal clear. Moving outwards in a radius from the fovea, the visual image is increasingly hazy, losing sharp focus as it fades into outermost peripheral vision. For example, when you look at this page of the book, the centre zone of perfect clarity see by your fovea is only about one forty-thousandth of the visual field (the entire area you can see). This means you can probably take in five to ten letters in perfect focus. To prove this, stare at the word *this* in this sentence. Keep staring. Notice that only a word or two remain crystal clear and the farther out your gaze extends, the less sharp it becomes.

The eye's physiology is such that in order to transmit useful images to the brain, the fovea fixates, as if taking camera snapshots, about four times every second. Thus the eyes take in the visual field in what can be likened to small visual gulps. Because of this, most of us are able to read only about one word per snapshot, or four words per second, which translates to about 240 words per minute. Despite this, numerous studies indicate that 'speed' readers – those who read far faster and with better comprehension than the average adult – do not read word by word.[55] Instead, most of them have expanded their senses to take in multiple words, phrases, sentences, and even paragraphs with each visual fixation of the fovea. The best among these advanced readers can take in five thousand words, or more, per minute with excellent understanding and retention.

You can learn to do this, too. Nearly any of us can. With a few simple visual exercises such as reading columns of letters on a page – focusing on the centre but taking in increasingly more letters and words with practice – the area the fovea can keep in perfect focus can be significantly expanded.[56] I've seen the pre- and post-results with many managers and professionals. The change can be dramatic. What's most interesting in terms of this chapter on opportunity-sensing is that many of these same people have told me that while expanding the way they read, other things have expanded, too, in the way they relate to people and circumstances. I recall a senior executive reporting to me how, in day-to-day conversations, he was better able to focus his attention on the speaker *at the same time* his peripheral vision took in more of the surrounding context and environment. He, like many others I have known, was relating to interactions – and the 'opportunity horizon' – in a *broadened sense*.

Similarly, I have heard enough first-hand reports to believe that, with practice, you can expand other senses not only to take in more information but also to perceive beyond the usual field of focus, to read between the lines and beyond the words, so to speak, in business settings and conversations. Through intuition and gut feelings, we can learn to notice, for example, more of the times to reach out to someone who is struggling, and to extend to him or her a kind word of acknowledgment and offer of assistance. Or we can 'catch people doing things right', to use Ken Blanchard's phrase, and offer on-the-spot praise instead of waiting for things to go wrong – which everyone seems to notice – and the blaming and excuses to start. In what other specific ways might you 'stretch your senses' of vision, hearing, intuition, and gut feelings, for example? How might you break out of old routines and have more fun, improving your work relationships and gaining broader access to the field of opportunities by more fully 'opening' – developing and expanding – your seven senses? Obviously, this is not an EQ-only process; it involves the five physical senses as well as gut instincts and intuitive flow, yet I believe these later two senses are the key to driving the whole process.

Extending Your Opportunity Horizon

A number of years ago, I gave a two-day presentation as part of the Arthur Andersen Masters Forum. James Kackley, a senior managing partner with the firm and director of the programme, was in attendance. During one of the breaks, Jim talked about what he had learned over the years about the need to distinguish clearly between focusing on *issues* – or problems – and seeking *opportunities*, and between *repeating* deepset habits and consciously *inventing* something new, in the way we approach a challenge, for example, or relate to another person, or learn. I've never forgotten that.

Most of us are quite good at noticing faults in other people and naming existing problems, for example, or at completing tasks and making routine decisions. In business, we're trained to do that. We're largely problem-focused and problem-centred. We can get stuck there, however.

Peter Drucker calls relegating the best people to a problem-fixing mode a 'deadly business sin'. He says that opportunities produce growth, whereas problem-solving is more like damage control.[57] At Arthur Andersen, for example, partners and engagement teams continue to commit to their long tradition of excellence in auditing historical financial statements. However, in recent years there has been a fast-growing demand for an added capability: to audit *forward*, to find every way to help clients improve business performance. This means, essentially, intuitively and analytically to detect hidden business risks as well as uncover every possible source, or direction, for new growth and value that gives clients a competitive advantage. Companies all over the world are responding.

At Hewlett-Packard (HP), one of America's most admired companies, managers and professionals watch the world with what is called *scanning*. They have developed this habit as a way to sense a wide variety of *possible* futures, and to use this to create outreach to invent new technologies, products and services, and improve work processes. Let Platt, Chairman and CEO, believes that scanning has been one of the keystones of HP's enduring profitability and advancement.[58]

For the most part, however, many of us still work by rote. We feel like we're on a treadmill or in a rut. We resist differing perspectives. We balk at change. We fail to grasp, for example, that we must understand the larger economic systems evolving around us and find ways to contribute. If not, we're fading or already finished. We just don't realize it yet.

Einstein quipped that the moon doesn't go away when we close our eyes.[59] Think for a moment about how many present-day inventions and services we take for granted were deemed by virtually everyone to be impossible a few short years ago. The few who kept their senses wide open, scanning for opportunities, found them. Think about the total number of works that an artist initiates in a lifetime. The quantity is staggering. Picasso is said to have sketched or painted more than 10,000 works. That's about the same number of new products launched in software stores each year.

It's insightful to note that Picasso continued to paint into his nineties and was said to have discarded about two out of every three of his paintings. We don't dwell on Picasso's creative 'failings'. Instead, we stand in awe of his successes. The same with Leonardo da Vinci. I keep a copy of his sketch books on my desk as a reminder. He clearly had a long time horizon, and was almost constantly imagining an array of intriguing possibilities, many of which would come to fruition long after the sixteenth century in which he lived. Best known as a painter, he also excelled as a sculptor, architect, musician, anatomist, botanist, engineer, geologist, and mapmaker.

At first people refuse to believe that a strange new thing can be done, then they begin to hope it can be done, then they see it can be done – then it is done and all the world wonders why it was not done centuries before.

Frances Hodgson Burnett, 1849–1924, English born US writer

Contrast this with the common present-day tendency to specialize in a single aspect of a single profession, and to think incrementally in straight, narrow lines, what Thomas Carlyle, in 1829, called *steam-engine intellects*.[60] In some companies, this means never venturing into unknown territory. It also means trying to avoid new product idea 'failures' and, instead, focusing on squeezing out every last penny from downsizing, cycle time reduction, and resource shifting. Not that any of these are bad ideas. It's just that I've never met anyone who wakes up in the morning excited to go after making an extra penny or an incremental improvement. As Meg Wheatley reminds us, 'The things we fear most in organizations – fluctuations, disturbances, imbalances – are also the primary sources of creativity.'[61]

Affecting the Future

In my experience, when people are asked to rate how they feel – most engaged and enthused to least engaged and enthused – when giving their best effort to a range of tasks, from the mundane to the creative, the answer rated most highly is 'Designing or discovering something new'.[62] Not statistical process control. Or generating reports. Or revising the old. When given the chance, and perhaps with some extra training or incentive, most of us love to stretch forward, to listen to our own inner sense of possibilities, and to spark and exude a passion about affecting – that is, shaping or influencing in some meaningful way – the future.

History supports us in this drive. Recall, for example, that until 1543, everyone assumed that the sun and planets went around the earth until Copernicus followed his intuition and asked the unorthodox question, 'What if we look at the entire universe from a different perspective? What if we put the sun at the centre of the movement of planets rather than the earth?' By scanning for other possibilities, and then bypassing the accepted facts of the day, Copernicus was able to sense, and then construct, what proved to be a far more useful and accurate model of what today we call the solar system.

Benjamin Franklin went to Boston in 1746 to witness a demonstration of electricity by a Scottish lecturer, Dr Adam Spencer.[63] Franklin became so intrigued with high-voltage static electricity that he immediately decided that he wanted to own Spencer's equipment. He approached the inventor and bought it all on the spot. One of Franklin's friends in England, Peter Collinson, sent him additional notes about the various electrical experiments being conducted there. Franklin at once took issue with the thinking of Europe's leading scientists who claimed that electricity was of two different types. Nonsense, Franklin's intuition told him. Electricity is electricity, and it flows, from greater charge to lesser charge, he believed. You can store it up here and let it jolt back when you draw the spark of an electric fire. The spark is what evens up all the charges that have been separated. Franklin's experiments set Europe buzzing. They wondered who this young upstart was, who had been studying electricity for only a few years. But his experiments couldn't be refuted, and they revolutionized the development of electricity.

Shortly after the beginning of the twentieth century, Albert Einstein triggered his own shift in scientific perception when he asked himself the question, 'What would it be like to run beside a light beam, at the speed of light?'[64] Einstein was keying into his intuitive sense that, contrary to accepted rationale, there might be a different, more fundamental relationship governing time and space, and by doing so Einstein turned accepted scientific 'fact' on its ear. He proved that the passage of time is relative and that the properties of an object were not absolute or fixed, but instead were relative to the position of the observer.

Many of us don't know that emotional intelligence was an integral part of Einstein's approach to creativity. According to Robert Dilts, author of *Strategies of Genius*, 'Einstein claimed to think primarily in terms of visual images and feelings. ... Verbal and mathematical representation of his thoughts came only *after* the important creative thinking was done.'[65] Einstein contributed his scientific prowess to what he called 'vague play' with 'feelings', 'signs', 'images' and other elements. 'This com-

Our company has, indeed, stumbled onto some of its new products. But never forget that you can only stumble if you're moving.

Richard P. Carlton, former CEO,
3M Company, 1950

binatory play,' he wrote, 'seems to be the essential feature in productive thought.'[66] It turns out that *emotional energy* is the stimulus for seeking hidden opportunities and the fuel for creative imagination.[67]

Einstein challenged Newtonian physics. The early Vikings challenged the seas. The American colonists challenged the feudal constraints and inherited privilege of European society. Picasso and other modernists challenged representational art. Galileo, Copernicus and Kepler challenged the centrality of Earth in the universe. Beethoven challenged his own deafness, as Milton did his blindness, and Hellen Keller both afflictions at once.

A small number of the most innovative and successful companies in the world, including, for example, Hewlett-Packard, Wal-Mart, Intel, Shell, 3M, ABB, and Creative Artists Agency, are constantly scanning for opportunities and developing new business advantages by leading the co-evolution of economic systems. That is, they search for every potential centre of innovation, both inside and outside their organizational boundaries, and orchestrate cooperative alliances of people and networks of firms that give rise to new industries and markets.[68] They identify and aggressively pursue unmet customer needs and untapped technologies.

Anita Roddick, founder of the internationally successful Body Shop, looked at Charles Revson's beauty-in-a-bottle philosophy, which peddled hope through cosmetics, and went the opposite way, literally, saying, 'I watch where the cosmetics industry is going and then walk in the opposite direction.'[69]

It is possible that most people working after the turn of the century will be working in industries that don't even exist now.

Nicholas Imparato and Oren Harai, authors of
Jumping the Curve

Contrary to the industry assumption that women are so lacking in self-confidence that they will pay inflated prices for simplistic formulations if advertising suggests they will become more attractive, Roddick believed that women have self-esteem and want simple, great scented, environmentally responsible products.

3M, consistently one of the world's best product innovators, now mandates that all units earn at least 30 per cent of annual revenues from products introduced within the past four years. The organization provides training and resources to support that goal, yet most new products result from the *informal interactions* of curious people at every level of the company, who are encouraged to spend at least 15 per cent of their time working outside their assigned project areas.

'Microsoft's only factory asset is the human imagination,' observed the *New York Times* writer Fred Moody.[70] SmithKline Beecham paid $125 million to Human Genome Sciences, a company whose only asset – it won't have a product ready for a decade – is a group of brilliant, inspired scientists. IBM didn't pay $3.5 billion for Lotus just to get its software and intellectual property; it was buying the untapped creative genius of one designer in particular, Ray Ozzie, creator of the powerful networking software Notes, and his tightly knit team. When entertainment moguls Steven Spielberg, David Geffen, and Jeffey Katzenberg formed Dreamworks SKG, they announced they would sell a one-third share in their new company for $900 million. They valued the new venture at $2.7 billion – and their own equity position at $1.8 billion – but not based on traditional capital assets. They had none. Quite a creative statement for a start-up with rented offices, leases on computers and copying machines, and virtually nothing in the way of traditional tangible assets. That's emotion-charged creative genius at work, backed by passionate belief and a driving sense of purpose and curiosity.

Either you learn to acquire and cultivate creative people or you'll be eaten alive.

Leon Royer, Executive Director, 3M

Here's another illustration of what I mean:[71] ABB, Asea Brown Boveri, is a worldwide electrical engineering company that provides power generation technology, electricity transmission and distribution systems, and a wide variety of electrically powered industrial equipment. Headquartered in Zurich and jointly held by Swedish and Swiss owners, it does business in 140 countries, and is widely respected for its innovative leadership.

In 1994, Paul Kefalas became CEO of ABB Canada at a time when that region was suffering from stagnant sales. The traditional approach to reviving revenues would have been to focus on product-improvement and try to decide what new offerings could capture the interest of the market, and then figure out how to produce them profitably. Kefalas went in a completely different direction. He asked his organization to explore what could be called its opportunity horizon, including the broadest business environment it hoped to serve in the future. What he wondered was, who will be the major shapers of the region's future? By seeking fresh insights into the influences and interests shaping industry in Canada, he was able to direct his management teams towards finding every creative way to set up learning partnerships with these leading companies in order to find ways that ABB could contribute to their success.

Prospects were selected because of their role in influencing the future, regardless of whether they happened to be ABB customers. Many of these companies would never have been reached through conventional product-centred sales initiatives. With those organizations that were willing, ABB assembled a team of experts from across ABB's units and arranged for them to work with the company's leaders to co-conceive creative ways to help the company seize unexpected opportunities and achieve its vision for growth. Doing business this way has produced a host of new opportunities and revenue streams for ABB Canada. More than a dozen major long-term customer-partnering arrangements, including several joint ventures, are underway, and sales have increased significantly.

$$Z \times (P + A + E) = OS$$

Zeigarnick × (Possibilities + Awareness + Engagement) = Opportunity Sensing

Consider this EQ equation which can be used as simple self-check in expanding your opportunity sensing capacities. Rate each factor on the left from zero (lowest) to ten (highest) scale. *OS* is the current capacity you have for *opportunity sensing*.

P represents your current field – or full range – of actual *possibilities*, including the opportunities, seen or unseen, that are available to you right now, whether or not you're aware of them. If, for example, you work in what feels to be a limiting or constrictive job at a company with low emotional intelligence, this number may be small, and perhaps only two or three; if, however, you work in a flexible, creative environment at a high EQ company, it may be virtually limitless and therefore rate a ten.

A represents your current *awareness* of the opportunities within your reach. Are you alert to the field of possibilities, however large it may be, or are you mostly on autopilot and out of touch with it?

E represents your current level of active *engagement* – how fully you feel committed to exploring the available possibilities in this specific circumstance. *Z* stands for the *Zeigarnick* Effect, which can be seen as an indicator of your present capacity to stay open and creative for as long as possible, right up to deadlines and performance points. When *Z* is zero, it indicates a strong urge for closure – to get things out of the way and over with, checked off your agenda or to-do list – and this can sabotage all the other factors in the equation, resulting in a zero for opportunity sensing.

The maximum score is 300. The lowest: zero. This equation happens to remind me of a cartoon I saw several years ago in the *New Yorker* which showed an angel hovering just outside the window of an office in which a manager or professional was sitting at a desk. The celestial spirit was holding a stick of dynamite labelled 'Innovate!' This represents a long-held view among many managers that when it's time to be creative, no problem, we'll just *get* creative. Unfortunately, with rare exceptions, it doesn't work that way. Innovation on demand doesn't pan out; you can't turn it on and off like a tap.

As individuals at 3M and other companies have discovered, to innovate consistently and effectively requires a personal – or, better yet, organizational – work culture in which opportunity-sensing is an everyday process, not an every-once-in-a-while special event. Try clearing your desk and sitting quietly with a pad and pen in front of you while commanding yourself to 'create something'. It rarely works. Most of us need to stay open to, or immersed in, the landscape of possibilities in order to have the best chance of landing new opportunities.

Let's say you're faced with a difficult collaborative project just before a key personal performance review, or are about to walk into a team meeting after your company has just lost a major customer or account, suffered a quality problem, or your boss has suddenly realized how badly the firm needs new ideas or sources of business revenue to avoid layoffs or to hold your own against an emerging, determined competitor. Normally, in such high-stress circumstances the brain tends to be *less* open or adaptable and is primed to *do more of the same, only harder.*[72] While such a tendency may have proved useful from an evolutionary perspective eons ago, in today's world it can loom up as a serious problem in business and career growth.

Using our hypothetical example above, take a few moments to give yourself a current rating in this EQ equation: *Zeigarnick* ×

(Possibilities + Awareness + Engagement) = Opportunity Sensing. Let's say it's right after lunch – which you've skipped, as you often do, because your morning meetings or tasks have run late – and you've been dreading this upcoming discussion or interaction. You feel a strong desire to get this settled in some way as quickly as possible, so your first *Zeigarnick* rating for openness is a three. Similarly, the actual field of possibilities – the *P* in our equation – feels very limited at the moment, and you're hoping someone else has a solution at hand. Score: another three. Turning to the rating of your present awareness, *A*, of the scope of possibilities, you decide there just *aren't* many opportunities here, and you're quite aware of that, so you give yourself a seven.

As for how wholeheartedly you're going to dive into the interactive project or meeting – the *E* for engagement in the equation – you find yourself feeling relatively hesitant. Thus, a four. Total score: 42 out of a possible 300. It could be worse, you say, which is true.

However, once the discussion or meeting starts, you feel yourself at a growing disadvantage. There's no end in sight. Tempers are flaring, and others are being controlling. You keep glancing at your watch, wishing all of these headaches were over. Now what?

Back to our equation. The factor with the most leverage is *Z*, the Zeigarnick Effect, which reflects your level of willingness in delaying closure until the last realistic moment and staying open to the widest range of possibilities. In many cases, your original score of three may be raised by choice. Here are several ways: one, take off your watch and slip it into your briefcase, pocket, or purse. Neurotic watch-watching can sink the Zeigarnick Effect faster than just about anything. Next, challenge yourself to get *really* curious about how long you might be able to stay *more* open and *more* creative between now and the end of the discussion or meeting. Actually, you want to *relax* your way into this. That is, you consciously release physical tension, for example, and stop putting up walls around your position or hurling mental darts at others in the room. At the same time, you make the choice to let go of incessantly searching for some close-in ending or on-demand solution and, instead, shift your senses into wondering what unconventional or unexpected ideas may be out there, just out of everyone's reach. Notice how that feels. Many executives and managers I've worked with report the perspective shift can be almost immediate.

This may bring your *Z* rating to an eight, let's say, at least for a while. Your opportunity-sensing score is now up to a 108 from 42, just from changing one variable. And this may prompt other changes as well. For example, with a higher Z rating, the more relaxed and alert you tend to be, which helps improve the accuracy of your assessment of the field of possibilities (when we're feeling anxious or tense, we tend to underestimate the possibilities).[73] Instead of a three, it's actually a five, you admit to yourself.

Now we're up to a total of 124. And, rather than feeling so compelled to protect yourself and wanting the discussion to end, your increased calmness and curiosity also raise your level of involvement or engagement (E), in this case from a four to a six, and it may go higher once you enter the dialogue and start asking a few creative questions, which no one else is doing yet. We're now at 140, which is a significant change, and with a level this high you'll likely find that exploring for new ideas and solutions feels more fun – even when there's a lot of conflict and discontent in the room – and, in turn, your openness and influence will be felt and more readily valued by others. This is an example of a very basic way to use an EQ equation to help you apply more of the capacities and principles of emotional intelligence to your daily work.

Now, let's take a real-life example of one of the companies with a top-notch system for opportunity sensing: the United Kingdom high-fidelity retailer Richer Sounds. Their anchor store is just across the Thames from Britain's Square Mile commercial centre, which happens to be one of the most expensive pieces of retail real estate on the planet. Averaging sales of approximately $26,000 US dollars per square foot, the store has earned an entry in *The Guinness Book of World Records* as the world's top retail outlet, all the more remarkable when compared to the UK's average standard of about $1,000 per square foot. With 200 employees and annual revenues of US $38.5 million, the company's twenty-six outlets emphasize the opportunity-centred ideas of founder and president Julian Richer:[74]

Richer's philosophy can be summed up in two ways: nonstop opportunity-sensing and respect. 'Respect for the individual has always been a guiding principle for me,' says Richer. ' "Do as you would be done by," should apply as much at work as in any other area of life.' Richer Sounds' employees – respectfully referred to as colleagues – experience this quality every day at work. In an industry with high turnover in personnel, Richer celebrates employee loyalty. Those who've been with the company over five years are invited for an anniversary lunch with the CEO at one of London's finest restaurants. 'The hire and fire attitude has no place in an organization that's serious about customer service,' he says, noting that turnover and shrinkage (a retail euphemism for employee theft) is far below the norm at Richer Sounds, which also maintains a hardship fund – 1 per cent of profits – which provides interest-free loans and grants for employees or members of their families falling on hard times.

Once every month, staff are given $5 to go to a local pub and sit quietly over a drink, thinking up new possibilities for improving the business. Ideas run from the practical to the inspired, including providing tape measures so customers can check equipment dimensions; placing comfortable chairs, coffee machines and complimentary snacks in stores; distributing mail-order catalogues; putting handles on boxes so purchases are easier to carry; and providing free bin liners so potential burglars can't identify customers' cargo. Each quarter the employee with the best suggestion wins a trip on the Orient Express, a retreat at a spa, or a day at the famous Brands Hatch motor racing circuit. Richer Sounds is recognized throughout the UK for generating more ideas per employee than any other company, and Richer will even pay half the price of a plane ticket to the United States if employees bring back notes on how US retailing techniques might be brought back to Richer Sounds as a source of improvement.

Every aspect of the company is marked by incentive and creative opportunities: in addition to soliciting feedback from mystery shoppers, telephone surveys, and associate directors, the company imprints all store receipts with a postage-paid form for customers to comment on service. Every time a customer marks 'excellent', that sales assistant receives a $5 bonus, regardless of the value of the transaction. If a customer says service was poor, the salesperson is docked $5. The money isn't actually withheld from wages, but any colleague in the red at months' end has some serious explaining to do. Scores are announced weekly. At the end of each month, the top three stores in the competition – dubbed the Richer Way League – win a car for a month. Two get Bentleys, one a Jaguar XJS convertible. The cars are for colleagues to use as they wish, and the company pays for petrol and will provide a part-time chauffeur for staffers who don't drive.

Richer also has the notion that work should be fun, and that everyone should do less of it. The company owns five holiday homes around the UK and Ireland, with plans for another in Paris. Any employee, together with their family and friends (and pets) can use them. It's first come, first served. If someone hasn't been able to get away all year, he or she might get preference over a colleague who wants to book a second holiday, but managers do not get any special treatment. It's all about respect and creative initiative.

Intuitively Scanning the Larger Field of Possibilities

As we saw in the preceding EQ equation, there are a number of emotional intelligence competencies that can be put to good, effective use when barriers get thrown in your way. Here's an example of a marketing team taking this kind of initiative:[75]

Hallberg Schireson, a marketing firm, had an account with a company known for its stain, but wanted to sell more of its paint. But the price was too high: $17 a gallon when other, similar paints were only $14 a gallon.

Why? asked Hallberg. Nobody at the company had an answer. Hallberg's curiosity got them intently involved with some creative questioning. The research and development people said, 'It's because we use more expensive ingredients.' Hallberg asked, 'Why?' 'There's some ingredient in here that's better, but we're not sure what it does.' Hallberg said, 'Can you find out?' R&D replied, 'It won't be easy, but we know it exceeds some sort of federal standards.'

Finally, with more than a little frustration and intense curiosity, the Hallberg marketers bypassed R&D. Instead, they went with the flow of events and took it upon themselves to look up these federal standards in thick manuals. The first thing they discovered, which surprised them, was that 80 per cent of paint jobs were over previously painted surfaces. Even better, they discovered that the expensive ingredient made paint stick more effectively to previously painted surfaces. So, where the research and development department had fizzled, the marketing firm came through, and discovered the best reason of all why Olympic paint was more expensive and why it was worth every extra dollar.

Sales skyrocketed, and have continued to grow ever since.

Let's consider several additional examples. One of the remarkable facts about First Direct, a bank in Great Britain, is that it can only be reached by telephone. It was created when its founders stared at what seemed the most daunting barrier to bank growth: time and convenience are money, and unless you build a branch office on every street corner – an obviously unfeasible scenario – customers who are busy professionals end up wasting both trying to conduct routine banking business. First Direct has half a million customers, many of them workaholics who carry, on average, a balance that is ten times higher than the average balance at Midland Bank, First Direct's parent, while overall costs per client are 61 per cent less. First Direct is now the fastest growing bank in the United Kingdom,[76] opening 10,000 new accounts a month in mid-1995, the equivalent of building two or three new branches every thirty days.

> *There is no master plan that can anticipate change. That is why my father counseled, 'Be in motion.'*
>
> Robert Galvin, CEO, Motorola

Richard Branson is another example of an executive who has worked hard to develop his intuition and opportunity-sensing capacities. He is the founder of the Virgin Group, the empire best known for its highly successful airline and Megastore retail chain. Branson's way of running his enterprises has made him not only one of the world's richest people but also an admired folk hero in the United Kingdom, even though he's had many failures. As publisher John Brown points out, 'The whole secret of Branson's success is his failures ... He keeps opening things, and a good many of them fail – but he doesn't give a f—. He keeps on going!'[77]

Branson has no traditional corporate headquarters, and has shunned many of the perks and status symbols of power. His last office was a houseboat on the Thames, even though he employs more than 6,000 people in more than sixteen countries. Decentralization is a passion of his, and he firmly contends that when there are more than seventy people in a building, they should be split into new, smaller teams or they lose their identity and creative commitment.

At the Virgin Group, informality (casual dress, the absence of hierarchy, a comfortable environment, and a lack of conformity) and real dialogue enable everyone to participate in seeking opportunities, flowing with challenges, and solving problems. Open, honest, lateral communication is the hallmark, and Branson sees Virgin as a boundaryless organization. He abhors narrowly defined job roles and encourages people to move around. He believes in organic growth and profitability, not in raiding other businesses to win market share. At the core of his working philosophy is the notion that when someone has a creative idea, that person should have full access to resources that could bring that idea to fruition. He encourages people to follow their intuition and take intelligent risks, to adapt, and create at all times. In this light, mistakes do not upset him; he loves to learn from them as he advances ahead. He says it is better to ask forgiveness than to ask permission. He rewards those who advance creative ideas: they receive a part of the profits. It's one of his ways to keep the top people becoming millionaires at Virgin, rather than out on his own.

What if your company has no such philosophy or creative vision? Then recall the stories of Rachel Carson, John Woolman, and many others throughout this book. Many important changes have begun with the ingenuity and commitment of a single individual. I also encourage you to reach out to those closest to you to discuss and develop some of these new competencies of emotional intelligence, putting them into practice one at a time. Looking ahead, such actions may change – or even save – your organization, or position you to move to a company that openly values such capacities.

EQ Map Connections: Opportunity Sensing
You may want to refer to the following scales of the *EQ Map* as points of reflection related in this chapter: emotional self-awareness, emotional awareness of others, creativity, interpersonal connection, outlook, intuition, and trust radius

---

EQ IN ACTION: *OPPORTUNITY SENSING CATALYSTS*

To heighten and expand your emotional-intuitive capacity to sense the widest range of possibilities and opportunities, consider the following:

Complacency can come about because of our own expertise. We can become so comfortable with it that we assume we know all there is to know and stop growing. We come up with no new ideas and are reluctant to consider new ideas from others. Meanwhile, the world has passed us by.

Robert J. Sternberg, Yale University

Make it a point to be surprised by something new every day.
If you stick close to shore you'll never sense the richness of the possibilities all around you. Ask a question you'd rarely ever ask, or express a deeply held belief. Listen to the story of a stranger. Walk through a different crowd, or park, or corridor. Sense what's unique about it, what's different, what's changing. Where are the hidden possibilities? Immerse yourself in them. Learn everything you can about them. If you're a leader, pepper people with information on future opportunities, on the specific rewards for seizing such

opportunities, and on the present-day inadequacies of the team or organization to pursue such opportunities.[78]

Champion creative unorthodoxy.
Many vital and lucrative discoveries have been accomplished by impassioned and unorthodox methods. The Wright brothers gave up trying to craft a stable flying machine, and succeeded only when they embraced the notion of an 'unstable' airplane. As Roger Schank, head of the Learning Institute at Northwestern University, reminds us:[79]

If an idea hasn't been proved, most scientists will not grant other scientists the opportunity to try to prove it. One has to show why something will work in order to be able to work on it. Further, one has to use the currently agreed-upon paradigm of research in order to be considered even eligible. Scientists are at least as rigid as everybody else. The sad fact is that most scientists have never done anything innovative in their lives. They simply follow the rules, and do what they are supposed to do.

Many important breakthroughs have been made using very unorthodox methods.

Consider Edison and the electric lamp. Edison tried and failed to make a lamp with hundreds of compounds before he came up with one that worked. There were many other scientists on this same goal, but they were all trying to make an electric lamp based on their theories of electricity, metals, and lamps. They wanted to be 100 per cent right about the theory before they tried anything in practice to see if it worked. They weren't willing to suggest, let alone try, things that might be wrong. Edison just stood at his workbench wiring things together, following his intuition and creative instincts, learning as he went, committed to finding something that worked.

Keep a Possibilities Journal.
Take a hint from da Vinci. His notebooks were a continuing source of inspiration in imagining the 'impossible'. You might begin by recording each evening the most surprising or emotionally moving experience that happened that day, and your response to it. After a week, you can reread your entries and begin to notice patterns of interest that may point the way to new ideas and pursuits in the future.

Remove 'mental locks' that inhibit the creative process.

In many cases, you can help the natural flow of emotional-intelligence-generated innovation if you remove as many barriers to it as possible. These 'mental locks' include:[80] everything is fine, follow the rules, to err is wrong, playing is frivolous, that's not my area, be practical, and I'm just not creative. In addition, see if you can spend a bit more time in the *creative spaces* that seem to stimulate your best flow of ideas: Chiat/Day, at its New York City headquarters, uses comfortable 'team and process rooms' instead of private offices, and a 'conversation area' instead of a conference room. Steelcase and Herman Miller, office furniture firms which specialize in such spaces, use such metaphors as 'harbours', 'oases', 'neighbourhoods', and 'activities' in place of hierarchical sterility.

If you see in any given situation only what everybody else can see, you can be said to be so much a representative of your culture that you are a victim of it.

S. I. Hayakawa, US Senator and educator

Take advantage of the exercise-EQ-innovation connection.

You may be surprised to learn that exercise can increase opportunity sensing and may generate surges of creativity in the workplace. So concludes Thomas Backer, research professor at the UCLA School of Medicine. 'In working with thousands of creative people, I now recommend a regular exercise programme as the single best way both to increase resistance to stress and to facilitate personal creativity.'[81] As noted in Chapter 2, regular exercise also contributes to emotional energy and resilience.

Rub elbows with highly creative people.

Hallmark, the Kansas City greeting card megafirm, encourages its artists to fly to museums anywhere in the world to stimulate their creative senses. Samsung, the electronics giant from Korea, regularly sends executives to visit design firm IDEO's Palo Alto, California headquarters to absorb creative spirit. Samsung maintains offices next door to IDEO yet they pay for the right to affiliate with IDEO's 'atmosphere'. Assess your own environment: does it enable you to make the most of your talents and interests? What significant, albeit small, changes could you personally make in your work atmosphere or environment? How, specifically, might you create more of your own opportunities rather than be limited by the circumstances in which you find yourself?

Vary your approach.

I often find myself recalling Abraham Maslow's observation: 'If the only tool you have is a hammer, you tend to treat everything as if it were a nail.' Begin a running list of opportunities, large and small, within current or future reach of you and your enterprise. Post it in a prominent place. Keep asking yourself, Am I seeking opportunities – and the opportunities *within* problems – with the same creative vigour and resources that I devote to fixing day-to-day problems?

Imagine your blessings.

One of the most unexpected ways I've ever found to expand the range and depth of my future opportunities is based on imagination and gratitude. It was shared with me a decade ago by Anees Sheikh, Chairman of the department of psychology at Marquette University, who advised, based on years of professional observation and experience, 'Don't just count your blessings, *imagine them*.'[82] He recommends writing down brief descriptions of ten specific blessings in your life. Recall another two or three additional blessings to this list each week. Once a day, perhaps during your five quiet minutes writing your EQ morning Notes (Chapter 1), sit relaxed in a quiet place and vividly imagine, and deeply feel, five of the blessings on your list for at least ten seconds. Dr Sheikh reports that in many cases he has seen this simple exercise progressively transform an individual's whole relationship with work or life, shifting from feelings of helplessness, martyrdom and self-pity to opportunity-seeking and increased resilience. In addition, he notes, people tend to become aware of the good things, the positive occurrences and creative opportunities in everyday life that, until now, they may have rarely noticed.

> *The world remains a boundless stage for discoveries to come … The most important words ever written on the maps of human experience are* terra incognita *– territory unknown.*
>
> Daniel J. Boorstin, The Discoverers

CHAPTER 16

Creating the Future

When most of us talk about change, we usually mean incremental change, theresult of a rational, sequential analysis and an orderly planning process. It is predominantly driven by intellect.

The future never just happens; it is created.

Will and Ariel Durant, The Lessons of History

Incremental change is short term, limited in scope, and tends to be reversible. We can abandon it and go back to the old ways of doing things. Through controlling – ourselves, others, and circumstances – we get stuck on the shadow side of this cornerstone of EQ. Robert Quinn of the University of Michigan Business School calls this the 'slow death dilemma'.[83]

Essentially, it's easier and safer to stay in the zone of comfort or certainty. We search for the painless fix. We confirm. If all goes well, we end up, at best, mediocre. We go through the motions, but deep down, we've quit trying to face the deeper challenges and possibilities. We take our pay cheques and ignore the nagging messages in our gut, the messages which call us to do whatever we can to transform ourselves and our circumstances.

In contrast, successfully intelligent leaders and managers continually question many of the assumptions that others accept. And beyond questioning assumptions, these men and women do not behave in fixed ways when they run up against the status quo: they challenge it perceiving the deeper risks and limitations, and in many cases find ways to transcend it. They have the courage to take creative risks. They allow themselves and others to make mistakes and explore new territories. Sometimes they fall flat on their faces. But they get right back up and keep wholeheartedly exploring. They know the future is not something we wait for; it is something we must actively help create. And emotional intelligence plays a vital role.

The Unifying Principle of Transformation

Growth is the single process that unites the feelings, thoughts, actions, and energies of every living thing. The nature of the living cell – of which we humans each have trillions – and of what we call 'human nature', are not something that *is* but rather something that is forever in the process of *becoming*.[84] We humans are given a significant role in determining ourselves through the way we choose to grow – through the unifying principle of transformation, as biologist and leadership researcher George Land calls it. Which is why one of the principal outcomes of this fourth EQ cornerstone is confluence, the drawing together of our capacities, diversified talents, dreams, and drives into a unified force for change and growth as a person, a family member, a business professional, and a citizen of humanity.

What we need is more people who specialize in the impossible.

Theodore Roethke, 1908–63, US poet and educator

In organizations, when leaders and managers ask people to change and to be more creative, it may sound like a wonderful idea. But deep down, it can feel mystifying or threatening, because to be creative is to entertain the possibility of not knowing, and the possibility not only of greatness but of failure. It takes emotional intelligence to engage in the change process known as creative transformation. It is major in scope, distinct from the past, and usually irreversible. The journey does not follow the assumptions, or neat line, of rational planning. It involves all the risks of venturing into unknown territory, and may require giving up most, and at times all, control. It builds on your depth of character and draws it full force into the risky intersections of change, fate, and the unwritten future.

'Being in connection with our emotional depths is critical to releasing our most powerful and creative forces,' says Michael Eisner, Chairman and CEO of the Walt Disney Company. 'Denying this deeper level leads to "disconnection". In effect, people lose touch with aspects of who they are. The result tends to be vulnerability, fear and denial, as well as superficiality, falseness and a mistrust of intuition, all of which can get in the way of deep, creative expression. Fear of criticism and lack of acceptance is a primary reason why people censor their feelings and intuitions and shut down their

The heart is the origin of creative impulses ... Everything is tested internally, sifted, and sorted, gold from dross.

Julia Cameron, author of The Vein of God

depths.... Trusting our deepest intuitions and instincts may mean over-riding contrary research, peer pressure, conventional wisdom or intimi-dation.'[85]

Similarly, creative transformation, which is, in essence, a shift in the formation of yourself, an idea, a product or service, or an entire organ-ization, has little to do with fair weather creativity, the kind that depends on long stretches of peaceful isolation and usually vanishes without a trace in the presence of conflict and turmoil. It is my contention that true, deep, EQ-related creativity simultaneously involves both thinking and non-thinking,[86] and is often initiated through emotional alchemy. It takes place progressively, across time and space. It is here that real growth can occur, of people and souls. It is here that your sense of humour is called upon. This is where you find out how far your emotional and intellectual intelligences can extend, and what you're made of. Things don't always turn out successfully, but this can work where nothing else will.

In physics, scientists talk about an electron field and, similarly, ideas and creative solutions operate in a collective field. By applying intuitive flow and each of the preceding fifteen competencies of Executive EQ, you are better able to tap into that field of unexplored opportunities, you are able to effortlessly shift perspectives, and sense unexpected ways to creatively transform difficult or complicated circumstances into some-thing of highest value in learning and, in many cases, to snatch success from the jaws of defeat, sometimes when no one else seems able to do it.

> *Creative people* always *encounter obstacles, and almost inevitably encounter resistance.*
>
> Robert J. Sternberg, Yale University

Not long ago, Ayman Sawaf, foun-ding Chairman of the Foundation for Education in Emotional Literacy was engaged by a national sales and mar-keting organization in trouble. Their sales force of several thousand was in turmoil bordering on rebellion. Revenues were way down at about $5 million, falling off over seven years from a peak of more than $50 million. Cash reserves and credit lines allowed for a three-month turnaround. If not, bankruptcy was probable. Downsizing and retrenchment had hit the company hard, costing it most of the best sales people and leaving facilities dilapidated. Few new products were in development. Many of the remain-ing sales people were angry, fearful of further cutbacks, and seemed to have lost all sense of mission or purpose, the spirit that had once infused this pioneering firm.

The first thing Ayman did was conduct an informal EQ survey (the Q-Metrics' *EQ Map™* and *Organizational EQ Profiles™* were in the early research and development phase at that time) on both current and former managers and sales personnel. He discovered, first and foremost, an overall lack of trust. Many sales reps had been with the company for years and felt entitled to high margins and benefits, which were gone. Although discount rates on products had been slashed, company profits continued to fall. Shipping response times were abysmal. And at the home office, ideas from the field were being ignored. Complaints went unanswered. Everyone seemed to be feeling undervalued. The headquarters and shipping staff were upset and resentful, expressing feelings such as, 'After all we've done for them (sales force).' The sales force was similarly stuck, complaining, 'After all we've contributed to them (headquarters administration).' Some sales directors felt like martyrs and they were furious about it, blaming everyone but themselves. Others felt victimized by circumstances. Everyone appeared to be waiting for someone else to step in and fix the problem – it was not *their* responsibility to do it, they reasoned.

Because there was no time to hire new talent, Ayman was granted senior management powers for a three month period. With the help of his wife, Rowan, he hired a training team and they travelled from region to region of the country, holding meetings and open, creative dialogues with sales groups. They infused a sense of enthusiasm and hopefulness as they instituted changes. They faced the truth about the company as perceived by the sales force. They listened carefully. Which was an unexpected change for the sales representatives. Many of them reported feeling valued by the company for the first time in a long time, and sales increased immediately. All because a leadership team listened to them and had the guts, ingenuity and wit to bring a disparate collection of people, product development and delivery issues, and marketing factors, together into a creatively contentious yet unified – and distinctly original – whole. The scientific name for this capacity is *esemplastic imagination*.[87]

Within a month, Ayman had received more than a hundred specific ideas from managers and sales reps alike on how to transform the company on a shoestring budget. Some sales people even flew to the home office at their own expense to join the 'roundtable dialogues' that Ayman initiated. For the first time in a long period, people were talking honestly and openly. Much of the anger and frustration were channelled into constructive action steps. Ways to cut overheads and speed services were implemented. Management

> *Reason is a narrow system swollen into an ideology. With time and power it has become a dogma, devoid of direction and disguised as disinterested inquiry. Reason presents itself as the solution to the problems it has created.*
>
> John Ralston Saul, executive and historian

announced via nationwide teleconference that the company was breaking out of its quagmire of unfairness and decline, beginning with a commitment to give rapid responses to all questions from the field, clearing up old broken promises and misunderstandings, and putting an end to expecting sales reps to contribute excessive time and energy without due recognition and remuneration. A new compensation strategy was announced and implemented.

'We've lost your trust,' admitted the CEO straight out, 'and we aim to win it back, one action at a time.' This process capitalized on many of the ideas Ayman had received, such as weekly conference calls involving management and each regional group of sales reps, a new series of audio sales tapes, and video presentations of each new product. Within forty days, the development teams had five new product lines underway at very low cost. At Ayman's requests, the accountants opened the financial books for all sales leaders to see, and to understand that fair commissions were being paid. Nothing was hidden, and as feelings of trust and confidence rose, this prompted more sales people to join in the transformation effort.

Ayman engaged the sales directors to work with him in planning and teaching regional trainings for 100 to 200 people each. Each region reshaped its purpose statement and began to map out opportunities to win new accounts and move the company forward. The specific strengths and distinguishing characteristics of each product line were clarified, and the firm's conceptual leadership role was affirmed. Feelings of pride began to return as the individuals valued each other. Over three months, revenues grew nearly a million dollars. In six months, revenues had doubled and at the time of this writing, were still rising.

What stories do you have of people who have faced up to what seemed an unfair or hopeless circumstances and followed their gut instincts or intuition – making a small change here, adding a specific feeling or action there – and began to turn things around, eventually transforming the situation? On a related note, you might consider the possibility of benchmarking the creative transformation (CT) capacities of your company, department, team, or core work group. On an informal basis, you might begin with what could be considered a CT audit, which examines the percentage of revenue that comes from products and services less than five years old, less than two and a half years old, and less than a year old. You can compare these figures to your competition in each market avenue using the same axes. Basically, you're developing a simple assessment scale to know how well you deal with problems and opportunities by transforming them into revenue-generating products and services that capture market share and advance your value as a professional and organization.

Turning Points

Over the years, I have listened to many leaders reflect on what they've learned from the 'break points' in their careers and of their organizations – the times when everything was suddenly on the line, when things ran out of steam or money, or ideas hit a wall and were rejected. A surprisingly large number of such situations end up turning into future successes. It's not that any of these men and women had fewer problems than the rest of us; they just found more solutions.

The future is not some place we are going, but one we are creating. The paths to it are not found but made, and the activity of making them changes both the maker and the destination.

John Schaar

It's remarkable how often we find it's not the good times that bring out the best in us but the experiences that physicists call bifurcation points[88] – life's unexpected 'collisions' with the barriers of time or circumstance. These are the moments we get brought to our senses, turned around, and launched in a new direction. Often it's one that wasn't even on our radar screen at the time. In fact, all the strategic planning in the world couldn't have picked it, which is just as well.

What we learn from creative transformation is that even if we don't win *this* sale or make *this* deal, or if we happen to lose a bunch of money or time, or find our path diverted or our expectations overturned, we shouldn't lose heart. We come to sense that, more often than not, if we apply our creative intelligence we can find some entrepreneurial way to transcend difficulties and remake ourselves and our organizations in the process, often better than before. And we have the guts, and gut instinct, to know when to pursue a goal alone, if necessary.

In a research seminar I attended in graduate school, a well-known authority on research methodologies told us about having to fund his latest studies himself. He gave other examples of this among world-famous scientists in many fields, including business. Why? No one wanted to fund them because the new work they proposed was groundbreaking, and in an area different from the ones in which they traditionally worked. The funding agencies had labelled these creative leaders and placed them in an 'approved' box, as if their expertise were linear and restricted. However, research shows that people do their most creative work when they love what they do.[89] If you love working in a small box or walking a narrow line, that's fine. But once you discover you don't love being in a box, you're faced with a choice: to let others keep you in it, or to step outside anyway, as did many of these individuals who went on to follow their passions and become famous in other fields or invent new approaches to solving 'unsolvable' problems.

When I think of people who 'followed their passions', I think of one of my friends, Esther Orioli, founder and President of Essi Systems, Inc., a San Francisco firm specializing in corporate performance measurements and training. Esther tells the story of how, fourteen years ago, she invested all of her savings – about $100,000 in all – in launching Essi Systems and developing StressMap™. She soon had fifty corporate clients and was generating $90,000 a month in sales. But she was quickly depleting her inventory and had no money for developing new products. Esther consulted with her financial advisors and wrote up a business plan, seeking a loan from a top bank in the bay area. The loan officer said she needed a co-signer.

No problem, thought Esther. One of her advisors was a multimillionaire and he had already agreed to add his signature as guarantee for a $300,000 loan. But the bank again said no, this time because the co-signer was not a member of her management team. 'Well,' replied Esther, 'I can make him part of the team.' Which she did.

But the bank rejected the loan once more. 'We want to wait two more years and watch your revenues,' they said. The millionaire friend called the bankers. They, in truth, had rejected Esther because she was a woman. So did five more banks in reviewing her loan request. Esther then turned to venture capital groups, who said they wanted 80 per cent of her company and, as their first action, they would replace her with a man as president. Esther said no. She valued herself. It was her company and her dream.

But she left the final meeting in a rage. She returned to her office and wrote a passionate letter describing her company and circumstances, mailing it to several hundred friends and acquaintances. Within days, money began arriving in the mail, which is yet another example of the power of constructive discontent. People sensed her passion and potential and withdrew funds from their savings accounts. This gave her an idea. 'You might as well roll over and play dead,' one of the venture capitalists had said to her. 'No, I'll play bank,' thought Esther now with a smile.

This is what she did. She started PlayBank™. Accepting money from individual investors, Esther paid 20 per cent annual interest and repaid the principal with a year. There is now a long list of people wanting to invest in Playbank™. For more than a decade, Esther has repaid investors on time and has never needed to go to any commercial bank for a loan, although many bankers have since approached her *wanting* to lend her money. Essi Systems now has 2,000 corporate clients in the US and 400 in Canada and, as one of a whole range of products and performance measurements, has sold nearly 500,000 StressMaps™.

That's creative transformation at work.

As it is in the next story about one of my mentors.

In 1966, aged seventeen, Nido Qubein left Lebanon with the equivalent of US $50 in his pocket, virtually no knowledge of English, and a dream of becoming a successful American citizen. He knew no one. His only plans were to travel 7,000 miles to attend Mount Olive College in North Carolina – and work very hard, and very creatively, which is exactly what he did. He worked part-time jobs while going to school, and summers as a camp counsellor. He earned a bachelor's degree in human relations and then an MBA from the University of North Carolina.

In 1971, he started a small consulting and publishing company, Creative Services, Inc., with $500 in savings. He worked diligently at perfecting his command of English, and in 1973 he began public speaking and consulting. Nido vowed to let nothing stand in his way. Again and again he transformed himself and his approach to business, learning every way to help each of a wide range of clients, from small companies to GE and AT&T, become more successful.

Over the years, he has published a dozen books, achieved ratings as one of America's top corporate speakers, and was recently inducted into the International Speakers Hall of Fame.

The future is not shaped by people who don't really believe in the future.

John W. Gardner, author of On Leadership

Along the way he became a partner in a $20 million-plus real estate firm, and a partner in the McNeill Lehman public relations and advertising firm. He also became director and major equity partner in Southern National Bank Corporation, a bank holding company which has grown from $100 million to $22 billion in assets. Aged twenty-four, he started the Nido Qubein Associates Scholarship Fund, which has raised nearly $1 million in college assistance for deserving students. Today, he is also Chairman of the economic development division of the High Point Chamber of Commerce.

The truth is, individuals of all backgrounds, and leaders at all levels in companies of all sizes, are committing themselves to playing an active, heart-felt role in creating the future. They are calling upon every aspect of their intelligence – emotional, practical, creative, and technical, among others – to lead the field and compete for new successes in the years ahead.

McKnight was curious: 3M didn't sell raw materials, so there was no

283

business to transact here. But, ever searching for new ideas that might propel the company forward, McKnight asked himself, 'Why does Mr Okie want these samples?' In this way, from a simple question, 3M found one of the most important products in its history, because Mr Okie had invented a revolutionary waterproof sandpaper that would prove of immense value to automobile manufacturers and repaint shops worldwide. It turned out that Mr Okie had asked for samples from numerous mineral and sandpaper companies but none – except for 3M – had bothered to ask why he wanted the samples. 3M immediately acquired the rights to the technology and began selling the new sandpaper. But McKnight transformed the transformation a second time; he didn't just sign an agreement with Okie, he hired him, and he moved to St Paul and became a key partner in developing new products for 3M until his retirement nineteen years later.

This leads to a great follow-up example of creative transformation at 3M: in 1924, the company was trying to advance beyond sandpaper and introduced a line of automobile waxes and polishes, but they proved to be a costly failure and were discontinued. Undaunted in the innovation-always atmosphere created by McKnight, a young 3M employee named Dick Drew was visiting a customer site – an auto paint shop – and overheard some angry cursing. Two-tone auto paint jobs were popular, but the improvised glues and adhesive tapes separating the two colours failed to mask properly, leaving ragged lines and blotches.

'Can't anyone give us *something* that works?' shouted the paint man.

'We can!' replied Drew. 'I'll bet we can adapt something in our lab to make foolproof masking tape.'

Listen to anyone with an original idea ... Encourage; don't nitpick. Let people run with their ideas.

William McKnight, 3M Company General Manager, 1914–55

Back at 3M, Drew discovered, however, that 3M had no such readily adaptable product in the laboratory. So, true to the spirit and inner drive of his company, he invented one: 3M masking tape, which would prove wildly successful.

In response to an opportunity hidden *within* a problem – a transformational strategy which would be repeated thousands of times at 3M in the years that followed – Drew had succeeded. Five years later, he did it again. Responding to complaints about poor quality packing tapes, Drew advanced the masking tape technology and created the first waterproof packing tape, which was a big success. But Drew had no idea that it would be used in hundreds of unexpected was by customers and – with 3M paying careful attention and asking McKnight's question, Why? – the packing tape was expanded into a line of tapes which would soon become the most important product line in the company by the mid-1930s and a household name: Scotch cellophane tape.

The point is, it wasn't planned. One obstacle revealed an opportunity, which led to other opportunities, and raised more questions about what was possible, tested the emotional adaptability and initiative of all those involved, and ended up ultimately revealing a host of unorthodox ways to work around related problems, and it sparked ideas about how to take a product and adapt it into a whole new market area.

This brand of innovation is alive and well at 3M, and has been embraced in various forms at many other organizations around the world. Even EDS, the computer outsourcing giant with $12.4 billion in sales for 1995, has become deeply committed to a creative transformation initiative called for by CEO Les Alberthal – to create a radically new identity as the world's most sensitive services company.[92]

This highlights a dramatic shift for this hard-driving culture. Starting in 1994, Alberthal began putting every EDS manager, starting with himself,

> *Whatever made you successful in the past won't in the future.*
>
> Lew Platt, CEO, Hewlett-Packard

through a series of transformational training sessions that delve deeply into the realm of feelings and creativity, to stimulate new ideas and greater sensitivity to colleagues, employees, and customers. According to Dean Linderman, a confidant to Alberthal who supervises leadership development: 'In an organization with a history of avoidance of the soft stuff, the heart-and-soul stuff, we've now said that not only is heart and soul important, but it's a prerequisite to take the corporation where we want to go.' In the case of EDS, thus far – and not unexpectedly – a number of the managers are reportedly not listening to their feelings primarily for fun; they're doing it because that's what is required to deepen and expand trusting relationships and generate future revenues.[93]

Which at least in part, may have things backwards.

Humour and Emotional Intelligence

One of the qualities I've often noticed in managers and executives with high EQ is a ready wit.[94] I believe this is no coincidence. However, I know men and women in

> *The compulsion to take ourselves seriously is in inverse proportion to our creative capacity.*
>
> Eric Hoffer, American sociologist

leadership positions who are, for lack of a better description, afraid of fun. 'There's more to life than business,' we all agree. But we don't act like it. Or at least not until we face a heart condition, a first grandchild, or some other soul-jolting occurrence. Better late than never, it seems, but why not sooner?

'Humour,' explains Dr Edward deBono, a physician and organizational authority on creativity, 'is by far the most significant behaviour of human intelligence.'[95] Studies show that a quick infusion of light-heartedness does more than boost your energy. It encourages intuitive *flow*, makes you more helpful toward others, and significantly improves intelligence processes such as judgment, problem solving, and decision making when you are facing difficult challenges.[96] It is a great aid to creative transformation.

And connection. Few things so instantly form a bond between people as laughter. People who've cultivated a light heart and a light touch are generally better able to be creative when the going gets rough and to bounce back faster from difficult circumstances. 'The person who has a sense of humour is not just more relaxed in the face of potentially stressful situations, but is more flexible in his approach,' says philosopher John Morreall. 'Even when there is not a lot going on in his environment, his imagination and innovativeness will help keep him out of a mental rut, will allow him to enjoy himself, and will prevent boredom and depression.'[97]

Unfortunately, many managers I know regularly complain that there's just no room anymore for spontaneous mirth in corporate life. Richard Branson is one of the chief executives who realizes this. He has worked to advance the Virgin Group as a community of successful people who help each other creatively at the same time they experience excitement and fun. Having fun is a central value in Virgin's company culture.[98] In the long run, Branson has found, people who have fun are usually more open with others, more creative and inclusive, and work harder.

Herb Kelleher, CEO of Southwest Airlines, has found much the same thing. His award-winning, consistently profitable carrier with more than $2.6 billion in sales, keeps humour alive as one of the firm's core values.[99] Southwest steadily wins the Department of Transportation's awards for best service, on-time flights, and superior baggage handling, and Kelleher was named best American CEO by *Fortune* magazine in 1994. That same year, 125,000 people applied for 3,000 job openings with Southwest. His secret to success? 'You can duplicate the airplanes. You can duplicate the gate facilities. You can duplicate all the hard things, the tangible things you can put your hands on. But it's the *intangibles* that determine success. They're the hardest to duplicate, if you can do it at all. We've got the right intangibles.'

The right intangibles, which – at Southwest Airlines and other leading enterprises – means inspired people. In Kelleher's cases, he 'cherishes and respects' his 18,000 employees, and his 'love' is returned in what he calls 'a spontaneous, voluntary overflowing of emotion'. That's actually more pragmatic than it may at first sound, and is based on a set of practices and core values, including humour, independence, and respect, which infuse every aspect of how Southwest is run, including how people relate to each other and to customers and suppliers. To make certain this set of values is *lived*, Kelleher recently appointed several dozen 'ambassadors' to help him monitor and reinforce it. He calls this group 'the most important committee in the whole company'.

At every level of Southwest, there is evidence that humour is infused into the inspiration to lead the field. Ascertaining whether an individual possesses such emotional intelligence begins when interviewers notice how applicants treat the receptionist who greets them. If they act self-important, and demand attention, 'they will not be hired,' says Kelleher. Moreover, people looking for jobs, from pilots to mechanics, are routinely asked, 'Tell us how you used humour to get out of an embarrassing scrape,' and, 'What is the funniest thing that ever happened to you?' And, on at least one occasion, applicants were tested to see how well they responded to a practical joke.'

The sense of fun imbues tough work experiences with a charge of healthy energy, and builds flexibility and adaptability to changing cir-

> *It is always fun to do the impossible.*
>
> Walt Disney

cumstances. 'The new goal in our society,' says corporate strategist Gary Hamel, 'is joy of use. We want our products and services to be whimsical, tactile, informative, and just plain fun. Any company that can wrap those attributes around a mundane product or service has the chance to be an industry revolutionary.'[100] Example? The most profitable food retailer in the United States: Trader Joe's, a cross between a gourmet deli and a discount warehouse. CEO John Shields calls it a 'fashion food retailer'. Seizing an area of the market essentially without competition, its seventy-four stores were averaging annual sales of $1,000 per square foot in 1995, twice the rate of conventional supermarkets. Why are customers attracted to Trader Joe's? As much for entertainment and fun, it seems, as for sustenance. The store stocks a wide range of rare and offbeat foods – raspberry salsa, jasmine rice, salmon burgers, for example – as well as a comprehensive selection of competitively priced staples. By transforming the hum-drum shopping experience into a culinary treasure hunt that's fun for people of all ages, Trader Joe's has more than doubled sales in the past five years to $605 million.

Humorous thoughts and, in particular, 'mirthful laughter' work their wonders by initially arousing and distracting the rational, linear mind while opening the heart and leaving us feeling alert yet relaxed.[101] 'We've always said that Silicon Graphics is all about making technology fun and usable,' says CEO Ed McCracken, 'and that means that working here should be fun. Too many corporations in the United States and Japan have cut the fun out of their businesses. ... Fun and irreverence also make change less scary.'[102] Scientists theorize that laughter and the sense of fun stimulate the production of brain catecholamines and endorphins which affect hormonal levels in the body, some related to feelings of joy, an easing of pain, and an enhanced sense of creativity and perspective.[103]

Consider the following example of creative transformation at work, succeeding in part *because* of humour, not in spite of it:[104]

A tale that once got out: Mercedes engineers, lobbying for zippier engines, 'disappeared' a Benz sedan for a few days. It returned with its hood chained shut, belly pan below, and its engine sounding stout. A few corporate fat cats raced it up the autobahn and Alps, and then rushed back to see what great advance was in there. The engineers unshackled the hood to reveal a BMW engine. Mercedes revamped its motors.

EQ Map Connections: Creating the Future

You may want to refer to the following scales of the *EQ Map* as points of reflection related to this chapter: emotional self-awareness, emotional expression, emotional awareness of others, intentionality, creativity, resilience, constructive discontent, outlook, intuition, trust radius, personal power, and integrity

---

One Feeling, One Choice, At a Time

Above my desk is a two-inch by three-inch display entitled 'DNA: The Blueprint of Life.' In the centre are three very thin, interwoven strands of what appears to be a cotton-like fibre. However, it is an actual specimen of plant-source deoxyribonucleic acid (DNA). Beneath the sample is written the following: 'The entire human population living on earth today received its hereditary characteristics through an amount of DNA equivalent to that embedded here.' It continues to surprise me each time

I look at it, as I have almost every day for nearly two decades. The point is this: we are more than our genes. We are more than a body with a brain. We feel. We intuitively create. We transform. We are beings with spirit.

As I noted at the outset of this book, studies suggest that a single person with a low EQ can lower an entire group's collective IQ.[105] Conversely, does it also hold that a single person with a *high* EQ may raise the group's IQ? Future research will tell us. One of the most heartening things I've learned in studying and mapping emotional intelligence in leadership and organizations is that through developing EQ, we each discover a wide range of previously untapped ways to make a meaningful difference in our work and life, even if we must begin to take action alone.

Imagine for a moment the one hundred trillion cells in your body. A solitary one of them can start a disease. On the other hand, a single cell anywhere in your body can initiate a healing process, eventually benefiting all of the other 100 trillion cells. Similarly, a change in a single feeling or attitude in one human being generates, in its own unique way, a transformative shift in the whorls of living energy that extend outward to touch all the rest.

Transformation takes place in the dynamism of an open biological and spiritual system. Individually we grow by learning, by expanding our capacities and enriching the lives of others. In this regard, each of us is an alchemist, an agent of creative transformation as we advance through our daily lives, making and remaking ourselves and our environment, abandoning transcending the *status quo* – if and when we dare – and creating what has been called the *status ascensium.*[106] We leave a unique sensory impression of our presence and influence, an imprint that will be felt, on some level and in some way, by our children's children, and their children. This is our legacy for having lived. It is not, then, a question of our power *to* influence or transform; it's a matter of how, exactly, we *express* that influence.

The secret of life, discovered four billion years ago in terrestrial seas, centres on the ability to build molecules according to need. Each of our cells contains the information needed to reproduce all of its component proteins, encoded in strings of nucleotides. DNA carries the hereditary codes passed from parent to child and generation to generation, forming a living link that ties us through time to the earliest cells on Earth.

DNA is perhaps the most beautiful and mysterious of our molecules, and its beauty lies not in its appearance but, more importantly, what is shaped and expressed within. DNA is composed of two long strands of nucleic acid, wrapped one around the other in a double helix. The sequence of the bases in each DNA strand is our genetic text, our purest source of promise and potential, holding the blueprint to build each of our proteins and renew our life. I like to imagine that, metaphorically, our emotional intelligence – both the light and shadow – is somehow intricately woven within the cells of the human heart in much the same way.

Creating an Emotionally Intelligent Future

Each of the notable men and women I have met over the years, including the Tibetan elder in the opening story of this book, has found his or her own way to keep in touch with the pulse of life, the inner spark which keeps them stretching, moving, adapting, growing, and taking on challenges. It is through humour and enthusiasm, as well as difficulties and doubts, and the courage to change, that we are each given the chance to learn from life's experiences and interact with them in ways that enable us to grow and learn, to listen and lead, and to live with creative spirit.

Following a speech he gave many years ago, John Gardner, professor of public service at Stanford, received a letter from a man who wrote to say that his twenty-year-old daughter had been killed in an automobile accident, and that he had found a paragraph from Gardner's speech transcript in her wallet.[107] The father was grateful that his daughter had kept it close to her and it told him something he might not otherwise have known about her values and focus:

Meaning is not something you stumble across, like the answer to a riddle or the prize to a treasure hunt. Meaning is something you build into your life. You build it out of your own past, out of your affections and loyalties, out of the experience of humankind as it is passed to you, out of your own talent and understanding, out of the things you believe in, out of the things and people you love, out of the values for which you are willing to sacrifice something. The ingredients are there. You are the only one who can put them together into that unique pattern that will be your life. Let it be a life that has dignity and meaning for you.

In his 1842 journal, Emerson wrote:

The tongue of flame, the picture the newspapers give, at the late fire in Liverpool, of the mountains of burning cotton over which the flames arose to twice their height, the volcano also, from which the conflagration rises toward the zenith an appreciable distance toward the stars – these are the most affecting symbols of what man should be. A spark of fire is infinitely deep, but a mass of fire reaching from earth upward into heaven, this is the sign of the robust, united, burning, radiant soul.

This was Emerson's image for the energy behind the poetic impulse as well as the leadership impulse, which were always for him not just a case of expression, but of continually connecting one's own small flame to the great central flames of life and the world.[108] Although we cannot predict the exact details of the future, we can have a hand in shaping the *heart* of the future, including its context of meaning, and our commitment and courage in advancing into the unknown.

Emotional intelligence is a primary source of these central flames in our lives, and is the source of the impulse that awakens us and inspires us to advance into the great unknown. But what about the executives who hedge every step, asking, 'Who else is already doing such a new thing, and doing it successfully, anyone?' A reasonable question, to be sure. A follow-up point to be considered, certainly. But as a lead-off question, it's dead-end. Second creative fiddle. Never first. And, in this way, many of us wait for others to lead, to take responsibility, to create the future. David J. Wolpe writes, 'There is a marvellous story of a man who once stood before God, his heart breaking from the pain and injustice in the world. "Dear God," he cried out, "look at all the suffering, the anguish and distress in the world. Why didn't you send help?"

'God responded, "I did send help. I sent you." '[109]

This is, it seems to me, as true in business as in life. This much we know: success in the Knowledge Era has become, in the words of John Seely Brown, Vice-President and chief scientist at Xerox Corporation, 'as much about the spirit of the enterprise as the economics of the business; as much about the positive energy it unleashes as the positive cash flow it creates.'[110] Business has become, in the last century, the most powerful institution on the planet. And the dominant institution in any society must take responsibility for the whole, to lead the way, by example, into the future. Every decision that is made, every action taken has to be viewed in light of – and in the context of – that kind of responsibility.

Emotions, like the eyes, have long been called a mirror of the soul, and it is in the human heart that we connect to our humanity and to the possibilities of greatness and service. 'Above all else,' it is written in Proverbs 4:23, 'keep watch over your heart, for herein are the wellsprings of life.' We must not let it be squandered through neglect or lost in the shadows of intellect.

How often do you, like most of us, ask yourself in the quiet dark of late night, 'What's it all for?' Most of our waking life is spent working. While we may tell ourselves it's just to earn a living, the heart knows it's engaged in a crucial struggle for its existence. William James, the father of American psychology, observed that the laws of habit – the small, moment-by-moment choices we either make or ignore every day – 'bear us irresistibly toward our destiny'. And it is the habits of the heart that, above all, give our lives meaning.

Ask yourself, What might be possible if everyone in your family developed more emotional intelligence? What if every member of your work team, organization, or community had a high EQ? How much more might you be able to give, learn, earn, cooperate, create, and accomplish through the rest of your life? The leaders of enterprise must find a way for the community of work to change. To create an organizational environment in which how we do business together is as important as what we produce, and how we serve others is as vital as how much we profit.

'Great ideas, it has been said, come into the world as gently as doves,' wrote Albert Camus in 1961. 'Perhaps, then, if we listen attentively, we shall hear, amid the uproar of empires and nations, a faint flutter of wings, the gentle stirring of life and hope. Some will say this hope lies in a nation, others, in a man or woman. I believe rather that it is awakened, revived, nourished by millions of solitary individuals whose deeds and works every day negate frontiers and the crudest implications of history. As a result there shines forth fleetingly the ever-threatened truth and each and every person, on the foundations of his or her own suffering and joys, builds for them all.'

I recall the words of the teacher Hillel in the first century AD: 'If I am not for myself, who will be for me? And if I am only for myself, what am I? And if not now – when?'

As I stated at the outset, the purpose of writing this book has been to raise and explore some potentially useful questions about the characteristics and values of developing and applying emotional intelligence in leadership, organizational learning, and life. It is my hope that these pages can serve as a starting point for a highly personal journey. The basic ingredients are here, inside your heart as well as your head. You are the leader. You are the process. As Mahatma Gandhi said, 'You must *be* the change you wish to see in the world.'

If not now – when?

READING LIST

Business as a Calling: Work and the Examined Life, Michael Novak (New York: Free Press, 1996).

Certain Trumpets: The Call of Leaders, Garry Wills (New York: Simon & Schuster, 1994).

Character First, Joseph W. Gauld (San Francisco: Institute for Contemporary Studies Press, 1993).

Common Fire: Lives of Commitment in a Complex World, Laurent A. Parks Daloz, Cheryl H. Keen, James P. Keen and Sharon Daloz Parks (Boston: Beacon Press, 1996).

Common Values, Sissela Bok (Columbia, MO: University of Missouri Press, 1996).

The Corporate Mystic, Gay Hendricks, PhD and Kate Ludeman, PhD (New York: Bantam, 1996).

Creativity in Business, Michael Ray, PhD and Rochelle Myers (New York: Doubleday, 1986).

Credibility, James M. Kouzes and Barry Z. Posner, PhD (San Francisco: Jossey-Bass, 1993).

Deep Change: Discovering the Leader Within, Robert E. Quinn, PhD (San Francisco: Jossey-Bass, 1996).

Descartes' Error: Emotion, Reason and the Human Brain, Antonio R. Damasio, MD, PhD (New York: Grosset/Putnam, 1994).

The Economics of Trust: Liberating Profits & Restoring Corporate Vitality, John O. Whitney (New York: McGraw-Hill, 1995).

Emotional Intelligence, Daniel Goleman, PhD (London: Bloomsbury, 1996).

The Empowered Manager, Peter Block (San Francisco: Jossey-Bass, 1987).

First Person: Tales of Management Courage and Tenacity, Thomas Teal (Boston: Harvard Business School Press, 1995).

The Heart Aroused, David Whyte (New York: Doubleday Currency, 1994).

The Heart At Work, Jack Canfield and Jacqueline Miller (New York: McGraw-Hill, 1996).

(integrity), Stephen L. Carter (New York: Basic Books, 1996).

Jamming: The Art & Discipline of Business Creativity, John Kao (London: HarperCollins, 1996).

The Language of the Heart: The Body's Response to Human Dialogue, James J. Lynch, PhD (New York: Basic Books, 1985).

The Leadership Challenge, James R. Kouzes and Barry Z. Posner, PhD (San Francisco: Jossey-Bass, 1995).

Leading Minds: An Anatomy of Leadership, Howard Gardner (London: HarperCollins, 1996).

Learning as a Way of Being, Peter B. Vaill, DBA (San Francisco: Jossey-Bass, 1996).

Managing the Equity Factor ... or 'After All I've Done for You ...', Richard C. Huseman, PhD and John D. Hatfield, PhD (Boston: Houghton Mifflin, 1989).

Meeting the Shadow: The Hidden Power of the Dark Side of Human Nature, Connie Zweig and Jeremiah Abrams (eds) (New York: Tarcher/Putnam, 1991).

The Moral Intelligence of Children, Robert Coles, MD (New York: Random House, 1997).

The New Paradigm in Business, edited by Michael Ray and Alan Rinzler for the World Business Academy (New York: Tarcher/Putnam, 1993).

Opening Up: The Healing Power of Confiding in Others, James W. Pennebaker, PhD (New York: Morrow, 1990).

The Origin of Everyday Moods, Robert E. Thayer, PhD (London: Oxford University Press, 1996).

The Passions: Emotions and the Meaning of Life, Robert C. Solomon, PhD (Indianapolis: Hackett Publishing, 1993).

Soar with Your Strengths, Donald O. Clifton, PhD and Paul Nelson (New York: Delacorte Press, 1992).

The Stuff Americans Are Made Of, Josh Hammond and James Morrison (New York: Macmillan, 1996).

Successful Intelligence, Robert J. Sternberg, PhD (New York: Simon & Schuster, 1996).

Taking Responsibility, Nathaniel Branden (Simon & Schuster, 1996).

Trust: The Social Virtues & The Creation of Prosperity, Francis Fukuyama (London: Viking, 1995).

The Vein of Gold, Julia Cameron (New York: Tarcher/Putnam, 1996).

When Elephants Weep, Jeffrey Moussaieff Masson and Susan McCarthy (New York: Delta, 1995).

You've Got To Be Believed To Be Heard, Bert Decker (New York: St Martin's Press, 1993).

NOTES

Prologue and Introduction

1. Mayer, J.D. and Salovey, P., 'The Intelligence of Emotional Intelligence', *Intelligence* 17 (1993): 433–42.
2. See, for example: Solomon, R.C., *The Passions: Emotions and the Meaning of Life* (Indianapolis: Hackett Publishing, 1993); Lazarus, R.S., *Emotion & Adaptation* (Oxford: Oxford University Press, 1991); Lazarus, R.S. and Lazarus, B.N., *Passion & Reason* (Oxford: Oxford University Press, 1995); Damasio, A.R., *Descartes' Error: Emotion, Reason, and the Human Brain* (New York: Putnam, 1994).
3. Institute of HeartMath (14700 W. Park Ave., Boulder Creek, CA 95006, 408–338–8700); Rein, G., Atkinson, M. and McCraty, R., 'The Physiological and Psycological Effects of Compassion and Anger', *Journal of Advancement in Medicine* (in press, 1996); McCraty, R., Atkinson, M. and Tiller, W.A., 'New Electrophysiological Correlates Associated with Intentional Heart Focus', *Subtle Energies* 4 (3) (1995): 251–68.
4. Burns, J.M., *Leadership* (New York: HarperCollins, 1978).
5. Sternberg, R.J., *Successful Intelligence* (New York: Simon & Schuster, 1996).
6. See, for example: Damasio, *Descartes' Error*.
7. Winter, A. and Winter, R., *Build Your Brainpower* (New York: St Martin's Press, 1986): 1.
8. See, for example: Gardner, H., *Frames of Mind: The Theory of Multiple Intelligences* (New York: Basic Books, 1983); Gardner, H., *Multiple Intelligences: The Theory in Practice* (New York: Basic Books, 1993); Perkins, D., *Outsmarting IQ: The Emerging Science of Learnable Intelligence* (New York: The Free Press, 1995); Goleman, D., *Emotional Intelligence* (London: Bloomsbury, 1996); and Sternberg, *Successful Intelligence*.
9. Sternberg, *Successful Intelligence*: 17.
10. See, for example: Perkins, D., *Outsmarting IQ*; Sternberg, *Successful Intelligence*; Farnham, A., 'Are You Smart Enough to Keep Your Job?' *Fortune* (15 Jan. 1996): 34–48; and Goleman, *Emotional Intelligence*.
11. See: Zukav, G., *The Seat of the Soul* (New York: Fireside, 1989): 105–6.
12. See, for example: Sternberg, *Successful Intelligence*; Whitney, J.O., *The Economics of Trust* (New York: McGraw-Hill, 1995); and Moore, J.F., *The Death of Competition* (New York: HarperBusiness, 1996).
13. See: Sternberg, *Successful Intelligence*: 11.
14. See, for example: Mehrabian, A., *Silent Messages* (Belmont, CA: Wadsworth Publishing, 1981); and Decker, B., *You've Got To Be Believed To Be Heard* (New York: St Martin's Press, 1992).
15. See, for example: Damasio, *Descartes' Error*.

16. Hammond, J. and Morrison, J., *The Stuff Americans Are Made Of* (New York: Macmillan, 1996): 197.

17. See, for example: Solomon, *The Passions*.

18. See, for example: Whitney, J.O., *The Economics of Trust* (New York: McGraw-Hill, 1996) and Fukuyama, F., *Trust: The Social Virtues and the Creation of Prosperity* (London: Viking, 1995).

19. See, for example: Perkins, *Outsmarting IQ*; Goleman, *Emotional Intelligence*; and Sternberg, *Successful Intelligence*.

20. Rosenthal, R., *et al.*, 'The PONS Test: Measuring Sensitivity to Nonverbal Clues', in McReynolds, P. (Ed.), *Advances in Psychological Assessment* (San Francisco: Jossey-Bass, 1977).

21. Argyris, C., *Knowledge for Action: A Guide to Overcoming Barriers to Organizational Change* (San Francisco: Jossey-Bass, 1993); Argyris, C., *Overcoming Organizational Defenses: Facilitating Organizational Learning* (Boston: Allyn and Bacon, 1990); Argyris, C. and Schon, D.A., *Organizational Learning II: Theory, Method, and Practice* (Reading, MA: Addison-Wesley, 1996).

22. The subject of group intelligence is presented by Robert Sternberg and Wendy Williams in 'Group Intelligence: Why Some Groups Are Better Than Others', *Intelligence* (1988).

23. Kelley, R. and Caplan, J., 'How Bell Labs Creates Star Performers', *Harvard Business Review* (July–Aug., 1993).

24. For information about learning materials, seminars, and workshops on emotional intelligence in business and organizations, contact the Learning Circle (142 North Road, Sudbury, MA 01776 USA; 508-371-8818; fax 508-371-5903; or http://www.learningcircle.com).

25. The self-scoring and computer-scored *EQ Map* (which include a colour printout of your results and a personal report) and *Organizational EQ Profiles* (for teams and companies) can be ordered from *Q-Metrics* (70 Otis St., San Francisco, CA 94103 USA; 415-252-8224; fax 415-252-5732; or http://www.eq.org).

The First Cornerstone: Emotional Literacy

1. I gratefully acknowledge Joseph W. Gauld, founder of Hyde School in Bath, Maine, for my deepened appreciation of the expression 'unique potential'.

2. See, for example: Solomon, R.C., *The Passions: Emotions and the Meaning of Life* (Indianapolis: Hackett Publishing, 1991).

3. The collection of research and perspectives which has most strongly influenced me on these points is Robert Solomon's *The Passions*.

4. See, for example: Sorokin, P.A., *Social and Cultural Dynamics*, Vol. IV (Bedminster Press, 1962): 746–64; Mishlove, J., 'Intuition: The Source of True Knowing', *Noetic Sciences Review* (Spring, 1994): 31–6.

5. See, for example: Parikh, J.D., *et al.*, *Intuition: The New Frontier of Management* (New York: Blackwell, 1994); Schultz, R., *Unconventional Wisdom* (HarperCollins, 1994); Agor, W., *Intuition in Organizations* (Sage Publications, 1989); Agor, W.H., *The Intuitive Manager* (New York: Prentice Hall, 1984); Rowan, R., *The Intuitive*

Manager (Boston: LIttle, Brown, 1986); The Intuition Network (Jeffrey Mishlove, PhD, Director, 369-B Third St, #161, San Rafael, CA 94901).

6. Wanless, D., in Farkas, C.M. and Debacker, P., *Maximum Leadership* (New York: Henry Holt, 1996): 152–3.

7. Marshall, C., in Farkas and DeBacker, *Maximum Leadership*: 152–6.

8. Oshry, B., *Seeing Systems* (San Francisco: Berrett-Koehler, 1995).

9. We have been using EQ Morning Notes as an executive development technique for a number of years. For a review of the psychological research on this subject, see Pennebaker, J., *Opening Up* (New York: Morrow, 1991). For general readers, one of the most useful and insightful approaches to this concept can be found in Julia Cameron's books, *The Artist's Way* (New York: Tarcher/Putnam, 1993) and *The Vein of Gold* (New York: Tarcher/Putnam, 1996).

10. Ray, M. and Myers, R., *Creativity in Business* (New York: Doubleday, 1987).

11. See, for example: Pennebaker, *Opening Up* and Francis, M.E. and Pennebaker, J.W., 'Talking and Writing as Illness Prevention', *Medicine, Exercise, Nutrition and Health* 1 (1) (Jan./Feb., 1992): 27–33.

12. I am grateful to Esther M. Orioli for the insights on this kind of simple, successful behaviour change process. See, for example: Orioli, E.M., *The StressMap 21-Day Rule Action Planning Workbook* (Essi Systems, Inc., 70 Otis St, San Francisco, CA 94103; 1993 and 1995).

13. Stewart, T.A., '3M Fights Back', *Fortune* (5 Feb. 1996): 94–9.

14. Huseman, R.C. and Hatfield, J.D., *The Equity Factor* (Boston: Houghton Mifflin, 1989).

15. See, for example: Thayer, R.E., *The Biopsychology of Mood & Arousal* (Oxford: Oxford University Press, 1992); and Thayer, R.E., *The Origin of Everyday Moods* (Oxford: Oxford University Press, 1996).

16. Dilts, R.B., *Strategies of Genius* Vol. II (Capitola, CA: Meta Publications, 1994); Pais, A., *Subtle is the Lord: The Science and the Life of Albert Einstein* (Oxford: Oxford University Press, 1982); Pais, A., *Einstein Lived Here* (Oxford: Oxford University Press, 1994); Einstein, A., *The World as I See It/Out of My Later Years* (New York: Philosophical Library, 1956).

17. Simon, H., *Hidden Champions: Lessons from 500 of the World's Best Unknown Companies* (Boston: Harvard Business School Press, 1996): 217, 232.

18. Decker, B., *You've Got To Be Believed To Be Heard* (New York: St Martin's Press, 1993): 117–20.

19. See, for example: Ray and Myers, *Creativity in Business*; Goleman, D., Kaufman, P. and Ray, M., *The Creative Spirit* (New York: Dutton, 1992); Catford, L. and Ray, M., *The Path of the Everyday Hero* (New York: Tarcher/Putnam, 1991); and Ray, M. and Rinzler, A. (eds), *The New Paradigms in Business* (New York: Tarcher/Putnam, 1993).

20. Kao, J., *Jamming* (London: HarperCollins, 1996): 48.

21. Thayer, *The Origin of Everyday Moods*: 183.

22. See, for example: Fritz, R., *Creating* (New York: Ballantine, 1991); and Fritz, R., *Corporate Tides* (San Francisco: Berrett-Koehler, 1996).

23. Gallagher, W., *The Power of Place* (New York: Poseidon, 1993).

24. See: Becker, F., *The Total Workplace: Facilities Management and the Elastic Organization* (New York: Van Nostrand Reinhold, 1990).

25. Royer, L., quoted in Stewart, '3M Fights Back', *Fortune* (5 Feb. 1996): 94–9.

26. Yhtyneet Kuvalehdet Oy, in Kouzes, J.M. and Posner, B.Z., *The Leadership Challenge* (rev. edn) (San Francisco: Jossey-Bass, 1995): 158.

27. See: Becker, F. and Steele, F., *Workplace by Design: Mapping the High-Performance Workscape* (San Francisco: Jossey-Bass, 1995): 83–4.

28. Coots, L., quoted in Becker and Steele, *Workplace by Design*: 138–9.

29. Moore-Ede, M., *The Twenty-Four Hour Society* (Reading, MA: Addison-Wesley, 1993).

30. See, for example: Moore-Ede, *The Twenty-Four Hour Society*: 55; Thayer, *The Origin of Everyday Moods*; and Solomon, *The Passions*.

31. Norfolk, D., *Executive Stress* (New York: Warner, 1986).

32. See, for example: Grandjean, E., *Fitting the Task* 4th edn (London: Taylor & Francis, 1988); and Moore-Ede, *The Twenty-Four Hour Society*.

33. See, for example: Grandjean, *Fitting the Task*; Moore-Ede, *The Twenty-Four Hour Society*.

34. See, for example: Thayer, *The Origin of Everyday Moods*.

35. Backer, T.E., 'How Health Promotion Programs Can Enhance Workplace Creativity', in Klarreich, S.H. (ed.), *Health and Fitness in the Workplace* (New York: Praeger, 1987): 325–37.

36. Maddi, S.R. and Kobasa, S.C., *The Hardy Executive: Health Under Stress* (Homewood, IL: Dow Jones Irwin, 1984).

37. See: Loehr, J.R. in Callan, K., 'Personal Power', *Success* (Sept., 1996): 22; Loehr, J.R., in Smith, L., 'Stamina: Who Has It, Why You Need It, How to Get It', *Fortune* (28 Nov. 1994): 127–40; Cooper, R.K., *Health & Fitness Excellence* (Boston: Houghton Mifflin, 1989); and Cooper, R.K., *Low-Fat Living* (Emmaus, PA: Rodale Books, 1996).

38. See, for example: Grandjean, *Fitting the Task*; Moore-Ede, *The Twenty-Four Hour Society*.

39. See: Grandjean, *Fitting the Task*; Jenkins, D.A., *et al.*, 'Nibbling Versus Gorging: Metabolic Advantages of Increased Meal Frequency', *New England Journal of Medicine* 321 (4) (5 Oct. 1989): 929–34; Edelstein, S.L., *et al.*, 'Increased Meal Frequency Associated with Decreased Cholesterol Concentrations', *American Journal of Clinical Nutrition* 55 (1992): 664–9.

40. See, for example: Chafetz, M.D., *Smart for Life* (New York: Penguin, 1993); Wurtman, J.J., *Managing Your Mind and Mood Through Food* (New York: HarperCollins, 1987); Wurtman, J.J., *The Serotonin Solution* (New York: Fawcett, 1996).

41. de Bono, E., *I Am Right, You Are Wrong* (New York: Viking, 1991): 1.

42. See: Isen, A.M., 'Toward Understanding the Influence of Positive Affect on Social Behavior, Decision Making, and Problem Solving: The Role of Cognitive Organization', Paper at the annual meeting of the American Association for the

Advancement of Science, Boston (11–15 Feb. 1988); Isen, A.M., *et al.*, 'The Influence of Positive Affect on the Unusualness of World Associations', *Journal of Personality and Social Psychology* 48 (1985): 1413–26; Isen, A.M., *et al.*, 'Positive Affect Facilitates Creative Problem Solving', *Journal of Personality and Social Psychology* 52 (1987): 1122–31; Isen, A. M., 'Positive Affect, Cognitive Processes, and Social Behavior', *Advances in Experimental Social Psychology* 20 (1987): 203–53.

43. See, for example: Jasnoski, M.B., 'Architectural and Interior Features Affect Mood and Cognitive Performance', *Journal of Applied Developmental Psychology* (1991); Kleeman, W.B., Jr., *et al.*, *The Interior Design of the Electronic Office: The Comfort and Productivity Payoff* (New York: Van Nostrand Reinhold, 1991).

44. See, for example: Kellman, *et al.*, *Interior Design of the Electronic Office*; Grandjean, *Fitting the Task*; Moore-Ede, *The Twenty-Four Hour Society*; Gallagher, *The Power of Place*; Kaplan, R., 'The Role of Nature in the Context of the Workplace', *Landscape and Urban Planning* 26 (1993): 193–201; Becker and Steele, *Workplace by Design*.

45. From *Wake Up America: A National Sleep Alert*, Report by the National Commission on Sleep Disorders Research (Presented on 5 Jan. 1993).

46. See, for example: Thayer, *The Origin of Everyday Moods*.

47. See: Hauri, P. and Linde, S., *No More Sleepless Nights* (New York: Wiley, 1990).

48. See, for example: Moore-Ede, *The Twenty-Four Hour Society*; Rossi, E.L., *The Twenty Minute Break: Using the New Science of Ultradian Rhythms* (New York: Tarcher/Putnam, 1991).

49 See, for example: Wegner, D.M., *White Bears and Other Unwanted Thoughts* (New York: Viking, 1989).

50. See, for example: Stenhouse, D., *The Evolution of Intelligence* (New York: Harper & Row, 1973).

51. I am grateful to Charlotte M. Roberts for inspiring me to explore this more deeply in my work with executives.

52. Halberstam, J., *Everyday Ethics* (New York: Viking, 1993).

53. See, for example: Brookhiser, R., *Founding Father: Rediscovering George Washington* (New York: Free Press, 1996).

54. Coffin, W.S., *Alive Now!* (May–June 1993): 37.

55. See, for example: Hammond, J., and Morrison, J., *The Stuff Americans Are Made Of* (New York: Macmillan, 1996): 197–8.

56. Kirkpatrick, D., 'This Tough Guy Wants to give You a Hug', *Fortune* (14 Oct. 1996): 170–8.

57. See: Parks, L.A., Keen, C.H., Keen, J.P. and Parks, S.D., *Common Fire* (Boston: Beacon Press, 1996).

58. Adapted from Branden, N., *Taking Responsibility* (New York: Simon & Schuster, 1996).

59. Zuboff, S. Quoted in Farnham, A., 'Are You Smart Enough to Keep Your Job?' *Fortune* (15 Jan. 1996): 48.

60. Institute of HeartMath (14700 W. Park Ave., Boulder Creek, CA 95006, 408–338–8700); Rein, G., Atkinson, M. and McCraty, R., 'The Physiological and

Psychological Effects of Compassion and Anger', *Journal of Advancement in Medicine* (in press, 1996); McCraty, R., Atkinson, M. and Tiller, W.A., 'New Electrophysiological Correlates Associated with Intentional Heart Focus', *Subtle Energies* 4 (3) (1995): 251–68.

61. McCraty, R., Atkinson, M., Tiller, W.A., Rein, G. and Watkins, A., 'The Effects of Emotions on Short-Term Heart Rate Variability Using Power Spectrum Analysis', *American Journal of Cardiology* (1995) 76 (14): 1089–93.

62. See, for example: Parikh, *et al.*, *Intuition*; Schultz, *Unconventional Wisdom*; Agor, *Intuition in Organizations*; Agor, *The Intuitive Manager*; Rowan, *The Intuitive Manager*; The Intuition Network (Jeffrey Mishlove, PhD, Director, 369-B Third St, #161, San Rafael, CA 94901).

63. Mishlove, J., 'Intuition: The "X" Factor in Business', *Journal of Creativity* (1995: refer to the Intuition Network, Jeffrey Mishlove, PhD, Director, 369-B Third St, #161, San Rafael, CA 94901); see also: Ray, M., 'Not Business as Usual', *Intuition* (1995): 28–53.

64. See, for example: Richardson, H.D., Jr., *Emerson: The Mind on Fire* (Berkeley, CA: University of California Press, 1995); Russell, P. and Evans, R., *The Creative Manager* (San Francisco: Jossey-Bass, 1992).

65. See: Parikh, *et al.*, *Intuition*: 30.

66. *International Journal of Scientific Education* 1995.

67. See: Wetherbe, J.C., *The World on Time* (Santa Monica, CA: Knowledge Exchange, 1996).

68. Stewart, T.A., '3M Fights Back', *Fortune* (5 Feb. 1996): 94–9.

69. Naito, H., in Farkas and DeBacker, *Maximum Leadership*: 104–7.

70. Adapted from Damasio, A.R., *Descartes' Error* (New York: Grosset/Putnam, 1994): 170–2.

71. Thompson, T., 'Feeling Smart: An Interview with Daniel Goleman', *Intuition* 9 (Feb. 1996): 28–31, 48–50.

72. Cramer, I., story in Dosick, W., *Golden Rules* (New York: HarperCollins, 1995): 80–1.

73. Kouzes, J.M. and Posner, B.Z., *Credibility* (San Francisco: Jossey-Bass, 1993): 30.

74. Platt, L., quoted in James, G., *Business Wisdom of the Electronic Elite* (New York: Times Books, 1996): 65.

75. Peterson, R., quoted in Peters, T., *The Tom Peters Seminar* (New York: Vintage, 1994): 240–1.

76. Federman, I., remarks to the Leavey School of Business and Administration, Santa Clara University, 2 April 1991.

77. Schultz, W., *The Human Element* (San Francisco: Jossey-Bass, 1995).

78. McCall, M.W., Jr. and Lombardo, M.M., *Off the Track: Why and How Successful Executives Get Derailed* (Greensboro, N.C.: Center for Creative Leadership, 1983).

79. 'Chrysler', *USA today* (17 May 1996): B1, 2.

80. 'The Man in Chrysler's Driver Seat', *Management Review* (Feb. 1994): 30.

81. Castaing, F., 'Small-Team Responsiveness', *Executive Excellence* (Aug. 1993): 10.

82. 'Crunch at Chrysler', *The Economist* (12 Nov. 1994): 81.

83. See, for example: Damasio, A.R., *Descartes' Error.*
84. See, for example: Mishlove, J., 'Not Business as Usual: An Interview with Michael Ray', *Intuition* 8 (1995): 28–31, 49–53; Ray and Myers, *Creativity in Business.*
85. Nair, K., *A Higher Standard of Leadership: Lessons from the Life of Gandhi* (San Francisco: Berrett-Koehler, 1994): 80–1.
86. Ryan, K.D. and Oestreich, D.K., *Driving Fear Out of the Workplace* (San Francisco: Jossey-Bass, 1991): 8.
87. See, for example: Ornstein, R., *The Evolution of Consciousness* (New York: Prentice Hall, 1991); Ornstein, R., *The Psychology of Consciousness* rev. edn (New York: Grosset/Putnam, 1997); Humphrey, N., *A History of Mind* (New York: Simon & Schuster, 1992); Sekuler, R. and Blake, R., *Perception* 2nd edn (New York: McGraw-Hill, 1990).
88. Adapted from Ryan and Oestreich, *Driving Fear Out of the Workplace*: 76–9.
89. Josselson, R., *The Space Between Us* (San Francisco: Jossey-Bass, 1992): 99.
90. See, for example: Bandura, A., *Self-Efficacy in Changing Societies* (New York: Cambridge University Press, 1995).

The Second Cornerstone: Emotional Fitness

1. See, for example: Whitney, J.O., *The Economics of Trust* (New York: McGraw-Hill, 1996) and Fukuyama, F., *Trust: The Social Virtues and the Creation of Prosperity* (London: Viking, 1995).
2. See, for example: Maddi, S.A. and Kobasa, S.C., *The Hardy Executive: Health Under Stress* (Homewood, IL: Dow Jones Irwin, 1984).
3. See, for example: Loehr, J.E., *Toughness Training for Life* (New York: Plume, 1994); Dienstbier, R.A., 'Arousal and Physiological Toughness: Implications for Mental and Physical Health', *Psychological Review* 96 (1) (1989): 84–100.
4. Ryan, K.D. and Oestreich, D.K., *Driving Fear Out of the Workplace* (San Francisco: Jossey-Bass, 1992): 8.
5. See, for example: Schultz, W., *The Human Element* (San Francisco: Jossey-Bass, 1995); Whitney, J.C., *The Economics of Trust* (New York: McGraw-Hill, 1996); Kouzes, J.M. and Posner, B.Z., *The Leadership Challenge* rev. edn (San Francisco: Josey-Bass, 1995); Rosen, R.M., *Leading People* (New York: Viking, 1995); Hendricks, G. and Ludeman, K., *The Corporate Mystic* (New York: Bantam, 1996); Block, P., *The Empowered Manager* (San Francisco: Jossey-Bass, 1987).
6. Conger, J.A., 'The Brave New World of Leadership Training', *Organizational Dynamics* (Jan.–Feb. 1993): 46–58.
7. Ryan, K. and Oestreich, D., *Driving Fear Out of the Workplace.*
8. Noer, D.M., *Healing the Wounds* (San Francisco: Jossey-Bass, 1993): 103.
9. Deming, W.E., *Out of the Crisis* (Cambridge: Massachusetts Institute of Technology Press, 1982, 1986): 59.
10. Herber, H., quoted in Hendricks, G. and Ludeman, K., *The Corporate Mystic* (New York: Bantam, 1996): 144–5.

11. See, for example: Hendrickson, P., *The Living and the Dead* (New York: Knopf, 1996).

12. I heard this story in October 1996 from Ian Bartrum, a faculty member at Hyde School, Woodstock, Connecticut.

13. See: Makihara, M., quoted in Kurtzman, J., 'An Interview with Minoru Malciharz', *Strategy & Business* (Winter 1996) 2: 86–93.

14. Hammer, M., *Beyond Reengineering* (London: HarperCollins, 1996): 171.

15. Handy, C., 'Trust and the Virtual Organization', *Harvard Business Review* (May–June 1995).

16. See, for example: Williams, R., *The Trusting Heart* (New York: Times Books, 1989); Williams, R. and Williams, V., *Anger Kills* (New York: Times Books, 1994); Eliot, R.S., *From Stress to Strength* (New York: Bantam, 1994); Siegman, A.W. and Smith, T.W. (eds), *Anger, Hostility, and the Heart* (Hillsdale, NJ: Erlbaum Publishing, 1994).

17. Williams and Williams, *Anger Kills*: xiii.

18. Williams, *The Trusting Heart*.

19. See, for example: 'Trust Traps', *Training & Development Journal* 48 (7) (1994): 11–12; Bunard, V. and Kleiner, B.H., 'Developing Trustful and Cooperative relationships', *Leadership & Organizational Development Journal* 15 (2) (1994): 3–5.

20. Driscoll, J.W., 'Trust and Participation in Organization Decision Making as Predictors of Satisfaction', *Academy of Management Journal* 21 (1) (1978): 44–56.

21. Decker, B., *You've Got To Be Believed To Be Heard* (New York: St Martin's Press, 1992): 50–1.

22. Collins, J.C. and Porras, J.I., *Built to Last: Successful Habits of Visionary Companies* (London: Random House, 1995): 32–3.

23. Frieberg, K. and Frieberg, J., *Nuts! Southwest Airlines' Crazy Recipe for Business and Personal Success* (Bard, 1996).

24. Decker, B., *You've Got To Be Believed To Be Heard*.

25. Messages destined for the cognitive, or intellectual, areas of the brain must first pass through the limbic system, including its fountainhead region known as the anterior cingulate cortex, and a related network that includes the brain's prefrontal cortices and sectors that map and integrate signals from throughout the body. Similarly, expressions of thought pass from the higher mind down through the limbic system and related structures as these messages and decisions are linked into working memory and converted into behaviour – body language, speech, or action.

26. Machado, L., *The Brain of the Brain* (Cidade do Cerebro, Brazil, 1990): 141.

27. Hainer, R., 'Rationalism, Pragmatism, and Existentialism', in Glatt, E. and Shelly, M., *The Research Society* (New York: Gordon & Breech Science Publications, 1968).

28. For an insightful introduction to this subject, see: Decker, B., *You've Got To Be Believed To Be Heard*.

29. Mehrabian, A., *Silent Messages* (Belmont, CA: Wadsworth Publishing, 1981).

30. Frieberg, K. and Frieberg, J., *Nuts! Southwest Airlines' Crazy Recipe for Business and Personal Success*.

31. See, for example: Armstrong, D.M., *Managing by Storying Around: A New Method of Leadership* (New York: Doubleday Currency, 1992); Schank, R.C., *Tell Me a Story: A New Look at Intelligence* (New York: Scribner's, 1990); Coles, R., *The Call of Stories: Teaching and the Moral Imagination* (Boston: Houghton Mifflin, 1989); Buckler, S.A. and Zien, K.A., *Journal of Production Innovation* 13 (1996): 391–405; Beach, B.K., 'Learning with Roger Schank', *Training & Development* (Oct. 1993): 39–44.

32. Armstrong, D.M., *Managing by Storying Around*: 21–2.

33. Adapted from Peace, W., 'Hard Work of Being a Soft Manager', *Harvard Business Review* (Nov.–Dec. 1991).

34. Adapted from Semler, R., 'Managing Without Managers', *Harvard Business Review* (Sept.–Oct. 1989) and Semler, R., 'Why My Former Employees Still Work for Me', *Harvard Business Review* (Jan.–Feb. 1994).

35. See, for example: Wills, G., *Certain Trumpets: The Call of Leaders* (New York: Simon & Schuster, 1994); Felder, D.G., *The 100 Most Influential Women of All Time* (New York: Citadel Press, 1996).

36. Fukuyama, F., *Trust*.

37. Lewis, C.S., *A Grief Observed* (New York: Bantam, 1976).

38. Ornstein, R., *The Evolution of Consciousness* (New York: Prentice Hall, 1991).

39. Warren McCulloch, *Embodiments of Mind* (MIT), quoted in Pribram, K.H., *Brain and Perception* (Hillsdale, NJ: Lawrence Erlbaum Publishers, 1991).

40. Pinker, S., *The Language Instinct* (New York: William Morrow, 1994).

41. Elgin, S.H., *Success with the Gentle Art of Verbal Self-Defense* (New York: Prentice Hall, 1989).

42. Tannen, D., *You Just Don't Understand* (New York: William Morrow, 1990).

43. Senge, P.M. in Dumaine, B., 'Mr Learning Organization', *Fortune* (17 Oct. 1994): 147–57.

44. Hammer, M., *Beyond Reengineering*: 164–5.

45. Sheff, D., 'Levi's Changes Everything', *Fast Company* (June–July 1995): 65–76.

46. Haas, R. in *Business Week* (1 Aug. 1994): 46–7.

47. This model was inspired, in part, by the writings of Dean Tjosvold in Tjosvold, D., *Learning to Manage Conflict* (New York: Lexington Books, 1993): 4–5.

48. Deutsch, M., 'Sixty Years of Conflict', *The International Journal of Conflict Management* 1 (1990): 237–63.

49. Moore-Ede, M., *The Twenty-Four Hour Society* (Reading, MA: Addison-Wesley, 1993).

50. Axelrod, R., *The Evolution of Cooperation* (New York: Basic Books, 1984).

51. Kalms, S., in Farkas, C.M. and DeBacker, P., *Maximum Leadership* (New York: Henry Holt, 1996): 7.

52. See, for example: Tanen, *You Just Don't Understand*.

53. Timmer, J., in Farkas and DeBacker, *Maximum Leadership*: 78–80.

54. Pascale, R., *Managing on the Edge* (London: Viking, 1990): 256.

55. Pascale, *Managing on the Edge*: 256.

56. Kiernan, M.J., *The Eleven Commandments of 21st Century Management* (New York: Prentice-Hall, 1996): 45–8.

57. Kume, T., in Kiernan, *The Eleven Commandments of 21st Century Management*: 46.

58. See, for example: Lloyd, D. and Rossi, E.L. (eds), *High Frequency Biological Rhythms: Functions of the Ultradians* (New York: Springer-Verlag, 1994); Rossi, E.L., *The Twenty Minute Break* (New York: Putnam/Tarcher, 1991); Rechtschaffen, S., *Time Shifting* (New York: Doubleday, 1996).

59. Erickson, F., in Rechtschaffen, *Time Shifting*: 22–3.

60. Roberts, C. and Ross, R., in *The Fifth Discipline Fieldbook* (London: Nicholas Brealey Publishing, 1994): 255–9.

61. Block, P., *The Empowered Manager* (San Francisco: Jossey-Bass, 1987): 96.

62. See, for example: Eliot, R.S., *From Stress to Strength* (New York: Bantam, 1995); Williams and Williams, *Anger Kills*.

63. See, for example: Podell, R.M., *Contagious Emotions* (New York: Pocket Books, 1992).

64. Arnold, W.W. and Plas, J.M., *The Human Touch: Today's Most Unusual Program for Productivity and Profit* (New York: Wiley, 1993).

65. Arnold and Plas, *The Human Touch*.

66. Binney, G. and Williams, C., *Leaning into the Future* (London: Nicholas Brealey Publishing, 1996): 105.

67. See, for example: Schank, *Tell Me A Story*.

68. Two of my favourite authors on stories are Rachel Naomi Remen and Clarissa Pinkola Estes. See: Estes, C.P., *The Gift of Story* (New York: Ballantine, 1993); Estes, C.P., *The Faithful Gardener* (New York: HarperCollins, 1995); Remen, R.N., *Kitchen Table Wisdom: Stories That Heal* (New York: Riverhead Books, 1996).

69. Handy, C., *The Age of Unreason* (London: Random House, 1988): 11–12.

70. Kennedy, W., in Cameron, J., *The Vein of Gold* (New York: Tarcher/Putnam, 1996): 192.

71. Ash, M.K. cited in Pelton, W.J., Sackman, S. and Boguslaw, R., *Tough Choices: Decision-Making Styles of America's Top 50 CEOs* (Homewood, IL: Dow Jones Irwin, 1990): 8–9.

72. Adapted from: Felder, *The 100 Most Influential Women of All Time*: 88–91; also see: Blackwell, E., *Pioneering Work in Opening the Medical Profession to Women: Autobiographical Sketches* (New York: Schocken Books, 1977).

73. Kornfield, J., story in Bryner, A. and Markova, D., *An Unused Intelligence* (Berkeley, CA: Conari Press, 1996): 61.

74. Jordan, M., *I Can't Accept Not Trying* (New York: HarperCollins, 1994).

75. Seligman, M.E.P., *Learned Optimism* (New York: Knopf, 1991): 207–17; Miller, S.M. and Seligman, M.E.P., 'The Reformulated Model of Helplessness and Depression: Evidence and Theory', in Neufeld, R.W.J. (ed.), *Psychological Stress and Psychopathology* (New York: McGraw-Hill, 1982): 149–79; Peterson, P. and Seligman, M.E.P., 'Causal Explanations as a Risk Factor for Depression: Theory and Evidence', *Psychological Review* 91 (3) (1984): 347–74.

76. Seligman, *Learned Optimism*: 112.

77. Adapted from: Enkelis, L. and Olsen, K. with Lewenstein, M., *On Our Own*

Terms: Portraits of Women Business Leaders (San Francisco: Berrett-Koehler, 1995): 125–33.

78. Holbard, G., 'Company Owners Strike It Rich', *USA Today* (17 Dec. 1996): 1A.

79. Mapes, J. J., *Quantum Leap Thinking* (Beverly Hills: Dove Books, 1996): 105.

80. Bateson, M.C., *Peripheral Visions: Learning Along the Way* (New York: HarperCollins, 1994): i.

81. Hammonds, K.H., 'Balancing Work and Family', *Business Week* (16 Sept. 1996): 74–80.

82. See, for example: Davidson, J., *Breathing Space: Living & Working at a Comfortable Pace in a Sped-Up Society* (New York: MasterMedia, 1991).

83. Gallup Survey, reported in Peterson, K.S., *USA Today* (21 Dec. 1992).

84. Myers, D.G., *The Pursuit of Happiness* (New York: Morrow, 1992); House, J.S., *et al.*, 'Association of Social Relationships and Activities with Mortality: Prospective Evidence from the Tecumseh Community Health Study', *American Journal of Epidemiology* 116 (1) (1982): 123–40; Berkman, L.F. and Syme, L.O., 'Social Networks, Host Resistance, and Mortality: A Nine-Year Follow-Up of Alameda County Residents', *American Journal of Epidemiology* 102 (2) (1979): 186–204; Eisenberg, L., 'A Friend, Not an Apple, A Day Will Keep the Doctor Away', *Journal of the American Medical Association* 66 (1979): 551–3; Cohen, S. and Wils, T., 'Stress, Social Support, and Buffering Hypothesis', *Psychological Bulletin* 98 (1985): 310–357; Caplan, G., 'Mastery of Stress: Psychological Aspects', *American Journal of Psychiatry* 138 (1981): 413–20; Lynch, J.J., *The Broken Heart: Medical Consequences of Loneliness* (New York: Basic Books, 1977); Jaffe, D.T. and Scott, C.D., *Take This Job and Love It* (New York: Simon & Schuster, 1988): 185.

85. Mackoff, B., *The Art of Self-Renewal* (Los Angeles: Lowell House, 1992).

86. Nagler, W., *The Dirty Half Dozen* (New York: Warner, 1991): 47–8.

87. Wurtman, J.J., *Managing Your Mind and Mood Through Food* (New York: HarperCollins, 1987); Wurtman, J.J., *The Serotonin Solution* (New York: Fawcett, 1996); Chaeftz, M.D., *Smart for Life* (New York: Penguin, 1993); Chafetz, M.D. (ed.), *Nutrition and Neurotransmitters* (New York: Prentice-Hall, 1992); Rossi, *The Twenty Minute Break*; Grandjean, E. *Fitting the Task*, 4th edn (London: Taylor and Francis, 1988).

88. See, for example: Miller, E.E., *Software for the Mind* (Berkeley: Celestial Arts, 1988); Sheikh, A.A. (ed.), *Imagery: Current Theory, Research, and Application* (New York: Wiley Interscience, 1984); Marks, D.F. (ed.), *Theories of Image Formation* (New York: Brandon House, 1986); Suinn, R.M., *Seven Steps to Peak Performance* (Lewiston, NY: Hans Huber Publishers, 1986).

89. Mackoff, B., *The Art of Self-Renewal* (Los Angeles: Lowell House, 1992).

90. Kaplan, R.E., *Beyond Ambition* (San Francisco: Jossey-Bass, 1991).

The Third Cornerstone: Emotional Depth

1. Shad, J., in Cox, A., *Straight Talk for Monday Morning* (New York: Wiley, 1990): 82–3.

2. Sun Tzu II drawn from: Cleary, T. (transl.), *The Lost Art of War by Sun Tzu II* (New York: HarperCollins, 1996); von Senger, H., *The Book of Stratagems* (New York: Viking, 1991); and Lau, D.C. and Ames, R.T., (transl.), *Sun Pin: The Art of Warfare* (New York: Ballantine, 1996).

3. Cited in Cleary, T. (transl.), Sun Tzu *The Art of War* (Boston: Shambhala, 1988).

4. 'The Master of Demon Valley', transl. in Cleary, T., *Thunder in the Sky: On the Acquisition and Exercise of Power* (Boston: Shambhala, 1993).

5. Ji, L., in Cleary, T., *Mastering the Art of War* (Boston: Shambhala, 1989): 96–8.

6. I am indebted to Joseph W. Gauld, founder of Hyde School, and Kenneth and Claire Grant and Paul and Laurie Hurd, for my deepened appreciation of the expression 'unique potential and purpose'. To learn more, see: Gault, J.W., *Character First* (San Francisco: Institute for Contemporary Studies, 1993).

7. See: Clifton, D.O. and Nelson, P., *Soar with Your Strengths* (New York: Delacorte, 1992): 36; Sternberg, R.J., *Successful Intelligence* (New York: Simon & Schuster, 1996): 49.

8. Clifton and Nelson, *Soar with Your Strengths*: 43–61.

9. Maslow, A., *Toward a Psychology of Being* (New York: Harper & Row, 1978).

10. Clifton and Nelson, *Soar with Your Strengths*: 33.

11. Amabile, T.M., *The Social Psychology of Creativity* (New York: Springer-Verlag, 1983).

12. Sternberg, *Successful Intelligence*: 219.

13. Bateson, M.C., *Composing a Life* (New York: HarperCollins, 1989).

14. Ohmae, K., *The Mind of the Strategist* (New York: McGraw-Hill, 1982).

15. Deming, W.E., *Out of Crisis* (Cambridge: MIT Press, 1983).

16. Michael Hoppe's story is told in Cameron, J., *The Vein of Gold* (New York: Tarcher/Putnam, 1996): 75–6.

17. Buechner, F., *Wishful Thinking* (New York: HarperCollins, 1973).

18. Collins, J.C. and Porras, J.I., *Built to Last: Successful Habits of Visionary Companies* (London: Random House, 1995).

19. Collins, J.C. and Porras, J.I., 'Building Your Company's Vision', *Harvard Business Review* (Sept.–Oct. 1996): 65–77.

20. See, for example: Hendrickson, P., *The Living and the Dead: Robert McNamara and Five Lives of a Lost War* (New York: Knopf, 1996).

21. Zukav, G., *The Seat of the Soul* (New York: Fireside, 1989): 64.

22. Cooper, K.H., personal interviews: May 1988 and February 1995.

23. Campbell, J. with Moyers, B., *The Power of Myth* (New York: Anchor/Doubleday, 1988).

24. To learn more, see: Leider, R.J. and Shapiro, D.A., *Repacking Your Bags: Lighten Your Load for the Rest of Your Life* (San Francisco: Berrett-Koehler, 1995); Kouzes, J.M. and Posner, B.Z., *The Leadership Challenge* rev. edn (San Francisco: Jossey-Bass, 1995).

25. Adapted from Felder, D.G., *The 100 Most Influential Women of All Time* (New York: Citadel Press, 1996): 104–7; also see: Brooks, P., *The House of Life: Rachel Carson at Work* (Boston: Houghton Mifflin, 1973).

26. *Nu Shu* drawn from Cheng, S-h., *Nu Shu* (Taiwan: Awakening Press, 1991); Metz, P.K. and Tobin, J.L., *The Tao of Women* (Atlanta: Humanics Ltd., 1995).

27. Sternberg, *Successful Intelligence*.

28. Peters, T., *The Pursuit of Wow* (New York: Knopf, 1995).

29. van Vlissingen, P.F., quoted in Farkas, C.M. and DeBacker, P., *Maximum Leadership* (New York: Henry Holt, 1996): 74.

30. Kaku, R., story in Farkas and DeBacker, *Maximum Leadership*: 3.

31. Hayek, N., quoted in Peters, T., *The Tom Peters Seminar* (New York: Vintage, 1994): 240.

32. Adapted from: Anderson, K., 'The Purpose at the Heart of Management', *Harvard Business Review* (May–June, 1992): 52–62.

33. Smithart, D., in Hammer, M., *Beyond Reengineering* (London: HarperCollins, 1996): 166.

34. See: Greenleaf, R.K., *Servant Leadership: A Journey into the Nature of Legitimate Power and Greatness* (Mahwah, NJ: Paulist Press, 1991); Quinn, R.E., *Deep Change: Discovering the Leader Within* (San Francisco: Jossey-Bass, 1996).

35. Greenleaf, *Servant Leadership*.

36. See, for example: Pennebaker, J.W., *Opening Up: The Healing Power of Confiding in Others* (New York: Morrow, 1990); Vaill, P.B., *Learning as a Way of Being* (San Francisco: Jossey-Bass, 1996).

37. This four-part model was clarified through a dialogue with Paul Hurd at Hyde School in Connecticut.

38. Nair, K., *A Higher Standard of Leadership: Lessons from the Life of Gandhi* (San Francisco: Berrett-Koehler, 1994): 77.

39. Schulze, H., 'Keep It Simple', *Executive Excellence* 12 (3) (March 1995): 12–13.

40. See, for example: Gauld, *Character First*.

41. See, for example: Schweitzer, A., *On the Edge of the Primeval Forest* (London: A. & C. Black, 1922); Schweitzer, A., *Out of My Life and Thought* (1931) transl. A.B. Lemke (New York: Henry Holt, 1990).

42. This exercise, which we have used for a number of years, is similar to a method suggested by Stephen Covey, Roger Merrill and Rebecca Merrill in *First Things First* (Simon & Schuster, 1994).

43. Kolb, D., in Srivastva, S. and Associates (eds), *Executive Integrity* (San Francisco: Jossey-Bass, 1988): 12–13; 68–88.

44. See: Solomon, R.C., *The Passions: Emotions and the Meaning of Life* (Indianapolis: Hackett Publishing, 1992); Rorty, A.O. (ed.), *Explaining Emotions* (Berkeley: University of California Press, 1980); Lazarus, R.S. and Lazarus, B.N., *Passion and Reason: Making Sense of Our Emotions* (New York: Oxford University Press, 1994).

45. Solomon, *The Passions*: xvii.

46. Srivastva and Associates, *Executive Integrity*: 7–8.

47. Carter, S. L., (*integrity*) (New York: Basic Books, 1996).

48. Carter, (*integrity*): 52–3.

49. Hendricks, G. and Ludeman, K., *The Corporate Mystic* (New York: Bantam, 1996): 31.

50. Hawley, J., 'What is Integrity?' in Canfield, J. and Miller, J., *Heart at Work* (New York: Macmillan, 1996): 26–7.

51. Torbert, W.R., *Managing the Corporate Dream: Restructuring for Long-Term Success* (Homewood, IL: Dow Jones-Irwin, 1987).

52. Personal interview, October 1996.

53. Waldrop, M.M., 'The Trillion Dollar Vision of Dee Hock', *Fast Company* (Oct.–Nov. 1996): 75–86.

54. As told to me by Esther M. Orioli, President of Essi Systems, Inc., in San Francisco, 4 October 1996.

55. Dolan, K., story in Godin, S., *Wisdom, Inc.* (New York: HarperBusiness, 1995): 42–3.

56. Gardner, J.W., *On Leadership* (New York: Free Press, 1990).

57. Hillman, J., 'The Cure of the Shadow', in Zweig, C. and Abrahams, J. (eds), *Meeting the Shadow* (New York: Tarcher/Putnam, 1991): 242–3.

58. See, for example: Zweig and Abrams, *Meeting the Shadow*.

59. Bly, R., *A Little Book on the Human Shadow* (New York: HarperSanFrancisco, 1988).

60. I gratefully acknowledge Esther M. Orioli for her insights on this subject.

61. Metzger, D., 'Writing About the Other', in Zweig and Abrams, *Meeting the Shadow*: 299–301.

62. Saul, J.R., *Voltaire's Bastards: The Dictatorship of Reason in the West* (New York: Free Press, 1992): 16.

63. Moore, J.F., *The Death of Competition* (New York: HarperBusiness, 1996).

64. Land, G.T., *Grow or Die: The Unifying Principle of Transformation* (New York: Wiley, 1973 and 1986).

65. Brandenburger, A.M. and Nalebuff, B.J., *Co-opetition* (London: HarperCollins, 1996).

66. See, for example: Wheatley, M.J., *Leadership and the New Science* (San Francisco: Berrett-Koehler, 1992); Wheatley, M.J. and Kellner-Rogers, M., *A Simpler Way* (San Francisco: Berrett-Koehler, 1996); Zukav, G., *The Seat of the Soul* (New York: Fireside, 1989); Harman, W. and Rheingold, H., *Higher Creativity* (New York: Tarcher/Putnam, 1984); Capra, F., *The Web of Life* (New York: Anchor Books, 1996).

67. Waldrop, 'The Trillion Dollar Vision of Dee Hock', *Fast Company* (Oct.–Nov. 1996): 75–86.

68. See, for example: Nair, *A Higher Standard of Leadership*.

69. Nair, *A Higher Standard of Leadership*: 59.

70. See, for example: Lynch, J.J., *The Language of the Heart* (New York: Basic Books, 1985); Pribram, K.H., *Brain and Perception: Holonomy and Structure in Figural Processing* (Hillsdale, NJ: Lawrence Erlbaum, 1991); Talbot, M., *The Holographic Universe* (New York: HarperCollins, 1991); Pinker, S., *The Language Instinct* (New

York: William Morrow, 1994); Ornstein, R., *The Evolution of Consciousness* (New York: Prentice Hall, 1991); Diamond, M.C., *Enriching Heredity* (New York: Free Press, 1988); Dossey, L., *Healing Words* (New York: HarperCollins, 1993); Coles, R., *The Call of Stories* (Boston: Houghton Mifflin, 1989); Schank, R.C., *Tell Me a Story* (New York: Scribner's, 1990).

71. See: Quinn, R.E., *Deep Change: Discovering the Leader Within* (San Francisco: Jossey-Bass, 1996): 101.

72. Institute of HeartMath (14700 W. Park Ave., Boulder Creek, CA 95006, 408–338–8700); Rein, G., Atkinson, M. and McCraty, R., 'The Physiological and Psychological Effects of Compassion and Anger', *Journal of Advancement in Medicine* (in press, 1996); McCraty, R., Atkinson, M. and Tiller, W.A., 'New Electrophysiological Correlates Associated with Intentional Heart Focus', *Subtle Energies* 4 (3) (1995): 251–68.

73. See, for example: Lynch, *The Language of the Heart*.

74. See, for example: Leonard, G., *The Silent Pulse* (New York: Bantam, 1981); Condon, W.S., 'Multiple Response to Sound in Dysfunctional Children', *Journal of Autism* 5 (1) (1975): 43.

75. See, for example: Damasio, A.R., *Descartes' Error: Emotion, Reason and the Human Brain* (New York: Grosset/Putnam, 1994) and Solomon, *The Passions*.

76. Adapted from Enkelis, J. and Olsen, K. with Lewenstein, M., *On Our Own Terms: Portraits of Women Business Leaders* (San Francisco: Berrett-Koehler, 1995): 93.

77. Feigon, L., *Demystifying Tibet* (Chicago: Ivan R. Dee, 1996).

78. McClelland, D. and Burnham, D., 'Power is the Great Motivator', *Harvard Business Review* (1976); reprinted Jan.–Feb. 1995.

79. See, for example: Lynch, *The Language of the Heart*; Pribram, *Brain and Perception*; Talbot, *The Holographic Universe*; Pinker, *The Language Instinct*; Ornstein, *The Evolution of Consciousness*; Diamond, *Enriching Heredity*; Dossey, *Healing Words*; Coles, *The Call of Stories*; Schank, *Tell Me a Story*.

80. Buckler, S.A. and Zien, K.A., 'From Experience – The Spirituality of Innovation: Learning from Stories', *Journal of Product Innovation* 13 (1996): 391–405.

81. Coles, *The Call of Stories*: 7.

82. Coles, *The Call of Stories*: 30.

83. Gardner, H., *Leading Minds: An Anatomy of Leadership* (London: HarperCollins, 1996).

84. See, for example: Kotter, J.P., *Power and Influence* (New York: Free Press, 1985).

85. Bennis, W., 'The Leader as Storyteller', *Harvard Business Review* (Jan.–Feb. 1996): 154–60.

86. Ulrich, H., *Management* (Bern, Switzerland: Haupt, 1984).

87. Deming, *Out of Crisis*: 66–7.

88. See, for example: Podell, *Contagious Emotions*.

89. See, for example: Thayer, R.E., *The Origin of Everyday Moods* (New York: Oxford, 1996).

90. McGee-Cooper, A., *You Don't Have to Come Home from Work Exhausted* (New York: Bantam, 1992): 245–62.

91. Paul, J. and Paul, M., *Do I Have to Give Up Me to Be Loved By You?* (Minneapolis: CompCare, 1983).

92. Podell, *Contagious Emotions*: 15.

93. Hsee, C.K., *et al.*, 'The Effect of Power on Susceptibility to Emotional Contagion', *Cognition and Emotion* 4 (4) (Dec. 1990): 327–40.

94. de Bono, E., *Serious Creativity* (New York: HarperBusiness, 1992).

95. See: Cohen, A. and Bradford, D.L., *Influence Without Authority* (New York: John Wiley & Sons, 1990).

96. Zeien, A., quoted in Farkas and DeBacker, *Maximum Leadership*: 64–7.

97. Adapted from Solomon, R.C., *Ethics and Excellence* (Oxford: Oxford University Press, 1993): 242–5.

98. Novak, M., *Business as a Calling* (New York: Free Press, 1996): 143–4.

99. Cited in Starke, L., 'The Five Stages of Corporate Moral Development', in Ray and Rinzler, *The New Paradigm in Business* (New York: Tarcher/Putnam, 1993): 207–8.

100. Adapted from Huseman, R.C. and Hatfield, J.D., *Managing the Equity Factor* (Boston: Houghton Mifflin, 1989).

101. See: Huseman, R.C., Hatfield, J.D. and Miles, E.W., 'Tests for Individual Perceptions of Job Equity', *Perceptual and Motor Skills* 61 (1985); Huseman, R.C., Hatfield, J.D. and Miles, E.W., 'A New Perspective on Equity Theory: The Equity Sensitivity Construct', *Academy of Management Review* 2 (1987).

102. Huseman and Hatfield, *Managing the Equity Factor*.

103. Watson, C.E., *Managing with Integrity: Insights from America's CEOs* (New York: Praeger, 1991): 30.

104. Dell, M., quoted in James, G., *Business Wisdom of the Electronic Elite* (New York: Times Books, 1996): 67.

105. Brown, J. and Isaacs, D., 'Merging the Best of Two Worlds', in Senge, P.M., Roberts, C., Ross, R.B., Smith, B.J. and Kleiner, A. (eds), *The Fifth Discipline Fieldbook* (London: Nicholas Brealey Publishing, 1994): 508–17. To learn more, contact: Juanita Brown and David Isaacs (Whole Systems Associates, 166 Homestead Blvd., Mill Valley, CA 94941).

106. Read, J., journal entry cited in Aliesan, J., *Grief Sweat* (Seattle: Broken Moon Press, 1991): 77.

107. Calloway, W., quoted in Farkas and DeBacker, *Maximum Leadership*: 81–6.

108. Novicki, C., 'Report from the Future: The Best Brains in the Business', *Fast Company* (Oct.–Nov. 1996): 27.

109. Capen, R.G., Jr., *Finish Strong* (New York: HarperCollins, 1996): xx.

110. Vanourek, R., in Spears, L.C., *Reflections on Leadership* (New York: Wiley, 1995): 300.

111. Adapted from Peace, W., 'Hard Work of Being a Soft Manager', *Harvard Business Review* (Nov.–Dec. 1991): 40–7.

112. MenTTium (8009 34th Ave. So., Suite 1350, Bloomington, MN 55425 USA; 612–814–2600).

The Fourth Cornerstone: Emotional Alchemy

1. Solomon, R.C., 'Sartre on Emotions', in Schilpp, P.A. (ed.), *Sartre*, The Library of Living Philosophers (LaSalle, IL: Open Court, 1977).

2. Autry, J.A., *Love and Profit* (New York: William Morrow, 1991): 23.

3. Csikszentmihalyi, M., *Journal of Humanistic Psychology* 15 (3) (1975).

4. Csikszentmihalyi, M., *Flow: The Psychology of Optimal Experience* (New York: HarperCollins, 1990).

5. Csikszentmihalyi, *Flow*: 213.

6. Csikszentmihalyi, *Flow*.

7. Planck, M., quoted in Heinberg, R., 'The Hidden History of Creativity', *Intuition* 8 (1995): 18–27.

8. Adapted from: Armstrong, D.M., *Managing by Storying Around* (New York: Doubleday Currency, 1992): 190–1.

9. Harmon, W.W., 'The 20 Year Present', *Public Management* (Jan.–Feb. 1980): 7.

10. Harmon, 'The 20 Year Present': 7.

11. Agor, W.H., *The Intuitive Manager* (New York: Prentice Hall, 1984): 8.

12. Mishlove, J., 'Intuition: The "X" Factor in Business', *Journal of Creativity* (1995: refer to the Intuition Network, Jeffrey Mishlove, PhD, Director, 369-B Third St, #161, San Rafael, CA 94901); see also: Ray, M., 'Not Business as Usual', *Intuition* (1995): 28–53.

13. Timmer, J., in Farkas, C.M. and DeBacker, P., *Maximum Leadership* (New York: Henry Holt, 1996): 78–80.

14. Pelton, W.J., Sackman, S. and Boguslaw, R., *Tough Choices: The Decision-Making Styles of America's Top 50 CEOs* (Homewood, IL: Irwin, 1990): 10.

15. Pelton, Sackman and Boguslaw, *Tough Choices*: 10.

16. See, for example: Vaill, P.B., *Learning as a Way of Being* (San Francisco: Jossey-Bass, 1996); Kao, J., *Jamming* (London: HarperCollins, 1996); Hamel, G. and Prahald, C.K., *Competing for the Future* (Boston: Harvard Business School Press, 1994); Conner, D.R., *Managing at the Speed of Change* (New York: Villard, 1994); Slywotzky, A.J., *Value Migration* (Boston: Harvard Business School Press, 1995).

17. Adapted from Pelton, Sonja and Boguslaw, *Tough Choices*: 10.

18. Damasio, A.R., *Descartes' Error* (New York: Grosset/Putnam, 1994): 188.

19. Mintzberg, H., 'Planning on the Left Side and Managing on the Right', *Harvard Business Review* (July/Aug. 1976): 49–58; see also Mintzberg, H., *The Rise and Fall of Strategic Planning* (New York: Free Press, 1995).

20. Mintzberg, H., 'The Rise and Fall of Strategic Planning', *Harvard Business Review* (Jan.–Feb. 1994): 107; and see: Mintzberg, *The Rise and Fall of Strategic Planning*.

21. Quinn, J.B., Anderson, P. and Finkelstein, 'Managing Professional Intellect: Making the Most of the Best', *Harvard Business Review* (March–April 1996): 71–80.

22. Example drawn from: Schon, D.A., *The Reflective Practitioner* (New York: Basic Books, 1983): 62–3.

23. McCracken, E., in Sherman, S., 'Leaders Learn to Heed the Voice Within', *Fortune* (22 Aug. 1994): 93.

24. Drawn from informal author interviews with 3M executives between 1990 and 1996; and from Schon, *The Reflective Practitioner*.

25. Palevsky, M., quoted in Pelton, Sackman and Boguslaw. *Tough Choices*: 32–3.

26. Ludeman, K., story excerpted with permission from Hendricks, G. and Ludeman, K., *The Corporate Mystic* (New York: Bantam, 1996): 114–15.

27. Zajonc, R.B., 'Styles of Explanation in Social Psychology', *The European Journal of Social Psychology* (Sept.–Oct. 1989).

28. See, for example: Mintzberg, 'Planning on the Left Side and Managing on the Right': 49–58; Hendricks and Ludeman, *The Corporate Mystic*; Kao, J., *Jamming*; Ray, M. and Myers, R., *Creativity in Business* (New York: Doubleday, 1986); Rowan, R., *The Intuitive Manager* (Boston: Little Brown, 1986); Goleman, D., Kaufman, P. and Ray, M., *The Creative Spirit* (New York: Dutton, 1992); Mintzberg, *The Rise and Fall of Strategic Planning*; Quinn, Anderson and Finkelstein, 'Managing Professional Intellect: Making the Most of the Best': 71–80; Cameron, J. *The Vein of Gold* (New York: Tarcher/Putnam, 1996).

29. Ray, M. and Myers, R., *Creativity at Work* (New York: Doubleday, 1986).

30. See: Parikh, J., *et al.*, *Intuition: The New Frontier in Management* (New York: Blackwell, 1994): 28–9.

31. Hendricks and Ludeman, *The Corporate Mystic*: 96–9.

32. See, for example: Pennebaker, J., *Opening Up* (New York: Morrow, 1991).

33. Russo, J.E. and Schoemaker, P.J.H., *Decision Traps* (New York: Doubleday Currency, 1989): 96.

34. See, for example: Jacobs, R.W., *Real Time Strategic Change* (San Francisco: Berrett-Koehler, 1994).

35. After using the term *time-shifting* in executive seminars for a number of years, we recently discovered that it also happens to be the title of an excellent book by Stephan Rechtschaffen, MD: *Timeshifting: Creating More Time to Enjoy Your Life* (New York: Doubleday, 1996).

36. Report by Banesh Hoffmann in Whitrow, G.J., *Einstein, the Man and His Achievement* (New York: Dover, 1967): 75.

37. One source of these notes is MRI in St Paul, MN: 612–738–6463.

38. McDaniel, T. Hughes Technical Management Systems. Cited in Wycoff, J., *Transformation Thinking* (New York: Berkeley, 1995): 103.

39. Morgan, M., Grumman Technical Services. Cited in Wycoff, J., *Transformation Thinking* (New York: Berkeley, 1995): 167–8.

40. See, for example: Jaques, E., *The Form of Time* and *Time-Span Handbook* (New York: Crane Russak, 1982); Lynch, D. and Kordis, P.L., *Strategy of the Dolphin* (New York: Morrow, 1988); Madridakis, S.G., *Forecasting, Planning, and Strategy for the 21st Century* (New York: Free Press, 1990); Maynard, H.B., Jr. and Mehrtens, S.E., *The Fourth Wave: Business in the 21st Century* (San Francisco: Berrett-Koehler, 1993); Siler, T., *Breaking the Mind Barrier* (New York: Simon & Schuster, 1990).

41. Luria, A.R., *The Human Brain and Psychological Processes* (New York: Harper and Row, 1966): 531.

42. Jaques, E., 'The Development of Intellectual Capacity: A Discussion of Stratified Systems Theory', *The Journal of Applied Behavioral Science* 22 (4) (1986): 364.

43. Matsushita, cited in: Kao, *Jamming*: 52–3.

44. Hamel, G., 'Strategy as Revolution', *Harvard Business Review* (July–Aug. 1996): 69–82.

45. This reflective time-shifting exercise was inspired in part by the writings of Elliot Jaques, *The Form of Time* (London: Heinemann, 1982) and *Executive Leadership* (Arlington, VA: Cason & Hall, 1991); by Gary Hamel and C.K. Prahalad in *Competing for the Future* (Boston: Harvard Business School Press, 1994) and 'Strategy as Revolution' in the *Harvard Business Review* (July–Aug. 1996): 69–82; and by Adrian J. Slywotzky's *Value Migration* (Boston: Harvard Business School Press, 1996).

46. See, for example: Hamel and Prahald, *Competing for the Future*; Slywotzky, *Value Migration*.

47. Hamel and Prahald, *Competing for the Future*: 17.

48. Cray, S., in Maney, K., 'Quest for Speed Drove Supercomputer Inventor', *USA Today* (25 Sept. 1996): 4B.

49. Rechtschaffen, *Time Shifting* (New York: Doubleday, 1996): 84 and 138–9.

50. Rechtschaffen, *Time Shifting*: 138–9.

51. Rechtschaffen, *Time Shifting*: 138–9.

52. See, for example: Nadler, G. and Hibino, S. with Farrell, J., *Creative Solution Finding* (Rocklin, CA: Prima Publishing, 1995).

53. Tetzeli, R., 'What's It really Like to Be Marc Andreessen?' *Fortune* (6 Dec. 1996): 159–67; *U.S. News & World Report* (27 May 1996): 65–6.

54. Tetzeli, 'What's It really Like to Be Marc Andreessen?': 159–67.

55. See, for example: McCarthy, M.J., *Mastering the Information Age* (New York: Tarcher/Putnam, 1991).

56. To date, my favourite practical guides for accelerative learning are: McCarthy, *Mastering the Information Age*; Gross, R., *Peak Learning* (New York: Tarcher/Putnam, 1991); and The Princeton Language Institute (ed.), *21st Century Guide to Increasing your Reading Speed* (New York: Dell, 1995).

57. Drucker, P.F., 'Drucker on Management: The Five Deadly Business Sins', *Wall Street Journal* (21 Oct. 1993): A25.

58. Platt, L., foreword to Hammond, J. and Morrison, J., *The Stuff Americans Are Made Of* (New York: Macmillan, 1996).

59. Einstein, A., quoted in Mitchell, E. with Williams, D., *The Way of the Explorer* (New York: Putnam, 1996): 119.

60. Carlyle, T., 'Signs of the Times, 1829', in *Thomas Carlyle Selected Writings* (Harmondsworth, England: Penguin, 1971).

61. Wheatley, M., *Leadership and the New Science* (San Francisco: Berrett-Koehler, 1992).

62. See also: Csikszentmihalyi, M., *Creativity* (New York: HarperCollins, 1996): 108.

63. See: Fleming, T., *The Man Who Dared the Lightning: A New Look at Benjamin*

Franklin (New York: Morrow, 1971); Flatow, I., *They All Laughed . . .* (New York: HarperCollins, 1992).

64. Pais, A., *Subtle is the Lord, The Science and Life of Albert Einstein* (New York: Oxford University Press, 1982): 131.

65. Dilts, R.B., *Strategies of Genius* Vol. II (Capitola, CA: Meta Publishing, 1994): 85–6.

66. Pais, *Subtle is the Lord*: 131. Also see: Dilts, *Strategies of Genius*; Wenger, W. and Poe, R., *The Einstein Factor* (Rocklin, CA: Prima Publications, 1996): 12–13.

67. See, for example: Averill, J.P. and Nunley, E.P., *Voyages of the Heart: Living an Emotionally Creative Life* (New York: Free Press, 1992); Kao, *Jamming*; Hendricks, G. and Ludeman, K., *The Corporate Mystic* (New York: Bantam, 1996).

68. To learn more, see: Moore, J.F., *The Death of Competition* (Chichester: John Wiley, 1996); Brandenburger, A.M. and Nalebuff, B.J. *Co-opetition* (London: HarperCollins, 1996).

69. Roddick, A., quoted in Hamel, G., 'Strategy as Revolution', *Harvard Business Review* (July–Aug. 1996): 71.

70. Moody, F. 'Mr Software', *The New York Times Magazine* (25 Aug. 1991): 56.

71. ABB story in Moore, *The Death of Competition*: 6–7.

72. See, for example: Ornstein, R., *The Evolution of Consciousness* (New York: Prentice Hall, 1991).

73. See, for example: Thayer, R.E., *The Biopsychology of Mood and Arousal* (New York: Oxford University Press, 1991).

74. Mitchell, L., 'Be Nice to Employees? It's So Crazy, It Just Might Work', *Fast Forward* 11 (3) (March 1996): 1–3. Excerpted with permission.

75. Adapted from Godin, S., *Wisdom, Inc.* (New York: HarperBusiness, 1995): 27.

76. First Direct, story in Hamel, G., 'Strategy as Revolution', *Harvard Business Review* (July–Aug. 1996): 73.

77. Brown, J., 'That's Rich', *Esquire* (British edition) (May, 1994): 52.

78. See, for example: Kotter, J., *Leading Change* (Boston: Harvard Business School Press, 1996).

79. Schank, R.C., *The Creative Attitude* (New York: Macmillan, 1988): 315–16.

80. Von Oech, R., *Public Management* (Jan. 1982): 7–9.

81. Backer, T.E., 'How Health Promotion Programs Can Enhance Workplace Creativity', in Klarreich, S.H. (ed.), *Health and Fitness in the Workplace* (New York: Praeger, 1987): 325–37.

82. Sheikh, A.A. (ed.), *Imagery: Current Theory, Research, and Application* (New York: Wiley Interscience, 1984): 516.

83. Quinn, R.E., *Deep Change* (San Francisco: Jossey-Bass, 1996).

84. See George Land's classic work *Grow or Die* (New York: Wiley, 1973, 1986).

85. Eisner, M., 'Growing Strong', *Executive Excellence* (Aug. 1996): 11–12.

86. Mishlove, 'Not Business as Usual: An Interview with Michael Ray', *Intuition* 8 (1995): 28–31, 49–51.

87. See, for example: Teal, T., 'The Human Side of Management', *Harvard Business Review* (Nov.–Dec. 1996): 37.

88. See, for example: Flach, F.F., *Resilience* (New York: Fawcett, 1988).

89. Amabile, T.M., *The Social Psychology of Creativity* (New York: Springer-Verlag, 1983).

90. Grove, A.S., *Only the Paranoid Survive* (London: HarperCollins, 1997).

91. Huck, V., *Brand of Tartan – The 3M Story* (New York: Appleton-Century-Crofts, 1955); Comfort, M.H., *William L. McKnight, Industrialist* (Minneapolis: T.S. Denison, 1962); *Our Story So Far* (St Paul, MN: 3M Company, 1977); see also: Collins, J.C. and Porras, J.I., *Built to Last: Successful Habits of Visionary Companies* (London: Random House, 1995).

92. Kirkpatrick, D., 'This Tough Guy Wants to give You a Hug', *Fortune* (14 Oct. 1996): 170–8.

93. Kirkpatrick, 'This Tough Guy Wants to Give You a Hug': 170–8.

94. See, also: Warren Bennis, writing in the *Harvard Business Review* (Jan.–Feb. 1996), who says, 'As my own study of dozens of contemporary leaders has revealed, whether in the arts, the political arena, or the corporation, leaders are almost always risk takers. They also tend to be curious, energetic, and gifted with an acute sense of humor.'

95. de Bono, E., *I Am Right, You Are Wrong* (New York: Viking, 1991): 1.

96. See, for example: Towler, J., 'Laughter is Profitable', *Canadian Banker* 97 (3) (1990): 32–33; Isen, A.M., 'Toward Understanding the Influence of Positive Affect on Social Behavior, Decision Making, and Problem Solving: The Role of Cognitive Organization', paper presented at the annual meeting of the American Association for the Advancement of Science, Boston (11–15 Feb. 1988); Isen, A.M., *et al.*, 'The Influence of Positive Affect on the Unusualness of Word Associations', *Journal of Personality and Social Psychology* 48 (1985): 1413–26; Isen, A.M., *et al.*, 'Positive Affect Facilitates Creative Problem Solving', *Journal of Personality and Social Psychology* 52 (1987): 1122–31; and Isen, A.M., 'Positive Affect, Cognitive Processes, and Social Behavior', *Advances in Experimental Social Psychology* 20 (1987): 203–53.

97. Morreall, J., *Taking Laughter Seriously* (Albany: State University of New York, 1983): 108.

98. Kets de Vries, M.F.R., *Life and Death in the Executive Fast Lane* (San Francisco: Jossey-Bass, 1995): 147–8.

99. See: Frieberg, K. and Frieberg, J., *Nuts! Southwest Airlines' Crazy Recipe for Business and Personal Success* (Bard, 1996); and Kelleher, H., in Farkas and DeBacker, *Maximum Leadership*: 86–90.

100. Hamel, G., 'Strategy as Revolution', *Harvard Business Review* (July–Aug. 1996): 72.

101. Lefcourt, H.M. and Martin, R.A., *Humor and Life Stress* (New York: Springer-Verlag, 1986); Nezu, A.M., *et al.* 'Sense of Humor as a Moderator of the Relation Between Stressful Events and Psychological Distress: A Prospective Analysis', *Journal of Personality and Social Psychology* 54 (1988): 520–5.

102. McCracken, E., quoted in Peters, T., *The Tom Peters Seminar* (New York: Vintage, 1994): 208.

103. Chapman, A., and Foot, H., *Handbook of Humor and Laughter: Theory, Research and Applications* (New York: John Wiley and Sons, 1982); Dillon, K.M., *et al.* 'Positive Emotional States and Enhancement of the Immune System', *International Journal of Psychiatry in Medicine* 15 (1) (1985–1986): 13–18; 'Laughing Toward Longevity', *University of California, Berkeley, Wellness Letter* (June 1985): 1; 'The Mind Fights Back', *Washington Post*; Brody, 'Laughter', *New York Times*.

105. The subject of group intelligence is presented by Robert Sternberg and Wendy Williams in 'Group Intelligence: Why Some Groups Are Better Than Others', *Intelligence* (1988).

106. I am indebted to George Land for this concept. See: Land, G., *Grow or Die* (New York: Wiley, 1986); or contact: Leadership 2000 (3333 N. 44th St., Phoenix, AZ 85018; 602–852–0223).

107. Gardner, J.W., 'Self-Renewal', *The Futurist* (Nov.–Dec. 1996): 7–12.

108. See: Richardson, R.D., Jr., *Emerson: The Mind on Fire* (Berkeley: University of California Press, 1995): 572.

109. Wolpe, D.J., *Teaching Your Children About God* (New York: Henry Holt, 1993).

110. Brown, J.S. and Gray, E.S., 'The People Are the Company', *Fast Company: The New Rules of Business* 1 (1) (Nov.–Dec. 1995): 78–82.

PERMISSIONS

Every effort has been made to obtain permission from the appropriate parties to include the cited works, but if any errors have been made we will be happy to correct them. We gratefully acknowledge the following permissions:

Excerpt from 'What is Integrity?' by Jack Hawley, in Jack Canfield and Jacqueline Miller, *Heart at Work*. Copyright 1996. Reprinted by permission of Jacqueline Miller and McGraw-Hill.

Excerpt from 'Dian Owen's Story' in *On Our Own Terms: Portraits of Women Business Leaders* by Liane Enkelis and Karen Olsen with Marion Lewenstein. Copyright 1995. Reprinted with permission of Berrett-Koehler Publishers.

Excerpt from 'Something unexpected happened' in *Transformation Thinking* by Joyce Wycoff with Tim Richardson. Copyright 1995. Reprinted with permission of the Berkley Publishing Group.

Excerpt from 'Threads' in *Love and Profit* by James A. Autry. Copyright 1991. Reprinted with permission of William Morrow & Company.

Excerpt/adaptation from 'First Person: The Purpose at the Heart of Management' in *Harvard Business Review* (May–June, 1992) by Kye Anderson. Copyright by the President and Fellows of Harvard College, all rights reserved. Reprinted with permission of *Harvard Business Review*.

Excerpt/adaptation from 'First Person: The Hard Work of Being a Soft Manager' in *Harvard Business Review* (November–December 1991) by William H. Peace. Copyright by the President and Fellows of Harvard College, all rights reserved. Reprinted with permission of *Harvard Business Review*.

Excerpt/adaptation from 'First Person: Why My Former Employees Still Work for Me' in *Harvard Business Review* (January–February 1994) by Ricardo Semler. Copyright by the President and Fellows of Harvard College, all rights reserved. Reprinted with permission of *Harvard Business Review*.

Excerpt from 'Emotions: Conventional vs. High-Performance Meaning' in *The Stuff Americans Are Made Of* by Josh Hammond and James Morrison. Copyright 1996. Reprinted with permission of Macmillan.

Excerpt from *Type 1 and Type 2 Situations* by Warren J. Pelton, Sonja

317

ACKNOWLEDGMENTS

The foundation for this book has been drawn together from the studies, experiences and insights shared by a wealth of individuals. It is with profound respect and appreciation that we thank the many researchers and specialists who shared their findings and wisdom with us, and whose knowledge and suggestions we have worked to review and distill.

The concept of 'emotional literacy' was first explored by psychologist Claude Steiner in the early 1980s. The initial pioneering studies on 'emotional intelligence' were conducted by Peter Salovey at Yale University and John Mayer at the University of New Hampshire. The discoveries and insights of Robert Solomon of the University of Texas at Austin and Antonio Damasio of the University of Iowa Medical School have served as special sources of reflection and consideration. Howard Gardner of Harvard University deepened and broadened the exploration horizon for all of us with his works on multiple intelligences, creativity, and leadership. Robert Sternberg at Yale University has done much to advance our understanding of practical, creative, and successful intelligence. Daniel Goleman deserves considerable praise for bringing the emerging field of emotional intelligence to the public's attention with such clarity and commitment.

Among the many other leaders, scientists, and educators whose professional initiatives, published works, or personal communications have informed and inspired us are: Kye Anderson, William Arnold, James Autry, Warren Bennis, Peter Block, Alan Briskin, Julia Cameron, Stephen Carter, Donald Clifton, Jim Collins, Mihaly Csikszentmihalyi, Bert Decker, Francis Fukuyma, John Gardner, Joseph Gauld, Gary Hamel, John Hatfield, Gay Hendricks, James Hillman, Richard Huseman, Joseph Jaworski, Prasad Kaipa, John Kao, Rushworth Kidder, Peter Koestenbaum, James Kouzes, Kate Ludeman, James Lynch, Martin Moore-Ede, Michael Novak, James O'Toole, Dian Owen, William Peace, Jeanne Plas, Jerry Porras, Barry Posner, C. K. Prahald, Robert Quinn, Michael Ray, Robert Rosen, John Ralston Saul, Ricardo Semler, Peter Senge, Robert Thayer, Dean Tjosvold, Peter Vaill, and David Whyte.

We have a special debt to those who reviewed and commented on parts of the manuscript: Deborah Kiley of Arthur Andersen and Andersen Consulting; Prasad Kaipa of Knowledge Architecture; Jerry de Jaaeger; James Kackley and Norm Carlson of Arthur Andersen; Esther Orioli of Q-Metrics/Essi Systems; Agnew Meek of 3M; Michael Ray of Stanford Graduate School of Business; Barry Posner of the Leavey Graduate School of Business at Santa Clara University; Charles Manz of the Arizona State University School of Management; Nancy Badore; Robert Webster of SmithKline Beecham; Eunice Azzani of Korn/Ferry International; Eldon McBride of Boeing; Russ Volckmann of the CPR Group; Larry Taylor of Pinkerton Security; Charlotte Roberts; Jacqueline Miller of Partnerships for Change; Gayle Holmes of MenTTium; Lucille Ueltzen of Octel Communications; Marie Kenerson of the Learning Circle; Brian Robb of the Carlson Companies; Jim White; Woody Numainville; Carol Kelsey and Dawn Sorensen of North Memorial Health Care; and James Ericson of the Masters Forum.

We are deeply grateful to the research and measurement team at Q-Metrics/Essi Systems, Inc., in San Francisco. From the moment we committed ourselves to embarking on an in-depth exploration of emotional intelligence in organizations and to developing the *EQ Map* and *Organizational EQ Profiles*, their heartfelt dedication and excellence in scholarship and science have been truly remarkable. In particular, we want to thank Esther Orioli, CEO; Karen Trocki, director of research; Sandra Trafalis, manager of research; Susan Yeres, Karla Carmony; Myron Binder; Paul Krawshuk; Brenda Aguilar and Guillermina Kirk.

The central integration of this book was improved significantly by an extraordinary ongoing partnership with Prasad Kapia, CEO of Knowledge Architecture, who created with us the *EQ-in-Action Pyramids*.

For design insights, networking, and valuable help in developing and marketing the core learning systems for emotional intelligence in leadership and organizations, Robert wishes to express his appreciation to Esther Orioli, Prasad Kaipa, Robert Bixler, Gwen Riscoe, and the Learning Circle: Rita and Bill Cleary, Marie Kenerson, Sandy Billings and Anne Starr.

Robert expresses his personal appreciation to the people of Tibet, and in particular those whose stories are shared in this book, who taught him about courage in the face of death, forgiveness in the face of betrayal, and that peace must be found first within ourselves before we can expect peace in the world. He also conveys his gratitude for the personal support, wisdom, and encouragement he has received during the course of this project from Larry and Lynn Taylor; Esther Orioli; Prasad Kaipa; Jim Ericson; Tom Miller; Nancy Badore; Harold Bloomfield and Sirah Vittese; Kathleen Dannemiller; Al Viswanathan; Karen Trocki; Michael Ray; Jim Kackley; Norm Carlson; Deborah Kiley; Ruth Hapgood; Elizabeth Wright; Nido Qubein; Brent and Dottie Williams; Ken and Claire Grant; Paul and Laurie Hurd; Ag and Peg Meek; Rita and Bill Cleary; Marie Kenerson; and Gayle Homes, Lynn Sontag, and the entire team at MenTTium.

Our literary agent, Stephanie Tade, has been a constant source of encouragement, insight, and creative initiative; in every respect she is a leader in her field. Martin Liu, publishing director at the Orion Publishing Group, and editorial assistant Louise Radford, have provided valued guidance and support at each stage of the research and writing.

Last, and most of all, we want to thank our families. Ayman expresses his appreciation and love to his father and mentor, Abdul Aziz Sawaf; his brothers, Omar and Bachar; and to his wife, Rowan Gabrielle. Robert expresses his love and gratitude to the memory of his grandparents; to his parents, Hugh and Margaret Cooper; his sister, Mary; brother, David; and to his son, Chris and daughters, Chelsea and Shanna. Through the entire research and writing process for this book it was his wife, Leslie, who, above all, provided the innermost circle of abiding love, friendship, laughter, and intelligence that enabled this project to be completed.

AN INTEGRATED EQ ASSESSMENT
AND INDIVIDUAL PROFILE

Mapping Your Emotional Intelligence

Norm Testing Version III.3

INTRODUCTION

Emotional Intelligence

Emotional intelligence is the ability to sense, understand and effectively apply the power and acumen of emotions as a source of human energy, information and influence. Human emotions are the domain of core feelings, gut level instincts and emotional sensations. When trusted and respected, emotional intelligence provides a deeper, more fully formed understanding of oneself and those around us.

About the EQ Map™

The instrument you are about to complete is extensively researched, statistically reliable and norm-tested on an employed workforce in the United States and Canada. Research for the creation of a special UK version will begin in Spring 1998.

The EQ Map ™ will help guide your exploration of emotional intelligence by plotting a sample of your personal performance strengths and vulnerabilities to identify individual and interpersonal patterns for success.

The EQ Map ™ Self-Scoring Version has two parts:

* The EQ Map™ Questionnaire will assist you in the assessment of the various components related to EQ and its inherent competencies.

* The EQ Map ™ Scoring Grid will visually map your personal performance, creating a personal snapshot of your current EQ strengths and vulnerabilities.

Completing Your EQ Map™ Questionnaire

Plan to spend at least 30 minutes completing the questionnaire. Start at the beginning. Complete each scale by circling the provided number (3,2,1,0) in the column which best describes your response to each statement or question.

Answer every question and complete the scales in the order in which they appear. Work quickly and be as honest with yourself as possible.

324

Finding Your Score

On each scale, add up the numbers circled in each vertical column, and place the total at the bottom of that column. Then add all the column totals together to get your Total Score for that scale. Write that total in the large circle.

Directly above the circle is a ruler with four levels. Your scores will fall within the ranges of one of these four levels. Locate the level your score falls into. Fill in the dot within that level. (Please refer to the example below). This will then help you to plot your position on the EQ Map ™ Scoring Grid found on pages 346 – 347.

Sample

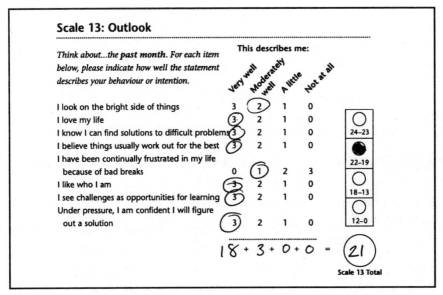

EQ Map™ Scoring Grid

You are going to transfer your scores from each scale of the questionnaire onto this grid, to give you an overall picture of your EQ performance levels. The Scoring Grid has four levels for each scale, just like the ruler. Transfer your ruler level from each of the scales by making a dot on the grid that matches your level on each scale. When you have transferred your level from each of the 21 scales, connect the dots on the EQ Scoring Grid to make a pattern. This line shows your individual EQ performance rhythm.

SECTION I

Current Environment:
Events, Pressures, & Satisfactions

Scale 1: Life Events

....

*Think about...the **past year**. For each of the work and personal events listed below, please indicate how much each has been a source of distress for you.*

	Great	Moderate	Little	None/ Didn't occur
WORK				
Fired, laid off, quit, or retired	3	2	1	0
New job or employer	3	2	2	0
New type of work	3	2	1	0
Downsizing or reorganization at my company	3	2	1	0
Some other change at work not listed above which caused you distress	3	2	1	0
PERSONAL				
Financial loss or diminished income	3	2	1	0
Death of a close friend or family member	3	2	1	0
Move or relocation	3	2	1	0
Your separation or divorce	3	2	1	0
Your marriage	3	2	1	0
Bought a new home	3	2	1	0
Crime victim	3	2	1	0
Birth of a baby, adoption, step-child(ren) or other person(s) added to the household	3	2	1	0
Involvement in a legal system	3	2	1	0
Serious personal illness or injury	3	2	1	0
Serious illness or injury of a close friend or family member	3	2	1	0
Some other change, not listed above, which caused you distress	3	2	1	0

○ 0–2

○ 3–7

○ 8–15

○ 16–51

....

\+   \+   \+   =   ○

Scale 1 Total

326

Scale 2: Work Pressures and Satisfactions

WORK SATISFACTIONS

*Think about...the **past month**. For each of the statements listed below, please indicate how true each is for you.*

	Very true	True	A little true	Not at all true
I enjoy my job	3	2	1	0
I have a supervisor whom I like and trust	3	2	1	0
I would rather make more money at a less interesting job	0	1	2	3
I believe in what my employer stands for	3	2	1	0
I have a good physical working environment	3	2	1	0
I receive adequate compensation for my work	3	2	1	0
I feel liked and valued by the people at work	3	2	1	0
I receive feedback about the quality of my work	3	2	1	0
I use my abilities and talents on the job	3	2	1	0
I participate in decisions about things at work which affect me	3	2	1	0
I am respected by people in the community for my job	3	2	1	0
When considering my contributions, I feel short-changed by my company	0	1	2	3
Resources are limited, I have to fight to get things	0	1	2	3

WORK PRESSURES

*Think about the **past month**. For each of the work pressures listed below, please indicate how much each has been a source of distress for you.*

	Great	Moderate	Little	None/ Didn't occur
Job security	0	1	2	3
Relationship with an immediate supervisor	0	1	2	3
Shifting priorities at work	0	1	2	3
Relationship with co-workers	0	1	2	3
Opportunity for advancement and growth	0	1	2	3
Too much work	0	1	2	3

Scale 2 continued

Control over my workload	0	1	2	3
Lack of job flexibility to deal with family and/or personal emergencies	0	1	2	3
Favouritism or unfair hiring and/or promotion policies at work	0	1	2	3
Constant monitoring of job performance by management	0	1	2	3
Boring or uninteresting work	0	1	2	3
Special recognition or award at my job	0	1	2	3
Pressure from competing deadlines at my job	0	1	2	3
Loss of commitment to work	0	1	2	3
Feeling bogged down in red tape and unable to accomplish anything	0	1	2	3
Flexibility hours of work	0	1	2	3
The commute to my job	0	1	2	3

○ 90–38

○ 37–24

○ 23–15

○ 14–0

Please total the values for *both* the Work Satisfactions and Pressure sections. This will be the score you plot on the Scoring Grid.

+   +   +   = ○

Scale 2 Total

Scale 3: Personal Pressures and Satisfactions

PERSONAL PRESSURES

*Think about...the **past month**. For each of the personal pressures listed below, please indicate how much each has been a source of distress for you.*

Great   Moderate   Little   None/Didn't occur

Financial difficulties	0	1	2	3
Increased caretaking responsibilities for an aging or disabled relative	0	1	2	3
Conflict with partner or spouse	0	1	2	3
Raising a child	0	1	2	3
Being separated from a spouse	0	1	2	3
Deteriorating personal health	0	1	2	3
Finding quality day care or problems with current day care situation	0	1	2	3

Scale 3 continued

Not enough time to spend with those closest to me	0	1	2	3
Dangerous or unsafe neighbourhood	0	1	2	3
Relationship with a close relative (parent, sibling, in-law)	0	1	2	3
Sexual conflict or frustration	0	1	2	3
Work-family conflict	0	1	2	3
Lonely or lack intimacy	0	1	2	3
Fertility or reproductive issues	0	1	2	3

PERSONAL SATISFACTIONS

*Think about...the **past month**. For each of the statements listed below, please indicate how true each is for you.*

	Very true	True	A little true	Not at all true
The people around me will take time for me when I need it	3	2	1	0
Those closest to me understand when I am upset and respond to me	3	2	1	0
I feel accepted and loved by those closest to me	3	2	1	0
The people close to me support me to do new things and make changes in my life	3	2	1	0
I spend quality time with friends/family	3	2	1	0
I am able to give what I would like to my friends/family	3	2	1	0
I can ask for help from my family and friends when I need it	3	2	1	0
I know that others are there for me	3	2	1	0

66–24
23–15
14–6
5–0

Please total the values for *both* the Personal Pressures and Satisfactions sections. This will be the score you plot on the Scoring Grid.

+ + + =

Scale 3 Total

SECTION II

Emotional Literacy

Scale 4: Emotional Self-Awareness

*For each item listed below, please indicate how well it describes the way you **currently** think or feel about yourself.*

This describes me:

Very well / Moderately well / A little / Not at all

	Very well	Moderately well	A little	Not at all
I can name my feelings	3	2	1	0
I've learned a lot about myself by listening to my feelings	3	2	1	0
I am aware of my feelings most of the time	3	2	1	0
I can tell when I am getting upset	3	2	1	0
When I am sad, I know the reason(s) why	3	2	1	0
I tend to judge myself by how I think others see me	0	1	2	3
I enjoy my emotional life	3	2	1	0
People who show a lot of strong emotion scare me	0	1	2	3
I often wish I were someone else	0	1	2	3
I pay attention to my physical state to understand my feelings	3	2	1	0
I accept my feelings as my own	3	2	1	0

○ 33–29

○ 28–24

○ 23–19

○ 18–0

+   +   +   =   ○

Scale 4 Total

Scale 5: Emotional Expression

....

*For each item listed below, please indicate how well it describes the way you **currently** think or feel about yourself.*

This describes me:

	Very well	Moderately well	A little	Not at all
I let other people know when they are doing a good job	3	2	1	0
I express my emotions even when they are negative	3	2	1	0
I let others know what I want and need	3	2	1	0
My closest friends would say I express my appreciation of them	3	2	1	0
I keep my feelings to myself	0	1	2	3
I let people know when uncomfortable feelings get in the way of our work	3	2	1	0
I have trouble reaching out to others when I need help	0	1	2	3
When interacting with others, I can sense how they are feeling	3	2	1	0
I would do anything to avoid looking foolish to my peers	0	1	2	3

○ 27–20
○ 19–17
○ 16–13
○ 12–0

....

+   +   +   = ○

Scale 5 Total

Scale 6: Emotional Awareness of Others

....

*For each item listed below, please indicate how well it describes the way you **currently** think or feel about yourself.*

This describes me:

	Very well	Moderately well	A little	Not at all
I can recognize emotions in others by watching their eyes	3	2	1	0
I find it difficult to talk to people who do not share my views	0	1	2	3
I focus on people's positive qualities	3	2	1	0
I rarely have the urge to tell someone off	3	2	1	0
I think about how others might feel before I give my opinion	3	2	1	0
No matter with whom I am speaking, I am always a good listener	3	2	1	0

Scale 6 continued

I can sense the mood of a group when I walk into the room	3	2	1	0
I can get new people I meet to talk about themselves	3	2	1	0
I am good at reading between the lines when someone is talking	3	2	1	0
I can usually tell how others feel about me	3	2	1	0
I can sense someone's feelings even if it is unspoken	3	2	1	0
I change my emotional expression depending upon the person I am with	0	1	2	3
I can tell when someone close to me is upset	3	2	1	0

○ 39–28

○ 27–22

○ 21–15

○ 14–0

....

+   +   +   =   ○

Scale 6 Total

SECTION III

EQ Competencies

Scale 7: Intentionality

*Think about...the **past month**. For each item below, please indicate how well the statement describes your behaviour or intention.*

This describes me:

	Very well	Moderately well	A little	Not at all
I can easily shut out distractions when I need to concentrate	3	2	1	0
I finish most things that I start	3	2	1	0
I know how to say no when I have to	3	2	1	0
I know how to reward myself after accomplishing a goal	3	2	1	0
I can put aside short-term rewards for long-term goals	3	2	1	0
I can completely focus myself on a task when I need to	3	2	1	0
I do things I later regret	0	1	2	3
I accept responsibility for managing my emotions	3	2	1	0
When faced with a problem, I like to deal with it as soon as possible	3	2	1	0
I think about what I want before I act	3	2	1	0
I can postpone my personal gratification for a greater goal	3	2	1	0
When I'm in a bad mood I can talk myself out of it	3	2	1	0
I get angry when I am criticized	0	1	2	3
I do not know the source of my anger in situations	0	1	2	3

○ 42–33

○ 32–27

○ 26–21

○ 20–0

+   +   +   = ○

Scale 7 Total

Scale 8: Creativity

*Think about...the **past month**. For each item below, please indicate how well the statement describes your behaviour or intention.*

This describes me:

	Very well	Moderately well	A little	Not at all
I've suggested innovative projects for my company	3	2	1	0
I participate in the sharing of information and ideas	3	2	1	0
I fantasize about the future to help me figure out where I am going	3	2	1	0
My best ideas happen when I am not really thinking about them	3	2	1	0
I've had brilliant ideas that came to me in a flash and were fully formed	3	2	1	0
I have a good sense of when new ideas will succeed or fail	3	2	1	0
I am fascinated by new and unusual concepts	3	2	1	0
I've implemented innovative projects at my company	3	2	1	0
I get excited by new ideas or solutions	3	2	1	0
I am good at brainstorming on a problem to generate options	3	2	1	0

○ 30–24
○ 23–19
○ 18–14
○ 13–0

+   +   +   = ○ **Scale 8 Total**

Scale 9: Resilience

*Think about...the **past month**. For each item below, please indicate how well the statement describes your behaviour or intention.*

This describes me:

	Very well	Moderately well	A little	Not at all
I can bounce back after feeling disappointed	3	2	1	0
I can accomplish what I need to if I put my mind to it	3	2	1	0
Obstacles or problems in my life have resulted in unexpected changes for the better	3	2	1	0
I find it easy to wait patiently when I need to	3	2	1	0
There is always more than one right answer	3	2	1	0
I know how to satisfy all parts of myself	3	2	1	0

Scale 9 continued

I am not one to procrastinate	3	2	1	0
I am afraid to try something again when I have failed at it before	0	1	2	3
I decide certain problems are not worth worrying about	3	2	1	0
I relax myself when tension builds up	3	2	1	0
I can see the humourous side of situations	3	2	1	0
I often put things aside for a while to get a perspective on them	3	2	1	0
When I encounter a problem, I focus on what I can do to solve it	3	2	1	0

○ 39–34
○ 33–28
○ 27–21
○ 20–0

+   +   +   =   ○

Scale 9 Total

Scale 10: Interpersonal Connections

*Think about...the **past month**. For each item below, please indicate how well the statement describes your behaviour or intention.*

This describes me:

Very well   Moderately well   A little   Not at all

I am able to grieve when I lose something important to me	3	2	1	0
I feel uncomfortable when someone gets too close to me emotionally	0	1	2	3
I have several friends I can count on in times of trouble	3	2	1	0
I show a lot of love and affection to my friends and family	3	2	1	0
When I have a problem I know who to go to or what to do to help solve it	3	2	1	0
My beliefs and values guide my daily actions	3	2	1	0
My family is always there for me when I need them	3	2	1	0
I doubt if my colleagues really care about me as a person	0	1	2	3
I have a difficult time making friends	0	1	2	3
I hardly cry	0	1	2	3

○ 30–28
○ 27–23
○ 22–18
○ 17–0

+   +   +   =   ○

Scale 10 Total

Scale 11: Constructive Discontent

Think about...the past month. For each item below, please indicate how well the statement describes your behaviour or intention.

This describes me:

	Very well	Moderately well	A little	Not at all
I can disagree effectively to bring about change	3	2	1	0
I would not express my feelings if I believed they would cause a disagreement	0	1	2	3
When it comes right down to it, I can only trust myself to get things done	0	1	2	3
I remain calm even in situations when others get angry	3	2	1	0
It is better not to stir up problems if you can avoid doing so	0	1	2	3
I have a hard time getting consensus from my work team	0	1	2	3
I solicit feedback from my peers on my performance	3	2	1	0
I am good at organizing and motivating groups of people	3	2	1	0
I enjoy the challenge of facing and solving problems at work	3	2	1	0
I listen to criticism with an open mind and accept it when it is justified	3	2	1	0
I let things build up to a crisis point before talking about it	0	1	2	3
When I make a critical comment I focus on the behaviour and not the person	3	2	1	0
I avoid confrontations	0	1	2	3

○ 39–34

○ 33–27

○ 26–20

○ 19–0

+   +   +   = ◯

Scale 11 Total

SECTION IV

EQ Values and Beliefs

Scale 12: Compassion

*Think about...the **past month**. For each item below, please indicate how well the statement describes your behaviour or intention.*

This describes me:

	Very well	Moderately well	A little	Not at all
I can see pain in others even if they don't talk about it	3	2	1	0
I am able to read people's emotions from their body language	3	2	1	0
I act ethically in my dealings with people	3	2	1	0
I would not hesitate to go out of my way to help someone in trouble	3	2	1	0
I take the feelings of others into consideration in my interactions with them	3	2	1	0
I can put myself in someone else's shoes	3	2	1	0
There are some people I've never forgiven	0	1	2	3
I can forgive myself for not being perfect	3	2	1	0
When I succeed at something, I often feel I could have done better	0	1	2	3
I help others to save face in a tough situation	3	2	1	0
I constantly worry about my shortcomings	0	1	2	3
I am jealous of people who have more than I do	0	1	2	3

36–33

32–29

28–21

20–0

+   +   +   =

Scale 12 Total

Scale 13: Outlook

*Think about...the **past month**. For each item below, please indicate how well the statement describes your behaviour or intention.*

This describes me:

	Very well	Moderately well	A little	Not at all	
I look on the bright side of things	3	2	1	0	
I love my life	3	2	1	0	
I know I can find solutions to difficult problems	3	2	1	0	24–23
I believe things usually work out for the best	3	2	1	0	
I have been continually frustrated in my life because of bad breaks	0	1	2	3	22–19
I like who I am	3	2	1	0	
I see challenges as opportunities for learning	3	2	1	0	18–13
Under pressure, I am confident I will figure out a solution	3	2	1	0	12–0

+ + + = ○

Scale 13 Total

Scale 14: Intuition

*Think about...the **past month**. For each item below, please indicate how well the statement describes your behaviour or intention.*

This describes me:

	Very well	Moderately well	A little	Not at all
Sometimes, I have the right answer without having the reasons	3	2	1	0
My hunches are usually right	3	2	1	0
I visualize my future goals	3	2	1	0
I can see the finished product or picture before it is completed	3	2	1	0
I believe in my dreams even when others can't see or understand them	3	2	1	0

Scale 14 continued

When faced with a tough choice, I follow my heart	3	2	1	0
I pay attention when things don't feel quite right to me	3	2	1	0
Once I've made up my mind I seldom change it	0	1	2	3
People say I am a visionary	3	2	1	0
When someone presents an opinion different from my own, I have a hard time accepting it	0	1	2	3
I use my gut reactions when making decisions	3	2	1	0

33–29

28–23

22–18

17–0

+   +   +   =

Scale 14 Total

Scale 15: Trust Radius

*Think about...the **past month**. For each item below, please indicate how well the statement describes your behaviour or intention.*

This describes me:

	Very well	Moderately well	A little	Not at all
People would take advantage of me if I let them	0	1	2	3
I trust until I have reason not to	0	1	2	3
I am very careful about whom I trust	0	1	2	3
I respect my colleagues	3	2	1	0
People similar to me at my company have gotten better deals (ie, raises, promotions, opportunities, rewards, etc.) than I have	0	1	2	3
The people I associate with are trustworthy	3	2	1	0
I seem to get the short end of the stick	0	1	2	3
Very little in life is fair or equitable	0	1	2	3
When something isn't working I try to come up with an alternative plan	3	2	1	0
When I meet new people I disclose very little personal information about myself	0	1	2	3

30–26

25–21

20–16

15–0

+   +   +   =

Scale 15 Total

Scale 16: Personal Power

*Think about...the **past month**. For each item below, please indicate how well the statement describes your behaviour or intention.*

This describes me:

	Very well	Moderately well	A little	Not at all
I can make things happen	3	2	1	0
Fate plays a strong role in my life	0	1	2	3
I find it useless to fight the established hierarchy at my company	0	1	2	3
Circumstances are beyond my control	0	1	2	3
I need recognition from others to make my work worthwhile	0	1	2	3
I am easy to like	3	2	1	0
I have a hard time accepting compliments	0	1	2	3
I have the ability to get what I want	3	2	1	0
I feel in control of my life	3	2	1	0
If I reflect on my life, I might find I am basically unhappy	0	1	2	3
I feel frightened and out of control when things change rapidly	0	1	2	3
I enjoy taking charge of things	3	2	1	0
I know what I want and go after it	3	2	1	0

39–34

33–29

28–24

23–0

+   +   +   =   ◯

Scale 16 Total

Scale 17: Integrity

*Think about...the **past month**. For each item below, please indicate how well the statement describes your behaviour or intention.*

This describes me:

	Very well	Moderately well	A little	Not at all
I am willing to admit it when I make a mistake	3	2	1	0
I feel like a fraud	0	1	2	3
If I no longer had passion for my work, I would change jobs	3	2	1	0
My job is an extension of my personal value system	3	2	1	0
I never tell lies	3	2	1	0
I find myself going along with a situation even if I know I don't believe in it	0	1	2	3
I exaggerate my abilities in order to get ahead	0	1	2	3
I tell the truth even when it is difficult	3	2	1	0
I have done things on my job that are against my beliefs	0	1	2	3

27–20

19–17

16–13

12–0

+   +   +   =

Scale 17 Total

SECTION V

EQ Outcomes

Scale 18: General Health

*Think about...the **past month**. Please indicate how often (if ever) you have experienced the following symptoms.*

	Never	Once or twice a month	Every week	Nearly every day
PHYSICAL SYMPTOMS				
Back pain	0	1	2	3
Problem(s) with weight (either underweight or overweight)	0	1	2	3
Tension headaches	0	1	2	3
Migraines	0	1	2	3
Colds or respiratory problems	0	1	2	3
Stomach problems (frequent gas, irritable bowel syndrome, or ulcers)	0	1	2	3
Chest pain	0	1	2	3
Unexplainable aches and pains	0	1	2	3
Some other kind of chronic pain not listed above	0	1	2	3
BEHAVIOURAL SYMPTOMS				
Eating (loss of appetite, overeating, no time to eat)	0	1	2	3
Smoking	0	1	2	3
Drinking alcoholic beverages	0	1	2	3
Taking tranquilizers	0	1	2	3
Taking aspirins or other pain killers	0	1	2	3
Taking other drugs	0	1	2	3
Withdrawing from close relationships	0	1	2	3
Criticizing, blaming or ridiculing others	0	1	2	3
Feeling victimized or taken advantage of	0	1	2	3
Watching TV (over 2 hours a day)	0	1	2	3
Playing video/computer games or using the Internet (over 2 hours a day)	0	1	2	3
Resenting people I encounter	0	1	2	3
Accidents or injuries	0	1	2	3

Scale 18 continued
EMOTIONAL SYMPTOMS

Trouble concentrating	0	1	2	3
Overwhelmed by work	0	1	2	3
Being easily distracted	0	1	2	3
Can't get things off my mind/constant worrying or dwelling	0	1	2	3
Feeling depressed, dejected, or hopeless	0	1	2	3
Feeling lonely	0	1	2	3
Mind goes blank	0	1	2	3
Feeling fatigued or overwhelmed	0	1	2	3
Trouble making up mind or making decisions	0	1	2	3
Trouble getting myself going or trouble calming down	0	1	2	3

0–8
9–18
19–31
32–96

+   +   +   =

Scale 18 Total

Scale 19: Quality of Life

*Please indicate how well each of the following statements describes the way you **currently** think or feel about yourself.*

This describes me:

	Very well	Moderately well	A little	Not at all
I am deeply satisfied with my life	3	2	1	0
I feel energetic, happy, and healthy	3	2	1	0
I have feelings of inner-peace and well-being	3	2	1	0
I would need to make lots of changes in my life to be truly happy	0	1	2	3
My life meets my deepest needs	3	2	1	0
I have gotten less than I hoped for out of life	0	1	2	3
I like myself just the way I am	3	2	1	0
Work for me is fun	3	2	1	0
I have found meaningful work	3	2	1	0
I am on a path that brings me satisfaction	3	2	1	0
I have made the most of my own abilities	3	2	1	0

33–27
26–22
21–17
16–0

+   +   +   =

Scale 19 Total

Scale 20: Relationship Quotient

*Please indicate how well each of the following statements describes the way you **currently** think or feel about yourself.*

This describes me:

	Very well	Moderately well	A little	Not at all
There are some people I connect with at a deeper level	3	2	1	0
I am honest with the people close to me and they are honest with me	3	2	1	0
I have deeply loved another person	3	2	1	0
I can usually find people to socialize with	3	2	1	0
I am able to make a long-term commitment to a relationship	3	2	1	0
I know I am important to the people closest to me	3	2	1	0
I find it easy to tell people I care about them	3	2	1	0

+   +   +   =

○ 21–20
○ 19–17
○ 16–14
○ 13–0

○ **Scale 20 Total**

Scale 21: Optimal Performance

This describes me:

*Please indicate how well each of the following statements describes the way you **currently** think or feel about yourself.*

	Very well	Moderately well	A little	Not at all
I am satisfied with my work performance	3	2	1	0
My co-workers would say I facilitate good communications among the members of my work group	3	2	1	0
I feel distant and uninvolved at work	0	1	2	3
It is difficult for me to pay attention to work tasks	0	1	2	3
In my work team, I am involved in decision-making	3	2	1	0
I have difficulty meeting commitments or completing tasks	0	1	2	3
My work performance is consistently the best I can do	3	2	1	0

+   +   +   =

○ 21–20
○ 19–17
○ 16–13
○ 12–0

○ **Scale 21 Total**

Thank you for your responses.

You have now completed the questionnaire portion of the EQ Map™.

To visually map your scores turn to the EQ Map ™ Scoring Grid on the next page and follow the instructions on page 325.

EQ MAP™

Scoring Grid

	Life Events	Work Pressures and Satisfactions	Personal Pressures and Satisfactions	Emotional Self-Awareness	Emotional Expression	Emotional Awareness of Others	Intentionality	Creativity	
	1	2	3	4	5	6	7	·8	
Optimal	☐	☐	☐	☐	☐	☐	☐	☐	☐
Proficient	☐	☐	☐	☐	☐	☐	☐	☐	☐
Vulnerable	☐	☐	☐	☐	☐	☐	☐	☐	☐
Cautionary	☐	☐	☐	☐	☐	☐	☐	☐	☐
	Current Environment			**Literacy**			**Competenc**		

METRICS

SCORING GRID

Interpersonal Connections	Constructive Discontent	Compassion	Outlook	Intuition	Trust Radius	Personal Power	Integrity	General Health	Quality of Life	Relationship Quotient	Optimal Performance
10	11	12	13	14	15	16	17	18	19	20	21
☐	☐	☐	☐	☐	☐	☐	☐	☐	☐	☐	☐
☐	☐	☐	☐	☐	☐	☐	☐	☐	☐	☐	☐
☐	☐	☐	☐	☐	☐	☐	☐	☐	☐	☐	☐
☐	☐	☐	☐	☐	☐	☐	☐	☐	☐	☐	☐

Values & Beliefs — **Outcomes**

EMOTIONAL INTELLIGENCE

INDEX

abdominal crunches 31
accountability 160, 171–4, 174
adaptability 127, 129, 131–3
Advance Micro Devices 55
advocacy 120–1
aesthetic judgement 6
Agor, W. 231
Alberthal, L. 285
alchemy 223–5
alertness 19, 30, 138, 228, 256
alignment 147, 173, 175
Allen, P. 151
ambiguity 245
amulets 88
Anderson, K. 167–9
Andreessen, M. 257–8
anger 34, 38–9, 122–4
applied integrity 177–95
appreciation 80
approach variation 275
Aristotle 6, 107, 123
Armstrong, D. M. 97, 99
Armstrong International 97
Arnold, W. 125
Arthur Andersen LLP 76–7, 90, 154
Asea Brown Boveri (ABB) 263, 264–5
Ash, M. K. 129
Aspen Institute 154
assumptions 276
AT&T 151
attention 242
attunement 153
authentic presence 69–86, 202, 208
authority 196–221
automated alarm signals 51
Autry, J. 224
awareness 112, 119
Axelrod, R. 114

Backer, T. 274
Bakken, E. 168
Bank of Montreal 216
Baron, G. 94
Barrett Browning, E. 145
Bateson, M. C. 135, 151
beacons of incentive 51

becoming 107, 277
believability 95
Bell, A. G. 151
Bendix Corporation 235
Bennis, W. 205
Bergson, H. 6
Bierce, A. 114
bifurcation points 281
Black, P. 122
Blackwell, E. 129–30
Blake, W. 107
blessings 275
blocks 238
Bly, R. 192
body language 21, 83, 95, 232
body sensations 13
Boeing Company 151, 190
Boorstin, D. J. 275
Boston College 187
bottom lines 106
Brandenburger, A. 197
Branson, R. 271, 286
break points 281
breathing spaces 136–9
bridges of trust 88, 89–91, 121
Brinker International 169
British Airways (BA) 9
British National Health Society 130
brothers' keeper principle 174
Brown, D. 150
Brown, J. 215, 216, 271, 291
Buechner, F. 153
business
    constructive discontent 121
    ecosystems 197
    inner side 45–9
    senses 238–9
    winning 87

California Job Journal 188–9
California State University 22
callings 147–8
Calloway, W. 215–6
calm-energy 22, 23, 25, 29
calm-tiredness 22
Campbell, J. 154

349

Camus, A. 292
capabilities 237
carbohydrates 138
Carlson, N. 76–7
Carson, R. 160–1, 170, 231, 272
Carter, S. 180–1, 185
Case Western University 179
cash-register honesty 3–5, 8
Cattabiani, G. 218–20
Centennial Medical Center 125
Center for Creative Leadership 55, 75
central callings 147
chain-dumping 207–8
challenges 113, 232–41
change 107, 276
chaos 197, 198–9
Chaplin, C. 3
charisma 93
China 147–8, 161–2, 202, 203
Chrysler 56–7, 59, 60, 110, 218
Churchill, W. 129, 231
clarification 120
clarity 84, 120
Clark, J. 257–8
Clifton, D. 150
Colby College 203
Coles, R. 140, 204
collaboration 22, 27
    creativity 113, 197
    decision-making 99
    entrainment 119
    environment 28–9
collective consciousness 205
Collins, J. 155
commitment 160–76
communication 65–6, 239
community 214–7, 220
compromise 114
conditioning 34
confidants 172
confidence 240–1
conflict 107, 197
confluence 224
Conger, J. 72
congruency 83–4
connecting 64, 71–7
conscience 160, 174–6, 179, 200, 205
consensus 111, 114
constructive discontent 107–26
contagion 207, 210
context 106
control 35
cooperation 114, 121, 197

Coots, L. 29
courage 79–81, 160, 163–9, 173, 175
Cramer, I. 52
Cray, S. 252
creativity 45, 107–8, 179, 209, 242, 263
    collaboration 113, 197
    future 276–92
    opportunity sensing 273
    tension 18–9, 24
    time-mapping 246–8
credibility 53, 177
Crick, F. 245
crises 128
Csikszentmihalyi, M. 227, 237
curiosity 133–5
cynicism 124, 133, 169, 211, 218
Czechoslovakia 196

damage control 34
Damasio, A. 140, 233
de Bono, E. 286
debate cultures 111
decision-making 49–51, 64–5, 99, 205
Decker, B. 21
defensiveness 121
delegation 102, 174
Dell Computers 214–5
Dell, M. 214
Deming Award 135
Deming Institute 190
deoxyribonucleic acid (DNA) 288–90
depression 20, 23
depth 143–5
DeSimone, L. D. 47
Dharma 203
dialogue 69, 71–9
    entrainment 119
    heated 114
    interruption patterns 36
Dickey, J. S. 175
Dilts, R. 263
direct knowing 230–2
discernment 180, 187
discipline 66
discontent 107–26
discovery 155–7
discussions 81–3, 114, 116
Dixons 114
Dolan, D. 189
Downing, W. 44
Drew, D. 284
Duke University 92
DuPont 136

Sternberg, R. 162
Stowe, H. B. 130
strategic planning 249
Strauss, N. 189
strengths 149–50, 155
stretching 237
study groups 140
suggestions 65
Sun Bin 147–9
Sun, D. 135
Sun Microsystems 110, 111
supervision 97
surprise 272–3
surveys 91–2

Taylor, A. 228–9
Taylor, F. 94
team architecture 29
teamwork 218
technical rationality 49–50
television 196
tense-energy 22–3, 29
tense-tiredness 22, 23, 29
tension 18–9, 137–8
Thayer, R. E. 22, 23, 24
Thurber, J. 51
Tibet 69–71, 87–8, 100, 201–3
time
    agreement 194–5
    horizon extension 248–50
    mapping 246–8
    saving 113
    shifting 242–54
    urgent movements 103
Timmer, J. 116, 232
Torbert, W. 187
Towson State University 66
tragedies 128, 134
transformation 170–1, 277–81, 289
transition times 137
triggers 14
Trudeau, G. 72
true voices 69
trust 112, 120, 279, 280
    radius 87–106, 187
    resonance 202
truth 7–10
Tu, J. 135
Tubman, H. 100, 170
Turner, T. 151
turning points 104, 281–5
type-1 challenges 232–41
type-2 challenges 232–41

Ulrich, H. 206
understanding 120
unique potential 147–59, 173, 174
United Auto Workers Union 56
United Kingdom 114, 125, 187
University of Chicago 227
University of Hawaii 209
University of Illinois 257
University of Michigan 114, 276
University of Pennsylvania 119, 133
University of Texas 54
unorthodoxy 273
untapped capacity 227
Unum Life Insurance 136

valence 197
values 34, 38, 72, 155
    congruency 83–4
    constructive discontent 112–8
    integrity 179
    resonance 199–200
Vanderbilt University 125
Vanourek, R. 217
vibrations 13
Vietnam War 11, 35, 77
Visa International 188, 198
Vlissingen, P. F. van 166
Voltaire 196
vulnerability 96

Wal-Mart 89, 132, 263
Walton, S. 89, 132
Wang Li 147–8
Wanless, D. 8
Warrington, J. 130
Washington, G. 38–9, 231
Watson, J. 245
weaknesses 150
Webster, R. 187–8
Westinghouse Corporation 97, 218
Whitehead, A. N. 6
Whyte, D. 88, 204
Wiener, N. 238
William, W. C. 204
Williams, R. 92–3
Wolpe, D. J. 291
Woolman, J. 170–1, 272
work
    breaks 30
    family balance 135, 136
    inner compass 151–5
    space 26–9
Worth Ethic Corporation 235

CONTACT PAGE

To order your own copy of the latest version of the computer-scored *EQ Map* (which includes a colour printout of your results and a confidential personal report), or to learn more about *Organizational EQ Profiles* for teams and companies, along with measurement-based training and development programs on emotional intelligence in your profession or business, contact:

Q-Metrics
70 Otis Street
San Francisco, CA 94103 U.S.A.
Toll-free in the U.S.A. and Canada: 1-888-252-MAPS (6227)
415-252-8224
Fax: 415-252-5732
Web Site on the Internet: http://www.eq.org

For information on core learning systems for emotional intelligence in leadership and organizations and on the availability of Robert K. Cooper and his associates for a wide range of private, public, and community programs including keynote speeches, seminars, conferences, workshops, leadership and executive development initiatives, and satellite broadcasts, contact:

The Learning Circle
142 North Road
Sudbury, MA 01776 U.S.A.
508-371-8818
Fax: 508-371-5903
Web Site on the Internet: http://www.learningcircle.com